Y0-BSE-836

SECRETS OF THE ORACLE:
A HISTORY OF WISDOM FROM ZENO TO YEATS

WITHDRAWN
UTSA LIBRARIES

WITHDRAWN
UTSA LIBRARIES

W. DAVID SHAW

Library
University of Texas
at San Antonio

Secrets of the Oracle

A History of Wisdom from Zeno to Yeats

UNIVERSITY OF TORONTO PRESS
Toronto Buffalo London

© University of Toronto Press Incorporated 2009
Toronto Buffalo London
www.utppublishing.com
Printed in Canada

ISBN 978-1-4426-4034-4

Library
University of Texas
at San Antonio

Printed on acid-free, 100% post-consumer recycled paper with vegetable-based inks .

Library and Archives Canada Cataloguing in Publication

Shaw, W. David (William David)
    Secrets of the oracle : a history of wisdom from Zeno to Yeats / W. David
Shaw.

    Includes bibliographical references and index.
    ISBN 978-1-4426-4034-4

    1. Wisdom – History.   2. Wisdom in literature.   3. Wisdom literature –
Criticism, interpretation, etc.   I. Title.

PN56.W54S53 2009   809′.93384   C2009-903900-1

This book has been published with the help of a grant from the Canadian
Federation for the Humanities and Social Sciences, through the Aid to
Scholarly Publications Programme, using funds provided by the Social
Sciences and Humanities Research Council of Canada.

University of Toronto Press acknowledges the financial assistance to
its publishing program of the Canada Council for the Arts and the
Ontario Arts Council.

Canada Council   Conseil des Arts   ONTARIO ARTS COUNCIL
for the Arts   du Canada   CONSEIL DES ARTS DE L'ONTARIO

University of Toronto Press acknowledges the financial support for its
publishing activities of the Government of Canada through the
Book Publishing Industry Development Program (BPIDP).

In Memory of My Daughter

'It is those we live with and love and should know who elude us'

Contents

Acknowledgments

'Eventually you discover that there isn't any accumulation of wisdom through continuity,' Northrop Frye warns, 'and that's where *real* wisdom starts. It starts in discontinuity, the acceptance of experience without a priori moral judgments (a time for all things)' (2002, 182). I started thinking about wisdom writing twenty years ago when studying the discontinuous prose of Carlyle's *Sartor Resartus* and the aphorisms of F.H. Bradley and Oscar Wilde. I was intrigued by the unheard words of Robert Browning's monologues, the withheld oracles of J.H. Newman, the wisdom of Koheleth, and the strangely self-withholding tetrameter quatrains that half reveal and half conceal the meaning of *In Memoriam*. Struck by Browning's curious combination of garrulousness and reserve, and by Newman's surprising remark (at the beginning of his most confessional book, the *Apologia*) that his secret was his own, I began to conjecture that obliquity might be a recurrent feature of the wisdom writing I admired. That body of writing has since expanded to include the majestic opening verses of John's Gospel and T.S. Eliot's enigmatic *Four Quartets*, the haunting coda of Norman Maclean's 'A River Runs through It,' and Lincoln's powerful Gettysburg and Second Inaugural address.

Oscar Wilde warns that 'all art is at once surface and symbol. Those who go beneath the surface do so at their peril.' Some scholars seem to think that if they take care of the surface of a text, its lexicon or syntax, what lies beneath the surface will take care of itself. I prefer to think that a scholar who risks a personal response to literature can study a surface that is intimate with its depths. For encouraging me in this task I am grateful to Richard Ratzlaff, Acquisitions Editor of the University of Toronto Press, and to his colleague, Lennart Husband. I also want to thank two anonymous readers of the manuscript for their large-minded understanding and support. When their wisdom could not save me from folly, their knowledge rescued me from error. My intellectual father is Northrop Frye, whose work informs everything I write. When I came to Victoria College in 1969, I held him in awe as the Coleridge of our age. After occupying an academic office adjoining his for more than twenty years, I came to know Frye as a humanist of great wit and feeling and finally as a friend. Portions of chapters 3, 4, and 5 originally appeared in my lecture, 'Renewing Thy Beauty: Tennyson's Afterlife from Hardy to Housman,' delivered at the Tennyson's Futures Conference at Oxford University, 27 March 2009. For permission to reproduce in chapter 2 parts of my essay 'Tennyson and Zeno: Three Infinities,' which appeared in the Tennyson Bicentenary issue of *Victorian Poetry* 47 (Spring, 2009), 81–99, I am grateful to the editors of that journal.

Half a century ago, when he was trying to put poetry in a test-tube in *Speculative Instruments*, I.A. Richards told his students that we had chosen the wrong profession. The future lay with science. A sharp and stirring exchange of ideas at a recent Tennyson conference at Oxford helped me refine some of my ideas and convince me that my choice of a career many years ago was not as perverse as Richards had predicted.

I am grateful for the counsel and support I have received over many years from my colleague Eleanor Cook and from my wife Carol, who had the good sense to convince me that the book's original title, *Descent of the Owl*, was a low point of folly, not the haunt of wisdom I intended. I also recall with gratitude the courtesy and patience of the scholarly custodian who showed me Newman's manuscripts and annotated books at the Birmingham oratory on Hagley Road, and who gave me a tour of the theologian's working library. I have a fond memory, too, of the student who shared my delight in the short stories of Norman Maclean and who presented me with a CD of songs on 'A River Runs through It' that he had composed and performed with other musicians. Since retiring five years ago, I have had less chance to refine my ideas in lectures or sharpen them on the whetstone of keener minds than my own. I say this, not to disarm predictable criticism of my book, but to acknowledge belatedly my indebtedness to colleagues I was close to and to students I have taught. If I were wiser, I would consign my notes on wisdom to a funeral pyre. Instead, I persist in the folly of brooding on wisdom's 'fierce dispute between damnation and impassioned clay.' Whether it be a mark of senility or a defence against time, I dream of being consumed like Keats – if not in another book then perhaps in another life – by the fire of Shakespeare.

SECRETS OF THE ORACLE:
A HISTORY OF WISDOM FROM ZENO TO YEATS

Introduction

Ostensibly a history, *Secrets of the Oracle* is also an elegy, a lament for lost wisdom, and a book on mystery attuned to words we overhear and to meanings that wisdom writers hold in reserve. Most votaries of wisdom are spies and secretaries, keepers of secrets. Their wisdom is to knowledge what the poetry of Hamlet and King Lear is to the prudential counsel of Polonius. When we eavesdrop on wisdom, its meaning is captured en passant, as a lucky event, or overheard in a reflection or aside, often when we least expect to discover it. The wisest answers are often a response to silent or unasked questions. In telling his audience at Gettysburg that the Union is dedicated to a new birth of freedom, Lincoln is giving a prophet's answer to the pacifist's question: what is the purpose of the great civil war? And when Lear says, 'Upon such sacrifices, my Cordelia, / The gods themselves throw incense,' he is giving the gods' answer to the question: what is the point of sacrificial love?

Conceived as a sceptic's companion to Charles Williams's *The Descent of the Dove*, this book traces the descent – both the lineage and decline – of wisdom. Like the dove at Pentecost, the owl of wisdom has been known to descend on John Milton, the Zen masters, and the sibyl of Amherst, Emily Dickinson. I have also detected accents of the owl in the bracing vocatives of Tennyson's Ulysses and in prophecies intoned by Matthew Arnold at Dover Beach and by Lincoln at Gettysburg. In studying the history of wisdom's two shaping forms, the oracle and aphorism, I argue that an important function of oracles is to clothe the dispossessed in glory and bathe them in revelation and light. What distinguishes not merely the aphorism and oracle but wisdom itself from folly is the power and wit of the expression. Like the quivering peals of the owl carried far into the heart of Words-worth's boy of Winander, a prophet's oracles sound and resound. A prophet is a raptor: like Athena's owl, he towers in pride of place before stooping to his prey. Aphorisms are stealthier. They enter the mind unawares and bite into our conscience like a snake.

More subject than oracles to the abuse of wit, the aphorisms in Alexander Pope's *Essay on Man* swell and sink in parody of John Milton's great surge of prophecy in *Paradise Lost*.

> Created half to rise, and half to fall;
> Great lord of all things, yet a prey to all;
> Sole judge of truth, in endless error hurled;
> The glory, jest, and riddle of the world!   (*An Essay on Man*, 2:15–18)

John Keats complains that 'with a puling infant's force,' Pope and his contemporaries 'swayed about upon a rocking horse, / And thought it Pegasus' ('Sleep and Poetry,' ll. 185–7). In his *Essay on Man* Pope places Milton's Adam and Eve on just such a horse and calls it wisdom. Without the oracles and aphorisms, however, we would be left naked on earth, since one result of technological revolution is the corrosion of visionary imagination and the treatment of revelation itself as a technology. Actuarial charts and statistics make an impact, but only oracles and aphorisms induce a tremor. We respond to great wisdom writing with the same twinge of awe that Hopkins feels when he reads Wordsworth's Intimations Ode. The poet of 'Spelt from Sibyl's Leaves' finds that his soul has been in a quiver, like a vibrating string, trembling between dread and subdued elation, ever since.

As a focus of verbal energy and authority, dropped into history from a different dimension of reality, the oracles and aphorisms discussed in this book form part of a personally selected kerygmatic anthology. My selections support the conclusion that the history of wisdom, though rich in its accidental varieties, is poor in its essential types. When Koheleth says that all is vanity, he is repeating the Buddha's idea that the world is full of emptiness. Since there is nothing new under the sun, including the saying there is nothing new, and since the wisdom of Koheleth was old even when the world was young, he appears to be a belated immigrant into realms of thought occupied before him by writers claiming to be wise. And yet his wisdom is more than a house of glass where a few familiar sayings appear to recede endlessly like an image seen in facing mirrors. For when Koheleth says, 'whatever it is in your power to do, do with all your might, for there is no doing, no learning, no wisdom in the grave where you are going' (Ecclesiastes 9:7-10), he is not merely saying 'eat, drink, and be merry, for tomorrow you die.' He is also implying that to do anything with enough intensity and power is to experience eternity compressed into a moment. When Norman Maclean and his father see Paul catch his last fish in 'A River Runs through It,' they are seeing not just the fish but the artistry of the fisherman. The moment itself may be fleeting. Yet it has lasted all the intervening years and enjoys an afterlife when Norm writes his story. As Koheleth knows, moments of our life can be eternal without lasting forever.

Though 'no kerygmatic canon can ever be drawn up,' since 'it would be impossible to find a committee to agree on the selections' (Frye, 2004a, 159), I for one hear a kerygmatic voice at the beginning of John's Gospel, in the Word who was in the beginning, who was with God and who also was God. I hear the voice again in words which echo John's Word in 'A River Runs through It' and T.S. Eliot's *Four Quartets*. Though few lines of inheritance are so transparent or direct, we are all heirs of wisdom, touched by words that reach down to us through time to remake our world and define who we are.

As in Zeno's paradoxes and F.H Bradley's antinomies, which show space and time are illusory and motion and change are unreal, the genius of wisdom writing is to shock as well as inform the mind. Like the koans of the Zen master and the parables of the Gnostic Gospels, the oracles and aphorisms of a wisdom writer jolt and transform a reader simultaneously. A writer who has no communion with the Muse produces sterile aphorisms: his oracles smoulder instead of burn. Whereas conservative wisdom is the attribute of George Eliot's Mr Brooke, a fossilized custodian of establishment values, radical wisdom is the attribute of adventurous innovators like Samuel Taylor Coleridge and Northrop Frye, who generate continuous mental energy. The conservative transmitter of ancestral wisdom depends on fixed boundaries as much as the radical transformer of wisdom depends on horizons that keep fading like the worlds glimpsed by Tennyson's Ulysses through the arch. Though these fundamental divisions are central to the experience of any wise person who wants to keep alive both the search for new horizons and a longing for ends, a love of wisdom must also be creative, and not simply erudite or learned. Wisdom is to poetry what knowledge is to history: a sense of the potential, not an understanding of what is actual or particular.

Like Tennyson's fabled city of art and culture in 'Timbuctoo,' Apollo's shrine at Delphi has fallen into ruin. Even the great temple of wisdom, the Parthenon at Athens, is now, as Keats says, the shadow of a magnitude. To repair the damage, writers from Jefferson to Lincoln, from Oscar Wilde to Bernard Shaw, invent their own oracles. Hegel says that the owl of Minerva rises when the sun sets. But he neglects to add that Minerva and her owl continue to cast a spell over votaries of the sun god. Wisdom writing is the homage prophets pay Apollo. Unlike Francis Bacon or F.H. Bradley, a wisdom writer is seldom a philosopher. More often he is a wise poet like William Blake or an oracle of wit like Northrop Frye, who offers the Muse the tribute of an owl.

Secrets of the Oracle explores the changing languages of seers and poets in an age beguiled by technocrats and sophists, when wisdom itself is in widespread retreat. Concentrating on Victorian and modern writers, I show how oracles and aphorisms lend majesty to Samuel Johnson's poem, 'The Vanity of Human Wishes,' and confer comparable authority on Tennyson's 'Ulysses' and George Eliot's *Middlemarch*. In the prose of Matthew Arnold, Thomas Carlyle, and Friedrich Nietzsche, wise words twist themselves into two-way aphorisms and writhe and coil as serpents of irony. To outwit oblivion a writer's wisdom need not be solemn. Witty Irish bulls detonate many of Bernard Shaw's oracles. And an alliance of wit and prophecy sharpens the aphorisms of Oscar Wilde, F.H. Bradley, and Canada's most celebrated wisdom writer and wit, Northrop Frye. Admittedly, few owls can swallow and digest the bulls of Groucho Marx. And not even a bull can crush a wily snake like Shakespeare's Iago, who speaks with the forked tongue of Apollo's priestess at Delphi, the serpent Pythia. Nonetheless, the wisdom writing studied in this book includes the Decalogue as well as the Sermon on the Mount, the Declaration of Independence as well as the Gettysburg Address. It claims the same privileged status in poetic, biblical, and modern political traditions as the Delphic oracle did in ancient Greece.

The monograph tests the thesis that wisdom writing individualizes the law and is geared toward the past: it speaks in aphorisms and proverbs. Prophecy individualizes the revolutionary impulse, and is geared toward the future: it communicates through oracles and visions. Jefferson is a wise writer and Lincoln prophetic. But if a wisdom writer is to present his ideas as a living presence with power to change us now, he must combine the capacity of Tennyson's Ulysses to interpret and explore with the rapture of Virgil's Sibyl, who 'swell[s] with the breath of the god yet fight[s] for control at every gasp' (Lipking, 1981, 90). Such a writer should have a genius for inventing oracles as well as a talent for minting fresh, arresting aphorisms. When the ghost of F.H. Bradley descends on T.S. Eliot or the shades of Thucydides and John Henry Newman speak through Arnold at Dover Beach, each poet serves as both an interpreter and an instrument of the precursor who possesses him. Ovid claims that authentic prophecy and genius are divinely inspired: 'Est deus in nobis.' Though Ovid's god is not a deity any more, 'only a psychological and subjective power,' Northrop Frye warns that its divine raptus 'is still numinous, still speaks with a mysterious and awful authority, and is still dangerous to trifle with' (1971, 65–6).

As a 'genius of the shore' (l. 130), the drowned Lycidas haunts his locality as a divinely appointed protector of all who wander by the perilous flood. And so a haunt or habit of the gods makes of such places as Delphi, the Sermon Mount, or the Lincoln Memorial in Washington a dwelling place or home. Of such god-haunted places we can say, with Wallace Stevens, that they are the home or 'haunt of prophecy.' Though Jesus will always be a genius loci of the Sermon Mount, and Abraham Lincoln of Gettysburg, there sound and resound through their haunts of prophecy the oracles of two precursors: Moses and Thomas Jefferson. Just as Jesus' Sermon on the Mount recalls and fulfils the Tables Moses receives on Sinai, so Lincoln's celebration in his Gettysburg address of a new birth of freedom confirms and enlarges the axioms of Thomas Jefferson. The Decalogue ratifies a preexisting moral order. And the Declaration of Independence reflects Enlightenment values. Quite different are the crucibles of paradox and irony that set apart the Sermon on the Mount and Lincoln's Gettysburg Address. Instead of merely mirroring the world, these reinvented oracles break it down and change it. Like a strong metaphor or paradox that uses shock effects to trigger new perception and insight, a reinvented oracle exercises both subversive authority and constructive power.

It is sometimes assumed that in removing a mask and baring his inmost thoughts to an audience, a Shakespearean character on his deathbed speaks as the playwright's mouthpiece or oracle. But any words Shakespeare's oracle speaks are self-concealing and elusive.

Just before he dies Hamlet hints that the secret most worth imparting is still to be revealed. 'Had I but time ... O, I could tell you / But let it be' (*Hamlet*, V.ii.339–43). As one critic says, 'Hamlet utters a total of almost twenty more lines after that "let it be," so that one can experience a certain frustration at not being told part, at least, of what is hinted' (Bloom, 2003, 114). Half in love with easeful death, Hamlet draws his last breath in pain, not to lighten the burden of the mystery, but to ask Horatio to speak wisely on his behalf. 'Absent thee from felicity a while / And in this harsh world draw thy breath in pain / To tell my story' (*Hamlet*, V.ii.358–60). Coming after the run of liquid consonants and unstressed syllables in line 359, the harsh spondees constrict like a noose. Instead of announcing what we already know, that the fell sergeant, Death, is strict in his arrest, Hamlet might have used his last remaining breath to draw together a few threads of wisdom from his great soliloquies. But just when Shakespeare seems about to admit us to an inner shrine, a curtain is drawn. Hamlet keeps his secret by displaying he has one. He hints at a meaning without announcing it. 'As obscure as life,' in Matthew Arnold's phrase, Shakespeare is a master of the oracle withheld. Openly secretive, the words we want to hear are seldom spoken.

Obliquity remains the core of any revelation. If wisdom writing is too direct, it may invade our space, like the pedantic Polonius, whom Coleridge calls 'the personified *memory* of wisdom' no longer possessed (1969, 115). A soliloquist who turns to lecture us directly may also substitute a church for a playhouse by turning a soliloquy into a sermon. If one is looking for great oracles in Shakespeare, one will not find them in the obvious places, not in the prophecies of the witches in *Macbeth* or even in the wise sayings of Prospero. They are to be found rather in the one thing that all the characters have in common, and that is the fact 'that no one but Shakespeare could have created them.' As Eliot says, 'the world of a great poetic dramatist is a world in which the creator is everywhere present, and everywhere hidden' (1961, 112).

It is useful to distinguish among a dramatic, a lyric, and a rhetorical voice in poetry, each of which possesses a special form of wisdom. Dramatic wisdom is the truth of contradictory qualities or opposites. As Stanley Wells explains, there is an 'openness to interpretation' in Shakespeare's plays, 'which helps explain the endless fascination they have exercised on audiences and performers alike. The actor playing Hamlet may emphasize the lyrical or the harsher aspects of the role ... Shylock may be presented as a figure of satire or may take on tragic

dimensions. Othello may be a noble Moor or a self-deluded murderer'
(2002, 22). By contrast, lyrical wisdom is the discovery that, though the
mind is its own place, each mind is unique: its qualities cannot be
imposed on a different mind. This is why a lyric voice in drama loses
much of its wisdom and reflective charm if we hear it principally as the
voice of a ventriloquist intoning through a puppet. When Romeo's
father speaks of the East beginning 'to draw / The shady curtains from
Aurora's bed' (*Romeo and Juliet*, I.i.42–3), what we hear is not a prosaic
old Montague but a lyrical Shakespeare talking through a mask. Only
in the balcony scene, when Romeo calls the light the East and Juliet the
sun, does the dramatic action catch up with the bridal metaphors of
the play. A third rhetorical form of wisdom exists in the gap between
applied and pure persuasion, between self-serving argument and rhetoric that is disinterested. Browning's would-be seducer in 'Two in the
Campagna,' for example, does not come out where he had planned.
Instead of completing his argument for free love, he says in conclusion:
'Only I discern – / Infinite passion, and the pain / Of finite hearts that
yearn' (ll. 58–60). No one has ever doubted the oracular finality of
these words. But like the 'deserts of vast eternity' that stretch before
Marvell's lover in 'To His Coy Mistress,' they surely do more to
congeal his mistress's blood than warm it.

    Secrets of the Oracle examines the difficult question of how an oracle
that reinvents its world can both *find* something and *recreate* it. How
can truth be discovered and refashioned at the same time? The verb
'invent' can mean opposite things. Though 'in-venire' is to 'come
upon' or 'find,' it can also signify 'create' or 'make.' An authoritative
oracle transmits what it receives. But if it is to speak convincingly to
each successive age, it will also need to remake or even revolutionize
what it finds and transmits. The words of power that Apollo speaks at
Delphi enjoy a supremacy over the divine words of lesser oracles. But
even Apollo's oracles have to be interpreted. And to interpret or reinvent an oracle is to risk becoming, as Blake says, idolatrous to one's
shadow. Gods punish boasts and oaths because, as words of power,
they threaten the gods' supremacy. And yet unless an oracle has been
fed by our own imagination, it is unlikely to strike us as almost a
remembrance. As Northrop Frye says, the sentences of the Sermon on
the Mount are words of power because, even as they 'seem to be
coming from inside ourselves, as though the soul itself were remembering what it had been told ... long ago' (1963b, 45), they have power
to change us now. Oracles 'present' the Word in a double sense: by con-

fronting or 'presenting' us with the Word, they make it a 'presence,' a living power.

An oracle may create a grotesquely distended image of its subject, as in a fun house of distorting mirrors. This is what happens to St Paul's words in the dream of Shakespeare's Bottom, or to Godbole's prophecies in the Marabar cave, where each echo generates another echo, like a snake composed of small snakes writhing independently. An oracle that generates antinomies or logical contradictions (like the attributes 'infinite' and 'absolute' often ascribed to God) may even create a flickering succession of two-dimensional images that fail to combine into the stable three-dimensional hologram it seems always on the verge of forming. Very different is the oracle that operates as a crucible to purify or refine the elements it first breaks down before combining into something unforeseen and new. Out of a broken whole such a reinvented oracle uses three sounds to frame, not a fourth sound, but a star. Examples include the Gospel paradoxes, the paradox of carnage and death begetting a new birth at Gettysburg, and even the 'terrible beauty' of a great elegy like Yeats's 'Easter 1916' or a tragedy like *King Lear*.

When repairing the oracles of Moses and Jefferson, neither Jesus nor Lincoln writes poems. But as Charles Williams says of St Paul, each 'uses words as poets do; [each] regenerates them' (1963, 15). Like all great prophets, Jesus and Lincoln possess a poet's ability to change the descriptive meaning of phrases like 'the kingdom of God' or 'a new birth of freedom' and to charge the words with extraordinary emotive power. In T.S. Eliot's phrase, they tongue 'the communication / Of the dead ... with fire beyond the language of the living' ('Little Gidding,' I. 50–1). Both are poets in George Eliot's sense: they have 'a soul so quick to discern that no shade of quality escapes it ... – a soul in which knowledge passes instantaneously into feeling, and feeling flashes back as a new organ of knowledge' (1956, 166). The most genuine language in poetry is unconsciously oracular, because in phrases like 'Ripeness is all' (*King Lear*, V.ii.11) or 'I have a journey, sir, shortly to go; my master calls me' (*King Lear*, V.iii.321–2) the reader is aware of more meaning than the speaker. Instead of merely predicting what will happen, the words expand like concentric waves, until they push against the vortex blocked off for us by death. Like Shakespeare's Bottom, we might all be prophets if we had wit to say what we dream or tell what we imagine.

1

Any presiding genius that is both supernaturally immediate and familiarly remote, like the archaic wooden image of Pallas Athene standing guard over Arnold's darkling plain in the poem 'Palladium,' holds a balance between hope and doom that justifies its claim to wisdom.

> Set where the upper streams of Simois flow
> Was the Palladium, high 'mid rock and wood;
> And Hector was in Ilium, far below,
> And fought, and saw it not – but there it stood!
>
> It stood, and sun and moonshine rained their light
> On the pure columns of its glen-built hall.
> Backward and forward rolled the waves of fight
> Round Troy – but while this stood, Troy could not fall.
>
> So, in its lovely moonlight, lives the soul.
> Mountains surround it, and sweet virgin air;
> Cold plashing, past it, crystal waters roll;
> We visit it by moments, ah, too rare!
>
> We shall renew the battle in the plain
> To-morrow; red with blood will Xanthus be;
> Hector and Ajax will be there again,
> Helen will come upon the wall to see.
> (Matthew Arnold, 'Palladium,' ll. 1–16)

A culture in which everyone was wise would never worship Pallas Athene as a god. But since we are never as wise as we should be, we deify Pallas, not as a goddess we can see in an image preserved in the Trojan citadel, as the ancients saw her, but as a power to see by.

The most familiar haunt of Matthew Arnold's ghost is the waves' retreat to the breath of the night wind 'down the vast edges drear' of Dover Beach. This desolate strand also turns out to be the haunt of two other ghosts – Thucydides and John Henry Newman, whose alarming words about a night battle on a darkling plain cause an odd, reverberating, reproachful lament to culminate in a sudden surge of terror. But there is another side to Arnold's story. For 'Dover Beach' also relieves the loss of faith by appealing to the love of the poet's bride and by making his language bracing rather than defeatist.

> Ah, love, let us be true
> To one another! for the world, which seems
> To lie before us like a land of dreams,
> So various, so beautiful, so new,
> Hath really neither joy, nor love, nor light,
> Nor certitude, nor peace, nor help for pain;
> And we are here as on a darkling plain
> Swept with confused alarms of struggle and flight,
> Where ignorant armies clash by night.   ('Dover Beach,' ll. 29–37)

The melancholy, long, withdrawing roar of the poem's penultimate stanza, which establishes an enchanting vowel music to lull the mind into oblivion, like one of Frost's snow poems, is confronted at last with firm resistance. To my ear Arnold's closing words never sink flatly into pessimism. What we hear is no dull tramp of stoic fortitude either, but an exquisite interlacing of parallel syntactic units and the motions of a freely fluid verse.

Arnold's echo of Newman's Oxford sermon on faith and reason (1839), which ends with a reference to Thucydides' account of the Syracusan disaster, dramatically reverses the import of the lover's plea to his bride. Like the wise Empedocles, Arnold is alerted to the danger of confusing the counsels of wisdom with the casuistry of sophists: 'Forsake / A world these sophists throng. / Be neither saint nor sophist-led, but be a man!' ('Empedocles on Etna,' ll. 134–6). Arnold's allusion to Newman and Thucydides also shakes him out of shallow doubt and scepticism. It warns him against the night battles of logomachy and invites him to use words lucidly and with precision. 'Controversy, at least in this age,' Newman had said, 'does not lie between the hosts of heaven, Michael and his angels on the one side, and the powers of evil on the other.' Instead, 'it is a sort of night battle, where each fights for himself, and friend and foe stand together' (Newman, 1887, 201). A prophecy of suicide on the darkling plain would be ignoble only if Arnold or Newman ever dreamed it was an option.

PART ONE

An Owl for Apollo: Wisdom and the Poets

In an unguarded moment John Keats admits that 'poetry is not so fine a thing as philosophy ... for the same reason that an eagle is not so fine a thing as a truth' (1978, 286). His verdict is surprising for a poet who insists that even 'axioms in philosophy are no axioms until they are proved upon our pulses' (1978, 273). But his odd preference for philosophy over poetry tacitly acknowledges the existence of two kinds of raptors: Apollo's eagle and Athena's owl. Unlike a poet who soars out of sight, a wisdom writer strides high and glides on the air before allowing his 'brute beauty and valour' to buckle or crumple by swooping down on his prey. Harold Bloom contends that 'wisdom writers are rarely philosophers' (2004, 208). But even as Apollo, the sun god, eclipses the face of Athena's owl, his wise poets and prophetic wits continue to flesh out her paradigms. In offering the tribute of an owl at Apollo's temple, Athena repays the debt philosophers owe poets. Since oracular writing tends to be philosophical in spirit, I want to consider in this first section the influence of five philosophers who are often considered oracular and wise: Friedrich Schleimermacher, Duns Scotus, F.H. Bradley, George Berkeley, and William James. What lines of inheritance can we trace between these thinkers and five prophetic poets? Though all poets are prophets of a sort, who depend as much on revelation and intuition as on analytic thinking, many of them are vehicles of the occult only by accident. In Browning, Hopkins, Eliot, Yeats, and Frost I have chosen poets whose oracles are steady and luminous rather than fitful and opaque.

1 Descent of the Owl: Philosophy among the Poets

According to Wallace Stevens, 'man is the intelligence of his soil, / The sovereign ghost. As such, the Socrates / Of snails, musician of pears, principium / And lex.' ('The Comedian as the Letter C,' ll. 1–4). But what is the point of being a legislator or a lawgiver, the roof and crown of things, if it forces one to be a ghost? Poets as dissimilar as the oracular Browning, the prophetic Hopkins, and the visionary T.S. Eliot try to avoid the pitfalls of solipsism by affirming the priority of God's existence. They seek in this ground of being an explanation of their situation that is neither less than human (a purely natural explanation) nor only human (a purely historical one). To explain how the infinite mind of God communicates with finite minds, Schleiermacher shows how human beings are instruments of their Creator, fluctuating like the dramatis personae in Browning's monologues between states of freedom and dependence. Hopkins, like Duns Scotus, seeks unmediated knowledge of God. But in aspiring too high, he is often left with an analogical or a merely equivocal understanding instead. The compound ghost in 'Little Gidding' is, I think, F.H. Bradley, Eliot's philosophical mentor, who exercises a lifelong influence over his most famous disciple. As for Yeats's debt to Berkeley, it seems to me an oddly double one: Augustan and Romantic. At first Yeats sees in Berkeley only the ghostly paradigms he discerns in Plato: a skeleton without flesh. Later he recognizes that Berkeley himself is an enemy of ghosts, of abstractions like substance, which he tries to exorcise from Locke's empirical account of matter. Like William James and the pragmatists, Frost also wages war against metaphysics and idealism by giving a sinewy new voice to philosophy's Rocky-Mountain toughs and sceptics.

1

For his audacious surmise that the world depends on a God of love, hidden 'behind the will and might,' but 'as real as they' ('A Death in the Desert,' ll. 500–1), Browning is indebted to the German philosopher Friedrich Schleiermacher. Browning owned W. Dobson's 1836 translation of Schleiermacher's *Introduction* to the *Dialogues of Plato*, and he was familiar as well with Strauss's discussion of the Christology of Schleiermacher in the third volume of *The Life of Jesus* (1846, 3:417–25).

At far-seeing speculative moments, the ghost of Schleiermacher can be heard speaking through Browning's Karshish and David.

> The very God! think Abib; dost thou think?
> So, the All-Great, were the All-Loving too –
> So, through the thunder comes a human voice
> Saying, 'O heart I made, a heart beats here!'
>
> ('An Epistle of Karshish,' ll. 304–7)

> I seek and I find it, O Saul, it shall be
> A Face like my face that receives thee; a Man like to me.
>
> ('Saul,' ll. 309–10)

Just as St Paul proclaims that his 'strength' was made 'perfect in weakness' (2 Corinthians 12:9), so David has already conceived a divine image that unites power and weakness, sublimity and pathos: ''Tis the weakness in strength, that I cry for! My flesh, that I seek / In the Godhead!' When Browning's David momentarily entertains the subversive hypothesis that he may actually surpass God in his capacity for love, he is trying to imagine what a feeling of total freedom, of love without restraint, would be like. But it is impossible to imagine such freedom because, as Schleiermacher explains, it is impossible to eliminate the consciousness of self. And as long as we retain any trace of self-consciousness, we retain 'a consciousness of absolute dependence' (Schleiermacher, 1928, 16). In contrast to an overreacher like Browning's Paraceslus, who is aggressively self-reliant, David is a passive recipient of vision. As the oracle in whom vision happens to take place, David is absolutely dependent, as Schleiermacher would say, on a power outside himself.

The 'stoop of the soul which in bending upraises it too' ('Saul,' l. 252) not only prefigures the Incarnation but also traces the curve of David's own exalted feeling of depending on another. When 'God is seen God' ('Saul,' l. 249), it is not because he is naturally immanent in creation, as Paley argues in his *Evidences of Christianity*. It is because, as Schleieremacher insists, each imperfection or feeling of dependence implies its perfecting counterpart in a God of power and love. Browning is always trying to replace the lonely God of Power with the loving God of Relationship. But he recognizes that the 'Face like my face' in 'Saul' (l. 310) is an elevation – the Face of the Other – and that it summons the self from on high.

Unfortunately, both Schleiermacher's theology and Browning's poem 'Saul' contain one serious flaw. The pieces of argument may dovetail like a parquet floor. But however artful the carpentry, the floor cannot bear the weight of the lofty conclusion it is designed to support. There is no logical way in which Schleiermacher can pass from a Christ who may never have existed except as an idea in his own mind to a Christ who really lived. The analogical argument in Browning's 'Saul' rests on just such a 'backward inference,' as Strauss calls it. As in ontological arguments for God's existence, all David seems to have proved is that if we think of God we must think of him as necessarily existing as a God who assumed human form. Otherwise, he could not have been crucified, and he would have been a lesser being than thousands of such rivals as the suffering David. 'Between the idea / And the reality,' however, 'falls the Shadow' (Eliot, 'The Hollow Men,' V.5–6, 8).

When St John compares his gospel's focusing of the eternal truths or 'stars' to the operation of an optic glass, he is conceding that any reduction to historic fact is the kind of licence appropriate to a poetic or narrative style. But 'chronology,' as Simone Weil reminds us, 'cannot play a decisive role in a relationship between God and man' in which 'one of the terms ... is eternal' (1974, 107). Even if the historical events which John has witnessed never occurred, he believes the logic of a 'love / Behind the will and might' ('A Death in the Desert,' ll. 500–1) would require him to invent them. The evangelist accepts the Christian oracles as a paradigm for the placing and timing of an eternal mystery. If the only decisive proofs of such a mystery are historical chronicles and archaeological discoveries, then faith is bound to atrophy: it lacks air to breathe and space in which to grow.

One important legacy of Schleiermacher's theology of dependence is Browning's belief that faith and reason depend upon each other. Faith without reason would be inhuman, and reason without faith illogical, since even the scientist's belief in the rationality of the world is a postulate of faith. In his realization that God is not indifferent, but lives, suffers, and hopes with us, Browning's David already anticipates the central teaching of Christianity, which makes God descend in sacrifice for man. Since David's faith harmonizes with man's needs, Browning believes it is a rational faith. Finite creatures depend upon an infinite creator. God responds to that dependence by becoming finite and opening man's finiteness to the breadth of his being.

Such openings may occur in the most improbable places. As infinity suddenly breaks through a smiling mask of imposture and pretence, we may glimpse God fleetingly in Mr Sludge's scams, which are his version of miracles or of events that create faith. In overhearing Blougram's musings on a flower bell, someone's death, a chorus-ending from Euripides, we momentarily eavesdrop on God's soliloquy. The opposite of a partisan, Browning performs on behalf of such casuists and cheats 'miraculous acts of imaginative generosity,' a phrase Stephen Greenblatt uses to describe Shakespeare's fashioning a comic genius, Falstaff, out of a scapegrace like Robert Greene (2004, 225). As G.K. Chesterton says, 'with Browning's knaves we have always this eternal interest, that they are real somewhere, and may at any moment begin to speak poetry. We are talking to a peevish and garrulous sneak; we are watching the play of his paltry features, his evasive eyes, and babbling lips. And suddenly the face begins to change and harden, the eyes glare like the eyes of a mask, the whole face of clay becomes a common mouthpiece, and the voice that comes forth is the voice of God, uttering his everlasting soliloquy' (1903, 172).

Though quacks and con men, casuists and tricksters, may all be masks of Browning's God, the poet himself remains a paradox. He has a great dramatic gift, except when writing plays. The most intellectual English poet since Donne, he shares the fideist's deep distrust of reason. A votary of Shelley, the 'Sun-treader,' Browning is a visionary with the soul of Caliban, a prophet on all fours. His Duke of Ferrara has an aesthete's disdain for money: he would like to pick it up, but not if he has to touch it. The poet who says, 'fancy with fact is just one fact the more' (*The Ring and the Book*, I.464) has a similar distrust of historical information. Though Browning wants facts to fortify his faith, he knows that sacred history is not world history. While an ark discovered on Mount Ararat might interest an archaeologist, it would not excite Browning. Just as Sir Thomas Browne thanks God that he never saw Christ or his disciples in the flesh, so Browning is afraid that if he had been in St John's place he would have missed the meaning of what he witnessed. Less important than empirical data is a prophet's capacity for spiritual vision, which transforms and enlarges everything he sees.

2

Like his favourite theologian, Duns Scotus, Gerard Manley Hopkins experiences, not a mere feeling of dependence on God, like Browning's Saul, but a direct and unmediated vision. 'I am all at once what Christ is, since he was what I am' ('That Nature Is a Heraclitean Fire,' l. 22). Unfortunately, one unforeseen consequence of this legacy is Hopkins's erratic veering between joy and despair. If the mind has mountains, cliffs of fall, it needs something sturdier than a rope-bridge to throw across the gorge. Scotus believes that the believer has direct access to God. But when his univocal concepts of God fail or betray him, there is no safety net, no middle ground of analogy, to break the poet's free fall through space.

According to Scotus, Aquinas's doctrine of the soul's hylomorphic composition degrades the soul beneath its natural dignity. The mind's darkened understanding of God is not, Scotus argues, a result of any defect inherent in the body or soul. There is no crack or flaw in the reflecting mirror itself. The obscurity is rather the result of a hindrance, of an intercepting veil placed between the mirror and its object. The veil is placed there forte ex peccato, as a result of sin, as Augustine had explained. And just as there is no material impediment or flaw that would distort the mind's knowledge of God, so there is nothing in the mind, Scotus concludes, to hinder its apprehension of individual things. Instead of moving slowly upward, from all visible phenomena, through choiring angels, to successively higher beings, as in the graduated analogical firmament of Aquinas and Aristotle, Scotus's idea of univocity may disclose in each created item a total image of the Creator. As a Scotist celebrant of the urgent univocity of being, Hopkins may leap all at once to God.

> In a flash, at a trumpet crash,
> I am all at once what Christ is,ꞌ since he was what I am, and
> This Jack, joke, poor potsherd,ꞌ patch, matchwood, immortal diamond,
>   Is immortal diamond.
>
> ('That Nature Is a Heraclitean Fire,' ll. 21–4)

The poet's recovery of his true identity is marked by strong reversion to truncated three-stress lines (ll. 21, 24). The reverberatory lift of the half-echoing internal rhymes, 'at a trumpet,' 'ash,' 'flash,' 'crash' (ll. 20–1), shows the firmness of the soul, staunch under attack. Linking solidity with finely faceted beauty, Hopkins's identification of his poor carbon or coal with immortal diamond confers on him the only genuine identity he knows: 'I am all at once what Christ is, since he was what I am' (l. 22).

Unlike Aquinas, who is more concerned with the essence of existence than with the existence of essences, Hopkins, like Duns Scotus, speaks sometimes as if existence itself were merely one of the many 'accidents' of a given essence or pitch. In insisting with Scotus that nothing can deprive each soul of its peculiar tone or pitch, Hopkins may be mistaking an accident of the soul for its essence. Or as Etienne Gilson puts it, 'the primacy of essence, which makes existence to be but one of its "accidents," appears in the doctrine of Duns Scotus as a remnant of the Platonism anterior to Thomas Aquinas. In a straight existential metaphysics, it would be much more correct to speak of the essence of an existence than to speak, with Duns Scotus, of the existence of an essence (*essentia et eius existentia*)' (Gilson, 1941, 69).

Another unspoken affinity between Hopkins and Scotus is a common neglect of their genius by pedants too blunted by learning or too dulled by talent to appreciate it. Or as Hopkins says of Scotus, 'a kind of feud arose between genius and talent, and the ruck of talent in the Schools finding itself, as his age passed by, less and less able to understand him, voted that there was nothing important to understand and so first misquoted and then refuted him' (1938, 201–2). In reading his friend Coventry Patmore's poetry Hopkins says he cannot always tell when an idea is difficult because it is obscurely expressed and when it is obscure because the thought itself is difficult. 'And so,' Hopkins tells Patmore, 'I used to feel of Duns Scotus when I used to read him with delight: he saw too far, he knew too much; his subtlety overshot his interests.' No slavish or pedantic clone of Scotus, Hopkins is sometimes more exasperated than beguiled by his mentor's niceties. In a letter of 3 June 1885, he tells Patmore that 'it is all one almost to be too full of meaning and to have none and to see very deep and not to see at all' (1938, 202).

When Hopkins makes the leap from matchwood to immortal diamond, it is not because each form of carbon participates in existence or being, as Parmenides and Aquinas both affirm. It is because Hopkins accepts, in Czeslaw Milosz's phrase, 'an additional metaphysical premise: something, strictly individual, unrepeatable, cannot ever be destroyed, because that would be senseless and unjust' (Milosz, 1988, 289). Though Hopkins's lines move from the concrete particular to the concrete universal, the individual is not blotted out. Alchemized from coal to diamond, Hopkins reaffirms the mystery of archetypal identity, a mystery that is celebrated not just in biblical myths but in all the ancient fertility myths of resurrection and rebirth.

Like Scotus, Hopkins aspires to knowledge of God that is more than analogical. But, paradoxically, in striving for unmediated vision, Hopkins in his darkest poems ends by seeing far less than Scotus. The fearful opening lines of 'Spelt from Sibyl's Leaves' capture most potently the moment of reversal, when plenitude turns to emptiness, and incremental naming gives way to an anarchy of sundered things in throngs.

> Earnest, earthless, equal, attuneable,' vaulty, voluminous ... stupendous
> Evening strains to be time's vast,' womb-of-all, home-of-all, hearse-of-all
>   night.   (ll. 1–2)

Each word is as discontinuous as an aphorism and each line as weighted with implication as an oracle. Impressions have to be absorbed into the mind one at a time, instead of being linked by an argument. As Frye says, 'the sense of extra profundity' comes 'from leaving more time and space and less sequential connection' at the end of each word and line (1971, 42). At first it seems that nothing could be more expansive and majestic than the adjectives modifying 'evening.' Assonance and alliteration bind together the semantically equivalent modifiers, making them all 'equal,' as Hopkins says, all predictably 'attuneable' to the delayed grammatical subject. But two oddities alert us to differences between the sibyl's darkly ominous naming and the sublime apostrophes to Christ at the opening of *The Wreck of the Deutschland*. There is an ominous double pause after 'attuneable,' which is marked by an extra stress sign, and after the adjective 'voluminous,' which is followed by triple dots. In the absence of a noun to which the adjectives can immediately attach themselves, the first line also threatens to collapse into one-word fragments. Straining to be expansively appositional, the oracular namer has forgotten for a moment how to name.

Even in filling the first line with no fewer than seven adjectives, three of them polysyllabic, the sibyl seems to be subsiding into darkness. In her world every discontinuous moment is just like every other. She allows a host of unnnamed attributes to drain away through the caesuras and triple dots, like stars that have been vacuumed down a black hole.

> Evening strains to be time's vast, ⏐ womb-of-all, home-of-all, hearse-
>   of-all night.   (l. 2)

The grammatical sundering of 'time's' and 'night' evokes an impression of magnitude. But instead of using tmesis to load every rift with ore, proclaiming the plenitude and bounty of the power she names, the sibyl's swift transit from womb to home to hearse enacts the rapid expansion and quick collapse of a whole universe. When the oracle finally supplies the suspended subject in the noun 'night,' it simply flaunts the power of the hearse to devour, not only the three parts of the compound in which it appears, but also the whole triad of compounds, including the womb and the home, of which it forms the final, all-consuming element.

Normally only a lunatic or child would take literally the metaphor of night as a hearse or tomb. But in Hopkins's bleakly gnostic testament, we can see what abysses open when 'metaphor is conceived as part of an oracular and half-ecstatic process' (Frye, 1963c, 127). As the sibyl moves toward the 'womb-of-all,' the 'hearse-of all,' night (l. 2), her oracle can do nothing to arrest the skid into emptiness. As one commentator says, Hopkins shows that any attempt to abolish differences by an unravelling of 'veined variety' 'destroys what it seeks in the very process by which its quest is conducted. For what is undifferentiated exceeds comprehension; indeed, it remains inaccessible to experience, quite as though it were nothing at all' (Bruns, 1974, 163).

Hopkins's inborn terror of living in the dark is the terror Kierkegaard associates with the 'night of the unconditional.' 'No night and no darkness is half as black,' explains Kierkegaard, as 'this darkness and this night where all relative aims (the ordinary milestones and signposts), where all mutual regards (the lanterns that generally help shed light on our way)' are dimmed or 'extinguished' (Kierkegaard, 1960, 159).

In his bleakest sonnets, Hopkins's efforts to harness the divine energy have the unforeseen effect of knocking down the scaffold of analogy, producing knowledge of God that is not univocal, as he had hoped, but incurably equivocal. In 'No Worst, There Is None,' for example, Hopkins is so totally obsessed by each exquisite and refined torture he thinks peculiar to himself that he loses sight of what connects him with Orestes and King Lear. In celebrating the *concrete* universal at the expense of the concrete *universal*, Hopkins loosens the archetypal bond.

And yet there is another explanation of Hopkins's loss of analogical grip. So overpowering is his fear of being annihilated by the pantheistic idols of the world, which his veneration of each unique item threatens to enshrine, that at times he veers too far in the other direction. Just as Francis Bacon generates an aura of wisdom by appropriating the Bible's rejection of idols, so Hopkins the Scotist sounds wise when staking everything on an unmediated, idol-free encounter with God. But in straining against every idol of the intellect in a bleakly agnostic oracle like 'Spelt from Sibyl's Leaves,' Hopkins swings so far out from every concrete signifier, beyond the last orbit of analogy, that he seems doomed to the fate of a stranded astronaut. The great void into which all analogies empty in 'Spelt from Sibyl's Leaves' is the contemplative poet's apophatic approach to God, the night in which all cows are black. Its traveller resembles one of Dante's lost souls, drifting forever in dark unpopulated space.

3

Though T.S. Eliot, the oracular poet of *Four Quartets*, is a disciple of Dante and the Christian mystics, he also inherits from the idealist philosopher F.H. Bradley, the subject of his Harvard doctoral thesis, large reserves of scepticism. It is precisely this scepticism that proves most congenial to Eliot's sense that human kind cannot bear very much reality. In later years Eliot conceded that he could no longer understand what he had once written about Bradley's theory of knowledge. Indeed anyone who has wrestled with Eliot's book *Knowledge and Experience in the Philosophy of F.H. Bradley* is likely to agree that Bradley himself is easier to understand than his commentator. But Bradley, like Dante, is Eliot's spiritual father. And when the 'unidentifiable' compound ghost chides Eliot in 'Little Gidding' for having forgotten 'my thought and theory,' adding that 'These things have served their purpose' (ll. 59–60), his rebuke is more appropriate to Bradley than to Dante. However radically Eliot may have refined the ideas of a master he studied and admired during his formative years, it is difficult to suppose that he could ignore or suppress that influence altogether. It seems safer to conclude that *Four Quartets* looks two ways at once. If the poem demonstrates Dante's theory that there is a divine order and only fools forget what it is, it also demonstrates Bradley's theory that a divine order exists, but only fools think they can describe that order or presume it is ultimately conceivable or known.

In his harrowing encounter with the phantom master in 'Little Gidding,' Eliot behaves as if he knew the nature of the ghost: he speaks as if the ghost were the result of a split personality. The poet himself assumes a 'double part,' and in his encounter with the phantom master he seems to be confronting a projection of himself. Perhaps the ghost is the image of the fulfilled T.S. Eliot, the genius who writes *Four Quartets*. Through the act of reinterpreting his past Eliot becomes Eliot. In one critic's words, 'that is the way that a poet comes into his own: in constant recoil from his earlier themes, in constant grasping toward the familiar ghost – that face like his but deeply lined – the future poet who has achieved his greatness' (Lipking, 1981, 10). But on closer reflection, neither Eliot nor the reader is quite so sure. If the voice that cries back is not a natural voice, is it imaginary or real? And how can we tell? What matters is less an answer to the question 'Who is the phantom master?' than an understanding of his postmortem status, which is also the question about his father's ghost that puzzles Hamlet. The power of the passage derives from Eliot's ability to minimize neither the sense of limitlessness and mystery nor the sense of precise definition. The ghost is said to be 'familiar' and 'intimate' as well as 'unidentifiable,' and his words compel 'recognition.'

The unforgettable lines on 'the gifts reserved for age' were written by Eliot to remedy what he felt to be 'the lack of some acute personal reminiscence.' But the moment we try to identify the private allusions we confront something limitless, beyond comprehension. The ghost considers how to culminate and then conclude, of how 'To set a crown

upon' a 'lifetime's effort.' The speech itself, however, does not conclude: it is broken off by the breaking of day; and though the phantom
master offers the poet 'a kind of valediction,' we are never told what
he says. The true 'crown' comes only in 'the crowned knot of fire' at
the poem's end. In the meantime, nothing truly ends or culminates.
Reading the master's prophecy is like waiting for the death of a dying
friend. We want the appalling disclosures to end, just as, almost from
the beginning of *Four Quartets*, we have wanted the poet's acute suffering to end.

The speech and description of the compound ghost are vivid and
intensely visual. And yet there is no one person we can picture. Yeats's
use of the dancer and the dance and his horror of being fastened to a
dying animal provide a link between the refining fire of art and the
anatomy of aging. But as a senior contemporary of Eliot, Yeats is too
young to be a mentor who rebukes his pupil for neglecting the
master's 'thought and theory.' Dante is ancient and venerable enough
to be a mentor; and he provides a link between the 'refining fire' of
Purgatorio and the amazed words in which Dante the pilgrim addresses his teacher Brunetto Latini: 'What! are *you* here?' But one problem with Dante's candidacy is that Eliot reverses the roles of master
and student. The poet's mentor addresses his pupil rather than the
other way round. And there is nothing uniquely Dantesque about the
ghost's disclosure of the gifts reserved for age.

As plausible a phantom master as any of the other candidates nom-
inated for the office is Eliot's intellectual father, F.H. Bradley. His
'thought and theory' were the subject of Eliot's doctoral dissertation.
Moreover, in renouncing professional philosophy for poetry and literary criticism, Eliot has 'forgotten' things which have nevertheless
'served their purpose; let them be.' Another point in Bradley's favour
is that, like the phantom master and Eliot, he has devoted himself to
purifying 'the dialect of the tribe.' In his fine essay on Bradley, Eliot
praises the philosopher for 'his great gift of style' (1932, 445). Bradley,
like Aristotle, is distinguished by his scrupulous respect for words.
And as Hugh Kenner has noticed, a pervasive influence of Bradley on
Eliot's style and sensibility is 'the disarmingly hesitant and fragmentary way in which [Eliot] makes a point or expresses a conviction.' Like
his sceptical mentor, Eliot often doubts 'he is quite the man to under-
take the job in hand' or devote 'an entire volume to 'notes toward the
definition' of a 'single word' like culture (Kenner, 1962, 41). A fourth
link between philosopher and phantom master is a common distrust

of sense impressions when torn asunder from what Bradley calls a
'finite centre.' Anyone who has read Bradley's scathing attack on Mill's
perishing impressions of sense in both *The Principles of Logic* and
Ethical Studies will perceive the link between the phantom master's
elegy on the failing senses and Bradley's epitaph for the fleeting atoms
of sense in Mill's associationist psychology. When such expiring atoms
are 'bodily buried in the past, no miracle opens the mouth of the grave
and calls up to the light a perished reality.' Bradley concludes that
Mill's 'touching beliefs' to the contrary 'may babble in the tradition of
a senile psychology, or contort themselves in the metaphysics of some
frantic dogma, but philosophy must register them with a sigh and pass
on' (1883, 280).

One of the great paradoxes in *Ethical Studies* is Bradley's wry reflection that if morality were ever to achieve its goals it would abolish
itself in the process. Though ideal morality tries to remove the distinction between the *ought* and the *is*, it must be preserved as the essential
condition of moral progress. This, I take it, is what Eliot means when
he says that 'Sin is Behovely' ('Little Gidding,' III.17). 'Where there is
no ought there is no morality,' and 'where there is no' sin or 'self-con-
tradiction,' Bradley says, 'there is no ought' (1876, 234). What is forever
unattainable, even in ideal morality, might possibly be attained in religion. But in a concluding chapter of *Appearance and Reality* called 'Ultimate Doubts,' Bradley announces that God's justice and personality
cannot be preserved as ultimate characters of the Absolute, which (in
Bradley's austere words) 'is not personal, nor ... moral, nor ... beautiful
or true' (1893, 472). This denial of God's ultimate reality shocked
Bradley's contemporaries: the Clarendon Press threatened to cancel
publication. And it is true: the negatives do fall with appalling force.
But so do the negatives in *Four Quartets*. Though Eliot never goes so far
as to deny God's ultimate reality, he retains large reserves of Bradley's
scepticism. 'Of wisdom,' Eliot reflects, 'Bradley had a large share;
wisdom consists largely of scepticism and uncynical disillusion; and of
these Bradley had a large share. And scepticism and disillusion are a
useful equipment for religious understanding; and of that Bradley had
a share too' (Eliot, 1932, 449–50).

Like his chorus in *Murder in the Cathedral*, Eliot would probably
argue against Bradley that those who seem to deny God's ultimate
reality 'could not deny, if [God] did not exist.' Moreover, 'their denial
is never complete, for if it were so, *they* would not exist' (*Murder in the
Cathedral*, concluding chorus, l. 5, my emphasis). What I am contend-

ing, however, is that if morality is a contradiction because man is a contradiction, then (Eliot would say) so is religious experience, and so are most efforts to describe it. The darkness of God may be the darkness that is light. But it may also be the darkness of mental emptiness, when 'the mind is conscious but conscious of nothing' ('East Coker,' III.22). 'I said to my soul, be still, and let the dark come upon you / Which shall be the darkness of God' ('East Coker,' III.12–13).

The phases of moral life that Bradley traces in *Ethical Studies* also appear in *Four Quartets*. In their mistaken (because one-sided) emphasis on morality's external and internal sides, respectively, both pleasure for pleasure's sake and duty for duty's sake remind Eliot, as they remind Bradley, what true self-realization is *not*. The self to be realized must honour communal loyalties and allegiances: it must be a product of what Bradley calls its station and its duties. The Mississippi River and the New England seacoasts, which Eliot knew as a youth, and a multitude of later English scenes have imbued the poet of *Four Quartets* with a vision of country and with a conscious refinement of specific times and places. In celebrating human community and 'the life of significant soil' in 'The Dry Salvages,' Eliot seems to be recalling the passage in which Bradley speaks eloquently of the citizen who 'appropriates the common heritage of his race.' Just as Krishna tells Arjuna to be loyal to his station and its duties, so Eliot announces that our destiny awaits us, not 'over a dark lake' or in some 'remote desert or city,' but 'Now and in England.' The patriot who 'grows up' in what Bradley calls 'an atmosphere of example and general custom' knows the partial truth of Bradley's epigram: 'To wish to be better than the world is to be already on the threshold of immorality.'

Though place and time *do* make a difference, Eliot tries to liberate himself from too local or partisan a view by seeking beyond love of country a form of Bradley's 'ideal morality.' He acknowledges at last the need for both the defeated and the victorious, for both strife and harmony, for both Royalist heroes like 'the broken king,' Charles I, and Puritan heroes like Milton, who 'died blind and quiet.' Torn between acute elation and absorption in grief, Eliot balances hope and despair, growing through discipline and prayer into the final 'sort of heavenly or at least more than human gaeity' he cherishes in Beethoven. At the close of 'Little Gidding' so compelling is Eliot's own sense of relief after great suffering that (even though the four quartets cannot be said to constitute a long poem) we feel we might be at the end of a tragedy or epic. We sense that these quartets are less an imitation of the Word than an expression of the kind of spiritual insight or prophetic vision that all the words in the Bible – from creation to apocalypse – exist to express.

4

Like their mentors Bishop Berkeley and William James, for whom abstract ideas are a major vice of the intellect, W.B. Yeats and Robert Frost both wage war against verbal bewitchment. In an effort to expel dead or departed fictions, Yeats tries to revive forgotten etymologies. And Frost, like the pragmatists, tries to explore and map out the consequence for action of the language he selects.

Yeats originally thinks of Berkeley as a Romantic idealist who denies the existence of a material world.

> And God-appointed Berkeley that proved all things a dream,
> That this pragmatical, preposterous pig of a world, its farrow that so solid
> seem,
> Must vanish on the instant if the mind but change its theme;
> ('Blood and the Moon,' ll. 25–7)

After reading Berkeley's *Commonplace Book*, however, Yeats changes his mind. He sees a new Augustan Berkeley, who values cultural robustness and sanity, and who never doubts the power of a sturdy sensuous world to breed life around him. The ghost that Berkeley tries to dispel most vigorously is the ghost of abstract ideas, especially the ghost of a fictitious materialism feeding off the lifeblood of the primary qualities. Bequeathed to later empiricists by Locke, material substance is the great chimera or wraith-rider Berkeley sets out to slay.

Just as Berkeley uses an idealist argument to authenticate the substantial world of everyday experience, so Yeats argues that in dreams begin responsibilities. There are two eternities, those of race and those of soul. And the poet's Irish identity is no less important than his inheritance of a portion of the great Animus Mundi. In 'The Circus Animals' Desertion' Yeats forsakes the 'masterful images' of Irish myth, images of Pateresque ecstasy and fairy fantasy, for the 'refuse or the sweepings' to be found 'in the foul rag-and-bone shop of the heart' (l. 40). Included in these sweepings are new definitions of such words as 'labour,' 'courtesy,' and 'ceremony.' When Yeats redefines 'labour' as 'blossoming or dancing where / The body is not bruised to pleasure soul' ('Among School Children,' ll. 57–8), he is animating a static, ceremonial world with a potential for passion and change. Commemorated in 'Sailing to Byzantium' as 'the artifice of eternity' (l. 24), this hieratic world is filled with 'Presences / That passion, piety, or affection knows.' But unless it is energized by living forms, unless it is as firmly embedded as a 'great-rooted blossomer' or as animated as a dance, it will turn into a mere 'ghostly paradigm' as remote from the contemporary world as medieval Byzantium or Rome.

Yeats's most balanced and considered view of Berkeley appears in his introduction to J.M. Hone and M.M. Rossi's *Bishop Berkeley: His Life, Writings, and Philosophy*. According to Yeats, the Berkeley disclosed in the *Commonplace Book* is an Irishman in revolt, a sceptic who found in the English Locke's abstract ideas 'the opposite that made [his] thought lucid or stung it into expression' (1931, xxi). Instrumental in changing Yeats's understanding of Berkeley are the many entries in the *Commonplace Book* which attack Locke's theory of ideas. In an intriguing essay, 'Was Berkeley a Precursor of Wittgenstein?' (Berkeley, 1993, 214–26, especially 220), Antony Flew argues that these entries anticipate Wittgenstein's warning about the power of words to mystify and confuse the mind. In entry 642, for example, Berkeley notes that 'the Chief thing I do or pretend to do is only to remove the Mist or veil of Words. This has occasion'd ignorance and confusion. This has ruin'd the Schoolmen and Mathematicians, Lawyers and Divines.' In entry 638 Berkeley is equally insistent that 'whatever word we make use of in matter of pure reasoning has or ought to have a complete Idea annexed to it, i.e. its meaning or the sense we take it in must be completely known.' We can observe Yeats heeding Berkeley's advice in the concrete images he attaches to words like 'custom' and 'ceremony,' which are made as immediate to our senses as a spreading laurel tree and rich horn.

In 'A Prayer for My Daughter' and 'In Memory of Major Robert Gregory,' Yeats revives forgotten etymologies that give new descriptive content to his prize words. In lines recording a growth in beauty and temper toward the 'hidden flourishing tree,' the father prays that all his daughter's

> thoughts may like the linnet be,
> And have no business but dispensing round
> Their magnanimities of sound,

Nor but in merriment begin a chase,
Nor but in merriment a quarrel.
O may she live like some green laurel
Rooted in one dear perpetual place.   ('A Prayer for My Daughter,' ll. 42–8)

The poet's bitter attack upon feminists like Maud Gonne, 'an old bellows full of angry wind' (l. 64), recalls Berkeley's attack upon abstract ideas in philosophers like Locke. In contrast to the shrill fanaticism of Maud Gonne, whose 'intellectual hatred' is accused of being 'the worst,' since it undoes the horn of plenty (ll. 57–60), Yeats's prayer moves from thoughtful meditation toward the quiet definition of 'ceremony' and 'custom' at the close:

Ceremony's a name for the rich horn,
And custom for the spreading laurel tree.   (ll. 79–80)

When Yeats says he would have his daughter 'in courtesy ... chiefly learned' (l. 33), he is celebrating an Augustan rather than a Romantic virtue, a value he associates with eighteenth-century aristocracy, courtliness and patronage. He is thinking of a mood or temper defined with precision in an earlier poem, 'In Memory of Robert Gregory,' where Lionel Johnson is said to be 'courteous to the worst' (l. 19). Death, by contrast, is 'discourteous' to the best, to 'Our Sidney and our perfect man' (ll. 47–8). The 'discourtesy' of Gregory's death has made Yeats discourteous, too, since his plan to commemorate other dead friends has broken down. The 'fitter welcome' he wanted to extend to them is now uncivilly withheld. Though 'courtesy' denotes gracious concern, it also evokes as a shadow meaning the tenure in medieval law by which a husband holds property inherited from a spouse. Gregory cannot share in that tenure; premature death has deprived him of his due. Embroidered upon an archaic legal meaning of 'courtesy,' the incivility is a breach of both decorum and law.

Though far removed from the high exaltation and ecstasy of 'The Second Coming,' the easy joy in 'The Gyres' mocks as well as invokes the solemnity of 'Old Rocky Face,' the oracle at Delphi.

The Gyres! the gyres! Old Rocky Face, look forth;
Things thought too long can be no longer thought,
For beauty dies of beauty, worth of worth,
And ancient lineaments are blotted out.   ('The Gyres,' ll. 1–4)

Yeats sometimes sounds like a ventriloquist intoning through a puppet. But usually the spirits he conjures from the cliff-face of mystery, 'Old Rocky Face,' are a hiding place of power, a shadow of lost knowledge. Does Yeats beget the oracle, or is the oracle the voice of a power that begets *him*? Yeats sometimes uses the voices as his mouthpiece. 'Out of a cavern comes a voice / And all it knows is the one word "Rejoice!"' ('The Gyres,' ll. 15–16). But in 'The Man and the Echo,' another poem on the Delphic oracle, old Rocky Face is strangely withholding, and refuses to answer either of Yeats's questions:

> O Rocky Voice,
> Shall we in that great night rejoice?
> What do we know but that we face
> One another in this place?   ('The Man and the Echo,' ll. 39–42)

When the owl descends, it is not as wisdom, the owl of Athena, but as a bird of prey that drops out of the sky and elicits from a rabbit a mad cry of pain.

> Up there some hawk or owl has struck,
> Dropping out of the sky or rock,
> A stricken rabbit is crying out
> And its cry distracts my thought.   ('The Man and the Echo,' ll. 45–8)

Though all that flames upon the night (including the fire-tongued oracles of great prophets and seers) 'man's own resinous heart has fed' ('Two Songs from a Play,' l. 32), Rocky Voice's self-begetting features exist in uneasy tension with the oracle's use by the god as an instrument of revelation. Yeats must live in the tension of this paradox, for if the oracle is not of his begetting, it is alien to his genius, like Berkeley's understanding of matter, which is a mere abstraction and chimera. Conversely, if the oracle is merely a voice of Yeats's begetting, it is a mere projection, and so in Berkeley's view no less defective. In the second case the oracle is the voice of a ventriloquist: in the first case, it is the speechless face of an idol. In C.S. Lewis's novel *Till We Have Faces*, the slab of stone that is worshipped in the priestess's house remains a mere idol until characters in the story try to give it an authentic countenance and name. When the god's baptism takes place, the object of worship turns into something immeasurably more demonic – or daemonic – than an idol. It becomes either a lustful

Shadow-brute or else Cupid himself, the resplendent god of love, a shining youth who enraptures Psyche and claims her as his ravishing (and ravished) bride. As Northrop Frye remarks of Apuleius's version of the myth, it is a 'lovely story' that 'floats like a soap-bubble up from [the] tale of Lucius transformed to an ass' (1976b, 154).

A prophet combines the seer's talent for hearing voices with a puppet's gift for being a passive and malleable instrument of transmission. As a receptacle of God's word, the priestess of Apollo at Delphi is a channel of revelation. To the degree she is a genuine prophet, she is always trying to reinvent the oracles by substituting for the copy speech of a puppet what Frost calls 'counter-love, original response.' But as the mouthpiece of a divine ventriloquist, the priestess may be too stupefied or stunned to know what she is saying. Like many prophet-poets, she is deeply divided. On the one hand, her oracles are projections. As a ventriloquist who is half-human, half-divine, she trains her voice to simulate Apollo's. On the other hand, like biblical prophets from Isaiah to St John she is also more than an impersonator or a verbal mimic. The priestess is a seer or visionary through whom the god speaks in sublime, beautiful, or grotesque oracles, and in whom authentic acts of 'counter-love' may also take place.

As Seamus Heaney says of Wordsworth's Boy of Winander, the seer may discover in the moment of 'baulked silence,' when the cliff-face refuses to return his mimic hootings, 'something more wonderful than owl-calls' (2002, 227). When the boy 'stands open like an eye or an ear, he becomes imprinted with all the melodies and hieroglyphs of the world; the workings of the active universe ... are echoed inside him' (2002, 227). Even when the oracle in 'The Man and the Echo' merely echoes the poet's most desolating words (the refrains 'Lie down and die' and 'Into the night'), Yeats never abandons the prophet's high vocation of bringing the soul of man to God.

> In a cleft that's christened Alt
> Under broken stone I halt
> At the bottom of a pit
> That broad noon has never lit,
> And shout a secret to the stone.   ('The Man and the Echo,' ll. 1–5)

Fortifying himself against any mindless assaults from the bleak oracle 'that's christened Alt,' Yeats moves from the shadow of his darkened pit into the light of vision. Despite the oracle's discouraging copy-speech, the poet's counter-speech is bracing and undaunted.

Yeats embraces random impressions of sense, not because he is willing to submit to them passively, but because he delights in transforming them into 'masterful images' cast by a cold eye on life and death.

> I balanced all, brought all to mind,
> The years to come seemed wasted breath,
> A waste of breath the years behind
> In balance with this life, this death.
>
> ('An Irish Airman Foresees His Death,' ll. 13–16)

Turning on the pivot of the late-breaking caesura, 'this life, this death,' the airman's audit looks back and forward at once. In both directions he sees only levelling stretches of sad waste time. Yet the provisional conduct and potential defeat of every life and poem is also beautifully offset by the triple chiasmus, which substitutes spatial envelopment and mental control for the aimless drift of images in time. The repetition in reverse order of phrases both wise and wrenching ('The years to come seemed wasted breath, / A waste of breath the years behind') allows the airman to anticipate and recall details of his life in acts of fearful premonition and dispassionate scrutiny of his past. Just as Berkeley's theory of knowledge uses the mind's mediations to master the linear drive of fleeting impressions of sense, so (as Helen Vendler has shown) tropes of balance and inversion allow Yeats to shape and celebrate bracing feats of mind.

Like Swift in his satire on the Academy of Lagado, Berkeley condemns philosophers who 'with a supercilious Pride disdain the common single informations of sense.' He attacks their grasping 'at Knowledge by sheaves and bundles ('tis well if catching at too much at once they hold nothing but emptiness and air' (entry 748). According to A.C. Luce, Yeats met 'the true Berkeley in the pages of "the *Commonplace Book* with its snorts of defiance."' Committed to showing the 'foul rag-and-bone shop of the heart' as well as 'the artifice of eternity,' the poet 'revelled in those notebooks, and from them he learned the simple truth which he expressed in the words, "Descartes, Locke, and Newton, took away the world ... Berkeley restored the world. Berkeley has brought back to us the world that only exists because it shines and sounds"' (Luce, 1945, viii), as it does so luminously in Yeats's best verse and prose.

5

Just as Yeats, the student of George Berkeley, is an unremitting critic of the abstract ideas that turn Maud Gonne into a Helen of social welfare dream, so Robert Frost's most influential mentor, William James, insists it is impossible to have a philosophically interesting theory of the dictionary meaning of a word. For James, as for Frost, a word's meaning is its consequence for action. As Frost's farmer says in 'The Mountain,' words are unstable, and 'all the fun's in how you say a thing.' To define the word 'home,' for example, in 'The Death of the Hired Man,' Warren translates the noun into a sequence of possible future acts: 'Home is the place where, when you have to go there, / They have to take you in' (ll. 118–19). In identifying the meaning of 'home' with its use, both Warren and his wife prove the truth of James's assertion that 'if I am lost in the woods and starved,' the 'true thought' about 'house' is 'useful,' 'because the house which is its object is useful' (James, 1911, 203). In his poem 'For Once, Then, Something,' Frost discovers 'an oracle at a well curb.' 'What was that whiteness?,' he asks, in a tone one critic describes as 'shrewdly realistic and dimly revelatory' (Brower, 1963, 136). 'Truth? A pebble of quartz? For once, then something' (ll. 14–15). Frost is a pragmatist among poets, a celebrant of both visionary vagrancy and everyday New England life.

In Frost's poem 'The Mountain,' many of the most idiosyncratic and memorable turns of phrase in the old farmer's speech stem from his pragmatic distrust of nouns. Substantives petrify action and block thought. They must be translated into chains of verbs that can be used and tested as blueprints for action. The speaker's confident use of nouns and demonstrative pronouns – '"What town is this?" I asked' – is quickly challenged by the farmer's surprising denial – 'There is no village' – and then by his amusing demonstration that words like 'village' are not inscribed for definiteness, only for reinvention. 'Village' has to be redefined to accommodate the novel fact that there are 'only scattered farms' in the town of Lunenburg. Even a noun with an apparently stable referent, the noun that gives the poem its title, is a convenient fiction for something too indefinite – and perhaps too numinous – to name. The farmer seems to realize that the mountain 'Hor' can be made a sign for anything: for the farmer himself, his town, even for the lure of the prophecies that are sometimes heard and made on mountain-tops. But he is reluctant to abet the speaker in his efforts to extract a single definite meaning from the word. For the essentialist notion that it is in the nature of mountain peaks to provide oracular visions, the farmer substitutes the more pragmatic, because empirically verifiable, notion that if there is a brook on the mountain, it must have a spring as its source. Like any self-respecting pragmatist, Frost's farmer establishes the conditions under which the truth or falsity of his statement could be established. The spring 'may not be right on the very top,' he concedes. But

'It wouldn't have to be a long way down
To have some head of water from above,
And a *good distance* down might not be noticed
By anyone who'd come a long way up.'   ('The Mountain,' ll. 69–72)

In answer to the question, 'how far is it around the mountain?,' the farmer turns a mere abstract number – five or six miles, say – into an entertaining account of how, if one were resolved to drive around Lunenberg, it would be barely possible to encircle the mountain without crossing the township boundary. Equally playful and more extravagant is his observation that the water in the mountain brook possesses the apparently magical property of being 'always cold in summer, warm in winter.' This arresting way of phrasing the matter allows the farmer both to grasp the pragmatic truth that propositions are called true or false for reasons of convenience or use and to restate the old axiom that all experience of temperatures is relative.

'I don't suppose the water's changed at all.
You and I know enough to know it's warm
Compared with cold, and cold, compared with warm.
But all the fun's in how you say a thing.'   ('The Mountain,' ll. 101–4)

Frost's playful account of a meteor's cosmic origins in his poem 'A Star in a Stoneboat' beautifully illustrates the immense delight or 'fun' of 'how you say a thing.' The meteoric stone used to build the wall is fancifully identified as the 'star' slipped 'from heaven' that 'softly' fell. Using available scientific evidence to explain the 'flying thing' with the 'long Bird of Paradise's tail,' Frost invites the labourer to prove the hypothesis of the stone's stellar origins by considering such data as the heat of the soil and the stone's magnetic properties. As cosmic matter, the 'star' in the 'stoneboat' is a microcosm of the earth itself. It makes concrete the mystery of the planet's stellar origins.

Frost's 'Mending Wall' is a boundary or definition poem that mini-mizes neither the advantages nor dangers of setting limits. To set a limit may provide a stay against confusion. But since a definition or a boundary may also seal truth off, Frost's speaker says, 'Before I built a wall I'd ask to know / What I was walling in or walling out.' To 'wall in' is to end the search for experiences that might better explain the meaning of being closed or open. Less concerned with producing true propositions than with finding new vocabularies and metaphors to keep inquiry going, a pragmatist resists any extravagant flight from the world, any form of premature pronouncement, that would bring inquiry to an end. What has been concluded, Frost would ask, that there is anything to conclude? Even when the desire to end is strongest, when the pull into wintry oblivion in 'After Apple Picking' or in 'Stopping by Woods on a Snowy Evening' is hardest to resist, Frost steadily opposes any oracle that offers closure prematurely. In 'Stopping by Woods on a Snowy Evening,' the puzzled horse, thinking it queer that its master should drift into reveries, assumes the role of an inquisitorial William James. The momentary surrender to the enchantment of the lovely woods is what James would call a form of 'moral holidaying,' a mental vagrancy or freedom to dream that has no 'cash-value' in the horse's practical arithmetic.

Equally playful in its blend of extravagance and homeliness is Frost's poem 'The Generations of Men,' an experiment in projecting and hearing voices. Behind the epistemological paradoxes that inform any debate about oracles (Are the voices overhead or projected? Do we find or invent them?), it is possible to hear the first tactical manoeu-vres in a game of courtship. The young woman of the Sark clan pre-dicts that the voices she and her young male cousin hear will be about themselves, because the voices exist, in true pragmatic fashion, as a consequence of their 'having been together.' The oracle seems 'to say: / Call her Nausicaä, the unafraid ... / Call her Nausicaä' (ll. 152, 160). Its ritual naming initiates a series of performative acts, which combine the petitions of courtship with the injunctions of a reinvented pastoral myth: 'And come and make your summer dwelling here, / And perhaps she will come' (ll. 166–7). Faith in a New England Ulysses and his cherished Nausicaä represents the kind of 'will to believe' that even a tough-minded sceptic must risk if she is to be authentically open to human encounter, 'unafraid,' as Frost's youth says, of 'an acquaintance made adventurously' (l. 153). Such oracular turns in poetry fascinate

Frost because they reflect our own intensified moments, our own capacity to take time out, to wander in imagination, and to think prophetically. As Frost says, 'they are most us.'

There are several ways a poem by Frost may die to time and acquire the over-meaning of a wise saying or oracle. One critic says of Frost's last line from 'The Wood-pile,' 'With the slow smokeless burning of decay,' that the 'sound carries an extraordinary authority and dignity because it has emerged out of the more sauntering vernacular movements at the beginning of the poem' (Poirier, 1977, 143). A loneliness in that line, which includes us unawares, sends another critic, Anthony Hecht, in search of some oblique 'under-thought' or 'over-meaning' that might account for its power. His intriguing suggestion is that the abandoned wood-pile, the 'handiwork' on which some craftsman spent himself, is Frost's own early poetry, which 'had gone virtually unnoticed during the poet's lifetime,' and which might 'be chanced upon by some stray wanderer long after the poet's death' (Hecht, 2003, 158).

In his book on pragmatism, James uses the adjective 'tough-minded' to describe the sceptical, experimental qualities he favours over the soft, visionary temperament of the idealist. Welcoming openness and risk, the 'typical Rocky Mountain toughs in philosophy' (1911, 12) mock the idealizing visionary impulse of their tender-minded counterparts. They consign the 'tender-foot's' extravagance or whim to a mere 'lady-land' of fancy,

'As't were the country of the Amazons
We men must see you to the confines of
And leave you there, ourselves forbid to enter.'

('West-Running Brook,' ll. 33–5)

In dramatizing the clash of tough and tender-minded speakers, Frost shows how every pragmatic critic of traditional philosophy faces a dilemma. If his language is too sceptical and tough, too purged of the idealist quest for truth, it will sound as indifferent or callous as the husband in 'Home Burial.' If his language is too oracular and playful, it will lack the blend of inner seriousness and homeliness that we value in Frost's best conversational poems. Whether a tender-minded philosophy appears in biblical prophecies or in the oracles of Absolute idealists, even in so gritty and tough-minded a philosopher as F.H.

Bradley, its monism is always the great enemy of pragmatists. For it forces premature closure, absorbs novelty and difference, and gives licence to unrestrained visionary vagrancy. Frost, like James, seeks a different universe. He is at home only in an open world whose intelligibility cannot be worried into being but must unfold by surprise, like the risky and imperfect art of writing poetry or making love.

2 Tennyson and Zeno: Three Infinities

The English poet most honoured and mocked in his lifetime for his vatic musings is Alfred Tennyson. In the tradition of wisdom writers from Virgil to the Zen Buddhists, Tennyson tries to master a plenitude of emptiness. Confronting the illimitable inane of Lucretius's universe and the huge whispering gallery of silence created by a knowledge of astronomy and a study of the earth's vanished species, Tennyson discovers that the way of wisdom requires large reserves of scepticism. But it also requires the imaginative play of a poet whose work is to expend energy for its own sake and find a way out of emptiness.

Though Tennyson left Cambridge without a degree because he refused to climb 'the apparently unscalable wall of mathematics' (Martin, 1980, 54), astronomy, physics, and the new geology of Robert Chambers and Charles Lyell continued to fire his imagination with thoughts of two immensities: the infinitely great and the infinitely small. As the mourner contemplates the fossil record and the long perspectives of the earth's history, sowing the dust of continents to be in *In Memoriam*, he hears a female harpy cry, like the sibyl in Heraclitus: 'A thousand types are gone; I care for nothing, all shall go' (56.2–4). The poem also plunges Tennyson into a second kind of infinity: into the vortex of an endlessly receding mindscape. Within Tennyson's picture of the earth is a picture of his own mind, and within that picture a picture of the mind that frames the pictures, and so on to infinity. In the third place, as a mystic who uses mantras to evoke God's presence, Tennyson is continually trying to map the coordinates of the Nameless of the hundred Names. Transformed by rapture and transfixed by awe, he is touched in turn by these three infinities: physical infinities of space and time, infinities of a mindscape, and the metaphysical paradox of a God who is absolute and infinite at the same time.

1

Tennyson most memorably evokes infinities of space and time in 'Ulysses,' where the poetry is distinguished by self-retarding motions that inch toward the end of a line by tiny increments, like Zeno's tortoise.

> Yet all experience is an arch wherethrough
> Gleams that untravelled world, whose margin fades
> For ever and for ever when I move.   ('Ulysses,' ll. 19–21)

In imitation of the 'untravelled world' that gleams alluringly before Ulysses, expansive open vowels with long quantities and voiced consonants begin to stretch and pull open the long central line. Readers can also literally see how the 'fading margin' of that world coincides with a slight fading of the poem's right-hand margin on the printed page. Indeed long vowels and assonance combine with the visual impact of the poem's 'printed voice' to create an impression of spaciousness so vast that Matthew Arnold felt 'these three lines by themselves take up nearly as much time as a whole book of the *Iliad*' (Arnold, 1960, 1:189).

It is as impossible for Tennyson's Ulysses to reach the untravelled world glimpsed through his arch as it is for Achilles to overtake the tortoise or for Zeno's arrow to reach its target. As in Zeno's third paradox of motion, which argues that an arrow in flight is always at rest, Tennyson often freezes motion into a still life or photograph that visualizes spatial effects through sound. Browning, by contrast, is always trying to free the arrow from the frame in which Zeno freezes it, and then to graph the trajectory it traces. A student of calculus would say that as a connoisseur of spatial effects and *opsis*, Tennyson is a poet of derivatives, who takes refuge from vertiginous movements by retreating to the still point of an instant in time, which appears like Zeno's arrow to possess no motion at all. Though Zeno's arrow must have instantaneous velocity, it is hard to determine at any given moment what that speed might be. To calculate such velocity we have to divide zero distance by zero time, which is an impossible operation. As a poet who traces movement in time rather than pattern in space,

Browning reverses this process by graphing integrals instead of derivatives. Out of a point in space he generates the volume of a sphere or a three-dimensional star, just as the student of calculus adds up pieces of area that have no volume in themselves to create a solid object that has three dimensions.

As in the hierarchical world of Pope's *Essay on Man*, where the chain of being is a ladder or the vertical axis of a graph, *In Memoriam*'s 'great world's altar-stairs that slope through darkness up to God' (55.15–16) approximate a 45 degree-slanted straight line. If x is the length of time Tennyson has travelled on the moving stair, then the function $f(x) = x$ tells us how high he has climbed. Matters become more complicated when the scale of nature turns into an escalator that may suddenly accelerate or abruptly slow down at any moment. Once Newton's laws of motion substitute changing velocity for constant velocity we require a function like $f(x) = x^2$ to plot Tennyson's new position on the escalator. We now need calculus to determine the velocity at which Tennsyon is travelling at any given place on the moving stair: in this case, a derivative of the function $f(x) = x^2$, namely $2x$. We also need calculus to determine the exact distance he has travelled. This distance turns out to be the antiderivative of the function, which is also the area under the graph of the sloping line.

In 'Ulysses' Tennyson creates an effect of infinite regress and vertigo by opening up three separate time frames. About to embark on his last voyage, the speaker recalls a time during his return to Ithaca when he was welcomed as a hero whose exploits from a still earlier period of his life were already known. Experiencing what it means to 'become a name' (l. 11), Ulysses has the odd sensation of confronting a legendary version of himself, a hero who once stepped out of Homer's pages, and from whom he is now many times removed.

The vortices in 'Ulysses' induce several forms of vertigo. Near the end of the poem Ulysses becomes for a moment his own audience. He observes himself drowning in a whirlpool or vortex of waves, dashed like Dante's mariner against the Mount of Purgatory.

> It may be that the gulfs will wash us down:
> It may be we shall touch the Happy Isles,
> And see the great Achilles, whom we knew.   ('Ulysses,' ll. 62–4)

At other moments Ulysses creates a vortex of dissolving time frames and events. Alive with both the clamour of war and empty windswept ruins, the spacious line 'Far on the ringing plains of windy Troy' (l. 17) collapses the space filled by years of conflict into a direct confrontation of pride and ruin. By combining battle on the darkling plain with a picture of Troy as the bare ruined choir of wasting winds, Ulysses allows the mind to cross great intervals of space and time. So voracious indeed is the whirligig of time that its vortex begins to induce the kind of vertigo Tennyson experiences in section 123 of *In Memoriam*. Here shocking pictures of hills as shadows and of solid land as mist run events together. It is as if the poet had just taken a time-lapse photograph of the earth extending over billions of years. Such pictures are not so much 'timeless' as 'timeful,' since they include an infinite regress of past and future snapshots of a given place.

Ulysses encounters a third form of vertigo in the prospect of passing 'Beyond the utmost bound of human thought' in a dizzying violation of the law of limits.

> And this gray spirit yearning in desire
> To follow knowledge like a sinking star
> Beyond the utmost bound of human thought.   ('Ulysses,' ll. 30–2)

Logically, the last line carries to a sublime depth of vision the contradictions of a bull. For if Ulysses is able to pass beyond a cosmic edge or limit, it cannot literally be 'the utmost bound' he claims it is. Instead, it is only one more end before the end, one more limit to be crossed before death closes all.

To sustain the sense of vertigo Tennyson allows the striking simile of the sinking star to fall two ways at once. Does the plummeting star trace the overreacher's manner of pursuing knowledge? Or does it trace the trajectory of the receding knowledge he pursues? In the first case, the vertigo induced by the falling star may be a product of Faustian arrogance. In passing beyond the utmost bound of human thought, Ulysses is passing into the *apeiron*, which for Aristotle can mean not only 'infinitely large' but also 'totally disordered, infinitely complex, subject to no finite determination.' In this interpretation, the vertigo Ulysses experiences is 'a privation, not a perfection' (Rucker, 1983, 3). Grazed by chaos in his brush with the infinite, Ulysses is unfit for future life in Ithaca. Alternatively, the vortex of the sinking star may dramatize the general paradox of the infinity of knowledge: Pope's paradox of hills peeping over hills and Alps on Alps arising.

In 'The Two Voices' Tennyson formulates the same epistemological paradox without any hint of criticism.

> 'The highest-mounted mind,' he said,
> 'Still sees the sacred morning spread
> The silent summit overhead.'   ('The Two Voices,' ll. 79–81)

The double trajectory of the plummeting star allows us to register simultaneously the sublime elusiveness of the goal and the ironic retreat of the goal, which like the flight of an asymptote from its curve continues to recede no matter how closely Ulysses approaches it.

Like the pure questing of Browning's Childe Roland, Ulysses' quest is Tennyson's version of the typical Victorian preoccupation with what Walter Houghton calls 'aspiration without an object' (1957, 291–7). To borrow Robert Frost's phrase ('Directive,' l. 49), the poem has a 'destiny' but no 'destination.' It foresees but impedes its own end. Accordingly, there are no past or future verbs at the end of 'Ulysses.' Instead, the speaker is absorbed into a cluster of timeless infinitives, poised between verb and substantive, between finite acts and endless questing. The poem's final phrases drift down, one by one, with as steady but unhurried a conclusion as any poem can have.

> that which we are, we are:
> One equal temper of heroic hearts,
> Made weak by time and fate, but strong in will
> To strive, to seek, to find, and not to yield   ('Ulysses,' ll. 67–70)

It is as if Ulysses, like Tennyson, were as reluctant to end his life as those final, tenseless infinitives – staring off into space and time – are reluctant to end the poem.

The paratactic syntax in line 5 of 'Ulysses' ('That hoard, and sleep, and feed, and know not me') and the infinitive triad of line 70, each capped by a negative construction, call to each other across sixty-five intervening lines of verse through an apparatus of allusion. Though audible only to attentive readers, they show how the echoes of Hamlet that resound subliminally ('What is a man, / If the chief good and market of his time / Be but to sleep and feed?' IV.iv.33–5) allow Ulysses, like his Shakespearean double, to be and not to be; to say opposite things simultaneously. As in the closing line of 'The Lotos-

Eaters,' 'O rest ye, brother mariners, we will not wander more,' words drag after them their own opposite, not for contradiction but development. In the verb of volition, 'we will not wander more,' the mariners evoke for a fleeting instant the resolute opposite of that irresolution and inertia into which they continue to subside. Similarly, even in Ulysses' defiant 'not to yield,' it is hard not to hear in the expansive infinitive the tranquillizing opposite of what Ulysses keeps asserting: the desire for oblivion of a mind half in love with easeful death.

2

I turn now from infinities of space and time to the infinite regress of Tennyson's mindscapes. Whenever the poet recalls with fond and exact scrutiny a place he once loved and cared for, it becomes a landscape of his mind. One distinguishing feature of such a mindscape is its inclusion of the recollecting mind in each local geography that it depicts. In section 101 of *In Memoriam*, for example, Tennyson anticipates a mindscape of neglect and oblivion after his family leaves Sombersby and the ancient garden-boughs and flowers fall into ruin. Anxiety can be felt in his equivocal syntax: 'And year by year our memory fades / From all the circle of the hills' (ll. 23–4). Is the possessive pronoun 'our' a subjective or objective genitive? Does the poet's memory of the hills fade, or the hills' memory of *him*? The second possibility is the more unexpected and disturbing. And yet even the hills' fading memory of the poet is a framing of the past that the poet himself has still to enclose within a second frame of his mindscape. Because Tennyson, even in grieving that the Somersby rectory is no longer loved and cared for, continues to love and care for it, he expects us to see why no picture of a once cherished place can ever be unhinged from a self-conscious mind. Indeed the picture within picture of a framed absence is always more vivid for Tennyson than an event he has experienced only once. Like the falling tree in an earless forest, the minimal unit of cognition is what a framing mind (God's or one's own) *perceives* to be real. The mind's power to frame its world is explored at length by Tennyson's friend, J.F. Ferrier, a Victorian George Berkeley, who publishes a series of seven articles entitled 'An Introduction to the Philosophy of Consciousness' in *Blackwood's Magazine* between February 1838 and March 1839. I explore the influence of Ferrier's idealism on Tennyson's mindscapes in *The Lucid Veil* (1987, 48–53).

The mourner's recollections of these remembered mindscapes

explain why *In Memoriam* is so recursive a poem, one that repeats, repeats, and repeats again, often with no relieving difference. A third anniversary of Hallam's death recalls a second anniversary, and a second anniversary recalls the original shock of the mourner's first hearing of Hallam's death. Such a poem of recursive mindscapes is clearly tracking, not only the progress of a dead soul, but also the successive surges of grief and melancholia that pass over and through the mourner like great shock waves or tremors. Just as the history of Christianity is more about the afterlife of Christ than about the life and death of its founder, so *In Memoriam* is as much about Hallam's afterlife in the mourner's mindscapes as it is about Hallam himself.

An important feature of *In Memoriam*'s mindscapes is the mourner's emblematic imagery for his own mind. The landscape of his past includes a picture of a forlorn yew tree, of an infant crying in the night, and of a burial ship, and each of these pictures includes other pictures of the same bleak image. The power of Tennyson's mind to generate recursive pictures of itself often induces a disturbing vertigo. In sections 54–6 of *In Memoriam* man, the self-conscious architect of mindscapes, turns out to be as far below the dinosaurs as he was once thought to be above them as 'the roof and crown of things.' At the bottom of the altar-stairs that slope through darkness up to God lies a false floor. And through an opening in that floor, man, the cosmic misfit, can fall in an apparently infinite descent far lower than the rest of the creation.

> And he, shall he,
>
> Man, her last work, who seemed so fair,
>   Such splendid purpose in his eyes,
>   Who rolled the psalm to wintry skies,
> Who built him fanes of fruitless prayer,
>
> Who trusted God was love indeed
>   And love Creation's final law –
>   Though Nature, red in tooth and claw
> With ravine, shrieked against his creed –
>
> Who loved, who suffered countless ills,
>   Who battled for the True, the Just,
>   Be blown about the desert dust,
> Or sealed within the iron hills?   (*In Memoriam*, 56.8–20)

In the first two quatrains a familiar feature of the appositional sublime, a use of widely spaced anaphora – 'Who built,' 'Who trusted,' 'Who loved' – gives man, God's noblest work, a spacious dwelling place in language. But, far from confirming that nobility, the run-ons between stanzas suspend man over an abyss of dizzying duration and depth. Amid physical infinities of time and space, the self-contained tetrameter quatrains of *In Memoriam*, with their included rhymes (*a b b a*), normally provide the mourner with a secure platform on which to stand. But now that floor is opening up. As the relative pronouns modifying 'man' begin huddling together, the repetitive contrasts, accumulative doubts, and bleak predicate of the quoted question mount to a crescendo of fear that is typical of the manic phase of depression and melancholia. Instead of providing comfort, the expansive appositions disclose a trap door through which man, God's last work of creation, 'who seemed so fair,' can plummet, like Milton's Lucifer, to new depths below.

Qualities of 'purpose, 'trust,' and 'love' that exalt man, that make him, as Hamlet says, 'noble in reason,' 'infinite in faculty,' angelic 'in apprehension,' 'the beauty of the world,' 'the paragon of animals,' also make him, as the merest 'quintessence of dust' (*Hamlet*, II.ii.315–19), the greatest anomaly in creation. In the next two quatrains the desolating thought that man's vision of cosmic harmony tragically unfits him for life and love in a world 'red in tooth and claw,' described by Erasmus Darwin as 'one vast slaughter-house,' collapses the expansive appositions into word heaps that are barely grammatical.

> No more? A monster then, a dream,
>   A discord. Dragons of the prime
>   That tare each other in their slime,
> Were mellow music matched with him.
>
> O life as futile, then, as frail!
>   O for thy voice to soothe and bless!
>   What hope of answer, or redress?
> Behind the veil, behind the veil.   (*In Memoriam*, 56.21–8)

Biologically considered, dragons of the primeval slime are better adapted to their environment than creatures whose dreams of design are unknown to their Creator. Though such a Creator is not malicious, he may not, as Einstein thought, be subtle either, but simply the 'Vast Imbecility' that Hardy fears in 'Nature's Questioning' (l. 13), a God who produces minds, but lacks one himself – a monstrous paradox.

The boldest explorer of mindscapes in Victorian poetry is G.M. Hopkins, who knows their terrors of recursive infinitude: 'the mind has mountains; cliffs of fall / Frightful, sheer, no-man-fathomed' ('No Worst, There Is None,' ll. 9–10). No sooner does Hopkins, the climber of mindscapes, plunge to a new depth of despair than he realizes there is always another depth, another lower level of grief and despair, to plunge to.

> No worst, there is none. Pitched past pitch of grief
> More pangs will, schooled at forepangs, wilder wring.
> Comforter, where, where is your comforting?   (ll. 1–3)

Such trap doors and vortices are also familiar to Shakespeare's Edgar, who asks the gods in *King Lear*:

> Who is't can say 'I am at the worst'?
> I am worse than e'er I was ...
> And worse I may be yet. The worst is not
> So long as we can say 'This is the worst'   (IV.i.25–8)

Even Christina Rossetti fears that the lowest place is still too high for her.

> Give me the lowest place: or if for me
>   That lowest place too high, make one more low
> Where I may sit and see
>   My God and Love Thee so.   ('The Lowest Place,' ll. 5–8)

> The lowest place. Ah, Lord, how steep and high
>   That lowest place whereon a saint shall sit!
> Which of us halting, trembling, pressing nigh,
>   Shall quite attain to it?   ('Called to Be Saints,' ll. 1–4)

More typical of the casualties among the mind's mountaineers is Milton's Satan, whose exploration of hell is a free fall through space. Satan's descent from one depth to a lower depth mocks the very idea of a 'lowest deep' or limit.

> Which way I flie is Hell; my self am Hell;
> And in the lowest deep a lower deep
> Still threatening to devour me opens wide,
> To which the Hell I suffer seems a Heav'n.   (Milton, *Paradise Lost*, IV.75–8)

Since each descent to a lower depth stands to its preceding depth as hell does to heaven, Satan's mindscape of hell includes within itself an image of each new hell to which he is falling, and within that image another image, in an endless regress of descents. A similar virus infects Tennyson's portrait of man, the 'roof and crown' of creation, who is also its most monstrous anomaly.

In 'The Ancient Sage' Tennyson provides in 'the abyss of all abysms' a basement or foundation for the mind's free fall through space. The quoted phrase refers also to the vortex of time, which is menacing because its fading memory of memories leaves only a faint wrack behind. Tennyson's 'passion of the past' arrests the regress, however, by giving each act of recollection as much distinct dignity and worth as the past it remembers. In 'The Lotos-Eaters' the past becomes dreadful when the mariners lose all memory of it. In *The Tempest*, by contrast, Miranda manages to dredge from 'the dark backward and abysm of time' (*The Tempest*, I.ii.49–50) some residual traces of what happened to her as a child. Logically, the line should read 'in the dark abyss of events that occurred far back in time, in the distant past.' But Shakespeare uses a daring combination of metonymy and hendiadys to turn 'back' from an adverb ('back in time') to a noun, 'the backward and abysm of time.' Time is still the dark behind of a monster both rapacious and menacing. But like the hollow form with empty hands in *In Memoriam*, time now has a wallet at its back in which to keep alms for oblivion. A magician like Prospero or a prophet like Tennyson may still redeem the unread vision of his past in a higher dream.

It would be a mistake to conclude, therefore, that all the infinite regresses in *In Memoriam* have a viral malignancy. After chronicling the earth's appalling dissolution in section 123, which is in danger of producing mere blackout and indifference, the mourner announces with Olympian serenity:

> But in my spirit will I dwell,
> And dream my dream, and hold it true;
> For though my lips may breathe adieu,
> I cannot think the thing farewell.   (*In Memoriam*, 123.9–12)

I used to think that 'dream my dream' was Tennyson's private joke. Instead of being unnerved by Pascal's fear of terrifying waste spaces, the mourner refuses to be undone by the deathly sublimities, even if it means retreating into solipsism. In 'dreaming his dream' and 'holding it true,' Tennyson seems at first to be embracing the narcissism of cognates. If so, we may discern a flicker of irony in the phrase 'dream my dream,' as the poet strives to stave off his loneliness, his terror of the isolating illusion to which the word 'dream' appears to consign him. I think now, however, that a more compelling way of reading the lines may illustrate a benign and more constructive use of infinite regress than we find in the downward spiral of section 56. Tennyson cannot 'think' Hallam's love and soul 'farewell,' not because it is too heartbreaking to do so, but because it is logically impossible.

As soon as Tennyson thinks of an absent Hallam, that thought becomes part of his own mindscape. Every future 'dream' or thought of that mindscape will include a 'dream' of Hallam, and a dream of the mourner dreaming of Hallam, and so on to infinity. When the mourner dreams his dream, he is not merely using cognate words. Instead, the grammatical object of a verb that describes a current dream of Hallam is another earlier dream: one of his many remembrances of Hallam. Section 64, where Tennyson thinks Hallam may be thinking of him 'as in a pensive dream' (l. 18), seems to anticipate *Through the Looking-Glass*, where the dozing Red King dreams about Alice, who is asleep and dreaming about the Red King. As one commentator notes, 'in both dreams, each dreams of the other, forming a pair of infinite regresses' (Gardner, 1996, 3). Unlike the malignant regress of section 56, however, the infinite regress of a dream about a dream is constructive. Shakespeare's Prospero says that we are such stuff as dreams are made on. But if our dreams are one of the things we dream about, then whatever the world in its endless regress of dreams is searching for must be substantial somewhere. It is as inconceivable to think otherwise as to imagine an infinite universe in which our planet should have no twin planet or double.

In other mindscapes Tennyson occasionally uses a regress of pictures to dramatize a perceiver's distance from the object perceived. In 'The Lady of Shalott,' for example, Lancelot is said to flash into the Lady's mirror from the river. The double nature of that mirroring – from bank to river to mirror – turns the water's reflecting surface into a mirror inside a mirror. The Lady of Shalott tries to shatter the regress of images by breaking her glass. More often Tennyson's distancing mindscapes are self-made. Nothing in Tennyson's stage plays is quite so touching or dramatic as the unactable moment in his idyll 'Lancelot and Elaine' when Elaine creates a mindscape in which Lancelot is conscious she is looking at him. In a regress of frames, Elaine knows Lancelot knows she is looking at him, and so cannot return her gaze.

> Then, when she heard his horse upon the stones,
> Unclasping flung the casement back, and look'd
> Down on his helm, from which her sleeve had gone.
> And Lancelot knew the little clinking sound;
> And she by tact of love was well aware
> That Lancelot knew that she was looking at him.
>
> ('Lancelot and Elaine,' ll. 973–8)

A stage play offers little opportunity for one-sided looking. But when Elaine looks at Lancelot in the poem, she reduces him to the quintessential object of her mindscape. Ashamed to return her look, he is powerless to disarm her unstated censure of him. The best comment on the passage comes from Christopher Ricks. 'The tact, the tenderness, the unmentioned bruises: to me the lines are unforgettable' (1972, 275).

3

In addition to charting physical infinities of space and time and recursive images of a mindscape, Tennyson also explores a third form of the infinite: an Absolute that is unlimited or boundless. In approaching what his Ancient Sage calls 'the Nameless of the hundred names' ('The Ancient Sage,' l. 49), as a curve approaches its asymptote, Tennyson cultivates two forms of contemplation, what mystics call cataphatic and apophatic meditation. Either he repeats a proper name or mantra that allows him to focus his attention on a specific word or sound; or else he tries to empty his mind of all content, until concentrated attention on no specific object allows him to pass 'into the Nameless, as a cloud / Melts into heaven' ('The Ancient Sage,' ll. 233–4). Section 95 of *In Memoriam* presents both contemplative activities with remarkable precision. Whereas the section's opening quatrains are elliptically sublime and apophatic, its closing quatrains, concentrating on the rocking elm trees and the swinging of the heavy-folded rose, are expansively sublime and strongly cataphatic. The words in Hallam's letters are said to be 'silent-speaking,' probably because Tennyson pronounces them subvocally. But as in any apophatic operation that empties the mind of content, the words are also said to be silent because they must be elicited as the voice of someone who has died since the letter was written. One result is that the letters act as an earplug to block out distracting gibberish or chatter. To approach the infinitude of 'boundless day' in the last stanza, Tennyson uses amplified repetitions that create simultaneous impressions of the bounded and the boundless. As the flaring lights of East and West join together to form a radiant centre, Tennyson moves from apophatic to cataphatic contemplation, from silent-speaking words to a breeze that breathes the words 'The dawn, the dawn,' yet so unobtrusively that we scarcely notice what has happened.

In an earlier experiment in contemplation, 'The Lotos-Eaters,' Tennyson combines the slow release of breath in a yoga exercise with repetitions that acquire the tranquillizing effect of a mantra. Like the regress of sounds that echo each other in an incantation or chant, the use of repetitions as rhymes in the proem's first four lines helps induce trance and hypnosis instead of mere inertia or torpor.

> 'Courage!' he said, and pointed toward the land,
> 'This mounting wave will roll us shoreward soon.'
> In the afternoon they came unto a land
> In which it seemèd always afternoon. ('The Lotos-Eaters,' ll. 1–4)

In the trembling, downward movement of the stream, Tennyson also uses sound to visualize tiny increments of change.

> And like a downward smoke, the slender stream
> Along the cliff to fall and pause and fall did seem.
> ('The Lotos-Eaters,' ll. 8–9)

The two extra syllables combine with the vertical pattern of falling and pausing to prolong the water's slow descent. Like a value moving toward its limit in calculus, the stream draws ever closer to falling without actually appearing to descend.

Most readers interpret 'The Lotos-Eaters' as Tennyson's indictment of hedonism. But if we concentrate on its diction and meter, we can see that the poem also resembles the yoga of breath control and incantation. The last line expands one of Tennyson's favourite mantras, 'No more,' into the resonant invocation: 'O rest ye, brother mariners, we will not wander more.' Also, by the time a member of the chorus reaches the first caesura in the concluding hexameter of each Spenserian stanza, he is barely breathing. He has slowed down even further by the middle of the line, and has all but exhaled his last breath by the time he comes to the line's late-breaking caesura. The ideal is to approach zero breathing, like a limit in calculus or the ghost of a departed quantity. The more slowly the breath can be released, as in a yoga exercise, the more relaxed and therapeutic the exercise will be. Like Wordsworth in 'Tintern Abbey,' Tennyson hopes that when 'the breath of [his] corporeal frame' is 'almost suspended,' he may be 'laid asleep / In body, and become a living soul' (ll. 43–6). The lotos-eaters are experimenting with what Dwight Culler calls the 'Zen Buddhist practice' of combining 'inhalations with rhythmic counting' (1977, 2). From the release of a modest amount of breath, these pauses proceed to a minimal release, and then to a release of breath that uses up all the speaker's energies. The Spenserian stanza ends as a yoga master might hope to relax his body and his will, or as a man might hope to die after expending all his powers without remainder.

Culler has shown how there survives in Tennyson 'something of the older conception of language as a magical instrument, a means of incantation or ritual' (1977, 4). Phrases like 'far, far away' and 'No more' moved Tennyson deeply, and often induced in him a trancelike state. In the song from *The Princess*, 'Ask me no more,' the incantatory refrain denies what it affirms. It dramatizes the moment of approach, when contact is about to occur but is still deferred. At a touch the woman will yield: delay will last only as long as her refrain 'Ask me no more' is allowed to continue. Indeed like many mantras, the refrain contains its own opposite: 'Ask me no more' is a petition to postpone indefinitely a convergence that seems fated to occur. Continued vocalization of a word may obliterate its meaning or induce a state of stupor in which 'Ask me no more' also means 'Ask me once more.' Changes of direction are equally predictable in 'Tears, Idle Tears,' where the same repeated phrase, 'the days that are no more,' achieves a precarious stability even as it tells us that nothing is stable. There is a wavering finality about each rising and sinking movement, as things merely graze us in passing, like tangents to a curve. As in 'Oenone,' a reader never knows whether he is rising on a crest or descending to a trough. Since each impression is countered by its opposite, we are always at some boundary between hearing and seeing, being happy or sad. Is a ship rising over the horizon at dawn or sinking with all we love below the verge?

Behind Tennyson's mantra, 'No more,' we can also decipher the wildweed-flower of his early lyric 'No More,' sadly reduced by the youthful poet from flower to proper noun.

> Oh sad *No More*! Oh sweet *No More*!
>   Oh strange *No More*!
> By a mossed brookbank on a stone
> I smelt a wildweed-flower alone;
> There was a ringing in my ears,
> And both my eyes gushed out with tears.
> Surely all pleasant things had gone before,
> Lowburied fathomdeep beneath with thee, NO MORE!

The mantra 'No more' is Tennyson's version of a demythologized name, like the flower hyacinth in Greek myth, which is inscribed with the letters AI of the word for 'Alas.' But the mantra also has power to reverse the fall from Eden into Babel, and from myth into time, by becoming, as we have seen, the germ of one of Tennyson's finest lyrics, 'Tears, Idle Tears.' As Geoffrey Hartman says of the author of Genesis, Tennyson has brooded on the name of the flower 'No More' until, like God brooding on the deep, he has made it pregnant. From the words which have been degraded from a name to a phrase, the precocious youth brings forth 'a new meaning' and 'world' (Hartman, 1970, 347).

To intimate what an experience of the Absolute might be like, Tennyson often tries to create situations in which it is possible, if only for an instant, to peer at once into two different worlds – the worlds of the infinite and the finite. Such situations sometimes occur in Tennyson's classical monologues, which try to reverse the fall into time. 'Tithonus' is Tennyson's version of Zeno's arrow. It is a story of a hero locked in time, frozen in a spatial frame like the Sleeping Beauty, unable to inch forward to the grave or reverse the fall into time by becoming once again the beloved consort of the goddess. There is nothing special about Aurora's cold beauty, which renews itself 'morn by morn.' And like the swan that dies after many summers, the one-way vector of 'earth in earth,' the cycle of the man who comes and ploughs the field and lies beneath, is too familiar to need comment. What is unique about Tithonus's perspective is his ability to stand outside his situation, making distinctions, and contriving a union of sensuous immediacy with permanence that arrests the flight of time's arrow. Though warm and passionate, like most things temporal, Aurora's heart is always 'renewed' and her 'bosom' always beating, for like the lovers on Keats's Grecian urn she is 'all breathing human passion far above.' Only when oblivion crystallizes with terrifying literalness into Tithonus's image of himself, 'earth in earth,' does there follow a touching change of focus, comparable to Keats's contemplating a cold pastoral on a marble urn. For a moment, however, before the arrow that is locked in time is released, Tithonus achieves a unique perception. Instead of seeing the world as either cold and enduring or as sensuous and perishing; as either John's Logos or Heraclitus's vortex, he sees it for a moment as both at once.

Such is the moment of fugitive enlightenment that Zen calls satori. In D.T. Suzuki's words, 'the oneness dividing itself into the subject-object and yet retaining its oneness at the very moment that there is the awakening of a consciousness – this is satori' (Suzuki, 1970b, 24). In his oxymoron for the Absolute, 'the Nameless of the hundred names,' Tennyson captures the fleeting instant of fluctuation Suzuki is describing. If the Absolute is nameless, how can it have a hundred names? And if it has a hundred names, how can it be nameless? Only at the instant of oscillation, I suspect, between the blissful moment of merging with the One and the moment of abrupt awakening when the mind draws back to reflect on its dream, and commit it to articulation in words.

The pulse and life-blood of Tennyson's poetry is this One–Many split. When drawn into the vortex of the world's multitudinousness, Tennyson is often overwhelmed by a panic-stricken sense of vertigo and loss. Pictures of an estranged place like the Somersby garden, 'familiar' now 'to the stranger's child' but unfamiliar to Tennyson, fill him with grief. 'Unwatched,' 'Unloved,' 'Uncared for,' the repeated negatives at the head of lines insist on saying. But also 'loved,' and deeply so, by the Zen master who uses his negative past participles as mantra-like chants to restore an impression of what is lost. 'No,' the repeated 'Unloved' keeps saying, but also 'Yes.' James Richardson notes that 'Tennyson's simplest and most profound delight in language is with its ability to say yes and no at the same time' (1988, 32). Like a master of satori, Tennyson finds he can remember Somersby best by seeming to forget it.

I find a similar power to look into two worlds at once in 'The Passing of Arthur,' where the certitude of 'saw' is immediately qualified by the provisional 'Or thought he saw' (ll. 463–5). The insistent pairing of 'clomb' and 'climb,' 'saw' and 'saw,' the passing 'on and on,' then going from 'less to less' before dissolving, show Bedivere looking harder and harder at a shrinking object. Arthur's miraculous vanishing 'into light' (l. 468) and Bedivere's hesitation and strain in tracking 'the speck that bare the King' (l. 465) appear to suspend the reader forever between real and visionary worlds.

A grasping of the world in the unity that divides it is also a recurrent feature of 'The Day-Dream.' Its elaborate nesting structure of frames inside frames creates an infinite regress, or *mise en abyme*, a term deriving from heraldry, where the recursive effect occurs in pictorial representations. Tennyson's speaker wants to tell a dramatic tale of fulfilled love as far away as possible from his own fond feelings for Lady Flora, his present auditor, and yet intimately in touch with them. To this end he writes a poem that half reveals the speaker's hidden motive and also half conceals it by moving resourcefully among a series of frames that refuse to end.

In 'Flower in the Crannied Wall' Tennyson uses an infinite regress to dissolve relations and put the mind in a trance by showing how the flower's meaning is derivable only from the whole, endlessly retreating horizon of the world it is in.

> I hold you here, root and all, in my hand,
> Little flower – but *if* I could understand
> What you are, root and all, and all in all,
> I should know what God and man is.
>
> ('Flower in the Crannied Wall,' ll. 3–6)

Initially, an idea of being spatially connected or rooted relates the flower to its crannied wall. The flower, after all, is said to be rooted in the wall: though both are intimately connected, they are still separate. In order to relate the rooted flower to the wall's other flowers, however, the poet must immediately invoke a second idea of being both rooted and detached, and then a third idea, and so on. Until the poet has related everything, he has understood and connected nothing. Since it is manifestly impossible to relate everything, and just as impossible to block the regress of relations once they are set in motion, either God and the mind must retreat from view down an endless vortex, or else we must conclude that relations are illusory. As a mystic who is ultimately a monist, Tennyson is tempted to embrace the second alternative by accepting the view of Parmenides, Zeno of

Elea, and of his intellectual ally, F.H. Bradley, that relations are deceptive. Only the movement from the multitude of particulars back to the One turns shadow into substance. Tennyson's reversion to unity drives the compulsive monism of the last line, where instead of writing 'I should know what God and man are,' he substitutes a singular for a plural verb. In the Epilogue to *In Memoriam* the fourfold repetition of 'one' in only two lines ('One God, one law, one element / And one far-off divine event') is further testimony to what M.H. Abrams calls the powerful 'monistic compulsion of the human spirit' (1989, 232). When looking down induces vertigo and looking up induces despair, the mourner in *In Memoriam* can only keep going by looking straight ahead. If it were not for his final apocalyptic vision of one far-off event, he might seem to be going round in circles, like a senile man who thinks his third or fourth repetition of the same memory is new.

Like F.H. Bradley some twenty-five centuries later, Zeno, a follower of Parmenides, tries to prove that motion and change do not occur. As Wesley C. Salmon explains, 'F.H. Bradley, while making no explicit mention of Zeno, uses thoroughly Eleatic arguments to support the conclusions that space and time, motion and change are unreal' (Salmon, 2001, 16). To make the claim plausible, Bradley, like Zeno, has to set afoot an infinite regress. According to G.E.L. Owen, the regress that Bradley and Zeno initiate is best understood as follows. 'Any two members of a collection must be separated from something if they are to be two things and not one; but by the same argument what separates them must itself be separated from each by something else; and so forth' (Owen, 2001, 151–2). Owen immediately goes on to observe, however, that 'this argument seems patently fallacious. For surely things may be separated by their common boundaries – by their edges, and nothing else' (2001, 152). Tennyson may not have read Bradley or Zeno. But the large number of books in Tennyson's library on Toaism, Buddhism, and Oriental thought supports the view that he was a lifelong student of Indian philosophy, which finds it hard to draw a horizon around its thinking. To conceive of anything in Indian philosophy is to initiate an infinite cycle, a regress of phenomena such as Bradley and Zeno set in motion.

I realize it is sometimes difficult to distinguish between the regress in a mindscape, the second category of the infinite, and the third category, the regress inside an Absolute that is infinite and boundless. The first kind of regress occurs in any self-representative system. The mind that tracks an experience is an important part of what is tracked. To move from this infinite mindscape to an Absolute Infinite is to move from epistemology to metaphysics, from a theory of knowledge to a theory of being. It is to pass from Tennyson's memory of his past in *In Memoriam* to his claim in 'Flower in the Crannied Wall' that under certain conditions a mind that has regressed infinitely might come at last to know what 'God and man is.' As Daniel Cohen observes in *Equations from God*, the Victorian mathematician Thomas Hill attacks Sir William Hamilton and H.L. Mansel for dividing the mind into two irreconcilable faculties, the infinite and the finite. Just as Hill demonstrates how mathematicians can use calculus to 'add together finite quantities' to 'approach the infinite' (Cohen, 2007, 60), so Tennyson believes that by marching through infinite regresses he can use reason as well as intuition to draw ever closer to a God who is boundless.

Clearly, however, the Absolute Infinite of Edward Caird, F.H. Bradley, and the English Hegelians is fraught with more contradictions than the infinite mindscapes of a subjective idealist like J.F. Ferrier or Pringle-Pattison. Moreover, since the idea of an absolute that is also infinite involves switching in quick succession between contradictory pictures, like Wittgenstein's duck-rabbit figure, it also requires verbal sleight of hand. The great crisis in Victorian agnostic theology arises from an inability to combine images of the absolute and the infinite in our understanding of God. In a seminal essay, 'The Philosophy of the Unconditioned,' a principal source of H.L. Mansel's and T.H. Huxley's agnostic theologies, Sir William Hamilton argues that God must be either absolute or infinite, discrete or boundless. To say he is both at once is like saying that matter is atomic and endlessly divisible, at once a particle and a wave. How can a subject possessing these contradictory predicates claim to be intelligible? Christopher Herbert finds it ironic that Mansel should base his critique of 'the philosophy of absolutes' squarely on Protagorean principles of relativity. 'Most modernistic of all,' Herbert claims, 'is Mansel's embrace of paradox as a necessary component of the scientific mode of knowledge' (2001, 388–9).

Fortunately, Tennyson is a more adventurous explorer of logical contradiction than Hamilton or Mansel. Ever willing to hover over contradictions and fluctuate between opposing states, his speaker in 'Tithonus' seeks the absolution of forgetting what he also remembers: 'I earth in earth forget these empty courts, / And thee returning on thy silver wheels' (ll. 75–6). Remembering a line from Dante, Tithonus forgets to forget. As Robert Douglas-Fairhurst observes, instead of erasing anything, Tennyson's 'earth in earth' does the opposite: it memorably brings to life again the phrase 'in terra terra' of Dante's St John (*Paradiso*, XXV.124) (2002, 229). Something similar occurs at the end of 'Demeter and Persephone,' where the great earth mother vows to obliterate from memory all desolating impressions of 'the Stone,' 'the Wheel,' and 'silent field of Asphodel.' But these images cannot be erased: even in resolving to forget them, she inscribes them forever on our minds. Only in *In Memoriam* does Tennyson acknowledge that every trade-off between the absolute and the indefinite, the discrete and the dissolving, entails an irreparable loss. At the climax of the elegy Tennyson had hoped to clasp Hallam's hand and listen to a voice that is irreplaceable and unique. But so diffused has that voice become that Tennyson can hear it only 'on the rolling air' or 'where the waters run' (130.1–2). Hallam has turned into something more cosmic and sublime than Tennyson anticipated. Intimacy and sublimity, the discrete and the diffuse, exist in inverse proportion and cannot be combined in a larger whole.

Fascinated by transitions and rates of change, Tennyson is the Ovid of a protean age of flux and evolution in the physical sciences. Charting the metamorphosis of the great chain of being into an escalator, he traces the slope of this moving stair as it ascends to new heights before plummeting down a vortex or disappearing through a black hole. I say 'ascend' or 'plummet,' because Tennyson is intrigued by the way a seemingly 'accidental variation' can be built into the program of a calculating engine, or what today we would call a computer. Tennyson owned a copy of George Babbage's *Ninth Bridgewater Treatise* (1838), which uses the analogy of the calculating engine to refute Hume's argument against miracles. When Robert Chambers introduces Babbage's example of the calculating engine into his hypothesis of development in *Vestiges of the Natural History of Creation*, he is not, like Babbage, trying to refute Hume by showing that unpredictable changes may have other causes than divine intervention. He is arguing instead that our historical era is 'only a small portion of the entire age of our globe. We do not know what may have happened during the ages which preceded its commencement, as we do not know what may happen in ages yet in the distant future' (Chambers, 1844, 152). Who indeed can assert with certainty that 'the great world's altar-stairs' will not turn at any moment into a wild careening roller coaster, doubtfully teleological, and frightening to contemplate?

David Berlinski believes that the calculus is 'a great and powerful theory arising at the very moment human beings contemplated the infinite for the first time: sequences without end, infinite additions, limits flickering in the far distance.' But then he adds, 'the simple melancholy fact is that outside the charmed circle of those working on the current frontiers, no one believes any longer that physics or *anything like physics* is apt to provide contemplative human beings with a theoretical arch sustaining enough to provide a coherent system of thought and feeling' (Berlinski, 1997, 304–5). Caught between worlds, Tennyson, I think, occupies a similar position in the nineteenth century. The world that retreats before Tennyson through Ulysses' arch is Zeno's world of Achilles and the tortoise, for it has no finish lines and no boundaries. Tennyson is torn between a lifelong interest in an Absolute Infinite in theology or metaphysics, on the one hand, and an obsession with sublime infinities of space and time in the physical sciences, on the other.

In section 123 of *In Memoriam*, which is Tennyson's 'farewell to continuity' (Berlinski, 1997, 304), the most fluid and solid elements are indistinguishable: 'The hills are shadows' (l. 5); 'They melt like mist, the solid lands' (l. 7). Though there is no end to change in such a universe, it may be preferable to Tithonus's unchanging world at a standstill through eternity. Aurora keeps returning on her silver wheels, and Tithonus grows tired of counting. He longs to forget her, but lacks the power to die. Even in *In Memoriam*, when infinities of space and time reach a zenith of magnificent absurdity, Hallam can at least die and annihilate the spectacle. Perhaps, as one critic suggests, 'that's the reason for death: to shake off infinity. Beckett's Murphy thought that the Resurrection was God overdoing things again' (Frye, 2004a, 259). If the God of *In Memoriam* is Paley's watch-maker, he is also a 'blind watch-maker,' as Richard Dawkins says. And if he is a poet, he is also a 'wild Poet,' working 'without a conscience or an aim.'

Like Lucretius and Zeno, Tennyson is an atomist whose 'finer optic' is attuned to discrete units of sensation. Browning, by contrast, is fascinated with waves of force and chromatic blending, like Clough and Swinburne. I have argued that Tennyson's focus on atomic parts is to the use of derivatives in calculus what Browning's evolution of solids out of two-dimensional shapes and points is to the use of integrals. But no calculus can determine the instantaneous velocity or plot the trajectory of the randomly accelerating atoms that 'holy Venus' lets loose in Tennyson's monologue 'Lucretius.' Though 'the abysmal terror of

"Lucretius" is redeemed,' in one critic's words, by 'a subcorporeal sort of infinitesimal sublime' (Tucker, 2007), the flaming atoms that the goddess sets streaming through an 'illimitable inane' resemble rapid fluctuations in the stock market. Their wild career traces a path too jagged and irregular for the smoother models of the calculus to quantify. The physics of Newton is designed to chart the dynamics of a continuously moving altar-stair that meets God at Ulysses' 'utmost bound of human thought,' or as a curve of a parabola meets its asymptote, at infinity. Perhaps fractals (or the computer simulations of a later age) provide the best model of Tennyson's post-Newtonian world of accidental variations in biology and of unpredictable changes in the history of the earth. In the world of Darwin, Chambers, and Lyell, species evolve randomly, and even solid lands shape themselves like clouds and disappear (*In Memoriam*, 123.8).

Since nothing is certain or permanent in such a world, Tennyson finds that the secret of wisdom is the detachment without withdrawal of a spokesman like Ulysses, in whom Tennyson claims to find more of himself than in all of *In Memoriam*. As Koheleth discovers in the wisest book of the Hebrew Bible, there is a time for all things, for touching the Happy Isles and for being washed down by the waves. Browning's Childe Roland is closest to his peers, the lost heroes of old, when they range themselves as ghosts along the hillside to view him for the last time. Ulysses, too, seems closest to his old friends, the mariners, when he can accept them as the spectral community they have become, and address them for a final time in a pep talk to ghosts. Honoured in his own day as a wisdom poet, Tennyson realizes that real wisdom starts with Ulysses' discovery that, despite his attempt to quest forever, it is impossible to travel endlessly. Only in a tranquillizing evocation of his end is it possible for Ulysses to be 'absolute for death.' Wisdom accepts the discontinuity of being whoever one is at the present moment, whether the wisest of the great Greek heroes or an old man 'made weak by time and fate, but strong in will / To strive, to seek, to find, and not to yield.' Absolved at last from endless striving, Ulysses must learn to relax his will and accept what is absolute and discrete in place of what infinitely recedes or dissolves. He must find joy, not in any timeless quest with his comrades, who lead too fading and ghostly an existence for communal enterprise, but in discovering a way out of emptiness by celebrating whatever is 'past, or passing, or to come.' When wisdom embraces experience as its own end, there comes the liberating sense of acceptance. As Cornelia Pearsall finely says, Ulysses tells his men 'that they are the sum of their losses, which is to say that what is taken *is* what abides' (2008, 199). To be wise is to accept the void of Buddhist thought, the world within nothingness, without any a priori judgment of it. Unlike the youth in 'Locksley Hall,' who says knowledge comes but wisdom lingers, Ulysses is no weary pessimist, tired of life, but a vigorous realist, committed to a life of continuous mental energy.

3 How Poets Die to Time: The Sublime Oracle

A culture and its oracles may die to time in three ways: by being destroyed by time; by being refined and enhanced by it; or by eluding and so escaping its ravages. If a culture is material and worships means instead of ends, its expense of spirit in a waste of shame is grotesque at best, since its quest for material well-being overshadows and obliterates any other goal. The shaping ends of a second phase of culture may be perfectly embodied in its science, politics, and art. Time may enhance or refine rather than waste such a culture, since its spiritual content and its material forms are in equilibrium. Instead of allowing its means to produce a grotesque distortion of its ends, as in the first phase of culture, or instead of celebrating a beautiful realization of its ends in its means, as in the second phase, a sublime culture defies means altogether. Its oracles are fading comets, which slip the leash of any orbit that might restrain them.

Each phase of culture is best expressed in its oracles, secular scriptures, and great prophetic poems. I first consider oracles that break their world apart by revolutionizing its values. Though a utopian vision may baffle the sage who tries to understand it, only a prophet of the sublime, who is neither a friend nor a victim of time, can escape its ravages. In the next chapter I go on to explore oracles like the one Keats associates with the Grecian urn: 'Beauty is truth, truth beauty.' Like a well-wrought urn, such an oracle is a friend of man, enhanced and refined by time as a dwelling place of the gods. Finally, in chapter 5, I examine oracles that are typical of a culture that is sense-bound and material, a victim of time. Haunted by sibyls and brides of darkness, its oracles from the grotto shrink the soul and atrophy the mind. Strewn with the ruins of time, a philistine culture is demonic. It is the grave of oracles; a wise one their temple; and a sublime culture the chrysalis at the moment of release, when a winged prophet comes to life or a god prepares to take flight from the world. A sublime prophet is too good for the world, and goes in the only way he can: out of it.

1

Some sublime parables by Blake and some visionary poems by Hopkins, Yeats, and Eliot must be perceived instantly and as a whole. They appear to be the verbal equivalent of a Gestalt. Teasing us out of thought as does eternity, they may stir our emotions while leaving us little to say. The aura of a meaning we cannot lay hands on is familiar to every admirer of poetry, music, and the visual arts. But without the stain of the poets' many-coloured glass, the white radiance of the wisdom writers would be as remote from us as the emeritus God of the Deists. They would be as aloof as the Logos in John's Gospel before it stoops to rise, 'Such ever was love's way' (Browning, 'A Death in the Desert,' l. 134). Until poets repair the oracles, wisdom is like God without the Word or eternity divorced from time. Paul's idea that we see through a glass darkly, per aenigmate, suggests that we entertain some oracles, 'not as the truth, but as something behind which the truth is to be found' (Weil, 1974, 120). An example is the Sermon on the Mount, which (as the oracle of a rabbi of genius) never merely echoes the Decalogue but gives it an extraordinary new turn.

An exile from paradise may drop some natural tears when forced to leave Eden. But like Milton's Adam and Eve, he will wipe them soon. For numinous moments are meant to be fugitive. As an instrument through whom the god speaks, Browning's Abt Vogler finds it wrenching to return to earth and impossible to integrate his sublime moments into 'the C Major of this life.'

> Well, it is gone at last, the palace of music I reared;
>   Gone! and the good tears start, the praises that come too slow
> ('Abt Vogler,' ll. 57–8)

To ascend to the god's shrine at Delphi or to scale Sinai or the Sermon Mount is a daunting task. And it is difficult to remain at such an altitude for long. Harvey Cox thinks that even the author of Matthew's gospel shows how hard it is to prolong and give body to a bracing vision. In the verse after the Sermon on the Mount concludes, the writer 'reports that the demanding crowds closed in once again, and among them there was another leper who wanted to be healed' (Cox, 2004, 153). To ease the jolt of returning to the everyday world is an occupation for a saint, or at least for a very skilful poet like Wordsworth or Housman, who knows how to master the prophet's art of grafting visionary onto clock time, or *kairos* onto *chronos*.

Such mastery can be studied in the sublime metamorphosis of Wordworth's Lucy in 'A Slumber Did My Spirit Seal,' which anticipates Housman's marvellous transformation of Dick in 'The night is freezing fast.' The second quatrain of Wordsworth's lyric assumes the form of a riddle: what better prophecy might repair the trite prophecy of the first quatrain? How might it totally reverse the import of everything the first prophecy implies?

> A slumber did my spirit seal;
>   I had no human fears:
> She seemed a thing that could not feel
>   The touch of earthly years.
>
> No motion has she now, no force;
>   She neither hears nor sees;
> Rolled round in earth's diurnal course,
>   With rocks, and stones, and trees.   ('A Slumber Did My Spirit Seal')

The lover's first prophecy is evasive. The truth he finds too painful to face and tries hard to deny is as immediate as a physical touch, the touch of a hand, and yet as strange and uncanny as the touch of time, which is not warm, like a lover's touch, but cold. 'Earthly' means earth-centred and earth-anchored, not merely *of* the earth but also *on* the earth and *in* it.

To repair the damage suffered by his first prophecy, by his foolish boast that Lucy is too pure to be seduced by any earthly rival, the lover substitutes in the second quatrain a grimmer but more potent prophecy. Just as the peace of a graveyard is often disturbingly at odds with the agitation that shakes a mourner's heart, so Lucy is securely and restfully enclosed within a turning world that, in its strenuous rotations, is the opposite of restful. In its magnificent tranquillizing evocation of the grave, however, the second prophecy mutes the agitation and subdues the rough diurnal motions of the earth. Though violence survives in the harsh spondees – 'No motion,' 'no force,' 'Rolled round' (ll. 5, 7), it is also tamed by Lucy's marvellous metamorphosis.

The second quatrain recovers an energetic forward movement. Its network of prepositions spin a protective web for Lucy: 'Rolled round in earth's diurnal course, / With rocks, and stones, and trees.' Just as Housman's Dick has learned to wear 'the turning globe,' and 'made of earth and sea / His overcoat for ever' (ll. 10–12), so Lucy has turned the rough earth into a vigorous protector. In full possession of the force and motion Lucy has lost, the masculine rocks and stones and the thrusting trees roll her round in a consummation that will last as long as the earth continues to hurtle through space. The grimness of the oracle is sealed off, as it were, by the action of an aggressively intrusive earth – by its power, not merely to enter the woman, but also to have the woman enter *it*. Having been propelled through space while being invaded, Lucy experiences the kind of calm vertigo that hurricane victims are said to feel when they find themselves at the still centre of a storm and live to tell of their ordeal.

Anthony Hecht praises the exquisite skill with which A.E. Housman uses 'subtleties of nuance' and 'delicate inflections of meaning' to create a comparably sublime metamorphosis in his lyric 'The night is freezing fast.'

> The night is freezing fast,
>   To-morrow comes December;
>   And winterfalls of old
> Are with me from the past;
>   And chiefly I remember
>   How Dick would hate the cold.
>
> Fall, winter, fall; for he,
>   Prompt hand and headpiece clever,
>   Has woven a winter robe,
> And made of earth and sea
>   His overcoat for ever,
>   And wears the turning globe.   (Poem XX, *Last Poems*)

As a wearer and weaver of worlds, Dick uses his 'prompt hand' and 'headpiece clever' – a strong, designing mind – to enter our space, envelop it, and finally take it over. A precedent for this slow enveloping is section 95 of *In Memoriam*, where Hallam and Tennyson are so enfolded or wound in each other that they seem to be wrestling, like Jacob and the angel. Another precedent is Wordsworth's Lucy, who is so strenuously embraced by rocks and stones and trees that in the diurnal course of the earth she resembles a projectile moving through space.

The rhyming units, which fall in the first stanza into three trimeter lines rhyming *a b c a b c*, are in unobtrusive conflict with the three syntactic units, each consisting of two lines terminated by either a semicolon or a period. Hecht implies that the same pattern persists in stanza 2. But in that stanza a stronger, more elemental force has already begun to override and blur the pattern. As Dick begins to dominate the seasons instead of allowing time and the seasons to dominate *him*, Housman removes the semicolons. There are no strong breaks between the three syntactic units of stanza 2. Instead, by replacing the expected punctuation mark at the end of line 10 with a graceful enjambment, the verb 'made' is allowed to await its surprising completion in 'overcoat,' its grammatical object. The major break in stanza 2 coincides with the semicolon after 'fall.' The rest of the stanza expands into a spacious sequence of principal clauses detailing the stages of Dick's wintry metamorphosis into a wearer and weaver of worlds.

The 'contrasting, almost competing, designs' that Hecht identifies as 'part of a complex, disorienting music' (2003, 98) account for what happens in the first half of the poem. But elements that compete with each other in the first stanza begin to pull together and cooperate in the second. Instead of expressing the 'disorienting music' of the first stanza as a 'dislocation' that is 'almost cosmic,' as Hecht says, the end of the poem does something altogether odder, I think, and yet strangely more harmonious. Housman makes the wearing of the earth, sea, and turning globe seem as natural yet restorative as the city's wearing the beauty of the morning 'like a garment' in Wordsworth's sonnet 'Composed upon Westminster Bridge.' As in Tennyson's 'Ulysses,' where the staccato energy of 'Come, my friends ... / Push off' (ll. 56, 58) is at odds with the long vowels of the slow-wheeling blank verse, so the urgency of Housman's 'Fall, winter, fall' yields to as slow and unhurried an expansion as any six-line stanza can sustain.

At first we are mildly puzzled by the identity of 'he' at the head of the second stanza. Is it a personified winter? No, it is Dick, but a dead Dick who has made of winter his winter coat 'for ever.' Indeed Dick and winter are as inextricably interwoven as Hallam and Tennyson, who uses chiasmus, the trope of reversing motion, to dramatize the two-way flow of their commingling. 'And all at once it seemed at last / The living soul was flashed on mine, / And mine in this was wound' (*In Memoriam*, 95.35–7). Chiasmus marks the elegiac pause. It is the trope of reflection, of the mind turning back on itself: 'earth and sea,' 'overcoat,' 'wears,' 'the turning globe' (*a b b a*). In both poets chiasmus creates a protective calm at the centre. In Housman's poem the seasons now reverse themselves. 'Fall' and 'winter' may fall as they wish, but they mute the dreaded 'winterfalls of old' by using rhyme to align 'the turning globe' with 'a winter robe' and by changing 'for he' into 'for ever.' Dick dies to change by using the earth itself as his protection against the winter cold he loathes. The triumph over winter is even more dramatic if we accept Hecht's ingenious alternative reading of 'Fall, winter, fall.' He says in a footnote that 'Richard Wilbur has plausibly suggested to [him] that "Fall, winter, fall" may be voiced in the imperative mood, as an intemperate petition, meaning, "Go ahead; do your worst"' (2003, 99). This reading would prepare for the cosmic drama of the coda by invoking the elemental language of a latter-day King Lear as he challenges the storm to vent its fury and destroy him if it will.

2

In sublime oracles words are important, not in themselves, but only as 'resonators for a centre,' a phrase Coleman Barks uses to describe the mystical verse of the Sufi poet Rumi, who bases his theory of language on the reed flute or ney. 'Beneath everything we say, and within each note of the reed flute,' Barks explains, 'lies a nostalgia for the reed bed. Language and music are possible only because we're empty, hollow, and separated from the source' (Rumi, 1995, 17). If 'all language is a longing for home,' then before the flute can overcome its separation from the reed bed, the source of its most haunting sound, it must exchange fire for wind. In Rumi's words,

> 'Few
> Will hear the secrets hidden
>
> Within the notes. No ears for that.
> Body flowing out of spirit,

Spirit up from body: no concealing
That mixing. But it's not given us

To *see* the soul. The reed flute
Is fire, not wind. Be that empty.'   ('The Reed-Flute's Song,' ll. 11–18)

Only to the sublime Sufi poet who loves emptiness better than plenitude and silence better than sound will the reed's 'pure hollow note'
seem too material to satisfy the ear and save the soul beside. Paradoxically, it takes an oddly mystic fish like Rumi himself to 'swim a vast
ocean of grace' and still somehow long for it ('The Reed-Flute's Song,'
ll. 39–40). When 'the grief-armies assemble' their vast platoons of
speech, Rumi refuses to go with them.

This is how it always is
When I finish a poem.

A great silence overcomes me,
And I wonder why I ever thought
To use language.   ('A Thirsty Fish,' ll. 27–31)

For Hopkins, as for Rumi, the words of even the most sublime poet
compose an elegy for what they signify. In *The Wreck of the Deutschland*,
where the poet is doubly removed from God by death and language,
the elegist must supplement God's silence with the silence of his own
self-effacement and humility. Dashes, hyphens, and caesuras mark off
places where 'the giant risen' can finally enter Hopkins's poem.

A vein for the visiting of the past-prayer, pent in prison,
The-last-breath penitent spirits – the uttermost mark
Our passion-plunged giant risen,   (*The Wreck of the Deutschland*, 33.5–7)

'The uttermost mark' is literally the dash that precedes the phrase – the
mark of ellipsis and caesura. It is the place of fracture, where life
breaks apart after being all but exhaled through the hyphens that
divide the monosyllables in the compound phrase: 'The-last-breath
penitent spirits.' The death of the penitent nuns is their first gasp of
spirit, meeting their Lord in the air. For the nuns' Purgatory is God
himself. Their risen giant appears in the break after 'spirits': he comes
to life in it, even as he comes to life from a tomb.

Wallace Stevens maintains that to be sublime an oracle must be the medium of a voice so pure and disinterested that it seems to come to the poet 'Without understanding, out of the wall / Or in the ceiling, in sounds not chosen' ('The Creations of Sound,' ll. 3–4). And yet an oracle that is 'better without an author' (l. 9), because it is too pure for any idea to violate, may be as deficient in meaning as an exhausted bell jar. When a sealed-off, hermetic poet like Stevens's X, presumably T.S. Eliot, tries to be 'intelligent / Beyond intelligence' (ll. 11–12) by speaking as 'an artificial man,' he forgets that 'speech is not dirty silence / Clarified' (ll. 12, 16–17). On the contrary, it is 'silence made still dirtier' (l. 17) by rooting itself in misery. Its anchor is the agony and strife of human hearts.

In the second section of 'Burnt Norton' Stevens's poet X locates silence at 'the still point of the turning world.' This stable point is to movement what silence is to speech. Just as without 'the still point, / There would be no dance, and there is only the dance,' so without the silence there would be no words, and there is only the Word. Amending Wittgenstein's aphorism that 'one must remain silent about that which one cannot utter,' Eliot shows that what is normally unutterable – the mystery of God's Word – can be expressed only in wisdom writing like *Four Quartets*, where literal silence is no longer possible.

One of the best comments on silence and wisdom comes from Simone Weil. 'When the intelligence, having become silent in order to let love invade the whole soul, begins once more to exercise itself, it finds it contains more light than before, a greater aptitude for grasping objects, truths that are proper to it' (1974, 131). Cautioning against premature speech in 'East Coker,' Eliot tells his soul to be still. It must be silent to hear the Word when it speaks. According to St John of the Cross, 'silence is God's first language.' Until we can accept the paradox that silence is its own opposite, the language of God, we can never recognize what Thomas Merton calls the 'little point of nothingness and of absolute poverty' which is also 'the power of God written in us, as our poverty' (Merton, 1989, 347). An essential condition of hearing oracles or of listening to the Word is a relaxation of the will. Instead of trying to take possession of time, which is the ego's revolt against death, the poet must let time go.

Eliot's most sublime meditation on words and silence appears in the fifth section of 'Burnt Norton.' The life of words is a continual death, he reflects. Under tension words 'slip, slide, perish, / Decay with imprecision.' But despite the cracking and breakage, phrases also exist within a pattern where the life of each word is preserved.

> Words move, music moves
> Only in time; but that which is only living
> Can only die. Words, after speech, reach
> Into the silence. Only by the form, the pattern,
> Can words or music reach
> The stillness, as a Chinese jar still
> Moves perpetually in its stillness.   ('Burnt Norton,' V.1–7)

Like a note in music, each word has value or meaning only in a context of other words and notes. A motionless jar may seem to move in an aura of diffused silence, in the stillness that surrounds it. With sleight of hand, however, Eliot qualifies the absence of motion in 'stillness' by using the temporal adverb 'still' to intimate an insistent stirring movement. The jar 'still / Moves perpetually in its stillness.' In a comparable way a presence like the air continues to surround and gently animate the words that, even as they reach into silence, manage to die for a moment to the rush of time.

3

Kierkegaard maintains that 'religious things have to do with a softly murmured soliloquy with oneself' (1960, 101). Few poets are more religious in Kierkegaard's sense, more Delphic and withdrawn in their silence and reserve, than Emily Dickinson, the sibyl of Amherst. Unfortunately, however skilled the sibyl may be in drawing the reader into her oracles, her riddles are seldom as successful in leading them on to a satisfying conclusion. As Philip Larkin complains, 'the amazing riches of originality offered by the index of her first lines is belied on the page ... Too often the poem expires in a teased-out and breathless obscurity' (New Statesman, 13 March 1970, quoted by Ricks, 1987, 274). Unlike Blake, Whitman, and some other prophetic poets, Dickinson never forgets that 'oracles stop speaking as soon as possible' (Tillotson, 1968, 85). But sometimes Dickinson's oracles stop too soon, before she quite earns the right to be silent. As one critic says, 'real silence' is not 'the stopping of speech,' not the arbitrary termination of it, but 'the end of speech' (Frye, 1976b, 188) that has reached its appointed end or destination.

At the conclusion of Frost's famous lyric 'Stopping by Woods on a Snowy Evening,' the repetition of the last two lines ('And miles to go before I sleep') allows the speaker to balance a literal description of the need to go on living with a drift into winter sleep. But a reader looks in vain for any comparable progression in Dickinson's lyric 'I shall know why.' When she says, 'I shall forget the drop of Anguish / That scalds me now – that scalds me now! (lyric 193, ll. 7–8), nothing in her repeated clause makes a literal meaning figurative. The pull in Frost's poem between a resolve to keep promises and a nodding off to sleep allows the poet to pass from a practical everyday predicament to a world of magic and spells. By contrast, Dickinson merely seems to end her poem too soon. Her cry that she is scalded is self-pitying and indulgent. Instead of allowing a drowsy current to pull her into the orbit of oblivion or easeful death, her cry does nothing to distil or concentrate her 'drop of Anguish' but merely rounds out the line.

It is hard, however, to dissociate obliquity from revelation. Because Dickinson is less articulate than Frost, she is often more obscure. But obscurity is one mark of her genius for prophecy. We eavesdrop on the sibyl, and overhear her greatness in words that withhold her wisdom and keep meanings in reserve. After quoting Ivor Winters's admission that, though Dickinson 'is a poetic genius of the highest order,' the 'ambiguity in one's feelings about her is highly disturbing,' Geoffrey Hartman remarks that 'this is itself honest criticism of a high order.' It is also criticism 'of an older order that separated beauties from defects and did not try to reach an understanding' of the intimate connection between the prophetic and oblique or the sublime and the repressed. As Hartman concludes, 'the least we can learn from interpretation as an art, as from humanistic discussion in general, is the quirky arbitrariness and relative mortality of judgmental edicts' (Hartman, 2007, 12).

A sublime oracle's slow attenuation of matter is most apparent in the spare, emaciated verse of Dickinson's lyric 'The Brain is wider than the Sky.' As syntax loosens and grammar falls away, the poet invites us to ponder the high mystery of the mind's relation to the sky, emptiness, and God. With daring brinkmanship Dickinson leads us to the verge of vacancy and beyond. What is wider than the sky, deeper than the sea, and weighs the same as God? By posing a little riddle, the oracle invites us to contemplate in the mystery of human consciousness something as invisible and silent as the earth's atmosphere, but no less encompassing as a result.

The Brain – is wider than the Sky –
For – put them side by side –
The one the other will contain
With ease – and You – beside –

The Brain is deeper than the sea –
For – hold them – Blue to Blue –
The one the other will absorb –
As Sponges – Buckets – do –   (lyric 632, ll. 1–8)

The brain is said to contain what the eye of an individual observer cannot see – the regions of interstellar space that are visible only to God. Dickinson creates a calm vertigo in this lyric. She conjures up images of vast measurement and immense weight only to cancel them out in the conceit of a tiny brain, the size of a small bucket or sponge, soaking up a whole ocean of water.

In a typical riddle there is an implied question, 'What weighs the same as God and contains both you and the sky?' The answer 'the brain' is wrong only because, as one critic says, 'it is an answer. The real answer to the question implied in a riddle is not a "thing" outside it, but that which is both inside and outside the poem' (Frye, 1976b, 147).

The Brain is just the weight of God –
For – Heft them – Pound for Pound –
And they will differ – if they do –
As Syllable from Sound –   (lyric 632, ll. 9–12)

Even as the sibyl of Amherst uses a suppressed enthymeme to tap obliquely the resources of her riddle, she is less interested in providing the right answer to the riddle than in exploring the absurdity of a world from which consciousness could be withdrawn. It would be like creating a great spectacle for which no audience exists. If Berkeley is right and the minimal unit of cognition is the world in union with a perceiving subject, then Dickinson's riddling definition of the human mind, though apparently extravagant, is also as sharply perceptive as it is arresting and strange.

Dickinson's odd, elliptical grammar often imparts a sibylline quality to her verse. In lyric 657, for example, she is said to 'dwell in Possibility.' We construe the preposition 'in' to mean 'within the region of,' 'in the imaginative domain of.' But when Possibility is immediately praised as a 'fairer House than Prose,' we discover that the preposition is also being used in a precise architectural sense. As we round the corners of successive lines, the building discloses exact information about its windows, doors, and roof.

In lyric 30 the unobtrusive surprise of the concluding adverb 'on' depends on our being tacitly aware how differently the word is used as a preposition twice before in the poem: 'So Sailors say – on yesterday,' 'So angels say – on yesterday' (ll. 5, 9). How odd and Delphic this repeated use of 'on'!

Adrift! A little boat adrift!
And night is coming down!
Will *no* one guide a little boat
Unto the nearest town?

So Sailors say – on yesterday –
Just as the dusk was brown
One little boat gave up its strife
And gurgled down and down.

So angels say – on yesterday
Just as the dawn was red
One little boat – o'erspent with gales –
Retrimmed its masts – redecked its sails –
And shot – exultant on!

The final protracted motion of 'on' propels the little boat beyond the limits of both the line-ending and the poem. In sharp contrast is the fearful downward drift of the adverb 'down,' twice used in a terminal position: 'And night is coming down!' (l. 2), 'One little boat gave up its strife / And gurgled down and down' (ll. 7–8). The eventfulness of the last stanza depends on our quiet surprise at the poet's breaking through the limits of the four-line stanza in a reversal of both the form and meaning of the middle quatrain. The lines are also alive with our sense of earlier prophetic uses of 'on' and 'down.' The full force of a protracted shooting 'on,' as an alternative to sinking 'down,' is achieved with perfect naturalness, as if the prepositions and adverbs were being used as tactful signposts in two oddly different versions of the same event.

In lyric 33, even hypothetical logic can be used as a stay against psychic erosion. The unchanging logical forms are as solid as bedrock or granite: if A were B (the opposite of A), then C; and if B were A (the opposite of B), then C also.

> If recollecting were forgetting,
> Then I remember not.
> And if forgetting, recollecting,
> How near I had forgot.
> And if to miss, were merry,
> And to mourn, were gay,
> How very blithe the fingers
> That gathered this, Today!

By pretending she is a logician constructing fanciful, contrary-to-fact hypotheses, Dickinson can gently remind her reader that she never in fact comes close to forgetting. Half whimsically, half plaintively, she intimates depths of grief by playing out a little exercise in logic, as if it were a game of cards. With unobtrusive dexterity, using forms that are too fixed and easy to be quite applicable to human grief, Dickinson retracts the whimsical hypothesis that she could ever be 'very blithe' or 'gay' while gathering flowers for the tomb of one she loves.

The power of lyric 45 depends upon a strong and precise impression of the other perfectly natural course the poem might have followed. Dickinson might have written: 'There's something quieter than sleep / Within this inner room! / She wears a sprig upon her breast.' Instead, she scrupulously avoids the personal pronoun. The poet seems about to speak of the dead woman's hand and face. But the impersonal pronoun 'it' and the riddling reticence of the clause, 'will not tell its name,' hold meaning in reserve. And they do so with a mild shock of surprise and with a sense that an alternative has been considered and rejected.

> There's something quieter than sleep
> Within this inner room!
> It wears a sprig upon its breast –
> And will not tell its name.
>
> Some touch it, and some kiss it –
> Some chafe its idle hand –

It has a simple gravity
I do not understand!

(lyric 45, ll. 1–8)

The caesural breaks in the second quatrain are silences that speak to us across death. They are oracles of our end, of 'something' that has disappeared into a world beyond words. We are invited to ponder the curious relation between the nameless spirit in the room and the qualities in the dead person that sustain or nourish it. 'Simple gravity' is not just a quality possessed by the woman while alive. The speaker's incomprehension, her inability to grasp its 'gravity,' its all but measurable weight, brings her face to face with a presence she can feel and all but touch.

I would not weep if I were they –
How rude in one to sob!
Might scare the quiet fairy
Back to her native wood!

While simple-hearted neighbors
Chat of the 'Early dead' –
We – prone to periphrasis,
Remark that Birds have fled!

(lyric 45, ll. 9–16)

There are moments when words like 'corpse' or 'dead woman' seem to be crying out to get into the poem. Yet Dickinson fends them off with sure and unobtrusive dexterity. The one blunt reference to death – 'The "Early dead"' – is associated with the empty chatting of 'simple-hearted neighbors.' When their rude speech threatens to dispel the magic by scaring the frail elfin spirit back to fairy land, Dickinson swiftly mutes its force by drawing a circle of words around death's uncivil intrusion and rude discourtesy: 'We – prone to periphrasis, / Remark that Birds have fled!'

Lyric 50 suggests that announcing one's death to strangers is a breach of decorum, the commission of an uncivil act. How should one have the effrontery, the 'face to die,' and then be bold enough to 'name it in the street'?

I will not name it in the street
For shops would stare at me –
That one so shy – so ignorant
Should have the face to die.

(lyric 50, ll. 5–8)

The mere lisping of the word is forbidden. Even an allusion to it in a riddle is too direct.

> Nor lisp it at the table –
> Nor heedless by the way
> Hint that within the Riddle
> One will walk today –   (lyric 50, ll. 13–16)

The sibyl's riddling use of 'Riddle' echoes Paul's comment that now we see in a riddle, or 'through a glass darkly.' But instead of quoting Paul directly, Dickinson shrouds her allusion in mystery. If death is an enigma, then, as Eleanor Cook explains, it is 'rhetorically a closed simile, where one term of the "like" is hidden' (2006, 107). Northrop Frye observes that 'the Sibyl of Amherst is no Lorelei: she has no Keatsian fairy lands forlorn or Tennysonian low-lying Claribels; she does not charm and she seldom sings' (Frye, 1963c, 201). Instead, she surprises her readers by using a sidelong allusion to the passage in Corinthians usually read at funeral services to make a riddling quotation even more oblique. With superb compression her oracle speaks of moving inside a Riddle which far exceeds the sibyl's own power to be oracular or riddling. Unfortunately, to enter the Riddle and walk inside it are not synonymous with solving anything. Since we can decipher only a fragment of the Riddle, it is hard to see how a mere metonymy, the part we can and do decipher, is also a synecdoche, a part we can use as a key to unlock the meaning of the whole.

Lyric 57 turns upon a pun: 'They may take the trifle / Termed *mortality*' (5–6). Though a term is a definition that sets limits or boundaries, the word 'trifle' is left unbound by being placed at the end of an unpunctuated line. In crossing the invisible boundary to an altered sense of 'termed,' we are reminded that 'termed' has its root in 'ending' or termination.

> To venerate the simple days
> Which lead the seasons by,
> Needs but to remember
> That from you or I,
> They may take the trifle
> Termed *mortality*!

We expect Dickinson to say that we venerate the simple days and seasons because we know they do not last. 'Death,' as Stevens claims, 'is the mother of beauty.' But the poet surprises us. Instead of producing change in the seasons, time takes something from us: nothing less than 'the trifle / Termed mortality.' In order to attain a more just assessment of life, less trifling than the short lease assigned by 'mortality,' we have to break down the definitions and the limits that they set, even if it means transgressing rules of grammar: 'from you or I.' Since we seldom think of life as 'a trifle,' we are shocked by the reversal. And yet the shock prompts us to recognize that, in defining life as mere mortality, we are assigning it too limited a term.

As an oracle of ends, the sibyl of Amherst is quizzically adept at giving a voice to silent-speaking words. In lyric 53 the semi-stutter of 'Our departed are' (l. 12) reads both as a chiasmic lament – 'Our departed Our' – and as an inchoate wail – 'Are departed are.' It is piercing both in its frail echoing and wavering finality. Since 'all the rooms' in Eden 'are full,' all our departed must be there, including 'One little mind from school.'

> Taken from men – this morning –
> Carried by men today –
> Met by the Gods with banners –
> Who marshalled her away –
>
> One little maid – from playmates –
> One little mind from school –
> There must be guests in Eden –
> All the rooms are full –
>
> Far – as the East from Even –
> Dim – as the border star –
> Courtiers quaint, in Kingdoms
> Our departed are.

Since they have not yet been admitted to Eden's guesthouse, the 'courtiers quaint' are as precariously stationed as possible. Dickinson is not interested in any simple, easy grandeur. A lesser poet would have ironed out the semi-stutters of 'Taken from men,' 'Carried by men,' 'Met by,' 'Our departed are.' But it is on such tentative pivot or hinge words that the soul's wavering entry into Eden is made to turn. Dickinson is a sibyl of oddly tilted wisdom. We can say of her riddling lyrics, a unique blend of intimate emotion and privacy, what Stephen Greenblatt says of Shakespeare's sonnets. They 'are a cunning sequence' of 'locked boxes to which there are no keys, an exquisitely constructed screen behind which it is virtually impossible to venture with any confidence' (2004, 249). A reader is continually thrown off balance by the oblique clarity and wistful strangeness of her oracles.

4

A sublime oracle gives us what John Bayley calls 'the momentary trick of angelic apprehension' (1981, 18). In his prophecies on the heath, Lear, a dispossessed king, inhabits a world in which dispossession no longer matters. As a king of space, Lear's consciousness fills and enlarges the play. As far away as possible from 'the agony and strife of human hearts,' Lear's imagination of living alone with Cordelia and of taking upon himself 'the mystery of things' is a godlike perception too good for this life. The mind's awareness of its freedom to wander in imagination tantalizes Lear. His sublime oracles conjure a world in which the burden of the mystery is momentarily lightened. In instants of surmise or visionary vagrancy, a prophet like Lear may suddenly open the door on a better world or cleanse our perceptions. Alternatively, he may simply dwell in possibilities by multiplying life's options. The more cribbed in and imprisoned the blinded Gloucester feels, the more freely he can leap with telegraphic economy from point to point in an enlarged understanding of his freedom to make a heaven of hell or a hell of heaven while Edgar is describing the cliffs at Dover.

Though Lear is Shakespeare's most sublime creation, he is only a foolish old man, a 'tattered coat upon a stick, unless / Soul clap its hands and sing, and louder sing / For every tatter in its mortal dress' (Yeats, 'Sailing to Byzantium,' ll. 9–12). Lear's arias at the centre of the play are operatic soliloquies, cosmic in scope, in which the king is not so much addressing the Fool as talking past him. The 'vaunt-couriers' of the storm are forerunners of thunder, but also boastful flatterers at court. Like these courtiers and couriers, all elements in the scene are allowed to run together. Is nature generating another race of men by scattering its seeds? Or is nature annihilating man by spilling seeds without inseminating anything? Is this an act of procreation or of cosmic onanism? The blows that level Lear are blows of language rather than natural assaults of the storm. Though two powerful metonymies, the storm's gross, full belly and the king's venerable white head, concentrate the conflict, the hammer blows that fall with greatest force are the spondees that reduce Lear to an 'infirm, weak, and despised old man' (III.iii.20). As a tattered coat upon a stick, Lear's greatest affinity is with the infirm and the poor. Unfed and without homes, they wear clothing which nevertheless has features of a house: it is full of windows or rents, and is looped like a blind which tries to hide the holes.

Whereas Posthumus is an unhinged scourge of women, an unbalanced misogynist, Lear after his exchange with the blinded Gloucester is a Job-like prosecutor. He uses the calamity that has overtaken Gloucester to grope his own way back to sanity. As a poet of cosmic inquisition, Lear is more a master of Aeschylus's sublimity and less a victim of Marlowe's rant than is Timon of Athens. There is reason in his madness and lucidity in his outrage. Lear first sweetens his imagination with a joke. Gloucester's purse, he says, may be light. But the sockets, the case and purse of his eyes, are heavy, because what they carry, his blinded eyes, have no light in them. Lear may dismiss as madness Glouceter's oxymoron of 'seeing feelingly.' But there is wise folly in his advice that 'a man may see how the world goes with no eyes' (IV.vi.153). The catachresis of looking 'with thine ears' can teach the blind man all he has to know. The usurer hangs the petty thief. The punisher of whores is more lecherous than the adulteress he stones. Rich apparel conceals vice just as surely as tattered clothes expose it. The blinded Gloucester should get glass eyes so that, like a dishonest politician, he can pretend to see things he does not. 'Bodily decrepitude is wisdom,' Yeats claims. Until the decay of his body releases him from prison, Lear is a Titan in chains. Only when his soul rages and his spirit soars can Lear launch the sublime reversals that playgoers associate with the Gospel parables and the Sermon on the Mount.

During the storm on the heath Lear vents his rage at filial ingratitude, man's inhumanity to man, and the pride of great ones. When he invites the winds to rage and blow, he is mirroring a grotesque need to howl in himself. Without a breaking open of his soul, which leaves him vulnerable, no healing can begin. But after the king himself becomes the storm and the tumult on the heath expresses the tumult in his soul, a more human Lear can be heard in the easier cadences of his verse. Speaking with new-found simplicity, Lear describes himself as a 'slave,' 'poor, infirm' and 'weak.' The perfect simplicity of such lines shuts out the mind while they liberate the spirit. As one critic says, 'it is surely impossible for anyone who cares about poetry to write about such moments without some expression of awe' (Kermode, 2000, 184).

In the most powerful apocalyptic scene in Shakespeare, Lear's reunion with his daughter, the king's torment on the heath is partially redressed by his angelic perception of Cordelia as a guardian spirit: 'You are a spirit, I know. Where did you die?' (IV.vii.49). Unforced and brief, the revelation scene is the most moving moment in the play, because, as John Bayley says, 'it is the only time the speech of father and daughter coincides. Neither is using words for effect or purpose, but like a kiss or a touch' (1981, 41).

Nevertheless, the wrenching truth in *King Lear* is life's capricious cruelty. Samuel Johnson could not remain in the theatre during the concluding scenes of the play. I think its devastating effect is best explained by Stephen Booth, who more than any other critic is aware that 'the power and intensity of our responses to the last moments in *King Lear* do not result from what happens.' They result rather 'from when and where it happens' (1983, 6).

What ought to be 'a smooth ceremony of conclusion' turns into something cosmically disturbing.

> KENT: Is this the promis'd end?
> EDGAR: Or image of that horror?
> ALBANY: Fall and cease!   (V.iii.263–4)

The 'symphonic ritual' of apocalypse does not merely describe events but 'takes them over,' as John Bayley observes (1981, 10). We are getting ready to leave the theatre, waiting for the play to end happily, as in all earlier versions of the story, when events begin to roll on interminably, like a Juggernaut, riding over every hope and expectation of happiness we have nurtured on Lear's behalf.

We grieve, as Booth says, for own vulnerability and for the fragility of things we cherish. We want Lear and Cordelia to be whole. Instead, the play gives us a broken whole. It pushes 'inexorably beyond' the whole it should be, 'rolling across and crushing the very framework that enables its audience to endure the otherwise terrifying' calamities it presents. After offering an action that promises to fortify our mind and enhance our soul, Shakespeare breaks and mutilates them both. He betrays our expectations by doing something we are never quite prepared for, no matter how many times we have read or seen the play. For strange as it may sound, Shakespeare 'presents the culminating events of his story, after his play is over' (Booth, 1983, 11). This is why we feel no deliverance from the destruction of evil characters in *King*

Lear. By thwarting our expectations they have also outwitted and humiliated us. Left to struggle on our own against this irony, we have to look in our heart and write our own oracles. As one critic says, 'it is partly because of this insistent challenge to the spectator's re-creative powers that the great tragedies are so endlessly fascinating to critics: merely to experience them seems to demand commentary as part of one's response' (Frye. 1967b, 120).

Iris Murdoch ingeniously suggests that 'tragedy must mock itself internally through being essentially, in its own way, a broken whole' (1992, 116–17). *King Lear* sets up expectations that it systematically disappoints. Instead of fulfilling its promises, it breaks them. The play's frustration of anticipated pattern or design extends from the generic promises Shakespeare seems to make to the way he breaks the tiniest details of his couplet form. When Albany, for example, the man of virtue and authority, seems about to distribute rewards at the end of the play by using a formal couplet to clinch a return of order, the audience reasonably anticipates a just and happy outcome.

> All friends shall taste
> The wages of their virtue, and all foes
> The cup of their deservings [bitter woes]   (V.iii.303–5)

But alas, the two last words are never spoken. At the moment we expect to hear them, Albany is interrupted by a spectacle too calamitous for words. He sees Lear carrying in the body of the dead Cordelia. Breaking off from the expected couplet, Albany can offer the audience only a shattered fragment. And yet the ruined couplet's promise of order, even when replaced by two anguished deictics ('O see, see!'), attests, as one critic says, 'to an orderliness in the play as play that persists even in defeat' (Booth, 1983, 27).

People, like relics and their dearest possessions, can be at once broken and whole. My daughter Margaret's contact lenses, and later her purple-framed glasses, were damaged or destroyed. But they were also restored. In a fit of anger and depression, her flute was crumpled into a tangle of tubes. But we bought another and a better flute. We adjusted it twice, and Margaret played it for her brother and sisters a few weeks before she died. In the end the flute, like the glasses, disappeared, as rare things tend to do. But they survive in our memory as sturdy reminders of what broken wholes may be. 'Give me the world if you must, but grant me an asylum for my affections.'

Sustaining the impression of a broken whole is *King Lear*'s heart-breaking demonstration that in their dreadful conflict with forces of evil good people suffer undeservedly. The play leaves an audience no shred of providential design, no tatter of poetic justice, to cling to. Instead, Lear's tortured reflections on injustice yield an oracular form of counter-truth. Northrop Frye compares these counter-truths to the 'sharp dissonances in classical music: however logical and right in their place, they are out of key with the whole design.' In such oracular dissonances, which can be rationalized as madness, 'we hear what is described at the end of *King Lear* as one of the results of undergoing a tragic experience, when we are able to "Speak what we feel, not what we ought to say"' (Frye, 1967b, 64).

5

In Amy Clampitt's elegy 'What the Light Was Like,' the parabolic structure of the journey out and back, including the inventory of familiar landmarks seen in reverse order, is the poet's way of allaying her fear of death. But her chronicle is never as seamless as she thinks. At the farthest reach of her parabola, she confronts the trauma of the sudden dash, the unexpected break or incision, which destroys the continuity of her narrative. At the end of the elegy we retrace the voyage out, but this time without the comfort of chiasmus. After taking us fifty miles beyond familiar landmarks (l. 60), the poet tries to imagine the imageless condition of being beyond all boundary lines, outside all restricted areas and limits. An experience of boundaries is threatening, not because it is the end of life, but because it is the most important moment *in* life. Like Emily Dickinson, Clampitt is inventive in thinking up ways to experience and yet survive the catastrophic moment. A torrent of images rushes in to fill the empty space at the centre. No one knows what precedes creation or follows apocalypse. All we know is that the vision finally ebbed. But did it ebb because of a plenitude of light, a halo gone berserk, like the somersaulting grandeur of the ocean at sunrise, which would resemble what the Bible calls the fullness of time? Or did it end in a void of emptiness, a moment of timelessness, expressing what Eliot calls the 'darkness of God,' by merging into a background of 'unreversed, irrevocable' night (Clampitt, l. 64)?

The God of *In Memoriam* may be a 'wild poet,' working 'without a conscience or an aim.' But at least he is not a super-craftsman God preoccupied with making things that are only well designed and useful, like the antiquated God of William Paley and the natural theologians. The mourner had hoped to talk with the dead Hallam as familiarly as Milton's swain addresses Lycidas. Instead, at the end of the poem, in the running waters and the rolling air, in the rising and the setting sun, he encounters something more Wordsworthian than Miltonic, more sublime than intimate, more cosmic than personal. The vaguely 'diffusive power' into which Hallam fades (*In Memoriam*, 130.7) dissolves our idols and warns us to be silent. Like the reader, the mourner comes to acknowledge the instability of his world, the idolatry of his beliefs, the narrowness of his commitments. Washed in the remotest cleanliness of a world that expels the poet and his images, as it expels the critic and his theories, Tennyson realizes that a sense sublime of something far more deeply 'interfused' has gently but irreversibly disturbed his poem and transformed its final vision.

Of the Christian virtues, we can say that the oracles of love are the most beautiful, because their spirit is incarnate. Conceived in darkness and born of vision, love celebrates the present. The most grotesque oracles are often oracles of faith, which is the substance of things hoped for looking for things not seen. Conceived in doubt and born of imperfect knowledge, faith looks to the past for a promised end. The oracles of hope are the most sublime, since like the voice Tennyson hears 'on the rolling air' (*In Memoriam*, 130.1) the spirit of hope is diffusive, ghostly, and devoid of any body. Conceived in despair and born of wisdom, hope looks toward the future.

4 Making Peace with Time: The Beautiful Oracle

'Beauty is truth, truth beauty,' Keats says, in one of literature's most famous aphorisms. Keats means, I think, that beauty is incarnated truth, which is beautiful only in a world where spirit is substantial. Despite his distaste for Hegel, the ghost of Hegel survives in George Santayana, who believes that everything in nature is lyrical and beautiful in its ideal essence, tragic and sublime in its fate, and comic or grotesque in its existence (Santayana, 1967, 142).

The Shakespearean soliloquist – Hamlet in 'To be or not to be' or 'How all occasions do inform against me' – begins as an explorer. His character is changing, myriad-sided, and responsive to earlier expressions of itself. Though conversion is usually withheld from such a speaker, explorers like Browning's David or Abt Vogler may also attain the more privileged position of the seer who aspires to sublime and exalted vision. At the opposite extreme are the mere muteness and unintelligibility of Browning's Spanish monk and Caliban. Initiated as a stammer from the mud or as a barely articulate growl, their speech is a struggle to emerge from the babble of autism and verbal muddle. Occupying a middle ground is the puppet manipulated by higher powers he cannot quite compass or control. At its most artful and contrived, puppetry can be a beautiful art, eloquently synchronized to ensure a coincidence of Andrea del Sarto's or Demeter's voice with the oracular voice of the prophet-poet, the ventriloquist behind the mask.

In his *Lectures on Aesthetics*, Hegel explains that God manifests himself as a grotesque animal god in ancient Egypt, then as a beautiful human god in classical Greece, and finally as the sublimely transcendent 'I am that I am' of Genesis – or the equally sublime God-man of Christian faith. In the last chapter I showed that the sublime Romantic art that Hegel equates primarily with music posits an imbalance between an increasingly attenuated sensuous form and a liberated spiritual content trying to free itself from matter. In the next chapter I turn my attention to grotesque oracles belonging to Hegel's ancient symbolical phase of art. Reversing the ratios of the sublime oracle, grotesque prophecies posit an imbalance between an attenuated spiritual content and the feel for dense, viscous things Browning associates with Caliban and his swamp. The present chapter concentrates on the beautiful oracle. According to Hegel, the truest expression of such beauty is to be found in the Greek statues of the classical period, which exhibit a perfect balance of spiritual content and material form.

Beautiful in the strict Hegelian sense, because of the reciprocity it achieves between an animating breeze and a landscape's material contours and forms, the prayer in section 86 of *In Memoriam* crosses with ease three successive stanzas.

> Sweet after showers, ambrosial air,
>   That rollest from the gorgeous gloom
>   Of evening over brake and bloom
> And meadow, slowly breathing bare
>
> The round of space, and rapt below
>   Through all the dewy-tasselled wood,
>   And shadowing down the horned flood
> In ripples, fan my brow and blow
>
> The fever from my cheek, and sigh
>   The full new life that feeds thy breath
>   Throughout my frame, till Doubt and Death,
> Ill brethren, let the fancy fly
>
> From belt to belt of crimson seas
>   On leagues of odour streaming far,
>   To where in yonder orient star
> A hundred spirits whisper 'Peace.'   (*In Memoriam*, 86. 1–16)

The growth from seeing into vision, from precise descriptions of 'the horned flood' and 'dewy-tasselled wood' into the intensifying consciousness of 'a hundred spirits' whispering 'Peace,' is beautifully expansive. The kernel of the sentence is 'Air, fan my brows.' But 'air' is heavily qualified by the clauses that come after, so that the mind has to double back on the sequence that advances and returns upon itself in a self-embedding manner. In the final quatrain the loose rhythm, without pauses we would could clearly call caesuras, together with the looser sound patterning and the larger syntactic units, establishes a growing, relaxed movement, leading naturally into the harmony of the hundred spirits whispering 'Peace.' The spaciousness and calm of the breeze's benediction are as much a function of the self-embedding syntax as they are of the sacramental images or the growing pattern of alliterating sounds. They help the poet cross breaks between quatrains and lines and achieve the sense of an easy growth in perception.

1

Northrop Frye coins the term 'outscape,' a variant of Hopkins's 'inscape,' to describe the haiku's 'convention of pure projected detachment, in which an image, a situation, or a mood is observed with all the imaginative energy thrown outward to it and away from the poet' (1957, 297). Section 121 of *In Memoriam* turns a mindscape into just such an outscape by projecting fleeting affinities of hope and despair in the poet's mind onto Hesper and the sun.

> Sad Hesper o'er the buried sun
>> And ready, thou, to die with him,
>> Thou watchest all things ever dim
> And dimmer, and a glory done.   (ll. 1–4)

Hopkins, a reluctant admirer of Tennyson, who dismissed *Idylls of the King* as medieval charades, declared of these lines' calligraphy of farewell: 'The maturest judgment will never be fooled out of saying that this is divine, terribly beautiful' (1938, 72). In its flickering hesitation, wavering in emphasis between 'a *glory* done' and a 'glory *done*,' Tennyson's outscape is as beautifully detached as a haiku and just as impersonal. Oscar Wilde says Meredith is a prose Browning, and so is Browning. We might say Hopkins is an aesthetic Tennyson, and so is Tennyson. Victorian beauticians may now be out of favour. But Tennyson's artifice will always have a future. In lines like these it is the artifice of eternity.

When the haiku poetess of Kaga writes a poem on the difficulty of seeing a cuckoo at night, she records that 'hearing a cuckoo cry, / I looked up in the direction / Whence the sound came: / What did I see?

/ Only the pale moon in the dawning sky.' Rejected by the Zen master for being too bound to a temporal sequence, the haiku must still liberate itself from linear transcription. D.T. Suzuki tells us that, after staying up all night to write a better poem, the author finally produces the following haiku, which her teacher accepts as a masterpiece (Suzuki, 1970a, 224–5).

> Calling 'cuckoo,' 'cuckoo,'
> All night long,
> Dawn at last!

By deleting the personal pronoun and replacing the three sentences of the original with mere syntactic fragments, the revised haiku fashions an inscape of feeling. Since haikus avoid egotism, their inscapes might more accurately be called outscapes. But they are outscapes with a difference. For they succeed to the degree they express and objectify authentic personal experience. As Suzuki says, there must be no 'mediatory agent' in a haiku 'between the artistic inspiration and the mind into which it has come' (1970a, 225).

In beautiful outscapes there is one perfection of the flesh and another of the spirit, but in the end both are united in a single harmony, where each can enhance and glorify the other. Such is the power of Hopkins's 'Hurrahing in Harvest' or 'The Grandeur of God,' where, as Coleman Barks says of the Sufi poet Rumi, 'the inner world is a weather that contains the universe and uses it as a symbolic language' (Rumi, 1995, 33). In creating a 'thou' world between the poet and nature, Rumi uses God as a metaphor to stabilize their union: 'Spring is Christ.' The beauty of their union is to the Sufi's poet's sacramental imagination what the sublime silence of 'The Reed-Flute's Song' is to a mystical or visionary imagination. Celebrating the reciprocal dependence of botanical, human, and divine orders, Rumi's rapture rivals the spring giddiness of Hopkins's reveller in 'Pied Beauty.'

> Spring is Christ,
> Raising martyred plants from their shrouds.
> Their mouths open in gratitude, wanting to be kissed.
>
> ('Spring Is Christ,' ll.4–6)

The oracle proclaims that 'there's no rest / except on ... branching moments' ('Spring Is Christ,' ll. 19–20) when the world rotates on flourishing axes of grace, and the 'wind is the Holy Spirit' and 'the trees are Mary' (ll. 11–12).

Though we may expect a 'branching moment' to culminate in an oracle or vision, its truest possessor may wish to disavow the role of seer altogether. Like the sheikh who played with children, Rumi's prophet may choose to hide his power and travel incognito.

> 'The people here
> Want to put me in charge. They want me to be
> Judge, magistrate, and interpreter of all the texts.
> The knowing I have doesn't want that. It wants to enjoy itself.'
> ('The Sheikh Who Played with Children,' ll. 41–4)

Whereas the knowledge laboriously acquired by lawgivers and rhetoricians is seldom a form of self-knowledge, the sheikh's way of knowing is a form of wisdom, a paradox of simultaneous self-consumption and self-replenishment.

> I am a plantation of sugarcane, and at the same time
> I'm eating the sweetness.'
> ('The Sheikh Who Played with Children,' ll. 45–6)

Such a self-inwoven metaphor 'both reconciles and opposes' since, as Christopher Ricks explains, 'it describes something both as itself and as something external to it, which it could not possibly be' (1987, 34). A crop of sugar cane cannot possibly eat or enjoy itself. Yet the liberal knowing the speaker seeks does just that. What he knows is its own reward, and its 'only real customer is God' (l. 52).

Like Rumi's god, the chaste, unravished bridegroom Hopkins celebrates in his most beautiful oracles may enter our soul in spring as we walk in an orchard or as we glean his harvest in autumn down all the glory of the heavens. Hopkins's lord of grace and bounty is irrevocably the being he is, pre-existing like the Logos by a final cause or end deeper than creation. Mediated through Thomistic interpretations of Aristotle as well as through Ruskin's theory of a penetrative imagination, Hopkins's celebration of inscape attests to the beauty, not of a more ideal but of a more essential world. Like Aristotle, the metaphysician who brought Plato's Ideas down to earth, Hopkins believes that Christ, as the procreator of a sacramental order, is the father and architect of a teleology that is immanent in all creation. By giving Aristotle's final and formal causes a dwelling place in matter, Christ has made clear to the popular imagination an eternal greatness incarnate in time and the world.

As unique as a scent or a musical note, the imagination of a Homer or a Shakespeare 'never stops at crusts or ashes, or outward images of any kind; it ploughs them aside,' as Ruskin says, 'and plunges into the very central fiery heart' (1903–12, 4:250). The penetrative imagination of a prophetic poet like Hopkins seizes in the object an indivisible unity that defies analysis. It is an actuality, an essence, something of which we can say nothing with literal truth except that it exists. All salient features of this penetrative imagination are present in great intensity and fusion in Hopkins's curtal sonnet, 'Pied Beauty.' Every detail of this exuberant *Te Deum Laudamus* proclaims an astonishing relation of sameness and difference that is cosmic in scope. The echoing and chiming of groups of dappled things turn the *concordia discors* of nature into a perfect analogy, a perfect reflecting mirror, of the Father's remarkable ability to unify diverse impressions in and through his Son.

In Aristotle's *Posterior Analytics* (II, 7), both Ruskin and Hopkins would have found the important distinction between what things are (the object of the descriptive sciences and of expository criticism) and the sheer fact of their existence, the mystery of their being this unique item and not that one. Hopkins may have assimilated his wonder at this mystery either through the medieval Aristotelianism of Aquinas, who seems like Ruskin to have been a thinker overcome with awe by the sheer reality of things, or else more directly through Ruskin himself. In 'Pied Beauty,' for example, microscopic impressions of rose-moles on a trout, 'fresh-firecoal chestnut-falls,' and of 'finches' wings' (ll. 3–4) are joined to impressions that are vast in scope. 'Dappled' is coupled with the vague noun 'things' (l. 1), and the variegated colours of the brinded cow are stretched into a Turneresque blending of the skyscape and the clouds. The variety of creation is fixed most definitely in the unique identity of what is 'counter, original, spare, strange' (l. 7). But no sooner is each item distinguished than a rapid multiplication of alliterating antonyms – 'swift, slow; sweet, sour; adazzle, dim' (l. 9) – begins to override distinction, celebrating the reversing flow of all beauty back to God.

The sonnet's culminating oracle is half prayer and half prophecy: 'He fathers-forth whose beauty is past change: / Praise him' (ll. 10–11). 'Couple-colour' (l. 2) becomes not just 'two-coloured,' but also,

because of its association with the brinded cows, a form of cosmic con-
joining – a coitus of sky and earth, a potential act of God's procreating
or 'fathering-forth.' Hopkins's groupings are potent, not merely as sets
of observed facts, but as alliances of analogy between fickle, freckled
things and God. Hopkins may not be able to explain how he, like the
fathering God, can progress from a tumult of diverse images, each
unique, to the unity of an inscaped world. 'Who knows how?' he asks
in wonder (l. 8). What is most mysterious and godlike about his oracles
is their ability to group together words and objects, through analogies
of sound and muscular sensation, until the procreating God and the
dappled, brinded things he fathers forth seem to conjoin, uniting physically as a single life-force.

2

Most visionary oracles are sublime, and most sacramental ones are
beautiful. But occasionally the ratios reverse themselves. Though Tennyson's dramatization of the hundred spirits whispering 'peace' in
section 86 of *In Memoriam* is steadily and luminously visionary, it
produces an oracle that is beautiful rather than sublime because of
its precise evocation of a local English landscape. Similarly, when
Geoffrey Hill in *The Mystery of the Charity of Charles Péguy* repeats
Rimbaud's desolating phrase, 'je est un autre' (9.32), even the anticipated grammar breaks down. Outwardly, everything appears lost. The
lines of men that in 7.28–9 had faltered and vanished into smoke now
seem totally erased. But because Hill celebrates in exquisite landscapes
and in lost French causes the transience and hence the seriousness of
beauty, even his annunciation of disaster is sacramental and beautiful
rather than visionary and sublime. By contrast, Hopkins's poems are
often too apocalyptic or visionary to be beautiful. But they are still
potently sacramental. Despite the 'wildfire' that leaves only 'ash' in its
wake, Hopkins's oracle in 'That Nature Is a Heraclitean Fire' is a
marvel of Incarnation: 'In a flash, at a trumpet crash, / I am all at once
what Christ is, since he was what I am' (ll. 20–2). The tidal surge and
flow of the seascapes in *The Wreck of the Deutschland* are tempestuous
and ravaging rather than pastoral and serene. Yet the heroic, Job-like
language of the nun's baptism of 'her wild-worst / Best' (24.8) evokes
a sublime sacramental world, even while tottering on the edge of frag-
mentation and collapse.

Balancing Keats's oracle 'Beauty is truth, truth beauty' is his more solemn prophecy: 'In the very temple of Delight / Veiled Melancholy has her sovereign shrine' ('Ode on Melancholy,' ll. 25–6). Harmonies of flesh and spirit are unstable and precarious. Sometimes beauty is only momentary in the mind, and in the flesh it is immortal. More often we are in love, but love what vanishes. What more is there to say?

A Victorian Keats, who writes his 'Ode to Autumn' in the monologue 'Tithonus,' Tennyson is a master of grave autumnal moods. 'The woods decay, the woods decay and fall.' The repetitions are relentless. 'Man comes and tills the field and lies beneath' (l. 3). The slow, deathward movement carries us down to the expiring swan, and composes a kind of epitaph for creation. The gnomic grandeur has an authority of reserve: there is as much reticence as emotion in the verse. These lines achieve their most potent afterlife in Hopkins's 'Spring and Fall.' It is his loveliest lyric and also his most oracular, because the ruin of its golden autumnal bower is also the ruin of paradise, the garden of Eden after the Fall.

> Márgarét, áre you grieving
> Over Goldengrove unleaving?
> Léaves líke the things of man, you
> With your fresh thoughts care for, can you?
> Ah! ás the heart grows older
> It will come to such sights colder
> By and by, nor spare a sigh
> Though worlds of wanwood leafmeal lie;
> And yet you will weep and know why.
> Now no matter, child, the name:
> Sórrow's spríngs áre the same.
> Nor mouth had, no nor mind, expressed
> What heart heard of, ghost guessed:
> It ís the blight man was born for,
> It is Margaret you mourn for.   ('Spring and Fall,' ll. 11–15)

Hopkins's most Tennysonian quality is his 'divine despair.' As in the 'happy autumn fields' of 'Tears, idle tears,' where as Christopher Ricks has said 'a most potent absence' is 'the absence of rhyme' (1972, 199), the beautiful autumnal paradise evokes a grief that seems at first unmotivated. But we are assured that as the young Margaret grows older she will weep again and know why. Strangely enough, the loveliest line Hopkins ever wrote – 'Though worlds of wanwood leafmeal lie' – is a lament for desolation and ruin. How is this possible? Part of the mystery lies in the contorted syntax of surrounding lines: 'care for, can you' (l. 4), and later 'what heart heard of, ghost guessed' (l. 13). The awkward grace of these lines finds release in an unforced succession of simple phrases: 'worlds of wanwood leafmeal lie.' The knot of syntax suddenly comes loose: the line unfolds with a natural grace and ease of movement. Though the leaves have fallen, the words themselves descend as slowly and majestically as a season might hope to pass. To give weight to the line Hopkins assigns a long quantity to each of the vowels in the unstressed phrases: to 'wood' in 'wanwood' and 'meal' in 'leafmeal.' The phrase 'Goldengrove unleaving' is itself 'unleaving': it endures in memory and will not leave a reader's mind. In the falling leaves, young Margaret half foresees 'the other fall we call the Fall.' Though the golden paradise is a ruin of time, like anything we love and lose it is 'unleaving.' It abides in the mind as a spot of time we cherish and remember. The world we love too well is made more lovely, partly because we know we must leave it soon. Though Hopkins and Tennyson were both dead when 'Spring and Fall' was finally published in the twentieth century, the two poets have less in common with Tithonus, 'earth in earth,' than with Aurora's return 'morn by morn' and the renewal of beauty for future generations.

If I were still trying to conduct a seminar in poetry, I would have to stay clear of many poems I used to teach, including this one. They mean too much to me now. My daughter Margaret used a bright autumnal palate in her paintings. Even when the pictures are dark in subject matter, they are adorned in the life-affirming arabesques of red, orange, and yellow colours that I shall always associate with 'Goldengrove unleaving.' What a contrast this poem makes to the psychiatric books, medical pamphlets, and *Merck Manuals* that keep piling up on my desk. I can seldom disinter such tomes from the tomb of their dull statistics and abstractions. I know now why Joan Didion's husband, John Gregory Dunne, strung together 'a kind of improvised rosary' of lines from Hopkins in the months following his brother's suicide (Didion, 2006, 32). Poets and prophets write a living language. Hopkins's words are proved on his pulses, carried alive into the heart with passion. 'Cor ad cor loquitur.'

Few oracles of early death are more beautifully conceived than Ben Jonson's Pindaric ode for Cary and Morison, whose cadences provide a soft landing for the poet by falling on the ear gently, as a man might hope to die. The power of poetry's measures and answered syllables to delineate 'the lines of life' (l. 64) is proved in the contraction and expansion of alternating short and long lines.

> A Lillie of a day
> Is fairer farre, in May,
> Although it fall, and die that night;
> It was the Plant, and flowre of light.
> In small proportions, we just beauties see:
> And in short measures, life may perfect bee.   (ll. 69–74)

The 'Lillie of a Day' is confined to a mere trimeter line, a sad contraction. But it dramatizes metrically the claim that the measures of a good life, like the measures of a fine epitaph, are assessments, not of length or size, but of 'how well / Each syllab'e answer'd, and was form'd, how faire' (ll. 62–3). Though Jonson never minimizes the breaks in continuity, he also beautifully develops the thought that, because Morison and Cary are united even by the rift that divides them, their perfection is a quality of proportion, of the aptness of what is done and wrought in season. Like Milton's 'Lycidas,' the words release emotion even as they control it, as I found when I tried to recite a few lines from this poem at my daughter's funeral.

As Imogen's grieving brothers chant over their dead sister one of the most beautiful songs in Shakespeare, they seem at first to be repeating the wisdom of Koheleth, who tells us there is a time and season for everything. But the charm of their song derives less from biblical wisdom than from the spell of a magician like Prospero.

> Fear no more the heat o' th' sun,
>   Nor the furious winter's rages;
> Thy worldly task hast done,
>   Home art gone, and ta'en thy wages.
> Golden lads and girls all must,
>   As chimney sweepers, come to dust.   (*Cymbeline*, IV.iii.258–63)

'Ta'en thy wages' look two ways at once. Imogen has earned a reward. But if the wages of sin is death, then her wages seem undeserved, since of all Shakespeare's heroines she and Cordelia are the most virtuous. 'Home art gone' promises domestic comfort. But this home is unhomely, a place where chimney sweepers and lads and lasses of fair and shining promise come to common dust in the end.

The song's first stanza consists of two lines of exhortation, two lines of consoling observation, and two lines of epigrammatic conclusion. In the two central stanzas the lines of exhortation increase from two to four. Only in the last stanza do the observations and epigrams yield to six lines of incantatory exhortation, which take over the whole poem.

> Fear no more the frown o' th' great;
>   Thou art past the tyrant's stroke.
> Care no more to clothe and eat;
>   To thee the reed is as the oak.
> The sceptre, learning, physic, must
>   All follow this, and come to dust.
>
> Fear no more the lightning-flash,
>   Nor the all-dreaded thunder-stone;
> Fear not slander, censure rash;
>   Thou hast finished joy and moan.
> All lovers young, all lovers must
>   Consign to thee, and come to dust.
>
> No exorciser harm thee!
> Nor no witchcraft charm thee!
> Ghost unlaid forbear thee!
> Nothing ill come near thee!
> Quiet consummation have,
> And renowned be thy grave.   (ll. 264–81)

From appeals to the dead, 'Fear no more,' the song passes to command of the elements: 'Ghost unlaid forbear thee! / Nothing ill come near thee!' As a spell against witchcraft, the imperatives are now too urgent for run-ons. Instead the brothers spin and let fall a magician's incantation, a protective web of trochaic chants for their sister. A rite of exorcism is beautifully in progress. Over the dead Imogen four echoing 'thee's cast a fond and lingering spell of feminine rhymes: 'harm thee,' 'charm thee,' 'forbear thee,' 'near thee.' Though time reduces everything to dust, against its reductive metonymies magic offers its own words of power, words that owe more to the enchanting wizardry of Prospero than to the wisdom of Koheleth or the stoicism of Seneca.

According to Theodore Spencer's lovely oracular lyric 'The day was a year at first,' childhood is a state or phase of imaginative existence. The more innocent and romantic the life of a child becomes, the more effortlessly its time frame expands until a mere day seems as ample and full of ease as a year spent in Eden.

> The day was a year at first
> When the children ran in the garden;
> The day shrank down to a month
> When the boys played ball.   (ll. 1–4)

The progressive shrinkage of time, at first from a 'day to a month' and then from a 'day to a week,' soon brings both a loss of leisure and a growth in stature and responsibility. For when 'the day was itself a day,' then 'love,' we learn, 'grew tall.'

> The day was a week thereafter
> When young men walked in the garden;
> The day was itself a day
> When love grew tall.   (ll. 5–8)

Finally, just as Eden sank to grief, so the disenchanted visionary subsides from romance and innocence into the high promise but eventual disappointments of youth and old age. We are shocked by the contrast between the speed at which time accelerates its pace and the pitiable limping of the old men in the garden, who inch grotesquely toward us.

> The day shrank down to an hour
> When old men limped in the garden.   (ll. 9–10)

Most appalling is the lyric's concluding oracle, which looks two ways at once.

> The day will last forever
> When it is nothing at all.   (ll. 11–12)

What is the prophet saying? When time is no time, why will the day that has been slowly and inexorably shrinking from the first quatrain of the lyric now 'last forever'? Is it because the everlasting day will no longer be ours – or anyone else's – to experience? Or will the day 'last forever' because at the end of the world, when time 'is nothing at all,' we shall regain an Eden more enduring than the one we have lost? Balanced on a knife-edge between hope and despair, the reader does not know whether to be glad or to grieve at such exquisite but panic-stricken awareness of the transience and hence the seriousness of beautiful moments and people.

5 The Ruins of Time:
The Grotesque Oracle

A grotesque oracle substitutes for a sublime intimation or a beautiful incarnation of the Word a distorting and distending echo of it. Like the dull 'boum' heard in Forster's Marabar Cave, a grotesque oracle sets loose an alarming reverberation whose centre is everywhere and whose circumference nowhere. At the edge of Mrs Moore's mind 'religion appeared, poor little talkative Christianity, and she knew that all its divine words from "Let there be Light" to "It is finished" only amounted to "boum"' (Forster, 1924, 150). The echo in the cave undermines Mrs Moore's hold on life because as the ultimate form of copy-speech it mocks 'pathos, piety, courage' by reducing them all to 'filth,' the lowest common denominator that Mrs Moore can discover in herself and the world. She is 'terrified over an area larger than usual,' because 'the universe, never comprehensible to her intellect,' offers in the dull echo of the cave, in its empty 'ou-boum,' no vestige of original response, no trace of the counter-love that might have given 'repose to her soul' (1924, 150).

1

Walt Whitman's poem 'Tears' is comparably grotesque, hollowed out, and eviscerated. One critic says of his poetry that 'even the dashes democratically [affirm] that all punctuation was created equal and that no clause should be subordinate to any other' (Lipking, 1981, 122). By the time Whitman has pronounced the last of his dark words, a listener has fully absorbed the independent life of each separate loss and woe.

O storm, embodied, rising, careering with swift steps along the beach?
O wild and dismal night storm, with wind – O belching and desperate!
O shade so sedate and decorous by day, with calm countenance and
   regulated pace,
But away at night as you fly, none looking – O then the unloosen'd
   ocean
Of tears! tears! tears!   ('Tears,' ll. 9–13)

Like most oracular poetry, 'Tears' is 'a series of utterances, irregular in
rhythm but strongly marked off from one another. We notice ... that the
end of every line has a strong pause – for, when the rhythm is variable,
there is no point in a run-on line' (Frye, 1963c, 134). The one exception
to this statement occurs at the end of the quoted passage, where
Whitman's run-on line wins assent to his agonizing pathetic fallacy by
directly identifying the ocean with the tears. A pathetic fallacy is
pathetic precisely because it is a fallacy. But since there is nothing fallacious about the shade's desperate mood swings, which are all too
descriptive of manic depression to be an illusion, the wind's unpredictable behaviour creates in 'the shapeless lump' with 'streaming
tears' a monstrous but credible persona. Whitman turns pity and fear
into a state of mind that binds us psychologically to nature's desperate
outpouring of despair instead of leaving us aesthetically detached, as
in Synge's tragedy *Riders to the Sea*, or as in a stormy seascape by
Turner.

Just as Aeneas visits the underworld to receive instruction from
Anchises' ghost on reincarnation and the future of Rome, so Eliot in
the third sections of 'Burnt Norton,' 'East Coker,' and 'The Dry Salvages' descends into a grotesque underground world to discover his
fate. In the first of the dark night passages, an underground train
carries lost, time-ridden passengers into a circle of distraction.

Neither plenitude nor vacancy. Only a flicker
Over the strained, time-ridden faces
Distracted from distraction by distraction

Filled with fancies and empty of meaning
Tumid apathy with no concentration   ('Burnt Norton,' III.10–14)

Moving from one station to another in the twilight of the London Tube,
the drifting passengers seem as lost and aimless as the crowds flowing
over London Bridge in *The Waste Land*. Without any acceleration of the

slow, weighted metre, the Tube takes the passengers down into a deeper 'world of perpetual solitude,' which acts upon them like a vacuum pump, leaving them in an exhausted bell jar, a dark night of the soul, which is neither in nor out of time.

Samson's cry of anguish, 'O dark dark dark,' launches the underground journey in 'East Coker,' where a repetitive circling movement leaves the traveller suspended, waiting for some energizing rhythm to break out. In the third section of 'The Dry Salvages,' the oppressed traveller in the London underground turns into a more hopeful figure, a traveller who appears first on a train and then on a ship. Since we 'are not the same people who left that station / Or who will arrive at any terminus,' we are privileged to carry our past with us and to hold out our hands to the future, like the dead souls in Virgil, who are in love with the farther shore.

> Here between the hither and the farther shore
> While time is withdrawn, consider the future
> And the past with an equal mind.   ('The Dry Salvages,' III.29–31)

Just as Aeneas descends to the underworld for prophetic reassurance, so Eliot descends on his own dark journeys to escape the fate of 'the houses' that 'are all gone under the sea.' Even as he moves into darkness, he wants assurance that the life of his poetry and the values of his civilization will somehow survive the general shipwreck 'between the hither and the farther shore.'

2

It has been said of Dickens that he dispensed with human nature by creating a community of eccentrics. Though his motive in killing Caesar is more grotesque and less intelligible than Cassius's motive, which is understandable personal animus, Brutus is nobler than Cassius and more rounded and complex than any character in Dickens. In his soliloquy in the orchard, Brutus aspires to be the Euclid of a new moral geometry, unique to the Stoics and himself. Yet the fragile web of hypothesis that Brutus spins is not as taut or as seamless as he thinks. Indeed Brutus has to concede that any argument against Caesar will have to be based on surmise rather than fact, on grotesque conjectures about what Caesar may become rather than on what Caesar is now. Surmise is as weirdly disjoined from fact in Brutus's soliloquy as remorse is disjoined from power in the Caesar Brutus says he fears. A.N. Whitehead claims that the major vice of the intellect is its intolerable love of abstraction. The extremities to which Brutus fears Caesar may run – 'these and these extremities' (*Julius Caesar*, II.i.31) – are as abstract in expression as all his other exercises in moral geometry and prophecy. In shocking contrast is the vividly realized malice of the serpent hatched from an egg, which Brutus wants to kill in its shell. Ironically, the most mischievous serpent hatched from Caesar's shell is Brutus himself, widely reputed to be Caesar's natural son.

Comparably grotesque is Othello's conviction that his wife will be as exquisite in her monumental beauty after death as she is in life. The idea is uncomfortably close to the reflection of Browning's strangler that Porphyria, his dead mistress, is alive. In combination with its midline caesura, the ritual repetition of 'Put out the light, and then put out the light' (*Othello*, V.ii.7) is weighted with intolerable double meaning. The idea of dimming a light before extinguishing a life is as ominously freighted as Frost's repeated line: 'And miles to go before I sleep.' The thought that a quenched light cannot be relit like a torch, or that a cut or plucked rose cannot be grafted back on a tree, is apt yet harrowing. And Othello's idea of stealing one more breath from the rose after he has stopped the rose's breathing altogether is as grotesque and odd as the conviction of Browning's lover that his mistress is glad he strangled her. Excruciating to the limits of endurance, the tears Othello weeps are said to be cruel. But Othello is less cruel to himself than he is to Desdemona. There is less in his sorrow that is 'heavenly' than hellish, despite his extravagant surmise that his love is like God's for his Son because 'it strikes where it doth love' (l. 22). Just as Othello and Desdemona divide a line of poetry between them before he takes her life, so Othello at the moment he kills himself achieves intimacy with Desdemona by executing an artistic chiasmus that reverses the circumstance of her death: 'I kiss'd thee ere I kill'd thee: no way but this, / Killing myself, to die upon a kiss' (ll. 358–9).

More grotesque than the soliloquies of Othello and Brutus are the speeches of a callous Cressida and a disillusioned Troilus. When Cressida decides to leave Troilus for Diomedes, her overheard soliloquy wittily mocks her duplicity by presenting her as a Janus figure, grotesquely looking opposite ways at once. She must be cross-eyed, since with one eye she looks back on Troilus while with the other – the eye of her heart – she roves in lust after Diomedes. Cressida wittily plays upon the double force of 'error.' A merely wandering eye is innocent enough. But when the eye that wanders leads the mind to err, the slippage from vagrancy to moral trespass, however disguised by Cressida's irresponsible word games and saucy overflow of wit, cannot escape censure. Stranger and more grotesque than Ariadne's metamorphosis into a spider is Cressida's transformation from faithful mistress into whore. Troilus's own assault of puzzled wit in response to this change is rivalled only by the riddling paradoxes of division in *The Phoenix and the Turtle*. He meditates on the mysteries of identity: of two in one; or (in this case) of one split into two.

Just as deft as Cressida in his playful use of logic, Troilus launches into a sorites, a chain argument in the form of abridged syllogisms that offer at least the promise of stable inference. Enfolding beauty in souls, souls in vows, vows in sanctimony, Troilus appears to be forging an unbroken sequence. But instead of ascribing to the first link in the chain, 'beauty,' what he ascribes to the last, as in a traditional sorites, Troilus breaks off the series. 'God's delight' is not repeated in the phrase that follows. What starts off as a sorites turns halfway down the chain into a string of hypotheses, each so transparently valid that its logical opposite defies belief. If *a* is true, its opposite, *b*, must be false. 'If there be rule in unity itself, / This is not she' (*Troilus and Cressida*, V.ii.141–2). If such opposites can both be true, then their defiance of the law of contradiction appears to evoke only the madness of discourse. Yet within such madness, chiasmus creates little oases of calm where the mind can turn back on itself and where reason can 'revolt/ Without perdition, and loss assume all reason / Without revolt' (144–6). Sorites is to logic what the great chain of being is to Renaissance cosmology. Heaven's bonds ought to reach down to sanction and embrace Cressida's vows to Troilus. But sunder one rung in the ladder and the whole chain falls apart. When the bonds are 'slipped, dissolved, and loosed,' as Troilus says, 'Things fall apart.' As in Yeats's 'Second Coming,' 'the centre cannot hold; / Mere anarchy is loosed upon the world' (ll. 3–4).

3

In his greatest monologues Browning prefers grotesque, unresolved, damaged subjects to dramatic artefacts that are beautiful or well made. Blocking out familiar, reassuring explanations of motive, Browning finds he can release a bizarre energy in Porphyria's lover that is not available in the raucous swearing song of the Spanish monk, even though the monk is outwardly more exuberant than the silent, self-withholding strangler. There is nothing remarkable about the monk's infantile jealousy or rage. But a strangler who wants to freeze his victim into an attitude of perfect beauty, who kills her because he wants to arrest time and turn an angelic instant into a 'moment one and infinite,' is no ordinary killer.

To portray the inward insurrections of a disturbed mind in 'Andrea del Sarto' and 'My Last Duchess' Browning uses two-way meanings, puns, and a radical excision of any obvious motive for addressing an auditor in words that seem to defeat the speaker's ostensible reason for speaking. If Andrea wants Lucrezia to stay at home, why insult her? If the Duke wants another marriage, why shock or intimidate the envoy trusted to negotiate it? We can say of Browning's excision of any obvious purpose for such self-defeating behaviour what Stephen Greenblatt says of Shakespeare. He 'found that he could immeasurably deepen the effect of his plays ... if he took out a key explanatory element, thereby occluding the rationale, motivation, or ethical principle that accounted for the action to be unfolded' (2004, 47).

Browning's early masterpiece, 'My Last Duchess,' stands in the same relation to 'Soliloquy of the Spanish Cloister' as a new Gothic creation like *Wuthering Heights* or *Villette* stands to the old Gothic fictions of Horace Walpole and Ann Radcliffe. Rapidly maturing as a poet of spooky, half-comic horrors in 'Soliloquy of the Spanish Cloister,' Browning soon replaces even the quieter, more chilling fantasies of the homicidal psychopath in 'Porphyria's Lover' with the interior, endlessly subtle seductions of Andrea del Sarto. Psychic shocks and disturbances that disrupt even the self-control of the smooth, autocratic Duke in 'My Last Duchess' correspond to the gradual displacement of ghosts and haunted castles in Gothic fiction.

We might suppose that the task of conveying an intense inner life is easier to achieve in a monologue than a play, where soliloquies and occasional asides to an audience are likely to sound contrived. But an early monologue like 'Soliloquy of the Spanish Cloister' shows that it is also easier to revel in a riot of sense and sound than explore any motive that is subtler than jealousy or more complex than brute lust or animal rage. Despite its staccato energy, 'Soliloquy of the Spanish Cloister' is too predictable a caricature to be a convincing sketch of the monk's internal quarrel with his rival. If the monk's mind is a theatre, its stage has been designed for a puppet show, not for the performance of a play like *Doctor Faustus*.

Or, there's Satan! – one might venture
    Pledge one's soul to him, yet leave
Such a flaw in the indenture
    As he'd miss till, past retrieve,
Blasted lay that rose-acacia
    We're so proud of! *Hy, Zy, Hine* ...
'St, there's Vespers! *Plena gratia*
    Ave, Virgo! Gr-r-r- you swine!   (ll. 65–72)

Though the monk's swearing song is a marvel of exuberance, his plan to dispatch Brother Lawrence to hell, as 'a Manichee,' is the mere prank of a juvenile delinquent. The trick is too playful and puerile, too transparent, to be evil. Yet all the mystery of the corrupted human will is in it. The quibbles that entrap divine love into imitating the Spanish monk are pretexts for sadism, wherever found. As theologically perverse in Browning's Johannes Agricola as in Dante's imagination of hell, the sadism of these quibbles is as repulsive to Browning as it is irresistible to T.S. Eliot. Despite a professed distaste for Donne the flesh-creeper and 'sorcerer,' Eliot is himself a sorcerer of the most exquisite and refined tortures, which he delights to conjure from the void beyond the death.

'Porphyria's Lover' marks an advance in Browning's ability to turn drama inside out by creating a theatre of 'Action in Character rather than Character in Action.' Though the speaker lacks the manic energy of the Spanish monk, he is also less boisterous and peevish. The turn from a spoiled, narcissistic child to a cold-blooded psychopath, who suffers from an impoverished range of emotions, is both deft and disturbing. Shortly after he murders his mistress, the lover presumes to look inside the corpse's mind and convince himself she is glad he strangled her. Like the Duke of Ferrara, the lover is strangely mesmerized by qualities in the corpse that he takes to be lifelike. Though the lover is safe for the moment, a hostile, avenging power may break into his world, turning his most angelic perceptions into demonic ones. His theatre is at once as precious to him as the 'smiling rosy little head' and as insubstantial as a mirage about to dissolve into air like his burning kiss.

Comparably grotesque is the soliloquy of Shakespeare's hunchback on his wooing of Anne in *Richard III*. His speech falls into the shape of a grotesque love sonnet, which is as displaced and malformed as his body. One fragment of the sonnet's concluding couplet is cast forward to the first lines of the soliloquy: 'Was ever woman in this humour woo'd? / Was ever woman in this humour won?' (*Richard III*, I.iii.228–9), and another is left stranded at the end: 'Shine out, fair sun, till I have bought a glass, / That I may see my shadow as I pass' (*Richard III*, I.iii.263–4). The love sonnet explodes in Donne-like fashion with an astonished expletive: 'My dukedom to a beggarly denier' (l. 252). To Richard's surprise, Anne finds him 'a marvellous proper man' (l. 255). The second quatrain, an inventory of the changes the lover will need to make in his wardrobe and his plan to buy a looking-glass, crosses the traditional break at the end of line 8, delaying the shocking turn of the sonnet's volta till the tenth line. The turn is literally his turning of his love's dead husband in his grave, and then his 're-turning' to his love in mock sorrow for her loss.

Just as an inspired cartoon is better than a dull fresco, so 'Porphyria's Lover' and 'My Last Duchess' are vastly superior to *The Inn Album* or *Red Cotton Night-Cap Country*. In 'My Last Duchess,' however, Browning wants to shake loose the dust of the grotto. Instead of sticking pins into a rival's effigy, like the court lady in 'The Laboratory,' the Duke of Ferrara renounces magic by exploring the two-way pull of a mind wavering between intimidation of his auditor and gestures of seduction and courtship. The Duke's speech bears unmistakable signs of both studied eloquence and gestures more grotesque, less supple and fluent. I am thinking of his sudden groping for words and his need to qualify an assertion in an afterthought or parenthesis, as if he were compassing some furtively subtle end, half hidden from himself.

Unlike the Duke of Ferrara, who is too conscious of impressing the envoy to allow his mind to wander, Andrea del Sarto broods obsessively. Though the Duke's apparent frankness and real reticence create a core of mystery in 'My Last Duchess,' Andrea fashions a miracle of disguise that is subtler and more precarious. As he broods about his crimes against King Francis and his parents, the burning bricks of the melancholy little house he built to be so gay reduce his mind to states of molten consciousness. Except as a last-minute effort to retrieve the power he feels slipping away from him, his dismissal of Lucrezia at the end of the monologue ('Again the Cousin's whistle, go, my love') is barely intelligible. By removing any strategic rationale for the Duke's verbal seduction of the envoy or for Andrea's oblique transfers of blame from himself to Lucrezia, Browning makes ulterior motives the focus of his monologues.

Like Andrea's feelings of guilt about his past, the Duke's last marriage has turned into a daily nightmare, ending only with the murder of his young wife. The distasteful task of negotiating another marriage revives memories of that nightmare, whose trauma must now be exorcised or tempered. Displayed on a wall, the 'faint / Half-flush that dies along [the Duchess'] throat' (ll. 18–19) is as much a pun on the painter's dyes as a comment by the Duke on the tragic precariousness of her beauty. With the flicker of a pun the killer aesthete revives the origin of 'infection' in 'inficere' or 'dye.' He diagnoses in a dying glow that stains his wife's throat an infection of her heart. Puns play a similar role in 'Andrea del Sarto,' where they alert us to subterranean motives, to the artifice behind the offhand tone, and to the bad faith of a seductive casuist. Half aware that the wife he cherishes has been bought at too high a price, he jokes that she is 'very dear, no less' (l. 32), smugly confident that she will fail to register his punning rebuke. Though Andrea is the admiring celebrant of his own Madonna, the architect of his own triumphalism,

> It is the thing, Love! so such things should be –
> Behold Madonna! – I am bold to say.   (ll. 58–9)

he is also his own harshest censor: 'All is silver-grey / Placid and perfect with my art: the worse!' (ll. 98–9). More prophetic than Andrea's apostrophe to the Madonna are his domestic but equally oracular pronouncements about his diminished expectations as both a painter and a husband. His acknowledgments of loss cut two ways at once.

> This chamber for example – turn your head –
> All that's behind us!   (ll. 53–4)

Does the preposition 'behind' have a spatial or temporal meaning? Is Andrea referring to the great canvases that are literally 'behind' them, lining the walls of his studio, and which Lucrezia could see if she bothered to turn her head? Or is he alluding to the more intimate pleasures of the marriage bed, which appear to have receded into a lost paradise for both of them?

4

As in music, the symbolism of grotesque oracles is 'unconsummated.' A grotesque dream or nightmare may have all the hallmarks of an oracle except one: an assigned connotation. What does the dream signify? What is it predicting or nudging us to recollect? Almost forty years after I left Ithaca, where I had taught for six years during the 1960s, a landscape of a recurrent dream and nightmare that had haunted me for decades suddenly materialized. There it was, a snow-filled, wind-beaten field and stretch of road winding high above the town, a desolate place I had forgotten I knew. Perhaps the Ithaca dream posed a menace all those years because I unconsciously associated it with rejection, loss, and the death of an early ambition. For in the days of my youth I had looked forward to a career in Ithaca, a place I loved, and for a future life there that was not to be. And yet half an hour after seeing the place I had been dreaming of for decades, I found myself in my car, trying to glimpse through a heavy snowfall the office where years and years before I had met friends and students in Goldwin Smith Hall. I realized then that the death of an early ambition was not the true meaning of my dream. It slowly dawned upon me, as I peered through the storm, why the scene of falling snow at the end of Joyce's story 'The Dead' had become over the years more powerful for me. It was an exact rendering of a terrifying 'spot of time' I had suppressed in my subconscious mind but which I was then reliving for the first time. For, strange as it sounds, the experience of peering through the storm from the window of my car in 2007 was an uncanny replica of an event that occurred in a late February afternoon in 1965. It was the day I received news of my father's unexpected death and had to drive from the same snow-filled place through a winter storm to help arrange and attend his funeral in Canada.

An unanswered prayer is like a grotesque dream, because one of its parts is suppressed or hidden: it lacks an assigned connotation. Yet even when a prayer receives no reply, the mere act of voicing the prayer may contain its answer. In his poem 'Love Dogs,' Rumi's unanswered suppliant is chided for praising a God who refuses to reply. When the petitioner stops praising Allah because he receives no answer, he is reproved by Khidr, the guide of souls, who explains to him that 'this longing / you express *is* the return message' (ll. 14–15).

The grief you cry out from
Draws you toward union.
Your pure sadness
That wants help
Is the secret cup.

Listen to the moan of a dog for its master.
That whining is the connection.

There are love dogs
No one knows the names of.

Give your life
To be one of them.   ('Love Dogs,' ll. 16–26)

In 'The Debtor Sheikh,' only the despair of the boy who has been refused his just payment melts God's heart and moves the wealthy Hatim to reward the plaintiff generously. 'If you want to wear a robe of spiritual sovereignty,' Rumi's oracle announces, 'let your eyes weep with the wanting' (ll. 89–90). The apparent absence in the world of God and justice is their actual presence. For the mere appearance of these things is never real. This, I think, is what Simone Weil means by her strange saying that 'any form of consolation in affliction draws us away from love and truth' (1974, 55).

Often a grotesque imbalance exists between a mind's godlike perceptions and the world it must inhabit. Trapped in several different perceptions of himself, Macbeth finds that only one self-perception, the image of himself as the relentless, unrepentant murderer, will serve his ends once he has killed Duncan. But as a living paradox, a warrior of angelic apprehension, Macbeth has been touched by other self-images, generous and humane ones. And negative capability does not allow him to surrender them easily after he murders the king. He retains a keen sense of the graces 'which should accompany old age, / As honour, love, obedience, troops of friends,' although he knows he 'must not look to have' them (Macbeth, V.iii.24–6).

A grotesque 'disproportion between agent and act' also prevents Hamlet from believing that 'the proper use of his capability and godlike reason' is to murder Claudius. Unable 'to convert an eggshell, like Claudius, into a great argument,' Hamlet has no way of 'accommodating his greatness to the rotten state of Denmark' (Bloom, 2003,

70). The 'mediations' and 'thoughts of love' that release Hamlet into what Bayley calls 'free intimacies of consciousness' (1981, 184) make it impossible for Hamlet to be purposeful or resolute in his desire to be avenged. Equally grotesque is the ghost of Hamlet's father, a king among men, scenting 'the morning air' like some primitive hound or wolf. An uncanny contrast exists between a ghost who can talk and a spirit who has disturbingly physical attributes. Though there is often some hint of comedy in the grotesque wordiness of a spirit who seems too incorporeal to talk ('Brief let me be'), there is also the mystery of each party's trying to understand the uncertain nature of its own way of being.

Most grotesque and harrowing is the fact that the death of a tragic hero like Hamlet or Macbeth, whose consciousness we inhabit, is also the death of our own consciousness. Instead of making an impact, like the death of Brutus, who is merely a stage-tragedy hero, the death of Hamlet induces a tremor. When Hamlet dies, something in each of *us* dies, too. This is quite different, I think, from Cordelia's death, which is too real to be acted out, too authentic for a play. We weep for Desdemona, precisely because we do not wholly believe in her stage-tragedy death. But Cordelia's death comes uncomfortably close to what Iris Murdoch calls the 'senseless rubble aspect of human life' (1992, 142). 'We go away' from the theatre 'uneasy, chilled by a cold wind from another region. Something of this unconsoling coldness is found in Greek literature' (1992, 121). Whereas actors have impressive lines to deliver at the end of *Othello*, *King Lear* offers few opportunities for eloquence. As John Bayley notes, 'an actor has nothing to look forward to at the end of *King Lear*. The dead Cordelia has subdued any possible initiative of the theatre.' But since 'the theatre can always fight back, even against Shakespeare,' Bayley suggests one ingenious, though grotesque, alternative to silence. 'An effective theatrical device – at least demonstrating the kind of difficulty that performance is up against – might be if Lear entered bearing in his arms not a live actress at all but some sort of dummy' (1981, 59).

If criticism struggles to say something important about *King Lear* that cannot be expressed in the language it must use, how can it also limit or define what is valuable in the play? And if criticism does manage to tell us what is happening, how can it also fulfill its function of expressing more than it says? What we define is not illimitable, and what surpasses what we say cannot be defined. As Jonathan Bishop says, 'this is the paradox of criticism, that it defines something more than can be expressed in the language available. We offer hypotheses when we have nothing better to say' (1972, xiii). The wisdom that draws a critic to the burden of the mystery precludes knowledge. But only knowledge demands involvement. Francis Sparshott formulates a version of the paradox when he says wisdom 'apart from the world is meaningless, but philosophy in the world must dissipate itself. The principle involved here was perhaps discovered and has certainly been most systematically studied by Marshall McLuhan: concentration varies inversely with involvement. It is the things that one cares most deeply for that one is casual about; what receives close attention is by that very act sealed off from the stream of living' (Sparshott, 1972, 131).

However bleak the pessimism of Philip Larkin or Sylvia Plath, their best poems are also triumphs of art that qualify the grimness of what they explore, like Shakespeare's best tragedies. Normally, any meticulous record of affliction is a means of exorcising, at least momentarily, the misery it inflicts. But in Larkin's 'Aubade' the impulse to exorcise is neutralized to the point that no relief is possible. On the contrary, at line 5, an 'unresting' force is unleashed as a 'death hound,' which, in Seamus Heaney's words, 'beats the bounds of our mortality, forcing its borders to shrink farther and farther away from any contact with consoling beliefs' (2002, 324). Heaney praises the technical perfection of Larkin's unnerving lines: 'yet the dread / Of dying, and being dead, / Flashes afresh to hold and horrify' (ll. 8–10). He observes that 'the word "afresh" (so joyful in "The Trees") is relocated in a context of horror.' He admires the way Larkin brings the word 'dread' into 'an almost catatonic confrontation with its full meaning' by rhyming it with 'dead.' He praises, too, the skill with which Larkin forces 'die' 'to live with its own emotional consequences' in the alliterating terror of 'to hold and horrify'(2002, 324–5).

Larkin allows the content of his oracle to be swallowed up in a great emptiness or void. As Heaney says, we are left 'like unwary surfers hung over a great emptiness, transported further into the void than [we] might have expected to go' (2002, 325). The only way such an oracle can defy the great Arctic freeze is by becoming what Heaney calls 'the definitive post-Christian English poem, one that abolishes the soul's traditional pretension to immortality and denies the Deity's immemorial attribute of infinite personal concern' (2002, 325). Heaney concedes that Larkin's bleak oracle 'does add weight to the negative side of the scale and tips the balance definitely in favour of chemical law and moral decline' (2002, 327). But even as it 'reneges on what Yeats called the "spiritual intellect's great work,"' Heaney insists that when a poem like 'Aubade' 'rhymes, when a poetic form generates itself, when a metre provokes consciousness into new postures, it is already on the side of life' (2002, 327).

Though Larkin refuses to 'make the Orphic effort to haul life back up the slope,' his oracle still defies entropy and dissolution by surprising us with a potent use of rhymes and by extending 'the fixed relations between words' (Heaney, 2002, 327). In his strong, aesthetic defence of Larkin, Heaney insists that a prophet, however bleak, 'opts for the condition of overlife, and rebels at limit,' whenever his 'language does more than enough, as it does in all achieved poetry' (2002, 327).

Helen Vendler makes a comparable defense of Sylvia Plath's 'Edge,' a poem of suicide and the murder of children, which like Larkin's 'Aubade' seems to betray 'the condition of overlife.' Far from advocating infanticide, however, Plath's elegy makes us feel, in Vendler's words, 'the sadness of the garden's extinction, as it bleeds out its colors and its fragrances' (2003, 147). Unlike the malign moon, 'staring from her hood of bone,' the mother feels the pain of life's losses and defeats. Though nothing can mute death's triumph, Plath also contrives to set against death's immobile, tomblike perfection the sensual beauty of the garden. However heartbreaking Plath's poem may be, Vendler is surely right to insist that its vision 'is authentic, irrefutable, and humanly true' (2003, 149). Like Heaney, Vendler believes that 'a poem is always a manifestation of living, even when its subject is death' (2003, 144).

Despite Vendler's defence, however, no art or poem can beautify violence or moderate the assault of sudden death. In the stunned paralysis following any unforeseen death, the weight of absence is the weight of what is lost, a vanished life. But it is also the weight of lost or missing purpose – the weight of an absurd world, a world drained of meaning, in which Sisyphus, forever pushing up his rolling stone, is Everyman. It is not what remains – the dark freight of my daughter's hearse on its way to the cemetery – that is heavy, but what is no longer there. Her flight as a toddler down the street to the butcher's shop now seems oddly premonitory. She leaves without warning or saying 'good-bye,' as if 'good-bye' were not worth while.

The last time I spoke with Margaret, two days before she took her life, she asked her oldest sister and me: 'Why is this happening? Why is this happening to *me*?' I don't know the answer to that question. And I don't know why daughters die before their fathers. But I do know that whenever I said 'good-bye' to Margaret at the hospital, she would say 'I love you.' O Margaret, my beautiful daughter, I love you, too. And what we love may be substantial somewhere. Camus says that the only serious philosophical problem is suicide, for it raises the question: is life worth living? Margaret's life was a tangle of absurd contradictions: the more creative she became, the less she could create. The more ambitions she had for her future, the more constrained she was by her disease. She possessed the terrible beauty of Yeats's martyrs in 'Easter 1916.' She experienced both the aspirations and frustrations of a Sisyphus or Tantalus.

In Christianity, only the Sermon on the Mount and Christ's words on the Cross spoke to me or came close to expressing what I felt when my daughter died: we perish each alone. I found more consolation in the great myths of paganism, especially in the story of Demeter and her daughter. I cannot grant Sylvia Plath the alleged beauty of her suicide poems, despite the stirring defence Helen Vendler mounts on their behalf. But I do take comfort from the two-way force of Randall Jarrell's reverberating phrase: 'the grimness, and the awfulness, and the untouchable sadness of things.' News often makes an impact. But since Margaret's death was the death of an important part of me, it also induced a tremor: there is forever the rumour of a tremor in the English verb 'remember': an abduction remembered.

As Dante shows in his wrenching descent to the circle of suicides, there will always exist the tug between pity and judgment, the impulse to embrace the anguish of the desperately ill and the impulse to blame or condemn them. The dual impulse to pity and yet judge survives but gets reversed in Samuel Butler's *Erewhon*, where the ill are put in prison for having committed a crime against life and where the criminally insane are consigned to hospitals, where their mental illness can be treated. In trying to mute the scandal and stigma attaching to suicide, Schopenhauer chooses the more neutral and soothing phrase 'voluntary death.' All suicides are voluntary deaths, but not all voluntary deaths are suicides. A martyr who submits to death dies willingly, but despite the claim of Eliot's fourth tempter in *Murder in the Cathedral*, he is not committing suicide. Yet if Christ is God's son, begotten of his Father before all worlds, then his voluntary death on the cross must in some deep sense have been the suicide of God.

In a world dark with griefs and graves, I can address God as lord of the universe or as 'sir,' but not as a father. It may be blasphemous to say so, but if God is a Father, he was much less a father to my daughter than I was. There are large parts of Scripture that remain deeply appealing to me. But I find it hard to say the Lord's Prayer. Its opening words, 'Our Father,' stick in my throat. If God is a father, his love is too partial. In one sense, an underworld descent is a quest for lost equality. Hell is a leveller, because no one knows how far we can drop. No worst, there is none. As Lear discovers on his heath, hell, infirmity, and death are democrats. But the descent can also generate new equality and tolerance, which is love at a distance. Descending to hell is a symbol of the wisdom Lear finds there: the instant of forgiveness when Cordelia destroys the law of cause and effect – 'No cause, no cause' – and saves her father. Like any oracle, this moment of love and forgiveness is discontinuous with the rest of Lear's life. But it will always be the moment his life has been about.

Before making the dreaded trip to Margaret's old hospital room to retrieve her effects after the funeral, I said something so true to the waitress at lunch that day, 'I'm sorry you're so busy,' that she burst into tears. She was crying, not from vexation, but from gratitude. She was grateful to me for acknowledging, as no one else had, the desperate situation of having to serve a whole restaurant of patrons by herself. It was her gratitude that made me mourn inwardly for her plight, which in a small though genuinely grievous way resembled my own. It is the kindness of people, the love I have done nothing to deserve or earn, or their gratitude for small things I have done, that makes me sad, perhaps because I am aware of a deep unworthiness in myself. Wordsworth puts this best. 'I've heard of hearts unkind, kind deeds / With coldness still returning; / Alas! the gratitude of men / Hath oftener left me mourning' ('Simon Lee,' ll. 93–6).

Though no poem can temper time's assaults, its imaginative power may make it easier to survive the blows. A memorable example is Thomas Hardy's poem 'During Wind and Rain,' an elegy on the ruins of time, where a blight that sickens and makes rotten induces a reaction that is close to physical nausea. 'Ah no; the years O!,' the poem's refrain alternately wails and intones. As Yeats says, 'Man is in love and loves what vanishes, / What more is there to say?' ('Nineteen Hundred and Nineteen,' ll. 42–3). It is not just the simple cycle of change that kills. It is the wrenching sadness and sense of waste that afflicts us like an attack of headache or nausea. The gentility of everyone we once loved and the courtliness of everyone we were close to seem hollowed out and vain.

> Ah no; the years O!
> How the sick leaves reel down in throngs!

> They clear the creeping moss –
> Elders and juniors – aye,
> Making the pathways neat
>   And the gardens gay;
> And they build a shady seat ...
>   Ah, no; the years, the years;
> See, the white storm-birds wing across!

> They are blithely breakfasting all –
> Men and maidens – yea,
> Under the summer tree,
>   With a glimpse of the bay,
> While pet fowl come to the knee ...
>   Ah, no; the years O!
> And the rotten rose is ript from the wall.

> They change to a high new house,
> He, she, all of them – aye,
> Clocks and carpets and chairs
>   On the lawn all day,
> And brightest things that are theirs . . .
>   Ah, no; the years, the years;
> Down their carved names the rain-drop ploughs.

> ('During Wind and Rain,' ll. 6–28)

In these lines Tennyson's panic-stricken sense of the transience and hence the seriousness of beauty acquires a harrowing afterlife unique in English poetry. I do not so much *hear* Tennyson as *over*hear him. Or perhaps I over-*see* him, since both poets use forms of time-lapse photography. Fearing that the Somersby gardens will fall into ruin, 'unloved,' 'uncared for,' Tennyson juxtaposes images of care and neglect. Over comparable pictures of neat pathways and gay gardens, Hardy superimposes images of sick leaves reeling down, of rotten roses ripped from the wall, and of a final removal of elders and juniors to the grave: 'Down their carved names the rain-drop ploughs.' The tetrameter line is at once an alliterative contrivance and a simple and direct evocation of nightmare. The superimposing of images is greatly speeded up in section 123 of *In Memoriam*: 'The hills are shadows, and they flow / From form to form, and nothing stands; / They melt like mist, the solid lands, / Like clouds they shape themselves and go' (ll. 5–8). Tennyson uses Lyell's *Principles of Geology*, not as a template to process data for a new theory of evolution, as Darwin does, but as an oracle of science to give authority to an ancient prophecy of Protagoras in the fifteenth book of Ovid's *Metamorphoses*. The result is a time-lapse photograph of the earth extending over billions of years.

'The isle is full of noises,' and not all readers will hear the same voice as Caliban. I, for one, hear an echo of Dagonet's song in Tennyson's idyll 'The Last Tournment': 'and the wan day / Went glooming down in wet and weariness' (ll. 214–15). Words in love with their own alliterative sound assume a mercenary, venal quality in 'The Last Tournament.' But in Hardy's poem Dagonet's 'death-dumb autumn-dripping gloom' (l. 750) is absorbed into a garden poetry of festive celebration familiar to readers of Tennyson's *Maud*. I hear an echo of *Maud*'s 'high Hall-garden' and of its dreadful counterpoint, the hollow behind the little wood, whose 'red-ribbed ledges' encroach on the garden and its 'high new house.' T.H. Huxley revises these images from *Maud* in the 1893 Oxford lecture he later publishes as his *Prolegomena* to *Evolution and Ethics*. The lecture's rigorous distinction between cosmic and ethical processes would have been as shocking to Hardy, had he heard it, as it was to Herbert Spencer. In separating the horticultural world of ethics from the struggle for existence in nature (Hardy's 'pet fowl' from 'the white storm-birds'), Huxley is substituting for an ethics of naturalism what Spencer calls a 'Pauline dogma of nature and grace' (Desmond, 1997, 598). To say that a Tennysonian nature, 'red in tooth and claw,' enjoys a future — an afterlife or posthumous existence — in Hardy is to say that there are poems by Hardy that are less Tennysonian imitations than an expression of the kind of sensibility part of *In Memoriam*, *Maud*, and 'The Last Tournament' exist to express. But if Tennyson had survived into a different age and ethos to write such poems he would not have been Tennyson.

Whatever the truth of the matter, the symmetrical grammar and phonetically paired lines of Hardy's lyric, like the poem's gay gardens and neat pathways, are touchingly at odds with the eerie, reverberating, reproachful lament that passes like a suppressed wail down each stanza's tremor of open vowels. Everyone agrees, I think, that Hardy is lashing out at something. Is he reproaching the culture of a garden world too refined and genteel to survive? Or is he striking out at envious and calumniating time itself, the years, the years? In a disillusioned but far more tranquil mood, Tennyson's lotos-eaters say that 'all things are taken from us, and become / Portions and parcels of the dreadful past' (ll. 46–7). Hardy's refrain is comparably disenchanted but much less restrained. Mounting to a surge of revulsion in each of the harshly stressed and alliterated final lines, his refrain is by turns plaintive, haunting, and verging on sickness and nausea.

In the last stanza, for the first time in the lyric, the rhymes in the opening and closing lines are faintly dissonant. 'Ploughs' is slanted away from its rhyme word 'house.' Heard in one tone, the refrain 'Ah, no; the years O!' is a deserved reversion of decadence to decay and annihilation; heard in another tone, it is a heartbreaking dramatization of the breaking points of the human voice: 'Ah, no; the years, the years.' I think we apprehend Hardy before we fully understand him. Even understanding what he says is an experience by acquaintance, not an inference by paraphrase or description. Torn between primitive exultation and a cry of pain, the speaker finds his emotional attachment to the dear dead people is strongest when he is about to look at their carved names on the grave and take leave of them for a final time. As in Feste's final song in *Twelfth Night*, which he is left alone on the stage to sing, the poise of festivity and blithe breakfasting, though under assault, is never lost. What keeps out the wind and the rain is the poet's art. 'For the rain it raineth every day' appears in the Fool's song in *King Lear* as well as in Feste's song in *Twelfth Night*. But it is Feste's song one mainly hears, with its beautiful and grotesque sadness of acceptance, though Hardy is less accepting, I think, than Shakespeare.

James Carse thinks we listen to wisdom poets like Hardy and Yeats because they offer us a kind of test. 'Selecting deeply vexing questions that rise from our very humanity,' from death, the ravages of time, the waste that kills, we press these questions against the poets 'to see how they meet our worldliness at its most intimate expression' (Carse, 2008, 161). Like Hardy, the aging Yeats who writes 'The Circus Animals' Desertion' discovers that his allegiances must be divided before he can find the heart to write. It is as if the poet must lose his voice to find it. Deserted by the 'masterful images' of Irish mythology, which he calls his circus animals, and fearing that a permanent isolation has set in, the seventy-three-year-old Yeats resolves to create authentic new prophecies out of Celtic legend and myth. Even oracles that are pieced together out of scraps, in the garbage dump of the heart, can be shored against the ruins of time and the fears and miseries of the poet's old age.

Yeats's poem 'News for the Delphic Oracle' shows how souls like Plotinus, with 'salt-flakes on his breast,' are generated out of water. Carried across the sea on the back of brute dolphins who 'pitch their burdens off,' such souls are left to founder in the flashing, fishlike foam. As one critic says, Yeats's oracle makes clear that 'nothing of the physical or concrete world is lost, or even sublimated, by the kind of redemption' described in this 'news for the oracle,' a grotesque pendant to 'Byzantium' (Frye, 1976b, 274). While love blinds Peleus's eyes with tears and Thetis's 'belly listens,' 'nymphs and satyrs copulate in the foam.' The import of Yeats's oracle (which is not *from* but *for* the priestess at Delphi) is the insight Yeats expresses in the last sentence of *A Vision*. As Frye explains in his essay on that work, 'the process of redemption is to be finally understood as an identification with Man and a detachment from the cyclical image he has created' (1976b, 274). This news from *A Vision* is also Yeats's 'news for the Delphic oracle,' and the news he delivers at the end of 'Two Songs from a Play': 'Whatever flames upon the night / Man's own resinous heart has fed' (ll. 31–2). Like the rationality of the universe, the wisdom of his oracles is a postulate of faith. It cannot be presupposed; it can only be proposed by a prophet like Blake or proved by a poet like Yeats who tests its vision and renews its life in words.

In 'Easter 1916' almost anyone from a madman to a drunken lout like MacBride can be made a hero, not because all things are equally noble, but because they are equally grotesque and indifferent. A 'terrible beauty' attaches to MacBride and his fellow patriots, not because they belong to a class of special people, but because they represent the special class of martyrs. In 'The Gyres' the Delphic oracle, which Yeats calls Rocky Face, commands lovers of horses and women to disinter from broken marble sepulchres the grotesque heroes of an unheroic age (l. 21). The purity of these heroes and martyrs would be less inviolable if it were not so arbitrary. Indeed the more damaged the rituals and the more compromised the myths, the more daring and resourceful the prophet has to be in restoring and burnishing the oracles, till they shine like revealed truth. Originating in the foul rag-and-bone shop of the heart, a grotesque oracle tries to salvage something of value from the scrap heap of even the most sadly reduced and diminished life.

From just such a junkyard Sylvia Plath retrieves the fantasized corpse of her father, with a 'stake' driven through his 'fat black heart,' in her elegy 'Daddy' (l. 76). Plath's portrait of her father has to be offensive enough to arouse outrage and dismay. But her hatred of the 'Panzer-man,' however brutalized, still preserves intact the *force* of what she loathes. The father she wants to kill is still a holy figure, a talisman or totem. Though he is a fallen god in whom elegy's traditional beauty and solace have been purified by irony, the religion of abomination. in which he plays the role of scapegoat clearly overlays a religion of the sacred.

Poems like 'Daddy' and 'During Wind and Rain' turn pain into pleasure, and so transform their subject. We exult in their aesthetic perfection lest we perish of their truth. As Harold Bloom confirms, 'ever since I was a small boy, I have judged poems on the basis of just how memorable they immediately seemed. It is distressing to reflect that what seemed inevitable phrasing to me (and still does) was the result of inescapable pain, rather than of what it seemed to be, bewildering pleasure ... Strong poetry is difficult, and its memorability is the consequence of a difficult pleasure, and a difficult enough pleasure is a kind of pain' (Bloom, 2004, 235–6). As Bloom also knows, however, a heroic and resourceful poet like Yeats can transform our 'casual comedy.' Finding grace in even the most grotesque oracle and pleasure in even the most acute pain, a prophet may discover that all has been 'changed, changed utterly' and that 'a terrible beauty' has been 'born' (Yeats, 'Easter 1916,' ll. 15–16).

PART TWO

Homage to Wisdom: From Delphi to Zen

Like a line from Shakespeare or the Bible that stirs us deeply – 'What a piece of work is man' or 'If I speak in the tongues of men and of angels, but have not love' – great wisdom writing launches an assault on our emotions that is immediate and commanding. However subtly a later analysis of the lines may modify the grand obviousness of the ideas, we can say of them what R.P. Blackmur says of 'language as gesture.' They create 'meaning as conscience creates judgment, by feeling the pang, the inner bite, of things forced together' (1954, 19). We respond at once to the majestic syntax of John's Gospel or to the architectonic, musical qualities of *Four Quartets*. A wisdom writer of genius has power to renew our spirit or shock us into recognition before we have time to study his words or understand fully what they mean.

The second section of the monograph compares the parables in the synoptic Gospels and the Gnostic Gospel of Thomas with the koans of Zen Buddhism. It explores 'counter-love, original response' in Wordsworth and Frost, and examines oracles of our end in Norman Maclean's 'A River Runs through It' and Joyce's 'The Dead.' Honouring the kindred points of heaven and home, Maclean, like his favourite poet, Wordsworth, sees with the eye of awakened imagination. But as a prophet of 'splendour in the grass' and 'glory in the flower,' he also tames the vagrancy of unworldly visionaries and dreamers. In Thomas Merton's view, 'to prophesy is not to predict, but to seize upon reality in its moment of highest expectation and tension toward the new. This tension is discovered not in hypnotic elation but in the light of everyday existence' (1981, 373). Often the passages I discuss are a blaze of glory, here and now, or else a hiding place of power for future restoration.

According to Shakespeare's John of Gaunt, truth lies upon 'the tongues of dying men,' which 'enforce attention like deep harmony' (*Richard the Second*, II.i.5–6). Each Beatitude or each of the logia from *The Secret Gospel of Thomas* has the force of a last or concluding word. But we do not have to wait till the hour of our death to die to error or to wake to truth. Enlightenment may come at any moment, like a thief in the night, when we least expect it. Indeed wisdom writing often confounds our expectations. In place of a final heroic scene, where Christ appears to the disciples on the road to Emmaus and later ascends into heaven, the Gospel of Mark ends in a mood of astonishment and puzzled wonder. The unsealed tomb and the enigmatic message from a youth dressed in white stage an open-ended drama of shock, surmise, and fear of the unknown.

The 'foretelling' aspect of oracles now belongs to the predictive power of science. A voice from Delphi may be 'innocent of prediction because it is itself the fulfillment of all the momentous predictions hidden in everyday life' (Merton, 1981, 373). But there is a second area for which the future is the only metaphor, and that is the area of the possible or potential, which is the most promising domain for wisdom writing and oracles. One critic says that hope is 'a virtue greater than faith, but one relating to the future as faith does to the past. As in Bunyan, we can be faithful only unto death, but hope goes through the Red Sea to the other side' (Frye, 2004a, 102).

6 Wisdom and the Logos: John's Gospel to *Four Quartets*

When the author of John's Gospel places himself at the beginning of time, he writes as an oracle of the Word who creates the world. This Word not only dwells with God but is also said to be God. It is as if a theoretical physicist were to describe the universe just before the Big Bang.

> In the beginning was the Word, and the Word was with God, and the Word was God. He was in the beginning with God; and all things were made through him. (John 1:1–3)

At the moment of creation, at the cliff-face of mystery, the God who is pure Being allows the Word to detach itself from God and enter the world it has created. But what could be stranger than the failure of the world to recognize the Word when it comes to live in it? 'He was in the world, and the world was made through him, yet the world knew him not' (John 1:10). According to Hegel, the road from the timeless heaven of Being to the earthly paradise of Becoming lies through a desert of Non-Being. The only way the pure Being of God can pass into the pure Becoming of the world is through Non-Being, the annihilation of the Word.

> He came to his own home, and his own people received him not. But to all who received him, who believed in his name, he gave power to become children of God. (John 1:11–12)

John knows that the world will try to reduce the Word to nothingness by destroying it on a cross and consigning it to the silence of a tomb. As one commentator notes, 'being ought to have a ground (the earth under our feet) and a source.' If the world rejects the Word, it would seem to have neither. As a vision, the Word's rejection is 'a devastation, an apocalypse at the wrong end of time' (Davenport, 1988, 77). But the oracle also foresees that for those who believe in the Word, for those who are reborn in its spirit as 'children of God' (John 1:12), the shadow of time will pass into the substance of a grounded prophetic vision.

Norm's father, the Presbyterian minister in *A River Runs through It*, tells his son that 'if you listen carefully you will hear that the words [of John's Logos] are underneath the water' (Maclean, 1992, 104). Like Reverend Maclean, Hopkins's nun in *The Wreck of the Deutschland* interprets the storm at sea as the word or news of God. Like a learned interpreter of both the book of nature and the book of God, she

> Read the unshapeable shock night
> And knew the who and the why;'
> Wording it how but by him that present and past,
> Heaven and earth are word of, worded by? –
>
> (*The Wreck of the Deutschland*, 29.3–6)

To call her destroyer her creator is not to be intellectually perverse but spiritually literate. For the nun knows she must 'word' or express her destruction by water as a word or decree of the same God who moved over the face of the waters in Genesis. This all-powerful, sometimes terrifying creator God is also the majestic Father of a Son, the Word or Logos who 'worded' the world into being in imitation of the creation of 'Heaven and earth' by verbal fiat in Genesis. Hopkins daringly identifies the God who says 'Let there be light' at the beginning of Genesis with the Word who was with God and who also *was* God in the Fourth Gospel. As Hopkins muses in one of his haunting devotional notes, 'God speaking to himself is Christ, but His Words projected beyond Himself form the universe' (1959, 129).

Comparably haunted are the oracles of Eliot's *Four Quartets*, where a foreordained future has already happened, and the seer gazes into a universe whose story he already knows. His fate is sealed, since 'what might have been and what has been / Point to one end, which is always present' ('Burnt Norton,' I.9–10).

> Time present and time past
> Are both perhaps present in time future,
> And time future contained in time past.
> If all time is eternally present
> All time is unredeemable.   ('Burnt Norton,' I.1–5)

The heavy footfall of the meter is appropriate to a poet who believes that the distinction between time past, present, and future is illusory. As in the world constructed by modern physics, where the geometry of space and time can be changed by the behaviour of objects moving inside its four-dimensional coordinates, we do not *become* but simply *are*. As Seamus Heaney says, 'the footfall of the word "time" echoes and repeats in a way that is hypnotic when read aloud, yet can be perplexing when sight-read for its meaning only.' Most oracular is Eliot's incantatory repetition of the words 'present,' 'past,' and future.' They go 'round and round, like a linked dance through the ear.' Equally bewitching is the way 'words going forward meet each other coming back. Even the word "echo" meets itself on the rebound. The effect,' says Heaney,' is 'of a turning and a stillness' (2002, 35).

> Footfalls echo in the memory
> Down the passage which we did not take
> Towards the door we never opened
> Into the rose-garden. My words echo
> Thus, in your mind.
>   ('Burnt Norton,' I.11–15)

The seer who turns his back on shadows and looks toward 'the door we never opened / Into the rose-garden' tries to abolish clock time by turning 'time future' and 'time past' into a time that 'is eternally present.' Though a seer who urges us to enter a rose-garden whose door remains unopened seems to urge the impossible, the consolation of a world that is imaginary is not an imaginary consolation. Unless an oracle's ghosts are ghosts of our own begetting, however, fed by our imagination and memory, it is hard to see how they can speak to our condition. On the other hand, if an oracle is only the shorthand of our brain, what authority can it claim? How can it begin to repair the damaged rituals of that vast panorama of futility and anarchy that Eliot thinks contemporary culture has become?

Four Quartets never rises to the oracular pitch of the Fourth Gospel. Instead, it celebrates in a sudden 'shaft of sunlight' and in 'the hidden laughter of children' a subdued surprise, something that happens providentially, when we least expect it. When the 'shaft of sunlight' returns in 'The Dry Salvages,' little at first is made of it. The wandering rhythm and wayward tone of the 'distraction fit, lost in a shaft of sunlight, / The wild thyme unseen, or the winter lightning / Or the waterfall,' mute the force of any sudden illumination or breakthrough.

> These are only hints and guesses,
> Hints followed by guesses; and the rest
> Is prayer, observance, discipline, thought and action.
> The hint half guessed, the gift half understood, is
>   Incarnation.   ('The Dry Salvages,' V.29–32)

By capitalizing the 'I,' Eliot restores 'Incarnation' to its use in 'Journey of the Magi': 'I had seen birth and death, / But had thought they were different' (ll. 37–8). Since 'Incarnation' denotes a mystery that makes an 'impossible union' actual, all the other timeless moments in *Four Quartets* acquire validity through the event announced in John's Gospel, the entry of the Word into the world. But the word 'Incarnation' is used lightly, even casually here, as something 'half guessed' and 'half understood.' As one critic says, the 'riddle-games' of Nicholas of Cusa, designed 'to express certain paradoxes in the nature of God,' are still haunting Eliot as he struggles 'to express the meaning of an incarnation which is neither in nor out of time' (Frye, 1976b, 145–6). Indeed in *Four Quartets* the Logos of the fourth Gospel occurs in a context that is just as appropriate to Krishna's experience as to Christ's.

Tennyson, too, displays a touch of 'genius' – an ability to join the self to greatness without violating its freedom – when he replaces Telemachus's bounded domestic world with the horizon of Ulysses's untravelled world, whose margins fade forever and forever as he moves. And in 'Tithonus' the poet once more proves his genius by substituting for the one-way journey of the speaker the daily return of the goddess, now feared, venerated, and spectacularly exalted by her earthly lover.

> Thou seëst all things, thou wilt see my grave:
> Thou wilt renew thy beauty morn by morn;
> I earth in earth forget these empty courts,
> And thee returning on thy silver wheels.   (Tennyson, 'Tithonus,' ll. 73–6)

In the two entwined but contrasting cycles of 'morn by morn' and 'earth in earth' Tennyson has joined, in eternal paradox, the brevity of love and the fragile strength of beauty soon to be forgotten and dissolved. We sense that this vision is not just an imitation of the prophetic coda of Keats's 'Ode to a Nightingale,' with its sudden thought of becoming 'sod' to the bird's 'high requiem.' Instead, in its celebration of an everlasting brevity, an eternal dawn, the coda captures the genius of all oracles. It is the kind of vision that every oracle – from the Sermon on the Mount to Lincoln's Gettysburg Address, from John's Gospel to Eliot's *Four Quartets* – exists to express.

Though a visionary genius like William Wordsworth or Percy Bysshe Shelley prefers poetry to discursive logic, a prophet-poet like Socrates or Jesus usually selects 'the lesser harmony' of prose. But these alignments may shift. The visionary Henry David Thoreau and Ralph Waldo Emerson are most at home in discontinuous, prophetic prose. And when such prophetic geniuses as Blake and Walt Whitman write prose, they seem, as Milton says of his own prose pamphlets, to be writing with their left hand only.

The great poets of Christian culture, from Milton and George Herbert down to Christina Rossetti and T.S. Eliot, all feel reluctant to assume the prophet's mantle, even though their best verse often culminates in a wise or witty oracle. In an age that owes as much allegiance to paganism as to a religion of the book, the prophet may find he is an anomaly, an exile, or even an apostate like Hardy or Swinburne. It is true that Swinburne's attacks on the 'pale Galilean' contain more thunder than lightning. And when, as an intoxicated atheist, he hymns the virtues of pagan fortitude and faith in man (his most congenial themes), Swinburne uses the oracles of Apollo to pervert Greek sentiment. Yet even in planting an epitaph on pagan culture in his poem 'The Last Oracle,' Swinburne continues to mourn the passing of its Delphic wisdom – what Wallace Stevens calls its 'haunt of prophecy' – in such laments as 'Hymn to Proserpine' and 'Hymn of Man.'

A great prophet or poet restores the oracles in a double sense: he both revives and reinvents them. Though Jesus says he comes not to abolish the law and the prophets but to fulfil them, his Sermon on the Mount appeals to the holiness of the heart's affections and the truth of a spiritual imagination. One commentator argues that 'Jesus does nothing new or unprecedented when he contrasts the practical, casuistic norms developed in the Torah with the pure will of God' (Ratzinger, 2007, 126), which Jesus expresses most powerfully in the Sermon. And yet the Sermon surely extends and completes the law that Moses receives on Sinai. Whereas Moses receives the Tables in a cloud, which obscures his view of God, the Son sees the Father face to face. In the Sermon on the Mount the Rabbi of Galilee gives the world a new Torah. He is the oracle of a God who is Father to a Son. Similarly, what we honour and remember in Lincoln's Gettysburg Address is not just its stirring revival of the founding fathers' faith that all men are created equal. What survives of Lincoln is his commemoration of something he has fathered as a leader of the war against slavery. It is one of the transforming moments he himself has changed: a new birth of freedom.

7 Gnostic Wisdom: Parable and Koan

Despite the riddling, gnomic quality of John's pronouncements on the Word, which sound more like an oracle by Plato than the judgment of a Hebrew prophet, 'it has not pleased God,' St Ambrose says, 'to save his people through philosophy.' This is lucky for the writers of the Gospels, who were not philosophers. The difference between the Christian and the classical virtues is the difference between the canticles of St Francis, which represent a 'religion of the heart,' and Euripides' 'religion of the head': 'O Zeus, whether thou be intelligence of mankind or compulsion of nature, to thee I prayed.' The Sermon on the Mount bears the same relation to the Law received at Sinai as Keats's belief in the holiness of the heart's affections bears to Kant's 'categorical imperative,' which exhorts us to make the maxim of our will the law of the universe. And yet the Gospel oracles are more than utopian visions. Since they are meant to change our lives, they have practical as well as imaginative appeal. Like a utilitarian who affirms the good of what is useful rather than the utility of what is good, a Christian does not live to prove the truth but proves the truth by living it.

1

Augustine says that in order to understand the Gospels we must first believe them. Since the first accounts of Jesus in the Gospels and the letters of Paul are 'all a blaze of holiness and miracle' (Wills, 2006, xxvii), we can confidently assume that whatever these writers say about the historical Jesus, it is always less, and never more, than what he was. But it is easier to believe and therefore understand the Gospels than it is to prove their truth by living it. On the one hand, Jesus exalts the oppressed: he assures them that the first shall be last and the last shall be first. On the other hand, he intimidates them by exercising an 'authority as arbitrary as God's in the Book of Job' (Wills, 2006, xvii). To rid Jesus of his paradoxes, of his puzzling silences and ironical replies, is to reduce him to platitude. But to restore him to his full and proper stature as 'a divine mystery walking among men' (Wills, 2006, xvii) is to transform him into a deep and living contradiction that no human being can possibly imitate. To prove the truth by living it we have to do incompatible things. We have to accept the insufficiency of the natural man and yet also believe that before Abraham was we were. In Wills's words, 'the only way we can directly imitate [Jesus] is to act as if we were gods ourselves – yet that is the very thing he forbids' (2006, xvii).

Jesus' oracles come as close as possible to inaugurating a way of life that has no defined contours. Rather than specifying what he means by a particular parable, the rabbi of Galilee prefers to point to the horizon of God's kingdom or reign (hence his preference for aphorisms, the horizon trope). Coleridge traces the etymology of 'aphorism' to the same Greek word as 'horizon,' the word that means 'bounded' and hence 'the limit of our vision' (1905, 17). In 'The Once and Future Testaments,' Robert W. Funk analyses the probative, testing quality of Jesus' aphorisms, which try to open or extend the boundaries of this vision. 'Jesus was a wandering teacher of wisdom. His voice emanates from a compendium of parables, aphorisms, and dialogues that can be isolated from the mass of tradition that accrued to his name. In those sayings, and correlative acts, we can occasionally catch sight of Jesus' vision, a vision of something he called God's domain or kingdom' (Funk, 2002, 550). Like Gary Wills, I prefer to use the less political word 'reign,' since, as Wills observes, anyone who tries 'to cram' the Sermon on the Mount 'within the structure of any state [is] making Jesus a king in Pilate's sense' (2006, 88).

Harvey Cox calls the Sermon on the Mount 'the most influential moral and religious discourse in all human history' (2004, 121). Though Cicero describes Rome as the 'light of the world,' Jesus proposes to replace the light of empire with another light, one that never was on sea or land, the consecration and the prophet's dream. Most original is Cox's interpretation of Jesus' blessing on the peacemakers, which harbours (he thinks) an understated irony. 'The empire's main claim to fame and legitimacy was that Rome and Rome alone was the peacemaker. It sustained the *pax Romana* under the magnanimous auspices of Caesar Augustus, a divine ruler' (2004, 125). In blessing the peacemakers, Jesus is making the bold claim that he and his obscure followers are the true makers of peace, not the armed forces of Rome. Rabbi Jesus is speaking about *shalom*, not *pax*. Shalom is peace 'nurtured by a loving god,' not an enforcement of peace in the name of a coercive emperor who called himself 'peace-bringer' while wading to his throne over the corpses of slaughtered multitudes (2004, 126).

Like the Gospels' riddling parables, the Beatitudes elude our grasp even as we reach out to embrace or take possession of them. The Sermon on the Mount keeps us slightly off balance by combining folly in one direction with wisdom in another. Though Nietzsche condemns the Beatitudes as a conspiracy of the sheep to convince the wolves that it is sinful to be strong, the precious nonsense of the meek inheriting the earth or of the poor in spirit possessing the kingdom of heaven is also a magnificent celebration of spiritual liberation. Looked at in one way, the replacement of Mosaic law with a law more subtle and exacting is an act of sublime folly. But looked at in another way, the Beatitudes are a liberal education of the spirit that replaces the law of moral command – 'thou shalt not kill' – with a hymn to the holiness of the heart's affections and the truth of a purified imagination.

Jesus can justify peace-making, poverty of spirit, purity of heart, by using an explanatory 'for' clause: 'for they shall be called the children of God,' 'for theirs is the kingdom of heaven.' Alternatively, he can use the 'for' clauses in an appositional rather than a causal way. He can use them, not to explain or justify anything by offering a reward, but in order to praise and celebrate qualities that are their own reward. Like a liberal education, purity of heart and poverty of spirit are self-justifying activities in no need of praise or explanation. But in case we are beginning to assume that purity of heart may liberate us from the law, the Sermon on the Mount invites us to ponder the sublime paradox of abolishing a law only to consummate or fulfil it. Instead of relaxing our will, the Sermon on the Mount has the opposite effect. It makes observance of the law stricter than ever: 'Think not that I came to destroy the law or the prophets: I came not to destroy but to fulfil' (Matthew 5:17).

A Gospel oracle may consist of one part wisdom to three parts folly or nonsense. It may resemble the famous Zen puzzle: 'What is the sound of one hand clapping?,' which as Cox observes 'can seem utterly silly or downright profound, or possibly both' (2004, 157). 'Zen tales are intended to rattle the way the hearer thinks and perceives the world. This was also Rabbi Jesus' style. Nearly all his stories end with a reverse loop. They leave the hearer not so much better informed as jolted' (2004, 157–8). As Cox says, often the point of the Gospel oracles and parables is not 'to drive home a moral point but to snare the listener into a change of consciousness' (2004, 157). A parable has less in common with a homily than with a Zen master's koan, which is meant to jostle the mind and unsettle the heart. The rich young man who is challenged to give all he has to the poor and follow Jesus (Mark 10:21) does not lack an understanding of the commandments. What he lacks is a power to transform his life. Unlike the stories told by 'desert fathers' and Sufi masters, the Gospel parables use what Cox calls a 'bait-and-switch technique' (2004, 156). They take us down a familiar path, 'and then, at the last minute, reverse the accepted social stereotypes and shake up the conventional world of his hearers' (156). Instead of the moral instruction the rich young man anticipates, Jesus offers him a crisis of choice. At stake is the future direction of his life.

Many of the most revealing oracles are self-withholding, and riddling. As Simone Weil astutely notes, Jesus' 'talk with Nicodemus' is 'very mysterious' (1974, 136). There is something furtive, even sinister, about Nicodemus, who as a 'ruler of the Jews' operates under cover and visits Jesus at night. When Nicodemus asks Jesus, as 'a teacher come from God,' to reveal God's secret, Jesus answers: 'Truly, truly, I say to you, unless one is born anew, he cannot see the kingdom of God' (John 3:3). Taking the oracle in its most literal sense, Nicodemus pretends to be puzzled. 'How can a man be born when he is old? Can he enter a second time into his mother's womb and be born?' (John 3:4) Having led the rabbi to the brink of intellectual absurdity, Jesus seems willing to play with him, leaving him to extricate himself as he can. Jesus may even have in mind the words of the wise man, 'Answer a fool according to his folly' (Proverbs 26:5), especially if the fool is prying and conspiratorial. So instead of telling Nicodemus that he has failed to understand the metaphoric language of his prophecy, Jesus delivers a second prophecy: 'That which is born of the flesh is flesh, and that which is born of the Spirit is spirit' (John 3:6).

If Nicodemus has taken the first oracle in a purely carnal sense, then the second oracle should teach him that the fault lies, not in the saying he should be born anew, but in his defective understanding of it. As Jonathan Bishop explains, 'men like Nicodemus have identified themselves with definitions they know too exactly. They want someone new to confirm a notion already fixed inside the heads of those who know best. For them revelation has become, quite unconsciously, technology.' The rabbi 'swallows a word, as it were, the wrong way, rejecting not simply the possibility of a meaning for imagination but imagination itself' (Bishop, 1972, 196–7). Instead of condescending to tutor Nicodemus or worrying over the wonder or obtuseness of a meddlesome rabbi, Jesus deepens rather than explains the mystery. 'Do not marvel that I said to you, "You must be born anew." The wind blows where it wills, and you hear the sound of it, but you do not know whence it comes or whither it goes; so it is with every one who is born of the Spirit' (John 3:7–8). Jesus draws Nicodemus on, step by step, not trifling with the subject, but making the mysteries of the Spirit as wayward as an unpredictable wind that keeps blowing where it will. 'Thy Father which is in secret' chooses to remain hidden. Jesus would rather perplex Nicodemus with a riddle than consolidate the mental level on which the rabbi is conducting his search. For the answer Nicodemus seeks is, in one critic's words, 'another way of trying to get control of things, the conceptual way, and renouncing it means, again, being set free to create. As Paul says, we see now in a riddle in a mirror, but we solve the riddle by coming out of the mirror, into the world that words and things reflect' (Frye, 1976b, 147).

If the oracles that continue through verse 21 are a part of Jesus' conversation with Nicodemus, as some interpreters maintain, then Jesus is not merely making fun of Nicodemus. For just as Jesus is unexpectedly generous to the rich young man, who is invited to give all he has to the poor and become a disciple, so he is astonishingly candid with the rabbi. Though Nicodemus, like the rich young man, is 'the patron of those who cannot quite encounter' (Bishop, 1972, 198), unlike his youthful counterpart, the rabbi is imaginatively transformed after his meeting with Jesus. At the end of John's Gospel we learn Nicodemus is the same person who appears to help bury Jesus with a large supply of myrrh and aloes (John 19:39). Such a transformation is not totally surprising, since even in mocking Nicodemus as a 'teacher of Israel' who fails to understand the key oracles of his faith, Jesus shares with this curious inquirer his most precious secret, which Luther calls the whole 'Gospel in miniature.' 'For God so loved the world that he gave his only Son, that whoever believes in him should not perish but have eternal life' (John 3:16).

No less puzzling than the parable of the dishonest steward (Luke 16:1–19), which seems to commend swindlers like the CEOs at Enron, is the parable of the wedding feast in Matthew 22:1–14. Having been invited to the feast at the last minute, guests who are improperly dressed are rebuked and punished with astonishing severity. The punishment of the substitute guests appears to be out of all proportion to their supposed offence. A more reasonable host would surely have reserved his anger for the guests who were invited originally but failed to show. Jesus seems to have spoiled a charming story of homeless people invited to a solid meal by committing his own offence against common sense and justice.

The surprise ending may leave us badly shaken. Instead of giving us a moral homily, Jesus hands us a puzzle or conundrum. An unpredictable, irascible Jesus emerges most strikingly in the Gospel of Mark, where his 'mood swings are like Hamlet's' (Kermode, 2005, 41). Northrop Frye finds the Gospels 'unpleasant reading for the most part.' He is disturbed by 'the mysterious parables with their lurking and menacing threats, the emphasis placed by Christ on himself and his uniqueness and on a "me-or-else" attitude, the displaying of miracles as irrefutable stunts, and the pervading sense of delusion about the end of the world' (Frye, 2004a, 109). Harvey Cox takes a more moderate line. He thinks that, like a Zen fable, Jesus' parables 'may be designed to short-circuit one's neuron paths and open the mind' (Cox, 2004, 163) to new possibilities. There are no tidy completions in the parables. As the Gospel oracles approach 'the threshold of the final mystery,' they 'end with a kind of question mark' (2004, 168).

2

How, then, are we to distinguish between a profound saying and a stupid one? What is the difference between a wise and a foolish oracle? Like Socrates, Cox takes comfort from the fact that 'perplexity and confusion are not always obstacles to learning. They are sometimes allies' (2004, 163). Since 'one of the most seductive temptations' in teaching is 'to explain too much,' Cox suggests that perhaps Jesus wanted to leave 'his hearers with their brows knitted and their heads shaking' (2004, 163). Instead of possessing a partial truth, Jesus' listeners must learn to appropriate a fuller truth by asking new and better questions. When Jesus speaks of God's coming kingdom, he is speaking of a kingdom we can enter while still alive. As an enlarged sense of the present moment, this future kingdom is a form of what Zen Buddhists call satori. The need to experience satori oneself, to respond to the 'reign of

God' (not in some future state but here and now), is central to everything Jesus says and does. The Resurrection looks backward: what is
immortal is not the life we are going to live after death but the life we
are exhorted to live now. Every crisis we have lived through in our
past and have died out of into a more stable future is a resurrection
that has already happened and is waiting to occur again. Jesus' parables are about something new and unprecedented that is taking place
now. Something, to be sure, is happening in the consciousness of the
listener. But it is also happening in the world. And the listener is
invited to be part of that change.

In several manuals on Zen Buddhism, D.T. Suzuki compares satori
to the breaking in pieces of rocks. Acquiring an enlarged sense of the
present moment is a form of mental upheaval: it may be as cataclysmic
as living through a tsunami or a hurricane. As Browning says about
resurrecting the deepest roots of his faith in *La Saisiaz*, it cannot occur
'without earthquake' (l. 616). The transformation of the Christian seer
or Zen master who in dying to time sees into the life of things is akin
to the change in consciousness that allows us to see a mathematical
problem or a logical puzzle in a new light and so solve it. But the transformation is not merely intellectual. To be complete it must include
psychological and moral change as well.

The most striking affinities with Zen occur in the secret Gospel of
Thomas, a Coptic text excavated in Upper Egypt in 1945–6, and dating
in its original Greek form to about 140 CE. In this text there is 'a strong
esoteric tendency to distinguish between an inner and an outer court
of hearers, or between deep and shallow comprehension of the same
doctrines.' As in Sufism and the Mahayana form of Buddhism, the
Gnostic gospels keep intact 'a secret tradition' that 'may serve as a
kind of back door or fire escape for a myth of freedom in persecuting
times' (Frye, 1971, 121–2). Whereas Jesus in the Synoptic Gospels
claims to say nothing in secret, the Gnostic gospels assume vestiges of
a mystery cult, which depends 'on a writing *secretary* or keeper of
secrets' (Frye, 2004b, 254).

One of the Gnostics' most shockingly open secrets is disclosed in
logion 61 of the Gospel of Thomas, whose first part describes Jesus'
climbing into bed with Salome. When Salome moves to exclude him
from her bed and table, Jesus pronounces an oracle: 'I am he who has
come forth from him who is Openness. I was given what came from my
Father.' When Salome replies, 'I am your disciple,' Jesus says to her:
'That is why I say when the disciple is open, he is filled with light.

When he is divided, he is filled with darkness.' All Salome has to do is walk through the open door in front of her. Donne's sonnet 'Show me dear Christ' extends to the church the same openness that the Gnostic Gospel attributes to Salome and Christ. As Christ's bride, the church is most pleasing to her bridegroom when she is most promiscuous, when she is widely embraced and open to most men. To be closed is to set up divisions or partitions, to banish the light of Christ from the warmth of one's hearth and home, and even from the intimacies of one's bed.

The Gospel of Thomas prefers solitude to companionship and depth to breadth. It is easy to spread out in a horizontal direction, but harder to move up or down vertically. As Jesus explains in logion 74, 'Many stand around the well, but there is no one to go down into it.' To be profound is to go deep by descending to the bottom of the well. And as Heraclitus says, the way up is also the way down. By definition, the multitude that throngs before the door of a bridal chamber cannot be solitary. Nor is it likely that an importunate suitor will be ingenuous or innocent. As Jesus says in logion 75, 'many stand before the door but it is the solitary ones and those who have become simple who will enter the bridal chamber.' Once again, as in the sixty-first logion, Jesus is using sexual intimacy as a metaphor for privileged admission to the secret chamber or inmost shrine of the oracle.

The Gospel of Thomas contains parables so enigmatic and riddling that Elaine Pagels compares them in her book *Beyond Belief* to Zen koans. Pagels finds 'unexpected spiritual power' in Thomas's oracle: 'If you bring forth what is within you, what you bring forth will save you. If you do not bring forth what is within you, what you do not bring forth will destroy you' (2003, 32). In other words, the imitation of Christ is not good enough for Thomas, since each believer must be the artist and architect of his own salvation. If you are loyal to your daemon, your daemon will save you. If you suppress or deny it, it will destroy you. The tenor of this oracle is closer to Emerson's essay on 'Self-Reliance' or to Blake's proverbs than to the canonical scripture it most resembles, the Gospel of John. As Pagels says, 'the strength of [Thomas'] saying is that it does not tell us what to believe but challenges us to discover what lies hidden within ourselves' (2003, 32).

3

At stake in the Gnostic gospels is the future course of Christianity. Western culture is at a crossroads. Is the new religion to be an experiment in self-enlightenment? Or is it to be a rescue operation? Is Gnosticism to be rejected as a heresy, as a mere parody of grace? Or is its appeal to self-development to be approved as a protest against later dogmas of original sin? Consenting to dwell in a world doomed to fall and fail, the God of Augustine and Calvin has stooped to rise: 'such ever was love's way' (Browning, 'A Death in the Desert,' l. 134). St John's oracle in Browning's poem makes clear to the popular imagination the truth of David's great paradox in 'Saul' that the 'stoop of the soul ... in bending upraises it too' (l. 252). In striking contrast, the Gnostic gospels proclaim that a pre-Adamic, Edenic world is already open to us. We need only knock and enter. Whereas a Platonist might accept Iris Murdoch's epigram that 'our world is elsewhere and it draws us like a magnet' (quoted by Pagels, 2003, epigraph), Thomas's Jesus is neither an exile condemned to live with 'fellow exiles' nor an iron filing drawn by an invisible force. Instead, in the Gnostic gospels the light that orders our chaos is a pre-created light that can never fail, since the glory that we trail in our wake precedes both Creation and the Fall. Indeed, as Harold Bloom explains, for the Gnostics 'Creation and the Fall were one and the same event' (2004, 261). In some forms of Gnosticism God even withdraws into himself to leave space for a material world. His withdrawal may help explain the visible darkness of creation in such Gnostic testaments as Hopkins's 'Spelt from Sibyl's Leaves' and in his dreadful sonnet, 'No Worst, There Is None.'

Browning has sometimes been accused of embracing the paradox of his pagan philosopher, Cleon, who argues that nothing succeeds like defeat and that 'most progress is most failure' ('Cleon,' l. 272). But the same might be said of Christianity, whose founder is a failed messiah. The meaning of Christ's failure is that no divine mediator can be expected to rescue humanity from its own cruelty and folly. As Cox says, 'Jesus was, in one sense, a colossal failure, but his "failure" forces us, even today, in a culture intoxicated by "success," to reexamine what we mean by that word' (2004, 218).

When Christ on the cross asks, 'My God, my God, why have you forsaken me?,' we may temper his agony by recalling the context of that cry in Psalm 23. After citing the opening line of Psalm 22, Jesus can, in Jeffrey Hart's words, 'triumphantly [skip] the rest of that Psalm – and say nothing. But the silence speaks.' Because Psalm 23, with its exalted poetry of peace and consolation, 'is vibrating there in the air around him,' Jesus can make his listeners 'fill in the silence, if only mentally, with what comes next' (Hart, 2001, 103). In his poem 'Saul' Browning goes one step further than Hart by reading into the Crucifixion a story of tremendous rivalry. If the Creator had not been crucified, he would have been a lesser being than thousands of such rivals as the suffering Saul. The words of great teachers reach into silence. In transmitting the shock of life-and-death issues, their sayings often replace demonstration with wonder and coercion with love and persuasive power.

A disturbing saying in Mark 4:12 suggests that Jesus' parables 'are intended not to open doors, but to lock them' (Ratzinger, 2007, 189). Only when the Crucifixion approaches does Jesus abandon the veiled discourse of his parables for plainer speech. Just as Abraham speaks with riddling irony when parrying his son's question about who will supply an offering for the sacrifice, so Jesus speaks in riddling parables about the terrifying mystery of the Father's sacrifice of his Son. As one commentator says, 'the failure of the Prophets is an obscure question mark hanging over the whole history of Israel, and in a certain way it constantly recurs in the history of humankind. Above all, it is also again the destiny of Jesus' himself, whose parables 'speak in a hidden way' of the mystery of his Crucifixion (Ratzinger, 2007, 189–91).

To Christ on the Cross, it must have seemed for the moment as if God has abandoned him. As Harvey Cox says, 'he must have felt, in his own way, that he had lost his faith. Of course, this is a paradoxical statement. How can God feel abandoned by himself? But the fact that we cannot grasp such an idea does not make it any less powerful' (2004, 266). Verging on sublime nonsense and folly, such bold paradoxes 'merely deepen,' as Cox says, 'the mystery of just how God was present in Jesus, and how God continues to suffer the grief and heartache of human existence' (2004, 266). In the end the Zen enlightenment of a parable or a Gospel oracle may not be enough. What we know is not merely satori (a transformation of consciousness) but an experience in which the whole world takes on a different appearance. Before we can take possession of peace or enlightenment, we may have to die to happiness, and descend into a hell of pain, injustice, and loss, as we do when our children commit suicide or are murdered.

Rudolph Bultmann believes that the Jesus of the Gospels, the rabbi of Galilee, is not a part of New Testament theology. He argues that Christian theology is an invention of St Paul, whose great oracles may sway us one moment and alienate us the next. As Anthony Hecht says, 'many a heart has melted' when it hears Paul's great hymn to love in 1 Corinthians 13:1. 'Though I speak with the tongues of men and of angels, and have not charity, I am as sounding brass, or a tinkling cymbal.' We cherish Paul 'for that exaltation of loving-kindness' (Hecht, 2003, 243). But as a trope of modesty, a confession of his own lack of merit when denied God's gift of self-effacing love, the disclaimer is less than convincing. Indeed Paul is notably lacking in humility and is often shockingly condescending. In Hecht's words, Paul's 'vituperations are almost as celebrated as his benedictions. In Galatians 1:8–9, he offers curses against any deviation from his theology, and in 1 Corinthians 16:22 he declares if any man love not the Lord Jesus Christ, let him be Anathema Maranatha, the final term being equivalent to "perdition at the coming of Christ the Lord"' (2003, 243).

As the prophet of a new order, exhorting his converts to burn their books from the steps of the temple, St Paul embodies in his art and life the genius of oracles. But it is only a short step from the flames at Ephesus (Acts 19:19) to the fires of the Inquisition and the witch trials at Salem. An age of reason may still be mesmerized by what it hates and fears in a zealous prophet. St Paul's search for truth is an effort of the imagination to overcome itself, to end its search for ends. And yet as every poet knows, it is also a feat that (if accomplished) would destroy the imagination in the act of consummating it. Only in the greatest prophet-poets, in Jesus or in Lincoln, are the prophet's spiritual authority and the poet's genius for joining the self to greatness without violating its freedom different expressions of the same power.

Just as Dante earns a place for himself in his own *Inferno* by turning his back on hell instead of harrowing it, so Paul gets trapped in his own machinery. Ironically, the Paul who exalts faith over morality and freedom over law also becomes a staunch defender of law when his teachings are absorbed into the body of scripture. More seriously, it is unreasonable for Paul to try to force something that cannot be coerced without losing its value. He says that God will hate anyone who refuses to love him. But love that is not given willingly is worthless. For the horizon of a love that retreats down a vista of negatives, that 'does not insist on its own way,' that 'is not irritable or resentful' (1 Corinthians 13:5), Paul substitutes the locked door of a prison. To be of any value, the love that God requires must be offered freely, not extracted by threatening to inflict its opposite, malediction and hate, which are alien to God's nature. Though Christianity can barely survive Paul's intoxicating zeal and condescension, its theology depends as heavily on his spiritual sorcery and charisma as an addict on opium.

Burton Mack has shown that Paul's praise of love 'fits uneasily in the context of an argument about the leadership gifts of preaching, prophecy, "tongues," healing, and so forth' (1990, 64). Though Paul wants spiritual gifts to edify the community, his encomium on love is part of an attack on spiritual middlemen that is more eloquently disinterested and far more universal in its appeal than Paul's more limited polemical purpose requires. His point is that all charismatic activity is mere noise without love. But the praise of love towers and soars above everything else in his letter. It is an oracle to end all oracles: indeed, it puts all other prophecies, including the one against abusing prophecy, in the shade.

Though Mack complains that Paul's claim that love is greater than faith and hope 'is neither supported nor developed' (1990, 66), it must be said in Paul's defence that he shows how love embraces and includes the two other virtues. There is at least an ingenious overlap in the definitions of faith, hope, and love. Agape for Paul is never a rigidly bounded term: it invades adjacent territory. Mack also argues that the only convincing example of the perfection of mind that love bestows is Paul's digression in verse 12 about 'fully understanding even as I have been fully understood.' But do we ever completely understand a theologian so subtle and complicated as Paul? And if we do, does the claim not beg the question? Even if we admit the autobiographical testimony as valid evidence, it seems dangerous to accept the exalted understanding of a spiritual genius like Paul as a highwater mark others can expect to reach before the tide of their faith begins to ebb or their zeal subsides.

From the sublime language of the Sermon on the Mount to the grotesque Zen koans of the Buddhists, oracles evoke a range of response from wonder to laughter. They may absorb a listener like a charm or wittily detach him like a riddle. Northrop Frye observes that 'those who consult oracles usually do so with a sense of uncritical awe, but oracles and oracular prophecies frequently turn on puns, ambiguous or double-faced statements, or sometimes, as in *Macbeth*, on quibbles that sound like feeble-minded jokes. There is a point at which emotional involvement may suddenly reverse itself and become intellectual detachment, the typical expression of which is laughter' (1976b, 137). The aim of Zen's frequent resort to riddles is to defeat the intelligence almost successfully. Sometimes, like the rabbi who recounts the parable of the wedding feast or the dishonest steward, the Zen master will tell a story that borders on nonsense. An example that Suzuki gives is the master who holds up his staff and says, 'If you have one, I give you mine; if you have none, I will take it away from you' (1970a,

7). Like the Gospel parables, enlightenment or satori often consists in a Zen koan's consequence for living. Suzuki recounts the story of the thief who teaches his son the art of burglary by robbing a house, locking his son inside a trunk in its attic, and then alerting the robbed family to the break-in. The father teaches his son the art of burglary by forcing him to be resourceful in a crisis. One critic quips that Zen 'is the gabbiest encourager of silence' he knows (Frye, 2004b, 21). Like Carlyle, who preaches the gospel of silence in twenty volumes, the Zen masters realize that the great secret held in reserve cannot be revealed until we tune out the gibberish and chatter. Though these masters may flood the world with books about silence, they realize that verbal instruction alone is like trying to catch a catfish with a gourd, and (as Josetsu's painting shows) it is always foolish and inept. Only by confounding or humiliating the mind can a Zen master awaken it to satori.

As liberating spiritual rhetoric that also baffles an interpreter, Jesus' parable of the wedding feast is a Zen fable in microcosm. We also hear a strange kerygmatic voice speaking through Jesus' challenge to the rich young man in the Gospels who wants to remain at the level of concepts. The rich youth wants to take part in an intellectual skirmish, but Jesus offers him enlightenment instead. For Jesus knows that as long as the young man stays with the law, he cannot reach enlightenment, or what the Gospels call God's 'Kingdom.' Everything in the Gospels depends on how we understand this Kingdom. One commentator, the current Pope, cites Alfred Loisy, who observes that 'Jesus preached the Kingdom of God, and what came was the Church.' The Pope concedes that 'these words may be considered ironic, but they also express sadness. Instead of the great expectation of God's own Kingdom, of a new world transformed by God himself, we got something quite different – and what a pathetic substitute it is: the Church' (Ratzinger, 2007, 48). Some interpreters follow Origen in locating the Kingdom of God in our inner being. I prefer to identify Jesus himself with the Kingdom, which is nothing less than the poet whose Sermon on the Mount repairs the Torah by giving the world a God of Love who is also Father to a Son.

8 Paradox and Oracle:
Crucible versus Mirror

What distinguishes, not merely the oracle, but wisdom itself from truism is the paradoxical force of the expression. 'The first shall be last' is a more arresting claim than 'the meek shall inherit the earth.' And 'he who would save his soul must lose it' is a more memorable (because more paradoxical) assertion than the truism that loss is a condition of spiritual growth. Central to any discussion of oracles and paradox is the contrast between mirrors and crucibles, between paradoxes that merely reflect or invert the world, as in a glass, and paradoxes that break it down and transform it, as in a mortar or a furnace.

1

An oracle may sound paradoxical by simply inverting a commonplace. When George Bernard Shaw announces that 'poverty, obedience, and chastity are the canonical vices,' he is merely mirroring the world by standing it on its head. Such a paradox is as easy to master as a chiasmus that presents YX after XY, its mirror image. Taking little ingenuity to perfect, tricks of inversion are best described by Richard LeGallienne, who claims that 'paradox with Oscar Wilde was only truth standing on its head to attract attention' (quoted in Hughes, 1975, 5). More impressive is the metaphysical paradox that charts the strange but necessary contours of an unfamiliar landscape. The best paradoxes are necessary because they are required by contradictions or riddles built into the structure of the mind and its world. Philip Wheelwright argues that a deep or true paradox is demanded 'by the complexity and inherent ambiguity of what is being expressed' (1959, 98). When Montaigne observes that 'a man who fears suffering is already suffering from what he fears' (quoted in Hughes, 1975, 33), what sets his aphorism apart from a simple paradox of inversion is not just the rhetorical wit of its chiasmus but the truth of its insight. Equally probing, I think, is Wilde's paradox that 'the well-bred contradict other people. The wise contradict themselves' (Hughes, 1975, 49). If well-bred people use contradiction to refine their insolence, the wise man uses it to prove the truth of Emerson's aphorism that consistency is the hobgoblin of little minds, adored by statesmen, philosophers, and foolish divines.

Pascal's paradox that 'God is not all-powerful as he cannot build a wall he cannot jump' touches on what is not merely unknowable but also unlimited in its subject (quoted in Hughes, 1975, 80). Unless God is free to abolish his own nature, it is true that a God who collapses all boundaries by being everywhere at once cannot build a border he is powerless to cross. Since God is powerless to be powerless, he cannot, Pascal argues, be 'all-powerful.' This paradox invites us to explore the meaning of 'power.' Can we stretch the word's meaning to include a power to abolish qualities that make God who he is, qualities of being everywhere as well as omnipotent? Or must we restrict the word 'power' to more conventional uses that allow theologians to reconcile it with traditional claims about God? Another paradox to tease us out of thought is Teilhard de Chardin's question: 'God loves everyone in the world who doesn't love himself. Does God love God?' (quoted in Hughes, 1975, 79). Since God is free of the vice of self-love, he presumably loves himself. But God's self-love immediately removes him from the circle of those whom God is said to love. If God loves himself, he is disqualified for love. And if God qualifies for love because he is someone 'who doesn't love himself,' he is by the very act of being loved made ineligible for love by committing the unpardonable act of loving himself.

Metaphysical paradoxes presuppose an analogical understanding of God and his attributes. A univocal knowledge of God could dispense with paradox altogether. A merely equivocal knowledge of God would be left with only the least cognitive form of paradox, the paradox of a logical contradiction or antinomy, which is a sign that our knowledge of God is imperfect. Midway between idolatry and scepticism is Aquinas's analogical understanding of God. Aquinas's analogy of being relies on paradox, because it assumes, like paradox, that, though our knowledge is partial, it is valid as far as it goes. As Kenner observes, 'paradox springs in general from inadequacy, from the rents in linguistic and logical clothing; paradoxy might be called the science of gaps' (1948, 17). The paradox that an equivocal knowledge of God claims *less* than can be known and that a univocal knowledge claims *more* leaves Aquinas's analogical understanding of God as a proper middle road.

Though G.K. Chesterton's paradoxes made him famous, he is also an outspoken critic of wits who abuse paradox. 'I know nothing so contemptible,' he protests in *Orthodoxy*, 'as a mere paradox; a mere ingenious defense of the indefensible. If it were true (as has been said) that Mr. Bernard Shaw lived upon paradox, then he ought to be a mere common millionaire; for a man of his mental activity could invent a sophistry every six minutes. It is as easy as lying, because it is lying' (1947, 15). The sad truth is, however, that too often Chesterton's own oracles build toward a paradox as a comedian builds toward the punch line in a joke. We can see what is coming miles in advance. More adroit is Chesterton's paradoxical definition of a theological word like 'dogma,' which reactivates the conflicting meanings of 'end.' For dogma, according to Chesterton, 'means the serious satisfaction of the mind. Dogma does not mean the absence of thought, but the end of thought' (1947, 43). In perfecting the final cause or goal of thought, dogma also ends or terminates the need for testing or refining what we think. Chesterton says that early in his career everyone assumed that 'my faith in the Christian creed was a pose or a paradox. The more cynical supposed it was only a stunt. The more generous and loyal warmly maintained that it was only a joke. It was not until long afterwards that the full horror of the truth burst upon them; the disgraceful truth that I really thought the thing was true' (1936, 172).

Despite Chesterton's jest about Shaw, the lifeblood of paradox is not a 'defense of the indefensible' but Chesterton's own undeniable talent for turning contradiction and reversal into a minor art. In an oracular paradox an apparent contradiction or bull uses resources of wit, irony, and persuasive redefinition to replace received opinion with insight and knowledge with wisdom. Or to put the point more simply and figuratively, a paradoxical oracle is a broken whole. If its truth were merely whole and unbroken, it might decline into a simple commonplace or platitude like 'whatever is, is right.' Conversely, if its truth were entirely broken or fragmented, it might deviate into an outright absurdity or bull. Such is Carlyle's outrageous claim that freedom is servitude, the bondage of 'Gurth born thrall of Cedric.' The best paradoxes and oracles combine the aptness of an analogy with the shock or surprise effect of a witty contradiction.

Comparison is to contradiction what analogy is to paradox. In using a reversal or inversion to contradict some received opinion or truth, paradox sends us in search of some unperceived analogy or unknown cause. Examples include Blake's proverb that 'Prisons are built with the stones of Law, Brothels with bricks of Religion.' Blake's oracle justifies the reversal by substituting a cause and effect of his own invention: 'The lust of the goat is the bounty of God,' 'The nakedness of woman is the work of God' ('Proverbs of Hell'). A paradox that lacks the justifying analogy or the ingenious reinvention of cause and effect might end in mere absurdity or in a simple violation of the law of contradiction. For instance, it is surely illogical or absurd to say that democracy is a failed form of dictatorship. By contrast, it is genuinely paradoxical for Carlyle to claim that democracy is the despair of finding heroes to govern you. The substitution of 'despair' for the expected 'hope,' and of 'heroes' for 'elected officials,' introduces that element of surprise which allows inversions of thought and feeling to rally support for Carlyle's bold redefinition of democracy. Conversely, a reversal that involves no contradiction may produce an elegant chiasmus. But the result is often more elegantly witty than paradoxical. Such is the casuist's self-consoling maxim in 'Andrea del Sarto': 'In this world, who can do a thing, will not; / And who would do it, cannot, I perceive' (ll. 137–8). This maxim is sententiously expressed, but its antitheses are too self-serving and studied to produce a wise oracle or paradox.

A logical absurdity may yield at most a jocular version of the bull: 'You have to be crazy to consult a psychiatrist,' 'I would never join a club that accepts me as a member.' In addition to the shock effect of a joke or a bull, a paradox has to reverse or invert its items. The mere reversal of a chiasmus, however, is not necessarily paradoxical. 'The first shall be last, and the last shall be first' is a genuine paradox. But most uses of chiasmus, as in the two lines just quoted from 'Andrea del Sarto,' are tidily elegant rather than wisely or wittily paradoxical. A paradox's reversal of received opinion or wisdom should in some sense justify the contradiction it expresses.

Such is the case with St Paul's great reversals in 1 Corinthians 15:51–6. 'For this perishable nature must put on the imperishable, and this mortal nature must put on immortality.' Only the transformation of what is perishable and mortal into their opposites can justify the ringing paradoxes of Paul's most famous oracle, which boasts that 'death is swallowed up in victory.' 'O death, where is thy victory? O death, where is thy sting?' Equally exalted is the climactic chiasmus in Browning's 'Abt Vogler.'

> And the emulous heaven yearned down, made effort to reach the earth,
> As the earth had done her best, in my passion, to scale the sky:
>
> ('Abt Vogler,' ll. 27–8)

Thrusting out with the fling of a great cantilever or arc, the lines offer the most superb chiasmus in all of Browning: 'emulous heaven,' 'earth,' 'earth ... in my passion,' 'sky.' Just as majestic is the ease with which Milton's poet-shepherd reverses direction in 'Lycidas.'

> For *Lycidas* your sorrow is not dead,
> Sunk though he be beneath the watry floar   (ll. 166–7)

Like faith, the language of revelation is performative. Its power to create the truth it celebrates makes it the birth and breeding place of Milton's most sublime prophecies and oracles.

When heavens open in 'Abt Vogler,' Browning's musician boasts of being touched by the finger of God, a flash of the will that can. Behind his image stand the gesture of Michelangelo's God, extending a finger to a beautiful but still soulless Adam in the Sistine Chapel painting, and the equally moving handiwork of God's finger in the majestic eighth psalm.

> When I look at thy heavens, the work of thy fingers,
>   the moon and the stars which thou hast established;
> what is man that thou art mindful of him,
>   and the son of man that thou dost care for him?
>
> Yet thou hast made him little less than God,
>   and dost crown him with glory and honor.   (Psalm 8:3–5)

Like the psalmist, a great wisdom writer opens doors. He finds a home inside a boundary, a 'bulwark' God establishes and defends because of his 'foes' (Psalm 8:2). But the psalmist also uses this bulwark, not as a prison, but as a place from which to break through limits by exploring and celebrating the glory of a God-given dignity unique to man. The subtlest exposition of this paradox comes from James Carse, who shows that if wisdom is confined to a bulwark of belief, or if it is freed from all such bulwarks, it ceases to be wisdom. As Carse argues, 'if belief were entirely horizontal it would be a wash of weightless and inconsequent ideas. Just as if it were entirely bounded it would become mindless chatter. The task is to find just the right way of blending what is certain with what is uncertain, the known with what is unknown; neither knowledge without wonder nor belief without horizon' (2008, 83).

The logic of paradox appeals to the mind. But when paradox is a heard event, it may also induce a tremor. We can hear such tremors in the wavering oracular voice of Samuel Johnson.

> For why did Wolsey near the steeps of fate,
> On weak foundations raise th' enormous weight?
> Why but to sink beneath misfortune's blow,
> With louder ruin to the gulphs below?
>
> ('The Vanity of Human Wishes,' ll. 125–8)

Johnson's wisdom rests safely on an axis of repose. He assures us in the coda that religion builds a ladder on which wavering man, deluded by wavering optical phenomena and wavering caesural pauses, can mount securely from the scorching 'torrent' (l. 346) to the fires of 'sacred presence' (l. 357). But breaking through the homily are moments of uncontrolled fear and trembling, when something he dreads touches a nerve: 'Yet hope not life from grief or danger free, / Nor think the doom of man reversed for thee' ('The Vanity of Human Wishes,' ll. 155–6).

Sometimes a tremor of awe may precede the impact made by the full comprehension of a paradox, as when Hopkins says in stunned wonder: 'I lay wrestling with (my God) my God.' Donne also achieves the combined effect of a blow or impact followed by a shock wave or tremor in 'A Litany': 'That our affections kill us not, nor die, / Hear us, weak echoes, O thou ear, and cry' (ll. 242–3). It is as if only the ear of God, a capacious power to hear and process all prayers, could catch and retain in Donne's sharp caesural breaks and daring metonymy the poet's faint, tremulous, endlessly receding echoes of the Word.

2

The case against a predictable oracle of inversion, which reflects the world in a mirror, is put most strongly by Hugh Kenner. He criticizes G.B. Shaw for turning his paradoxes into 'the mirror of the social structure he abominates, because in reversing it he reflects it unchanged' (1948, 10). It is one thing for the Sermon on the Mount or Lincoln's Gettysburg address to allude to an earlier tradition in order to reinvent and transform it. But what if Shaw alludes to a maxim only to invert it? What if, instead of displacing or revolutionizing a social structure or system, he merely perpetuates it in a mirror image? A paradox of mere inversion tends to feed incestuously off a precept or a commonplace. Examples include Shaw's warning not to do unto others as you would have them do unto you, because their tastes may be different, or F.H. Bradley's wry reminder that all things come to the man who waits for them, among other things death. Unlike a paradox of inversion, which leaves the deep structures of its world unchanged, a crucible of paradox breaks down the world in order to remould it from inside.

Chesterton's novel *The Man Who Was Thursday* seems to build at first on a simple paradox of inversion. Except for Gregory, all the anarchists are policemen in disguise. The President of the anarchists, Sunday, turns out to be the chief of police who persuades the other anarchists to become officers in his force. But until we penetrate his mask, Sunday seems at once everything and nothing. Possessing the apparent indifference of Job's God, the god of nature and the Stoics, he displays few attributes of a providential deity. The first time we read Chesterton's tale, we savour its mystery: Sunday seems a paradox of negative capability. The next time we read it, having solved the mystery of the masks, we respond more to its paradoxes of inversion. Instead of showing that apparently virtuous, respectable people are criminals, as in most detective stories, Chesterton does the opposite: he presents the more reassuring mirror image of anarchists who are policemen.

Instead of merely inverting what it reflects, an oracle may see the world through a bifocal lens. From Augustine to J.H. Newman, the paradox of the double audience allows writers of confessions to profess their faith and confess their failings at the same time. Profession without confession would be empty, and confession without profession blind. The trick is to be universal and particular, disinterested and partisan, simultaneously. To see the world through a bifocal lens, however, may distort a speaker's vision. The more Browning's Andrea del Sarto tries to defend his life and art by blaming his wife Lucrezia for his failures, the less successful he can be in persuading her to spend the evening with him.

Whereas the paradoxes of an apologist are conservative in temper, designed to consolidate support for received doctrine or tradition, a subversive paradox is radical in both tone and temper. Its purpose is to attack or contradict accepted opinion. Some of the Gnostic gospels subvert the authority of orthodox theology. And Nietzsche's paradox of the ethical immoralist depends in part on a subversive redefinition of both ethics and morality. 'A criminal,' says Nietzsche, instead of glorying in his immorality, 'is frequently not equal to his deed; he makes it smaller and slanders it' (1989, 85). A version of his paradox goes back to St Paul, who exalts faith over morality and law. In *Beyond Good and Evil* Nietzsche scandalizes a reader by claiming that 'the lawyers defending a criminal are rarely artists enough to turn the beautiful terribleness of his deed to his advantage' (1989, 85). At first it seems outrageous for Nietzsche to praise the art of an ethical immoralist by associating his crimes with the 'terrible beauty' Yeats associates with the Irish martyrs in 'Easter 1916.' But Nietzsche is redefining morality to mean mores or custom, and ethics to mean the promotion of more abundant life and great-souled deeds. Instead of merely shocking a reader, Nietzsche's paradox becomes an instructive exercise in the art of changing the emotive and descriptive meanings of a charged or loaded word.

Often the so-called contradictions of a merely verbal paradox dissolve like sugar in water or a fogbank in sun. Thomas Fuller's jest that 'many would be cowards if they had courage enough' (Hughes, 1975, 34) sounds paradoxical only if we forget that it may take more courage for a pacifist to risk being called a coward than to fight as a solider. If empiricists base their knowledge on fugitive impressions of sense, then it is a paradox more verbal than real for George Santayana to denounce 'the bankruptcy of their enterprise. Immediate data are the counters of experience, but they are the money of empiricism' (1967, 194). Less entangled in logomachy is Santayana's paradox that, though 'there is a sense of safety in being and not thinking which probably all the animals know,' the disadvantage' of such 'radical empiricism is that it shuts out experience' (1967, 201).

Some paradoxes are more amusing than instructive. To say 'a banker will lend you money only if you can prove you don't need it' (Hughes,

1975, 18) tells us less about principles of banking than about the comedy of being denied credit when one wants it and of being offered it when one doesn't. As Frost quips, all the fun's in how you say a thing. 'In Leningrad freezing point is called melting point' (Hughes, 1975, 57), and it is hard to say whether 'a person who bathes particularly often' is 'particularly clean or particularly dirty' (Hughes, 1975, 68). Equally amusing is Ionesco's joke that 'the French word for London is Paris' (Hughes, 1975, 43), or Daniel Boorstin's jibe that 'the celebrity is a person who is known for his well-knownness' (Hughes, 1975, 51), as if fame were only a shimmering mirage, a reflection seen in facing mirrors.

A paradox may sometimes defend its use of contradiction by showing how a serious approach to language, which censors all but one meaning, inhibits the polysemous (often contradictory) meanings that are inseparable from any resourceful use of words. As Wilde says, 'seriousness' in this sense 'is the only refuge of the shallow' (Hughes, 1975, 12). Paul Valéry's observation that 'Achilles cannot defeat the tortoise if he thinks of space and time' (Hughes, 1975, 25) shows how the apparent contradictions of Zeno's paradox can be resolved only by another paradox. This is the paradox of awarding victory to the tortoise by tricking Achilles into thinking space and time are endlessly divisible.

The witty observation that 'everyone believed in God's existence until it was proven in the Boyle lectures' has the shock effect of a paradox. But the shock depends on a false equation of belief and proof. The paradox evaporates once we recognize that, unlike Robert Boyle's law on the compressibility of a gas, which requires the assent of all right-thinking chemists, no experiment to prove God exists can be conducted in a test tube. Even if a lecturer in the series Boyle endows were able to prove God exists, his proof would have to be logically coercive, and so an occasion for counter-arguments by sceptical opponents. One logical corollary is that any free assent to the proposition 'God exists' is bound to disappear whenever a Boyle lecturer tries to coerce it in the manner of a proof.

Other contradictions, however, may take strong chemicals to dissolve. One such solvent is what Keats calls 'negative capability,' or the paradox of masks. A playwright like Shakespeare, who can be Iago as well as Imogen, cultivates a form of art that is generous or inclusive enough to contain its own contraries. As Wilde explains, a truth in art is one whose opposite is also true. Moreover, images in the unconscious are often said to mean opposite things simultaneously. As a paradox of negative capability, even Chesterton's Sunday in *The Man Who Was Thursday* appears to be capacious enough in mind and body to absorb most contraries in himself, so that his irony is invisible. As a character in a nightmare, he is also capable of generating the double, sometimes opposite, meanings that often appear in dreams.

By contrast, there are other paradoxes that no solvent can dissolve without eroding their subject. These include the physicist's 'wave-particle' theory of light, the theologian's paradox of a 'First Cause' or 'Unmoved Mover,' and Zeno's paradoxes of motion. The paradox that Achilles can never overtake the tortoise that crawls past him while he sleeps, or that the released arrow can never reach its target, results from the fact that time is an illusion and that the arrow, like the runner, is always at rest. Similarly, when Kant shows that the attributes of a God who is at once absolute, infinite, and a First Cause are contradictory, the result is either unbelief or fideism. The noumenal subject becomes a ghost, and the intelligible world of the conceptual understanding remains the mere mask of a ghost. This is the central paradox of F.H. Bradley's theory of knowledge: a denotation or a 'that' can only be gestured at, and a connotation or a 'what' can be described only in antinomies that concede the philosopher's failure to exhaust the mystery and complexity of his subject.

Equally intractable are the paradoxes arising from Plato's teaching that to be wise is to follow the injunction Apollo inscribes on his temple at Delphi: know yourself. To know oneself is to know how little one knows. But it takes some degree of knowledge to know this. As Montaigne says, 'one has to push at a door before realizing that it is closed to one.' From this truth there arises 'the Platonic paradox that those who know have no need to inquire because they know; and those who do not know have no need either, since in order to inquire one has to know what one is inquiring about' (Montaigne, 1958, 356). Even the wise saying of Koheleth that all things have their season prompts Montaigne's amused aside that we 'may say the Lord's prayer at the wrong moment' (1958, 225). A wise man also knows when to conclude his formal pursuit of wisdom. 'One may always continue to study, but not to go to school. How ridiculous is an old man learning his A B C!' An aging scholar with one foot in the grave, who continues to write in his dotage, might wish to heed Montaigne's advice. 'Here is a man learning to talk, when he should be learning to be silent for ever ... Our studies and ambitions ought sometimes to have a feeling of age' (1958, 226).

In his Gettysburg address and later in his Second Inaugural, the trauma of a great civil war seems to unnerve Lincoln. For a moment during his Inaugural address, Lincoln's grammar wanders. Does God support the North or the South? Perhaps he is indifferent and supports neither side in the conflict. To know God's will is to know the unknowable. Prepared to present his argument disjointedly, Lincoln never tries to resolve the inconsistencies. Indeed, unhinged by the enormity of the carnage, he is not quite sure how to manage the consolations of either an elegy or a eulogy. Paradoxically, the more resolute Lincoln tries to be the more irresolute he sounds. Yet the momentary wavering and irresolution also suggest that Lincoln is a strong mourner who never oversimplifies the work of mourning.

In 'Easter 1916' Yeats acknowledges that even a drunken, vainglorious lout like Macbride can become a hero. But how exactly is the casual comedy transformed? Is it possible for an atrocity like the Holocaust or the terrorist attack on the Twin Towers to acquire the 'terrible beauty' Yeats associates with the Irish martyrs? In *Four Quartets* beatitude is always receding from the poet, who composes a music of suffering out of broken allusions to broken people who are still mysteriously 'united in the strife which divided them' ('Little Gidding,' III.25). And in *King Lear*, as Iris Murdoch observes, Shakespeare 'almost breaks the art form, and a surviving Lear would break it altogether. (As his crying continues on and on.) The metaphor of the broken circle, the cracked object, occurs to us especially I think here, where the satisfying calming completeness of art is internally contradicted by absolute contingency and humiliating death' (1992, 120). One paradox of great art is that it 'cannot help changing what it professes to display into something different' (1992, 122). Less important than Childe Roland's discovery of the Dark Tower is the change it produces in his consciousness, which is both a cause and effect of his discovery. Frye speaks of 'the Gnostic fallacy of diving for the pearl at the bottom of the sea. There isn't any pearl at the bottom: it's suffered a sea-change into the sea itself' (2000, 460). Any transformation into the rich and strange may produce powerful aesthetic effects. But in a poem that portrays the Holocaust or dramatizes the atrocities of genocide, these sea-changes may be morally offensive. If Shakespeare can transform and make bearable the terrible scene in *King Lear* where Gloucester's eyes are put out, it is because his imagination revolts against the horror of the scene. As Northrop Frye says, what Shakespeare presents 'is not the paralyzing sickening horror of a real blind-

ing scene, but an exuberant horror, full of the energy of repudiation'
(1963a, 41).

3

When we pause to consider what will survive of us, we confront at last
the 'paradox of ends.' I use the term to include two paradoxes: the
unforeseen discovery that in our end is our beginning, and the unsettling possibility of there being nothing behind the veil that is not
already in front of it. Sooner or later we come face to face with three
conflicting end games. And each scenario corresponds to a different
oracle or precept of wisdom: to an oracle of emptiness, to an oracle that
mirrors a scheme of salvation already worked out for us by someone
else, and to an oracle that challenges us to work out our own salvation.
   Hopkins's bleak oracle in 'Spelt from Sibyl's Leaves' predicts that
our sole legacy will be whatever darkness we encounter this side of the
vale of soul-making. Despite the longing of Virgil's dead souls to reach
the farther shore, nothing awaits them there. 'Our evening is over us;
our night whelms, whelms, and will end us' (l. 8). St Paul's oracles
about the resurrection of the body foresee a very different end. His
victory over death mirrors the victory already achieved for him by
someone else. A third kind of oracle sees the world as a crucible, as
what Keats calls a vale of soul-making. In a world of refining pain,
each pilgrim has to forge in the smithy of his soul the uncreated end
game of his pilgrimage. Only when the oracles scorch and sear the soul
do their questions become real and start to purge the pilgrim for the
first time. In 'Little Gidding,' T.S. Eliot insists there is no escape from
the crucible: 'We only live, only suspire / Consumed by either fire or
fire' (IV.13–14). 'The intolerable shirt of flame' that burns and sears the
flesh can also heal and purify it. A similar paradox transforms the fire
of the destructive dive-bomber into the eternal Pentecost, the perpetual descent of the dove in tongues of flame. Fluctuating between 'pyre
and pyre,' only a refining crucible has power to redeem the poet,
saving him 'from fire by fire.'
   Cynthia Bourgeault associates oracles of soul-making with Christian
Wisdom, and she believes Wisdom's death knell was sounded 'in the
infamous doctrinal squabble between Augustine and Pelagius in the
late fifth century' (2003, 17). Maintaining that 'it was both possible and
necessary for people to embark on the quest for perfection,' Pelagius
insisted 'that *theosis* (the Greek word for "divinization," or the full real-

ization of the divine image and likeness within the human person) was the whole point of our earthly pilgrimage.' Bourgeault reminds us that 'Augustine was horrified by this idea, and his counterproposal, which became the doctrine of Original Sin, carried the day' (2003, 17). As a result of 'this watershed dispute,' Jesus 'was repositioned from *moshel meshalim* (teacher of wisdom) to mediator, and the spiritual journey was reframed from a quest for divinization to a rescue operation' (2003, 17). Paradoxically, Pelagius and the Gnostics offer a more reasonable interpretation of redemption than Augustine and Calvin. For Augustine and Calvin 'those elected for salvation are,' as one observer notes, 'not so much redeemed as rescued. A man rescued from a shipwreck is simply pulled out of the water; but redemption means fulfilling what one formerly was, as well as separating it from the demonic or parody-world of evil. A redeemed slave has his bondage annihilated, but his essential human life is fulfilled' (Frye, 1991, 6).

A Wisdom tradition survives in the Gnostic Gospels, which often surprise us with their deft reversal of a common image. Instead of rapping on the outside of a door to gain admission to a house, we are told in the sixty-first logion of the Gospel of Thomas to knock from inside. 'Jesus said: He who seeks will find. To him who knocks from the inside, it will be opened.' But if we are already inside the house, why should we knock? The answer is that all divinity is interior. To be open to Jesus and the Father of Openness from whom Jesus was sent forth, a disciple must make of the self not a prison house but a temple, where every treasure of the spirit is waiting to be claimed. In Thomas's Gospel, Jesus often sounds like a Platonic sage with an original doctrine to expound. The reverse is true in the Synoptic Gospels, where Jesus is 'original only as a strong story-teller, and his doctrines are commentaries on the Old Testament, echoing those of contemporary rabbis' (Frye, 2004a, 154).

As the light which illuminates all men, and who is united with the All, the Gnostics' Jesus can say he is both Alpha and Omega: 'The All came forth from me and the All ended up in me.' 'Split some wood, I am there. Lift a stone, you will find me there' (logion 77). As ubiquitous as Whitman's Oversoul, Jesus lurks in the world's inmost crannies and nooks. Whether in a fragment of the wood we split or in the stones we lift, Jesus is always lying in ambush for us. As in logion 113, 'the Kingdom of the Father is spread over all the earth and men do not see it.' This is equivalent to the aphorism of the video artist that Pagels uses as an epigraph in *Beyond Belief*: 'There is an invisible world out there, and we are living in it' (2003, 1). Since last things are present now, there is no eschatology in the Gospel of Thomas. The kingdom of God is immanent in creation: it already exists in the scattered particles of light that are the Father's most precious possession. This idea can be found in the Gospel of Philip: 'Those who say that the Lord first died and (then) arose are wrong. For he first arose and (then) he died ...' (104. 15ff.). The chiasmus marks the Gnostics' reversal of received opinion: in this case, their belief that Jesus was resurrected, not after he died, but on the near side of the grave. 'What is immortal is not the life we are going to live after death, but the life we have lived. The Resurrection must be *retrospective*' (Frye, 2004a, 143).

The influence of the Gnostic gospels can be clearly discerned in Blake, for whom God is the eternal self and worship of God is self-development. Blake's true gods are the Muses. As his most original expositor explains, this is 'what Blake meant by saying you're not a Christian if you're not an artist, though I certainly wish he'd said it in a more cautious way' (Frye, 2000, 670). Like Blake, many thinkers and poets who find 'themselves at the edges of orthodoxy' (Pagels, 2003, 150) sympathize with the Gnostics' claim that the light that dwells in each of us is the source of all creative power. The Gnostic gospels also extol the same spark of pre-created light that Hopkins praises in 'Hurrahing in Harvest' when he gleans our Saviour 'down all that glory in the heavens' (l. 6). If creation is abdication, then God is all-powerful only in the sense 'that his abdication is voluntary. He knows its effects, and wills them,' as Simone Weil conjectures (1974, 48). Even if God has abandoned the world in creating it, he still 'keeps under his care the part of Creation which is himself – the uncreated part of every creature. That is the life, the Light, the Word; it is the presence here below of God's only Son' (Weil, 1974, 48). The light that is in us and in Jesus is not a part of the fallen world. It is prelapsarian. In Hopkins's curtal sonnet 'Pied Beauty,' as in the creation story in Genesis, an exuberant *Te Deum Laudamus* is about to consecrate creation as a fathering forth of God. But Hopkins uses the rapid multiplication of antonyms to override the unique identity of what is 'counter, original, spare, strange' (l. 7). He celebrates instead the reversing flow of a beauty which, since it precedes creation, is past all change, and can turn with a preordained ease and grace of movement back again to God.

The oracles of Augustine and Calvin reject as a parody of grace any appeal to man's divinity in protest against the dogma of original sin. Such theologians see man only as a mirror of the first Adam. Instead of exhorting us to imitate or mirror Christ as a second Adam, their oracles advise us to supplicate him as a saviour, as part of a 'rescue operation.' But the promise of salvation may prove intellectually and spiritually disabling. Augustine's *deus ex machina* is always in danger of becoming a *deus in machina*, stuck in a machine of predestination and election. An antidote exists in oracles that operate as crucibles, like the oracles of the Wisdom writers and the Gnostics. Arching over Plato's trinity of the good, the beautiful, and the true is the bridge of soul-making. For the categories in Plato's trinity are also aspects of making. And they invite us to refine and purify our lives by experiencing to the full the pain and mystery of existing in a world where we, too, are makers – artists and architects of our own salvation. The soul-making endorsed by this second kind of oracle assumes, like Pelagius and the Gnostics, that the total creation we have made out of nature will be our passport into whatever New Jerusalem awaits us on the farther shore. Since the only Kingdom of God is the one we ourselves create as we make our way to the Celestial City, our end will prove the truth of the Mad Hatter's paradox in *Alice in Wonderland*. 'How you get there is where you'll arrive.' Our destination depends upon the journey that we take.

9 Copy-Speech and Counter-Love: Wordsworth and Frost

What poets seek in nature is neither copy-speech nor a tyrannical power that dominates them from outside but a form of 'counter-love, original response' (Frost, 'The Most of It,' l. 8). William Wordsworth may want to prove that he is 'lord and master over outward sense.' But by turning nature and the language of the sense into a form of copy-speech, he finds in the Boy of Winander passage from book 5 of *The Prelude* that he is merely creating his own counter-tyranny. 'The Idea of Order at Key West' is Wallace Stevens's attempt to glimpse the ocean as 'water never formed to mind or voice, / Like a body wholly body, fluttering / Its empty sleeves' (ll. 1–4). Though this 'veritable ocean,' inhuman, moved by the wind to make a 'constant cry' (1–5), is a cause of cries in us, it is also staunchly independent of us and prior. The sea is not just a mask for a ventriloquist who tries to speak through it. But neither is the singer a mere mouthpiece for the sea.

The 'grinding waters and the gasping wind' can be heard stirring in the poet's song. And yet the sudden appearance of triple rhymes ("heard," "word," "stirred") in a blank verse poem also shows how 'medleyed sound' can subdue the 'ever-hooded, tragic-gestured sea' to some semblance of consonance and order. If we hear the singer of the sea and not the sea (l. 14), what are to make of Stevens's earlier claim that the ocean's cry 'was not ours although we understood' it? (l. 6) In performing a delicate balancing act, hovering between self-projection and entry into the authentic 'genius of the sea,' Stevens is trying to etch, as sharply as possible, the ocean as it is, with a touch of real surf and 'sunken coral' in it. Only the mind's capacity for fine and multiple response, in which every impression is clear and distinct, can draw out the ocean's 'ghostlier demarcations' or order its words in 'keener sounds.'

No one who reads Stevens can think an observer should do nothing but merely wait for the ocean to be heard or the sky to be seen. The need to respond and create is central to everything he writes. In the sea the singer finds a replica of her own language and moods. Is this because another maker, secular or divine, has been there before her? Or is it because, as Aristotle thinks, nature has already been organized into properties that are found in their purest form in art? Whatever the reason, the maker's words find in the sea and its language a 'blessed rage for order' that is the truest attribute of the human mind itself. As Frost would say, 'it is most us' ('West-Running Brook,' l. 72).

'The genius of the sea' is something that is being fashioned, not just in the consciousness of the singer or her listener, but in the world itself. Like an oracle or a lesser deity, the singer is 'the single artificer of the world / In which she sang' (ll. 37–8). It is her 'voice' alone that makes 'the sky acutest at its vanishing' and measures 'to the hour its solitude' (ll. 33–5). When she sings, something new and unprecedented is happening, both in the world and in her, and we, too, can be transformed by it.

Knowledge is discovery, but wisdom is remembrance. A thinker who struggles to understand the world, like Stevens's singer, lives in a hemisphere of youth and inexperience. But as the thinker ages, the left side of her prefrontal cortex, where the patterns of experience come to reside, becomes just as active as the right hemisphere. The increased activity of the brain's left side, which can be observed in PET scans and MRIs, is one neurological manifestation of wisdom. Pattern recognition and the mind's power to contribute to experience such essential ingredients of its own knowledge as Kant's forms of space and time make the mind lord and master over outward sense. Wisdom has more in common with Kant's theory of knowledge than with Bentham's or Mill's. It gives the mind a measure of omnipotence, since what we encounter in the world is already present in us. We can say of wisdom what Keats says of great poetry: it strikes us as almost a remembrance.

1

A divine ventriloquist may be too close to his puppet and an emeritus god too remote from his creation to offer counter-love, original response. The god of Delphi and the prophets should occupy an appropriate middle ground. To find this ground a poet may have to experiment with a variety of tones that are critical of prophecies and sceptical of Delphic oracles. What we hear at first may sound less like a prophet than a wayward pilgrim. I am thinking of Browning's sceptical Arab physician, Karshish, for example, or of T.S. Eliot's bewildered wise man. Equally vagrant is Christina Rossetti's bruised lover in the devotional poem 'Twice,' or even the angry plaintiff of Hopkins's sonnet 'Thou art indeed just, Lord.' As a puppet, the oracle faces a dilemma. If he is too pliable a puppet, he may dwindle into a mere votary of the god. But if he is too energetic, he may take on independent life. He may be too unpredictable, too possessed by the imp of the perverse, to qualify as a mouthpiece of the higher power.

Oracles of destiny or fate may rob the present of immediacy. As shadows or figural types of Christ, Old Testament characters like Noah, Joshua, and Joseph in Keble's cycle of devotional poems, *The Christian Year*, lack substance and autonomy. Equally immaterial and spectral is Virgil's Aeneas, who obeys the oracles that adapt him to each occasion and that shape his destiny as founder of Rome. As one critic concludes, 'the *Aeneid* is a melancholy epic, whose most famous lines return to tears, silence, and deprivation. Destiny prevails, but destiny does not consult the feelings of the hero' (Lipking, 1981, 82).

Milton's oracles bear least resemblance to a puppet's when his breakthroughs are uncertain and his prophecies prove difficult to sustain. Only after two earlier failures does Milton's uncouth swain finally achieve catharsis in 'Lycidas.' Milton places a frame around the end of his elegy but not around its beginning. To secure the conclusiveness of the closing lines he steps out of a picture frame into a world that claims to be less fictional. This gesture is conclusive because it is the third and final time he passes from a lower world into a higher one. Earlier in the elegy, after the shepherd-poet laments that the death of his fellow poet Lycidas is premature, Phoebus Apollo, the god of poetic inspiration, encourages him to renounce earthly ambition. 'Fame is no plant that grows on mortal soil,' Phoebus warns him. 'Of so much fame in Heaven expect thy meed' (ll. 78, 84).

The shepherd-poet steps out of a shadow world of make-believe and artifice for a second time when forced to admit that Lycidas's bones have been washed far away, hurled 'beyond the stormy Hebrides' (l. 156), or possibly brought to a more restful grave near Land's End. The consolations of pastoral elegy, including the vain custom of heaping flowers on an empty grave, are frail and unavailing. Only 'the dear might of him that walked the waves' can give the elegist the confidence and strength to pass from 'the bottom of the monstrous' sea to the streams of paradise. And the apotheosis, when it comes, is more imposing for being difficult to achieve. As the uncouth swain, Milton's puppet, begins to speak in unison with the prophet behind the mask, the clinching of the simple rhymes locks the moment of slow turning and majestic reversal into a lucid affirmation. The mounted corpse towers magisterially, looking far beyond the auspices of its chiming couplet (ll. 171–2).

> For *Lycidas* your sorrow is not dead,
> Sunk though he be beneath the watry floar,
> So sinks the day-star in the Ocean bed,
> And yet anon repairs his drooping head,
> And tricks his beams, and with new spangled Ore,
> Flames in the forehead of the morning sky;
> So *Lycidas* sunk low, but mounted high,
> Through the dear might of him that walk'd the waves
> Where other groves, and other streams along,
> With *Nectar* pure his oozy *Locks* he laves,
> And hears the unexpressive nuptiall Song ... ('Lycidas,' ll. 166–76)

If rhyme binds the corpse to the spangled ore of the sun, flaming in the forehead of the morning sky, syntax and logic also unite Lycidas to the dear might of a greater Sun, Christ, and to the inexpressible nuptial song of Revelation. The reflections of the sun's glory and the greater glory of the Son have power to illuminate and enlighten. But their might, like the ruth that melts the angel (l. 163), can be petitioned and sustained only because the mourner now speaks in unison with the prophecies in Revelation and with Milton's own oracles.

In order to merge the two identities, those of the puppet and the sublime ventriloquist who speaks and pulls the strings, a third and final transition must be made. To ensure that the poet's last words are conclusive Milton has still to shatter the illusion that the poet of 'Lycidas' is an 'uncouth swain.' To this end Milton takes off the pastoral mask and speaks to us directly for the first time. As in a valediction or recessional, which takes a receding view of the action as a whole, Milton allows the consolations of elegy to pass through and beyond the poem's pastoral frame. The traditional language and ancient symbols become a form of liturgy, releasing emotion even as they control it.

As a 'genius of the shore,' Lycidas is welcomed into a world we all now inhabit. When the shepherd-poet wipes 'the tears forever from his eyes' (l. 181), he is experiencing a catharsis that Milton wants each reader to share. In our own world, which is no longer the pastoral world of sheep and shepherds, it is important that we, too, be able to lay our grief aside and face the future with renewed hope. We, too, should be able to say, not just with an 'uncouth swain' but also with Milton himself, the prophet-poet of 'Lycidas,' 'Tomorrow to fresh woods, and pastures new' (l. 193). The elegy's last words are also its most conclusive. They show for a third and final time that there is an invisible world outside our own world. By moving out of picture frames, we can exchange margin for centre, shadow for substance, and inhabit a more meaningful space even now.

At the end of lyrics by Donne and George Herbert, after wandering far apart with little prospect of converging, the voices of God and his wayward prophet may be heard to sound for a moment in unison. Herbert's devotional lyric 'Denial' laments the distance that continues to separate the poet from God. Though Herbert yearns to be God's oracle, and numbs 'both knees and heart in crying night and day, "*Come, come, my God, O come!*" (ll. 13–14), God fails to hear him. Unless God speaks through his oracle and allows the words of Herbert and his Maker to chime in harmony, the poet's soul will remain 'untuned, unstrung' (l. 22). By a marvel of verbal grace, however, such mending of Herbert's rhyme does take place in the lyric 'Jordan (I).' In the last line the poet can 'plainly say, *My God, My King*,' without being punished, as he fears, by loss of rhyme. For 'King' manages to rhyme with two other words in the last stanza, 'sing' and 'spring' (ll. 21, 23–5). However 'fierce and wild' Herbert may grow, there is always a chance he will hear 'one calling, *Child*!,' and respond by saying '*My Lord*' ('The Collar,' ll. 35–6).

In its slow but steady progression, Donne's sonnet 'Show me, dear Christ, thy spouse so bright and clear' is closer in spirit to Herbert's lyrics than to Hopkins's. Donne grows in intimacy with God by becoming a courtly lover, a shining and amorous knight in arms.

> Betray kind husband thy spouse to our sights,
> And let myne amorous soule court thy mild Dove,
> Who is most trew and pleasing to thee, then
> When she'is embrac'd and open to most men   ('Holy Sonnet 179,' ll. 11–14)

The loving graces that temper the dignity of Donne's and Herbert's God are absent in Hopkins, the angry inquisitor, whose last-minute convergence with Christ's voice in 'Thou art indeed just, Lord' is far more precarious and unstable. Indeed it is hard to exaggerate the difference in tone between the cold, distant 'Lord' of justice in Hopkins's opening line and the gracious 'Lord of life' who sends his 'roots rain' in the moving conclusion to the sonnet.

At the climax of most dramatic monologues a divine ventriloquist and his puppet can be heard speaking in unison. But the oracle is most effective if both before and after their moment of union the two voices begin to diverge or pull apart. In Browning's 'Saul' David's voice remains vibrant with prophecy. His oracle, 'See the Christ stand!,' seems to resonate endlessly in a world tremulous with feeling, transformed by love and desire. But in monologues like 'Fra Lippo Lippi,' 'An Epistle of Karshish,' and 'Cleon,' Browning traces an inverted U shape. After ascending with effort to a mount of vision, the prophet climbs down from his pinnacle reluctantly. Having scaled the heights, he has difficulty returning to 'the C Major of this life' ('Abt Vogler,' l. 96).

As forms of one-sided communication, the prophet's oracle and the poet's dramatic monologue have curious affinities. In an oracle, a ventriloquist god, speaking through the mouthpiece of a puppet, responds to the inquiries of a silent auditor or suppliant. In a dramatic monologue, a speaker, not to be identified with the poet behind the mask, takes part in a one-sided conversation with a silent auditor. The U shape described by an oracle, in which a god condescends to answer a suppliant, and the inverted U form described by a dramatic monologue, in which a speaker rises to an oracular strain, meet at one point only. They touch at the nadir of the oracle and the zenith of the dramatic monologue. After Apollo prophesies through his oracle at Delphi, which is located in the foothills of Mount Parnassus, he withdraws to Olympus, the mountain of the gods. While prophets climb Parnassus, speakers in monologues descend from Delphi to a lower world. Like the modern pilgrim to Delphi or the chastened mourner at the close of 'Lycidas,' only speakers who allay their fears, renew their hopes, and keep their oracles in repair can make their way 'Tomorrow to fresh woods and pastures new.' Shy of bardic presumption, seers like Browning and the early T.S. Eliot turn to monologues in order to keep faith with an observed world of delinquent monks and baffled magi. As prophets, however, they are also drawn to a very different world, frightful and estranging. Overpowered and engulfed, the raised spirit may suffer the fate of Lazarus in Browning's monologue

'An Epistle of Karshish': in being raised from the dead by a Nazarene sage, he is spiritually razed or raped. And yet the personification of God as the sage who raises Lazarus from the dead also reaches beyond personification to an affirmation of miraculous identity.

> This man so cured regards the curer, then,
> As – God forgive me! Who but God himself,
> Creator and sustainer of the world,
> That came and dwelt in flesh on it awhile!
>
> ('An Epistle of Karshish,' ll. 267–70)

Just as the priestess of Apollo is inseparable from the god who speaks through her, so the sage not only personifies God: he *is* God.

2

Emerson's most paradoxical expression of counter-love and original response is 'Brahma,' a poem that for years disturbed and haunted Frost. Bound by rhyme into the unity that Brahma says they share, even opposites like 'shame' and 'fame' are shown to serve a common end (l. 8). Superior to both 'the red slayer' Siva, the Hindu god of destruction, and the meek Christian God, Brahma shocks us with his open syntax, which (like his theology) looks two ways at once.

> They reckon ill who leave me out;
> When me they fly, I am the wings;
> I am the doubter and the doubt,
> And I the hymn the Brahmin sings.
>
> ('Brahma,' ll. 9–12)

The primary meaning of the phrase 'me they fly' is 'flee from me.' But we cannot quite banish from our mind a wilder shadow meaning: we fly Brahma as we might fly a colossal eagle or aeroplane. And that possibility is strengthened, not weakened, when Brahma announces that he is the wings and that in him all distinctions of grammar, all differences between subject and object, plural and singular, are annihilated. Brahma is part of the individual – he is both 'the doubter' and his 'doubt.' But like the Möbius strip on which a line can be traced forever, Brahma is also the whole of which the individual is only a part.

It took Robert Frost years to make his peace with this poem. The first time he read the last stanza of 'Brahma' 'he blacked out,' he says, 'as if he had bumped his head and he only came to dazed.' Like most members of Emerson's audience when he addressed the Harvard Divinity School, Frost says he was angry and asked 'if anybody had a right to talk like that' (1968, 96).

> The strong gods pine for my abode,
>   And pine in vain the sacred Seven;
> But thou, meek lover of the good!
>   Find me and turn thy back on heaven.   ('Brahma,' ll. 13–16)

'What baffled me,' says Frost in another essay, 'was the Christianity in "meek lover of the good"' (1968, 114). It was a dark saying he had 'to leave the clearing of to time.' If Frost had been told that the paradise sought in vain by the 'meek lovers' of Christianity, by the Muses, and by the gods of ancient Greece is the Nirvana of the Buddhists, that information would have robbed him 'of the pleasure of fathoming depths for himself.' Even when he had lived enough to return to 'Brahma' and grapple with it, Frost still entertains the dark suspicion that Emerson, the former Unitarian minister, is a blasphemer. In urging disciples to turn their back on heaven, Emerson's Brahma is being disloyal. 'Be as treacherous as you must be for your ideals, but don't expect to be kissed good-by by the idol you go back on' (Frost, 1968, 118).

In the Boy of Winander passage from *The Prelude* the failure of the owls' boisterous halloos to respond to the youth's mimic hootings signals a return to the mere copy-speech of an empty echo after an interlude of renovating counter-love and original response. When the owls no longer respond, something seems to die in the celestial fount. But as the boy trembles on the brink of silence, an experience more profound than the responsive echoes of the birds is 'carried far into his heart.' A silence that 'baffles his best skill' to revive the quivering peal of the owls' 'long halloos' gives way to the voice of mountain-torrents, audible only to his inward ear. And at that moment, as a kind of visual replica of the lost echoes, the solemn imagery of the rocks, woods, and uncertain sky, 'received / Into the bosom of the steady lake,' enters into the boy's unconscious mind.

It seems, then, as if silence can have two results. It can be the threshold to moments when the youth dies to sound and sight into a profounder mode of consciousness, or it can be a prelude to literal death. In the first case, luminous auditory or visual experiences no longer seem to share in the discourtesy of death. Remote mountain-torrents become audible, and even a picture of the landscape is imprinted on the youth's unconscious mind. The receiving element embraces and protects what it receives, just as the 'bosom of the steady lake' tranquillizes and calms an 'uncertain heaven.' Alternatively, just as the 'long halloos and screams and echoes loud' of the owls are taken from the boy, so the boy himself is taken from the world before he is twelve years old.

In the youth's death the poet contemplates something that has died in himself. His faith in the power of any 'concourse wild / of jocund din' to renew itself seems jeopardized. The baffling silence that baffles the boy's best skill to revive the quivering peals of the owls is exactly replicated in the poet's gentle shock and bewilderment when he stands transfixed and mute before the young boy's grave. His fixed stare recalls the odd immobility of Matthew in 'The Two April Mornings,' when he looks and looks and looks again at his dead daughter's counterpart or double, yet does not wish her his.

The gentle shock that accompanies the owls' failure to respond to the boy's mimic hootings is followed by a deeper shock. The real surprise is that during the interval of silence a voice of mountain-torrents is carried far into the young boy's inward ear. As the poet stands mute and stares for a full half-hour into the youth's grave, what (if anything) does he discover? Is it some equivalent of the voice of mountain-torrents carried alive into the heart? Or is it an image of an uncertain heaven received into its bosom by the steady lake? About this mystery the poem is silent. And its silence baffles the best skill of every reader. What Wordsworth hears across the silence of the boy's death is more than a surge of great melancholy or emptiness. It may be a prophecy of being and nothingness, an oracle of God's creation *ex nihilo*, which Frye calls 'the verbal message everybody wants to kidnap but can't get hold of' (2004a, 232). All we can say with certainty is that the failure of the echo to renew itself seems to undermine the poet's hold on life. Like Mrs Moore in the Marabar cave, the poet is 'terrified over an area larger than usual; the universe, never comprehensible to [his] intellect, offer[s] no repose to [his] soul' (Forster, 1924, 150). Perhaps the best explanation of the poet's 'standing dumbly, a full half-hour, at the boy's grave' comes from Geoffrey Hartman. 'Wordsworth,' he suggests, 'injects a new emphasis on inwardness. The strange half-hour pause suggests that he looks not only at something external, a grave, but also at something within, his former heart' (1964, 21).

The finest transformation of copy-speech into counter-love takes place in Frost's masterpiece, 'The Most of It,' where the important change comes almost as an afterthought. Just as the querulous solipsist is about to accept the truth that nothing in the universe will ever answer back, a modest change occurs, signalled at first by nothing more significant than a subordinate clause introduced by a tentative conjunction, 'unless.' This clause, which starts unpromisingly, steadily expands, however, riding over line endings and culminating in a series of mythic, almost biblical anaphoras ('And landed,' 'And stumbled,' 'And forced'), which overshadow everything else in the poem.

> And nothing ever came of what he cried
> Unless it was the embodiment that crashed
> In the cliff's talus on the other side,
> And then in the far-distant water splashed,
> But after a time allowed for it to swim,
> Instead of proving human when it neared,
> And someone else additional to him,
> As a great buck it powerfully appeared,
> Pushing the crumpled water up ahead,
> And landed pouring like a waterfall,
> And stumbled through the rocks with horny tread,
> And forced the underbrush – and that was all.   ('The Most of It,' ll. 9–20)

The tone of quiet understatement returns only in the poem's last four words: 'and that was all.' But for Frost's lonely egoist this is surely enough – far more, indeed, than anything he had reason to expect at the beginning of the poem.

An unsettling ambiguity disturbs the verb 'keep' in the opening line: 'He thought he kept the universe alone.' Does the sceptic 'keep' the universe in the sense that he lives there or inhabits it? Or is he its keeper or custodian? If he is so bold as to think he is a surrogate god, the sole creator and sustainer of the world, then he will be shocked to learn that the space he inhabits is a mere acoustic chamber. For unlike the Boy of Winander, the only voice he can hear is a 'mocking echo of his own / From some tree-hidden cliff across the lake.'

The solipsist resembles Frost's half-mad egoist in 'Any Size We Please,' who, indulging in absurd theatrics, stretches out his arms 'to the dark of space' and 'in infinite appeal' speaks one word: 'Hell.' But unlike this 'outpost sentinel,' the egoist in 'The Most of It' is not constrained to shrink inside himself. He substitutes for the sentinel's 'space all curved,' which is 'wrapped in around itself and self-befriended,' a world of 'counter-love, original response.' When a force larger than himself, identified initially as a mythic presence, an impersonal 'it,' powerfully appears in the form of a 'great buck,' the observer is shaken out of his complacency. He realizes with a shock that he does not, after all, keep the universe alone. The world is larger than he is, and betrays his expectations in ways that both alarm and console him.

Reuben Brower observes that, 'though the listener' in 'The Most of It' 'does not get what he wants, the "embodiment" comes with such liveliness and objective force ... that the irony is not altogether unmitigated' (1963, 134). In other poems Frost's speakers often stumble upon rare discoveries when they least expect to. A typical example is 'For Once, Then, Something,' which Brower calls 'an oracle from a well-curb.' He praises the 'beautifully contrived ambiguity of tone and feeling in the poem's last four words': 'For once, then, something.' In staring down the well and reporting what he sees, the observer makes us feel, like Wordsworth's Boy of Winander, that 'he is looking into an "uncertain heaven" of the mind, into a reality more than physical' (1963, 137).

Richard Poirier ingeniously suggests that the young man in 'The Most of It' 'is an Adam without an Eve' (1977, 160). 'He wants to keep the universe without spending very much on it.' Poirier points out that 'the poem exists within a large poetic context of "echoing" that has been best located in English poetry by John Hollander and Angus Fletcher' (1977, 162). The young man in Frost's poem 'will not let himself be satisfied with anything that comes back to him, echo, silence, or embodiment.' But Poirier believes that there is something potently oracular about this poem, a masterpiece that 'creates adherents rather than readers,' possibly because it contains 'a vision of some fabulousness beyond domestication' (1977, 165).

In 'The Poetry of Amy Lowell,' Frost says we 'throw our arms wide with a gesture of religion to the universe; we close them around a person' (Frost, 1968, 71–2). In the first ten lines of 'The Most of It,' Adam without his Eve throws his arms wide, in a gesture to the universe, then closes them again, around not a woman but an animal. Just as Thoreau can get more pleasure from a morning with a chickadee than most men can get from a night with Cleopatra, so Frost's youth is more enthralled by a brief encounter with a buck than by a rendezvous with Eve. The phrases about 'counter-love, original response' strike

Poirier as peculiar. 'Their technical angularity makes it sound as if a prescription were being called for. And "original response" is close to oxymoronic since to call for a sound that has an unprecedented origin is to deny its capacity to be "re-sponsive," a word that in the Latin sense means to pledge back something that has once been received' (1977, 166). Poirier concludes that the young man's demands are both 'wonderful' and 'impossible.'

The great buck which pushes the crumpled water ahead of it then pours it on land like a waterfall tells the solipsist in all but words that no man keeps the universe alone. In his own brute way, the animal is the paratactic embodiment of might and force. He is the answer to the solipsist's prayer that he should have more than his 'own love back in copy speech.' The speaker is a kind of backwoods Lambert Strether. And as Poirier says, 'the poem is exciting for the largeness of its embrace, and because the man is beautifully anxious that "life" be allowed to exalt and enrapture itself' (Poirier, 1977, 166). In a world of damaged oracles, the buck allows the sceptic to feel a sublime twinge and shudder. He also gives the youth something that no prophet or beautiful woman, no god from Mount Olympus or Delphi, from Sinai or the Sermon Mount, can give him. And that is the gift of 'counter-love,' a power expressed as pure elevation – as the Face of the Other. It summons the self from on high like the voice that speaks to Job through the whirlwind or to Karshish through the thunder.

10 'A River Runs through It' and Joyce's 'The Dead'

An oracle is the acoustical equivalent of an inscape. Just as Hopkins causes the veined variety of things to rhyme and chime in Christ, so an oracle uses the charms of consonance and the binding spell of assonance, alliteration, and other 'under-ear activities' to echo and reecho a voice first heard at Delphi, Sinai, or the Sermon Mount. When end words in a story or a poem become oracles of our end, they usually resonate with other prophetic cadences and tones. As an oracle of our last end, Joyce's closing words in 'The Dead' have power to revive and expand the meaning of phrases used earlier in the story. And in Norman Maclean's 'A River Runs through It,' the coda is biblical. Its paratactic syntax and meditation on the Logos echo the opening lines in John's Gospel. 'Under the rocks are the words, and some of the words are theirs.' But it is hard to decide whether the happy solemnity of the words is bracing or defeatist. All we can say is that the spectacle of 'all things merging into one' absorbs the shock of death by recalling earlier breaks in the story when death comes unawares, casually, almost as an afterthought or as a tragedy that is unforeseen.

1

Introduced as an uncivil intrusion, as something both unnecessary and avoidable, Paul's brutal murder is all but buried in the middle of a paragraph that opens with a celebration of his artistry and grace as a fisherman. Since the wish for 'three more years' is half prayer and half prophecy, it allows Norm to pass from eulogy into elegy with beautiful naturalness and ease of tone.

At the time, I was surprised at the repetition, but later I realized that the river somewhere, sometime, must have told me, too, that he would receive no such gift. For when the sergeant early next May wakened me before daybreak, I rose and asked no questions. (Maclean, 1992, 111)

A prophetic voice can be heard sounding and resounding in these lines. We hear it first in Paul's strange fantasy, twice repeated, that he needs three more years before he 'can think like a fish.' Paul's charisma is associated with the luck and grace of heroes in romance, whose destiny is prophesied by some kind of oracle. We hear a prophetic voice again in a chain of eerie echoes – 'somewhere, sometime' – that is made even stranger by Norm's later realization that a voice he ascribes to the river is trying to tell him something he cannot quite formulate. When these 'under-ear activities,' as Seamus Heaney calls them (2002, 373), combine with echoes of speaking waters and of meanings only half understood or evaded in the mind, they do more to explain the poetic energy of 'A River Runs through It' than any summary of its plot.

Unless a repetition is transformed in the telling, it may remain a mere hollow echo, the copy-speech of a ventriloquist. In order to resonate prophetically, the repetition must sound like an oracle. It must come from outside the ventriloquist, as a form of counter-love or original response. Such are the phrases, cadences, and syntax associated with Norm's father, who announces prophetically that Norm will understand what happened to his brother only when he makes up 'a story about it and the people to go with it.' We know that these words are prophetic, because they continue to echo and reverberate in Norm's mind years after they were spoken. Indeed they seem to be the genesis of the story he is writing. Though his father's voice is heard *in* the story-teller's voice, its potency is linked to oracular uses of 'beautiful,' 'grace,' and 'art,' and to homiletic transitions like 'So it is' (89) or 'For' (111), which are difficult to paraphrase. A reader never hears these words merely *as* the words of the teller. Rather, they are Norman Maclean's way of moving forward the premonitory 'under-ear activities' once he and his story get ahead of the narrative and he finds himself out on a limb of conjecture or surmise.

The oracles we remember in 'A River Runs through It' are enigmatic and riddling. Even Paul's most transparent remarks have openings at their centre that take Norm through and beyond them. His stories tend to wander in and out of Norm's mind, coming to life with unforeseen possibilities just when he thinks he has forgotten them. An anecdote that begins as a factual report about chasing a rabbit with a car's headlights ends as a confession about failing to see a right-angled turn in the road that the rabbit is alert enough to spot. The missing event is the wreck of Paul's car, which costs him the price of a rebuilt one to repair. As a representative anecdote, the story's two-way meanings echo and reecho in Norm like some haunt of prophecy, since he is never quite sure how to interpret it.

> I rode part of the way down the Blackfoot wondering whether I had been told a little human-interest story with hard luck turned into humor or whether I had been told he had taken too many drinks and smashed hell out of the front end of his car. (1992, 16)

Offered as frail and tentative networks of connection, the two-way anecdotes are Paul's honour-bound way of letting Norm know 'that he lived other lives, even if he presented them to [him] as puzzles in the form of funny stories.' Even a 'human-interest story' can become prophetic when it leaves Norm bewildered about what precisely his brother is trying to tell him. As oracles of his 'last end,' Paul's stories continue to darken for Norm with disturbing counter-truths long after their teller is dead.

The power of Norm's father to speak *through* and *to* his son is clearest in 'USF 1919: The Ranger, the Cook, and a Hole in the Sky,' where he assumes the status of the Old Testament God addressing Job from the whirlwind. 'Then I think it was my father who spoke out of the whirlwind of my mind, and said to me, as if he had just written the Bible, "Be ye compassionate"' (1992, 230). Since Reverend Maclean knows nothing about cards, Norm is half amused by the odd commingling of impertinence and authority in his father's rebuke. The oracle warns Norm not to 'rejoice because someone with great gifts in handling cards turned out not to be even a good card player on account of something little (so he said) inside him.' Yet instead of merely repeating his father's words, Norm allows his soul to rhyme and chime with them until they begin to acquire for him the moral authority of Moses at Sinai or of Jesus on the Sermon Mount. Just as Kant is moved by the precept 'act as if the maxim of thy will were the law of the universe,' so Norm comes to life at the touch of his father's biblically cadenced words.

Though strict and Puritan in his demand for discipline, Norm's father generously extends the word 'grace' to include the gracious behaviour of civilized people. It even embraces the bounty of nature, which proves 'gracious' to Reverend Maclean and his sons whenever they walk together beside Montana's Big Blackfoot River or fish on summer days that 'are almost Arctic in length.' Though theological grace finds a counterpart in the grace of art, the clergyman insists that all forms of grace are hard to acquire. 'To him, all good things – trout as well as eternal salvation – come by grace and grace comes by art and art does not come easy' (1992, 5). The father's flexible use of words like 'grace' and 'beautiful' tempers the theological austerity of a Presbyterian minister with the healing power of Wordsworth. For the closed end games of Puritan theology, with its rigorous distinction between the elect and the damned, they substitute the more tolerant, open-ended oracles of a bountiful and generous religion of nature. The father's important distinction between the achieved and the provided explains how the beauty of the Bitterroot Mountains and the Big Blackfoot canyon is the art of God, a gift provided, whereas the art of fly-fishing or of story-telling is one of the achieved perfections.

Oddly, however, the more entranced Norm becomes by his father's words, the less he seems to understand what they say. When pushed by his father to tell all he really knows about his dead brother, Norm replies 'he was a fine fisherman' (1992, 112). 'You know more than that,' his father prods him. 'He was beautiful.' When Norm tells his father that Paul should have been 'beautiful' because his father taught him, the father becomes strangely silent, as if a better answer must await deeper understanding.

> 'My father looked at me for a long time – he just looked at me. So this was the last he and I ever said to each other about Paul's death.' (1992, 112)

The dash at the centre of that first sentence takes a reader through and beyond it. Despite the fixity of his father's stare, Norm is made aware of a daily beauty surrounding both Paul and his father, which fuels his love for each of them. Art and fly-fishing are the occasion of grace, not its cause. If they were causes of grace, they would replace the religion of Norm's father with the magic or mystique of a four-count rhythm. As in art and fly-fishing, so in people he loves, Norm often discovers a grace that educates intelligence into spirit and that allows him to explore in his writing hiding places of power. Though his father's last oracle about his son's 'last end' looks off into space, Norm now realizes that further understanding will come only when he accepts his father's challenge to write a story about Paul.

The story writing itself is Norm's delayed response to his father's strangest, least understood oracle.

> Once ... my father asked me a series of questions that suddenly made me wonder whether I understood even my father whom I felt closer to than any other man I have ever known. 'You like to tell stories, don't you?' he asked, and I answered, 'Yes, I like to tell stories that are true.'
>
> Then he asked, 'After you have finished your true stories sometime, why don't you make up a story and the people who go with it?
>
> 'Only then will you understand what happened and why.
>
> 'It is those we live with and love and should know who elude us.' (1992, 112–13)

In context, the last sentence of this prophecy refers most immediately to Norm's imperfect understanding of his father. The call for a short story or novel that will disclose the truth about their family for the first time is an astonishing request from someone who has devoted his life, not to a study of secular letters, but to meditation upon the New Testament in its Greek original. Indeed Norm wonders for a moment if he has ever truly understood the man he feels closest to. But as a connoisseur of grace wherever he can find it, in art and nature (as well as in theology), the father may be making a more reasonable request than his son suspects.

When Norm writes a fiction about people he lived with and loved but who continued to elude him, he is not merely writing a story with a known outcome or a predetermined end. On the contrary, in relating imaginatively, instead of factually chronicling, the history of his mother's one-sided love for her younger son and the tragedy of that son's murder, Norm is freshly touched by it. When Norm accepts his father's challenge by telling difficult and fugitive truths about his family in a story he makes up, we can hear a new and backward-reaching intimacy enter his voice. He responds to the tragedy from his newfound talent as a writer. Only when Norm accepts his father's challenge and makes up a story 'and the people who go with it' does he discover what really happened. If he had written an autobiography, he would have reported only what he saw happening. As Oscar Wilde says of music, the oracular passages of 'A River Runs through It' create for Norm 'a past of which [he] has been ignorant, and fills [him] with a sense of sorrows that have been hidden from [his] grief' (quoted in Frye, 2004a, 191).

As forgotten truths begin to come into focus for Norm, he realizes that 'one of our ultimate troubles was that I never wanted to hear too much about my brother' (1992, 26). Writing the story may not allow Norm to understand his brother better. But it may allow him to understand better why he failed to understand. As his father explains, 'help' is 'giving part of yourself to somebody who comes to accept it willingly and needs it badly.' Using an old homiletic transition that gives the oracle its prophetic cadence, 'So it is,' he said, 'that we can seldom help anybody. Either we don't know what part to give or maybe we don't like to give any part of ourselves. Then, more often than not, the part that is needed is not wanted' (1992, 89). Norm commands and moves the reader most when he unexpectedly reverses roles and plays the part of counsellor and guide to his father. When he tells Reverend Maclean that 'you can love completely without complete understanding,' his father confirms the wisdom of the son's saying by acknowledging, 'That I have known and preached' (1992, 112).

'We had the experience but missed the meaning,' says Eliot in 'The Dry Salvages' (II.45). One of the 'sudden illuminations' that comes into retrospective focus for Norm is the sad and disturbing truth that his mother was more carefree and intimate with Paul than with any other man, including her husband and her older son. After Paul is murdered, Norm tells us that his mother 'was never to ask me a question about the man she loved most and understood least. Perhaps she knew enough to know that for her it was enough to have loved him.' And then comes Norm's most wrenching discovery. Revealing as much about failures of love in his father as in himself, he arrives at the painful but also strangely liberating truth that Paul 'was probably the only man in the world who had held [his mother] in his arms and leaned back and laughed' (1992, 111).

Resonating most deeply with the story of its own telling is the haunting conclusion of 'A River Runs through It.' Even in conducting his own end game, Norm does everything in his power to delay and postpone it. Though he admits that 'nearly all those I loved and did not understand when I was young are dead' now, he assures us that he 'still reach[es] out to them' (1992, 113). This Virgilian gesture of stretching forth his hands in love of the farther shore harks back to an earlier moment in the story when Jessie and Norm say to each other, 'Let's never get out of touch' (1992, 85). In a daring crossing of the two time frames, the retrospective narrator then adds, 'And we never have, although her death has come between us.' The breaching of boundaries by a touching of souls who cannot be separated, even by death, may defeat the understanding almost successfully. But the last lines of the story vindicate Norm's claim by using the parataxis of four biblical conjunctions to blur the boundaries imposed by time itself, the great river that in running through, over, and between the two lovers might seem to annihilate everything of value.

> Then in the Arctic half-light of the canyon, all existence fades to a being with my soul and memories and the sounds of the Big Blackfoot River and a four-count rhythm and the hope that a big fish will rise. (1992, 113)

By repeating the four prophetic 'and's, the biblical cadences acquire their own 'four-count rhythm.' But the river is not just Robert Frost's 'cataract of death that spends to nothingness.' Earlier in the story Norm's father had been reading in his Greek New Testament the passage from John's Gospel which says 'the Word was in the beginning.' He explains cryptically that he 'used to think water was first, but if you listen carefully you will hear that the words are underneath the water' (1992, 104). To affirm the priority of universal change is to mistake the shadow of running waters for the substance of rock. It is to mistake the oracles of Heraclitus for the wisdom of John.

If Norm like his father is 'haunted by waters,' it is not because they seriously, sadly run away to fill the abyss's void with emptiness. It is because 'on the rocks are timeless raindrops,' ripples once made by the flow of water over mud which has since petrified into rock. Earlier in the story Reverend Maclean's imagination had been 'stirred by the thought that he was standing in ancient rain spattering on mud before it became rocks. "Nearly a billion years ago," I said, knowing what he was thinking' (1992, 92). Made biblical by its short coordinate syntax and its stern parataxis, the story's coda resonates with this earlier moment, a Wordsworthian 'spot of time,' and with the Logos of John's Gospel.

> Eventually, all things merge into one, and a river runs through it. The river was cut by the world's great flood and runs over rocks from the basement of time. On some of the rocks are timeless raindrops. Under the rocks are the words, and some of the words are theirs. (1992, 113)

A shudder of pre-Socratic awe runs down these lines. We tremble before the words like a guilty thing surprised, as John trembles before the terrible majesty of a Word that came into a world that knew it not. In John's Gospel the Word comes from and goes back to a world of mysterious remoteness, while the spirit that works within Norm, the story-teller, shaping his use of words, speaks in a language that is as geologically accurate as it is hallucinatory and prophetic. Wary of apocalyptic presumption, Maclean finds that by substituting a remote cause for a present effect, the bold metalepsis of the 'timeless rain-drops' allows him to take part in a seemingly endless story. His chron-icle opens toward the horizon instead of closing on a boundary. Reaching forward to embrace the testament of future story-tellers, the story's ending also moves back through layer after layer of geological history until it reaches in the world's foundation 'the basement of time' itself.

In their endings talented authors often exercise what Nietzsche calls the 'faculty of oblivion' in order to rid themselves of disappointment and a vague but nagging sense of failure. The deaths of his father and mother, his wife and his brother Paul, have all created a huge whis-pering gallery of silence for Norm. At the end of the story the narrator does not so much deny the past as reshape it. His mother always felt that he, not Paul, was the loser in the family. But by trying to prove to his mother, now a silent auditor, that she was wrong, Norm also proves she was right. Until Norm is obsessed by the fear that he is actually the less gifted and handsome son, he lacks the necessary incentive to prove his worth. And yet the more the future English pro-fessor and writer of short-story fiction is recognized as a winner, the more he also knows himself to be a loser.

Norm must prove again and again, both to himself and to his visible and invisible witnesses, that he is not what they think he is. He is a person of promise, just as worthy if not so brilliant as his brother Paul, who is an artist not only of fly-fishing but also of a generous and recep-tive hospitality to life. As Seamus Heaney says of Norman MacCaig, the art of a poet or a story-teller is like the art of 'a great fisherman, a master of the cast, of the line that is a lure.' Maclean has the 'power to get a rise out of the subject.' He has mastered, like his brother Paul, the angler's art of 'coming in at an angle' (Heaney, 2002, 399) by writing a story to exorcise a demon. When he allows the past to be past, Norm can also at last relinquish the desire to play over and over again the same self-destructive script. As the surviving brother, he no longer needs to defend his title against the fair and shining Paul, the young Apollo of the family, the beautiful misfit and loser who may also be the winner in the only sense that finally matters.

2

Since a short story achieves a maximum predetermined effect with a minimum of material, its last words often resonate strangely with spells cast by earlier sections of its narrative. We sometimes experience these spells as tricks of diction and cadence, or as intoxicating verbal charms. From 'the dark odorous stables where a coachman smoothed and combed the horse or shook music from the buckled harness' (Joyce, 1962, 30), the speaker in James Joyce's 'Araby' conjures a marvel of tactile and aural sensations. In a culture that keeps alive the power of spoken words, all language is 'grammarye,' oracular, enchanting, magical, like the runes of Norse poetry. Though the 'dark muddy lanes' with their rowdy gangs threaten violence, the fantasy of running 'the gauntlet of the rough tribes' turns the brutality and squalor of Dublin life into an adventure in the binding power of words.

Joyce's short story is a contest between threatening impressions of blindness, claustrophobia, and frustration, on the one hand, and a growth into erotic sensibility and an imagination of freedom, on the other. The main release from a hostile, constrictive culture is the story-teller's talent for casting verbal spells and charms. Most magical is the sound of the word 'Araby,' the name of the bazaar which 'cast an Eastern enchantment over' the youth (1962, 32). But when he finally arrives at the bazaar and 'looks humbly at the great jars that stood like eastern guards at either side of the dark entrance to the stall' (1962, 35), the spell he associates with allurement and mystery soon dissipates. A passport to adventure turns into an edict of exile, a harsh decree of banishment instead. Because the stern eastern guards have less in common with an enchanted Oriental garden than with the flaming brands of Milton's cherubim, who drive Adam and Eve out of paradise, they condemn the youth to disenchantment and exclusion from the charmed world he wants to enter. Instead of escaping from a sterile culture, he is left to wander in a maze, a 'creature driven and derided by vanity' (1962, 35), who consumes his life in chasing phantoms.

In most of his short stories Joyce is deeply ambivalent about the redemptive power of love: is it an altar stair that slopes through darkness up to God? Or is it an uneven roller coaster, doubtfully teleological and frightening to contemplate? The end games of Joyce's love stories often seem to promise freedom and release. But in 'The Boarding House,' the landlady who traps Mr Doran into marrying her daughter reduces sex to imprisonment. His shot-gun marriage is a fixing of boundaries rather than an opening of horizons. In another short story, 'A Painful Case,' which terminates in suicide and despair, a pilgrim who tries to ascend a Platonic ladder of love is plunged into darkness instead. The 'adventureless tale' of Mr Duffy's life is a chronicle of negatives, which fall on the ear with appalling force:

> He had neither companions nor friends, church nor creed. He lived his spiritual life without any communion with others, visiting his relatives at Christmas and escorting them to the cemetery when they died. (1962, 109)

Mr Duffy's first faltering ascent of love's ladder is the friendship he forms with Mrs Sinico, his intellectual companion and confidante. But even as he shares intimacies of consciousness with her, he hears a voice he recognizes as his own 'insisting on the soul's incurable loneliness' (1962, 111). We hear in the cadences of this voice the same condescending reserve and the same distancing habit of mind that mark Duffy's imperfect sympathy with the Irish Socialists, whose cause he embraces in theory only. 'He felt that they were hard-featured realists and that they resented an exactitude' he associates with the mincing precision of his own patrician mind, 'the produce,' he disdainfully reflects, 'of a leisure not within their reach' (1962, 111).

When Mrs Sinico becomes unexpectedly passionate, pressing his hand to her cheek, an embarrassed Mr Duffy recoils from her overtures. With Jamesian discretion, he composes a *bon mot* to fence off any progression of friendship into the greater intimacies of sex and romantic love.

> 'Love between man and man is impossible,' he hears himself saying, 'because there must not be sexual intercourse and friendship between man and woman is impossible because there must be sexual intercourse.' (1962, 112)

This oracle of self-serving prudence and timidity precipitates a disastrous downward spiral that ends with Mrs Sinico's suicide at a railway station. The newspaper column recounting her death is a repelling inventory of her physical injuries. It sounds like an autopsy or a coroner's report, in coarse contrast with the elegance and poise of Duffy's high-toned conversations with her.

Most inhuman and jarring, however, is Duffy's revulsion as he reads the paper. 'What an end! The whole narrative of her death revolted him and it revolted him to think that he had ever spoken to her of what he held sacred' (1962, 115). Unforgiving and supercilious, Duffy uses the chiasmus of his carefully calculated turn upon the hinge word 'revolted' to contrast Mrs Sinico's degradation of herself with her greater degradation of *him*. Only when Duffy begins to feel ill at ease with the thought that his friend's desperate end game has ended her life, turning her into a mere wraithlike memory, does it occur to him that his own obliteration will be no less complete. 'His life would be lonely too until he, too, died, ceased to exist, became a memory – if anyone remembered him.' As life winds down, the halting clauses contract in length, as if the speaker were drawing each breath with effort. Though the phrases broken apart by commas almost stop after 'too,' the speaker's flagging pulse starts up again in a flutter of synonyms – died,' 'ceased to exist,' 'became a memory' – before expiring altogether at the end of the next clause. And yet Duffy's ending is not total despair. Even as the void descends and Duffy experiences a silence of pure emptiness, for the first time he achieves in memory an intimacy of sound and touch that he never achieved with his friend in life. 'At moments he seemed to feel her voice touch his ear, her hand touch his' (1962, 117). In a last retrospect, more charitable than anything that precedes, Mr Duffy comes to see that, because he has denied the 'one human being' who 'had seemed to love him ... her life and happiness,' he is a lost soul himself, an 'outcast from life's feast' (1962, 117).

A more open and hopeful end game takes place in 'Eveline,' where, after a tentative commitment to her lover, a young Dublin woman wavers with indecision when the moment arrives to escape with him to South America. A parable of Joyce's own decision to seek exile outside Ireland, the story balances threatening images of closure with welcoming images of openness and freedom. But even at the end of the story, it is uncertain which force will prevail. Balancing Eveline's descent into darkness after the death of her mother and her favourite brother is the shining promise of her marriage to Frank, who is said to be 'very kind, manly, open-hearted,' and who wants her to live with him in an exciting foreign land.

As an Irish Ulysses who has sailed through the Straits of Magellan and tells strange tales of the 'terrible Patagonians,' Frank exerts a strong magnetic pull on Eveline. But her father's opposition to the marriage and her own memories of past happiness in Dublin when her mother was alive pull her in an opposite direction. Will removal from Dublin be an expulsion from Eden, like the first Eve's? Or is exile the only alternative to her mother's fate, a 'life of commonplace sacrifices closing in final craziness' (1962, 40)?

Joyce's end game is the drama of a mind torn apart, pulled two ways at once, self-divided in its loyalties. As Eveline makes her way to the boat to join Frank for the voyage to South America, she feels that instead of being rescued she is drowning.

> All the seas of the world tumbled about her heart. He was drawing her into them: he would drown her. She gripped with both hands at the iron railing. (1962, 41)

Like her crazy mother, Eveline sends out amid the seas a 'cry of anguish,' which is balanced by a swift progression in intimacy in the cry that comes to her from her equally desperate lover: 'Come,' Frank urges, 'Come,' 'Eveline,' 'Evy.' Drained of life and resolve at the climactic moment, Eveline seems frozen, 'passive, like a helpless animal.'

> He rushed beyond the barrier and called to her to follow. He was shouted at to go on but he still called to her. She set her white face to him, passive, like a helpless animal. Her eyes gave no sign of love or farewell or recognition. (1962, 41)

Since shouting is normally an energetic, boisterous activity, the use of the verb 'shout' in the passive voice is odd and disturbing. Joyce makes the pervasive paralysis even more stunning by allowing a march of short coordinate phrases to constrict like a noose in the final sentence. Using echoing negations, strange inversions of grammar, and the binding spell of an oracle's 'under-ear activities,' Joyce mines his story with depth-charges. Everywhere in *Dubliners* we feel the torpedo touch of his own impending exile.

3

The shadow of exile falls most ominously in Joyce's most famous and prophetic short story, 'The Dead,' in which Gabriel Conroy feels increasingly alienated by a need to play-act at his aunts' Christmas party and to fend off the shrill verbal assaults of Miss Ivors, a vocal Irish nationalist. Gabriel hopes to recover a more genuine identity by sharing a few moments of intimacy with his wife Gretta after they return to their hotel. As he prepares for that moment, Gabriel lingers with fond scrutiny over Gretta's slow undressing and her warm response to his overtures. As in a slow-motion seduction scene, he looks forward to calling

> her softly:
>   'Gretta!'
> Perhaps she would not hear at once: she would be undressing. Then something in his voice would strike her. She would turn and look at him ... (1962, 214)

As Gabriel half expects, Gretta is slow to answer him when the anticipated moment comes. But the apparent similarity between the loving dalliance he looks forward to and his wife's strained, distanced gaze implies a total reversal of everything his marriage ought to stand for.

> Gabriel paused for a few moments, watching her, and said:
>   'Gretta!'
> She turned away from the mirror slowly and walked along the shaft of light towards him. Her face looked so serious and weary that the words would not pass Gabriel's lips. No, it was not the moment yet. (1962, 216)

Inventing small talk to fill the silence, Gabriel now replaces the innocent delay of dalliance with a delay that seethes with anguish and barely suppressed scorn. In a 'fever of rage and desire' he longs to possess his wife. But he struggles to hold his lust at bay because he realizes that 'to take her as she was would be brutal. No, he must see some ardour in her eyes first.'

The domestic drama takes an unexpected turn when Gretta comes to Gabriel freely, as he had hoped, kisses him gently, then assures him he is 'a very generous person.' But this is as intimate and tender as she becomes. No sooner does Gabriel's heart swim 'over with happiness' as he draws his wife toward him than their domestic war breaks out on a different front. Breaking loose from his embrace, Gretta throws herself on the bed, hides her face, and admits that the song Bartell D'Arcy sang as they were leaving the party has overwhelmed and unhinged her. As Gabriel goes over the brim, Gretta goes over the top.

In a subtle interplay of new tenderness and old jealousy, Gabriel questions Gretta about the young boy, Michael Furey, who sang the song that reduces her to tears. '"Someone you were in love with?" he asked ironically.' When Gretta tells him she can see the boy's eyes plainly, Gabriel accuses her of being in love with Michael. As if deaf to the charge, Gretta says in a tone of oddly distant rapture that she used to go walking with Michael when she lived in Galway with her grandmother. Yielding to a surge of blind rage and jealousy, Gabriel betrays his suspicion that Gretta's interest in a walking-tour in Galway is only a pretext to visit her lover.

> A thought flew across Gabriel's mind.
> 'Perhaps that was why you wanted to go to Galway with that Ivors girl?' he said coldly.
> She looked at him and asked in surprise:
> 'What for?'
> Her eyes made Gabriel feel awkward. He shrugged his shoulders and said:
> 'How do I know? To see him, perhaps.'
> She looked away from him along the shaft of light towards the window in silence.
> 'He is dead,' she said at length. 'He died when he was only seventeen. Isn't it a terrible thing to die so young as that?' (1962, 219)

Talking past her husband, estranged from him by her sad, excruciating reverie, Gretta answers his questions with wrenching effort. There is a raw, jagged rhythm to the few words she manages to drag forth. Stunned, broken phrases like 'What for?' or short, hallucinatory statements like 'he is dead,' 'he died when he was only seventeen,' are fragments of an interior dream world Gabriel is barred from entering.

Gretta is unprepared for the irony that edges her husband's voice with suspicion and disdain. And Gabriel is even more shocked to discover that the youth his wife is ravished by is chaste and dead. Compared with the boy from the gasworks, who is separated from Gretta, not by the Conroys' home wars, but by the more inscrutable divide of death, Gabriel realizes he is only a clownish figure, trying to idealize his lusts and play a humiliated fool's part to amuse his aunts. Far from achieving the hoped-for truce, Gabriel's attempt to learn more about his dead rival brings the home wars to a new pitch. When Gabriel asks if her young lover died of consumption, Gretta says 'I think he died for me.' The thought of doing battle with a spectral Romeo, a shivering youth who courted Gretta from the end of a garden and died as a result, is more unnerving than the challenge of facing a flesh-and-blood rival. An amorphous terror seizes Gabriel as he registers the futility of trying to whip a fog or defeat an 'impalpable and vindictive' ghost that seems to be 'gathering forces against him' in a phantom world.

Humble and abashed now, all Gabriel can offer Gretta is the attentive ear of a counsellor and friend. When Gretta chokes with sobs, face downward on the bed, Gabriel holds her hand gently. At the end Gretta is alone in her grief. Equally isolated in a spectral world, where ghosts are more palpable than living people, Gabriel lets his wife's hand fall. 'Shy of intruding' on an experience he cannot share, he walks quietly to the window. As Gabriel begins feeding like a vampire off the life-blood of a ghost, he senses that his own identity is now just as spectral to his wife as Michael's is to him.

> He thought of how she who lay beside him had locked in her heart for so many years that image of her lover's eyes when he told her that he did not wish to live.
>
> Generous tears filled Gabriel's eyes. He had never felt like that towards any woman, but he knew that such a feeling must be love. (1962, 223)

We want Gabriel to say that now, for the first time, he can love his wife as intensely and disinterestedly as Michael did. But that is not what he can bring himself to say. As the second paragraph goes on, Gabriel seems to be confessing that, unlike his dead rival, who did not want to live without Gretta, he is incapable of feeling that way toward any woman, now or in the past. Banished by his own oracle, Gabriel is consigned instead to a 'a grey impalpable world' in which he seems to fade out and dissolve like a ghost.

When Bartell D'Arcy sings *The Lass of Aughrim*, he moves Gretta to tears precisely because he gives a staged performance in which the tenor himself is not moved. But young Michael Furey's singing is not a feat of art. Instead of merely moving Gretta, his words touch her. Gretta responds from her own centre to a centre of feeling in someone who reaches her even now, across the fearful divide of death, out of a transforming power to love. Gabriel tries to move his wife, as D'Arcy does in his song. But though artifice can move people, it seldom touches them. The artful moves of the caring husband are shattered by his wife's memory of Michael's touching her from a distance, a gesture which changes her from inside. To reach out to lovers, friends, or parents who are dead, as most mourners do in elegies, is to communicate with a mere wraith or ghost. But Gretta is bound to Michael by an eternal tie no eye can see, stretching across the space where 'the vast hosts of the dead' dwell, and into 'whose wayward and flickering existence' Gabriel can feel his own identity beginning to merge.

Whereas Michael's love for Gretta dwells in an ennobling world of adventure and romance, Gabriel's sexual longing for his wife belongs to a petty world of domestic comedy, shame and intrigue. In Gabriel's anticipation and plotting of his sexual possession of Gretta after their return from the party, Joyce invites us to contemplate a terrible potentiality of all thwarted longing and desire. Gretta is so touched by her memory of the young tenor who sang to her shortly before he died that sex with her husband now seems deformed and degraded. Sex has turned into a mere power play, in which Gabriel is the winner and she the defeated adversary. Michael's song has touched Gretta from a distance. But by shrinking to zero the distance that keeps growing between husband and wife, Gabriel's desire to be sexually intimate with Gretta reduces his hunger for love to a mere piece of failed acting. On such a stage neither husband nor wife can move or touch the other.

A writer like Joyce or Maclean is so attuned to the rhythms of prophecy or the cadences of John's Gospel that an oracular voice can be heard breaking through. Each story combines the epigrammatic weight of an oracle with the cumulative drive of a small tragedy or epic poem. 'The journey westward' that Gabriel feels he must now take is not the journey west to Galway, the county of genuine Gaelic culture, that Miss Ivors upbraids him, as a mere West Briton, for failing to take. Nor is it the mere journey home to Monkstown where he and Gretta live. The journey westward is also a journey into loneliness and death. In slow, spectral phrases, weighted with alliteration and chiasmus, the prophecy of a 'last end' sets up a disturbing tension. It contrasts warm and familiar impressions of lamplight, windowpanes, and a little gate with dark images of stormy waves, treeless hills, and barren thorns, all cold and distant. As Gabriel takes a last receding view of a world that once seemed solid, but that now begins to fade and dwindle, he is left alone with the relics of the living and 'the vast hosts of the dead.'

A few light taps upon the pane made him turn to the window. It had begun to snow again. He watched sleepily the flakes, silver and dark, falling obliquely against the lamplight. The time had come for him to set out on his journey westward. Yes, the newspapers were right: snow was general all over Ireland. It was falling on every part of the dark central plain, on the treeless hills, falling softly upon the Bog of Allen and, farther westward, softly falling into the dark mutinous Shannon waves. It was falling, too, upon every part of the lonely churchyard on the hill where Michael Furey lay buried. It lay thickly drifted on the crooked crosses and headstones, on the spears of the little gate, on the barren thorns. His soul swooned slowly as he heard the snow falling faintly through the universe and faintly falling, like the descent of their last end, upon all the living and the dead. (1962, 223–4)

Words wander in and out of the mind like an unheeded prophecy that becomes pregnant with meaning only after it begins to drift away and fade. The cadenced repetitions of phrases used earlier in the story now compose a prophecy that foretells with lucid poignancy 'the descent' of a 'last end' upon 'all the living and the dead.' As an oracle of our last end, the coda of 'The Dead' has a power to reverberate and expand. As Frye explains, an oracle is a prophecy or a vision 'that begins to speak only after we have exhausted its explicit meaning. From that explicit meaning it begins to ripple out into the remotest mysteries of what it expresses and clarifies but does not "say"' (1991, 83). Mary Jane originally uses the phrase 'last end' to explain to Mr Browne why Carthusian monks sleep in their coffins: it 'is to remind them of their last end' (1962, 201), she tells him. Presumably, if 'all life death does end, / And each day dies with sleep,' repose at the end of life, like rest after labour, is a consummation devoutly to be wished. The hand that Gabriel lets fall gently for fear of intruding on a private grief is evoked for a last time in the snow that is said to be 'falling softly upon the Bog of Allen and, farther westward, softly falling into the dark mutinous Shannon waves.' Though the entire passage is hallucinatory, it has ballast and weight. As Seamus Heaney says of Simone Weil's *Gravity and Grace*, the visionary, dreamlike world 'is imagined within the gravitational pull of the actual and can therefore,' despite its spectral qualities, 'hold its own and balance out against the historical situation' (2002, 259). In composing its lovely chiasmus of alliterating sounds, even the gentle motions of the snow, 'falling faintly through the universe and faintly falling,' exist in a state of reversible equilibrium, like an oracle that faces two ways at once.

What we love deeply, we may not understand. And what we understand or know we may not fully value. Just as a mathematician can use calculus to fashion out of infinitesimals a solid object, so out of light that is diminished into points Browning's St John can fashion the three-dimensional volume of a star. Like Shakespeare's pole-star, however, the worth of John's star may not be known, although its height is taken. In *The Cloud of Unknowing*, God must be approached through love, not knowledge. At the moment Norman Maclean realizes he may never have understood his father, he also tells us that his father is the man he feels closest to and loved most in his life. Gabriel thinks he knows his wife inside out, her every mood and gesture. But when she tells him about her spectral teen-age Romeo, the long dead Michael, his hunger for her love is quickened by the space in which the person he thinks he knows best fades into a ghost. Gabriel is wise enough to realize that he loves his wife most deeply in the space of his unknowing.

PART THREE

Owls, Bulls, and Serpents: Wisdom or Guile?

This third section of the monograph examines both the wisdom of Pytho, the serpent slain by Apollo and later used by the god as his oracle, and the wit of exuberant Irish bulls. Whether we hear the prophet-poet's voice in the Gospel oracles or the Gettysburg address, in the oracles of 'Abt Vogler' and 'Saul' or in Blake's *Jerusalem*, how are we to distinguish a wise owl from a foolish one? And how can we tell the difference between the sophistries and jests of an Irish bull and the guile of a prophet who speaks with the forked tongue of Apollo's priestess, the serpent Pythia?

In an age of evolutionary theology, Apollo may pitch his temple in the mud-bound swamp of Browning's Caliban, which breeds at first only nonsense and folly. Even in Abraham's assurance to Isaac that God himself will provide a burnt offering, Kierkegaard finds it difficult to distinguish between an inspired prophecy, which bears the mark of exalted genius, and a joke. Like Flaubert's association of the parrot with the Holy Ghost, Tennyson's obsession with the flower in the crannied wall and with mantra-like repetitions of proper names throws over an apparently trite object or an empty phrase a halo of the sacred. The smallest leaf or flower has power to utter something stupendously important. Only our prodigious stupidity has prevented our hearing or understanding what the oracle has to say.

In emerging from the inane, plunging stormfully across the astonished earth, then plunging again into the inane, Carlyle's pilgrim in *Sartor Resartus* seems to be passing from one emptiness to another. Is his passage as transient or fugitive as the flight of Bede's bird into the mead hall, then out again into the night? Or is the apparent emptiness of the 'inane' a hiding place of power? What operation of sense or faith allows the 'inane' to grow, first into an interesting uncertainty, then into an incomprehensible certainty, and finally into a radiant dwelling place of God?

11 The Wise Owl:
George Eliot's Arrested Wit

Whereas an oracle of simple assertion or decree is a broadcasting megaphone that amplifies the voice of an ascendant sage and his adherents, an oracle that invites a listener's participation and response looks several directions at once. It should be sharply pointed enough to skewer the attention of a wayward mind. But if such an oracle is to command wide assent, it must also appear to be judicious and wise. As Johnson both affirms and illustrates in *The Preface to Shakespeare*, once 'the pleasures of sudden wonder are ... exhausted,' a wise oracle must appear to 'repose' with authority 'on the stability of truth' (1959, 241).

Combining stability and repose in equal measure, Johnson's definition of wit is wisely oracular. True wit, he insists, rotates securely on an axis of truth, whose poles are the new and the natural, the surprising and the just. When Johnson in his *Dictionary* defines an uxorious man as someone 'infected with connubial dotage,' we are shocked by the energy of his contempt. Is his wording not more arresting than just? Without accusing Johnson of serving up as a maxim or a general truth his own disenchantment with marriage, we may feel in his equation of marital enslavement with senility a personal anxiety seeping through. If his definition is memorable, it is not because it is just, but because it registers the painful truth of Johnson's own crumbling marriage to Tetty. Though Johnson was distraught when his wife died, toward the end of her life she 'was always drunk,' according to Robert Levet, 'and reading Romances in her Bed, where She killed herself by taking Opium' (quoted in Bate, 1975, 237).

Unlike Johnson's prudential wisdom, which preserves as well as subverts authority, the wisdom literature of the Book of Job 'touches upon sublimity, of a highly negative kind: "Will he make a covenant with thee?" Even as a child,' writes Harold Bloom, 'I blinked at this divine sarcasm. As a bombardment of exuberances, it is unanswerable, and substitutes power for justification' (2004, 18). Many of the Book of Job's oracles seem more self-destructive than wise. When God speaks to Job from the whirlwind, he asks Job

> where shall wisdom be found? and where is the place of understanding? Man knoweth not the price thereof; neither is it found in the land of the living.

Though Bloom maintains that 'the Book of Job offers wisdom,' he admits that 'it is not anything we can comprehend. Hence the superb poem of chapter 28:12–18, which gives us no choice except yielding to its eloquence' (2004, 20). But if wisdom is as elusive as God says it is, how can we say that the oracles in Job are wise? Would a wise God justify a tyranny over man of unpredictable violence and cruelty? In telling his victims to submit to him and obey him without expecting him to love them in return, is Job's God not, in effect, confirming Yeats's insight that 'Wisdom is the property of the dead, / A something incompatible with life' ('Blood and the Moon,' ll. 49–50)?

Northrop Frye maintains that the wisdom of Koheleth, the preacher in Ecclesiastes, consists, by contrast, in his injunction to 'live joyfully' (9:9). 'The secret of wisdom is detachment without withdrawal.' Or 'to put Koheleth's central intuition into the form of its essential paradox: all things are full of emptiness' (1982, 123). Whereas Frye discerns in Koheleth a constructive prophet who transforms 'the conservatism of popular wisdom into a program of continuous mental energy,' Harold Bloom broods upon Koheleth's 'sense of life as a waning but extraordinary gift.' He sees in Ecclesiastes only 'the wisdom of annihilation, of Hamlet and Lear, and perhaps of Shakespeare himself' (2004, 23–4, 31).

Many of Shakespeare's wisest soliloquies are meditations on time. The most reflective of them touch on Ecclesiastes' insight that time, like death, is the great leveller: there is nothing new under the sun, including the reflection there is nothing new, which was old when Koheleth said it. To reflect on time is to abate its terrors. It is to flow with time and be part of its passage. Though time is the remorseless devourer in Ulysses' great speech in *Troilus and Cressida*, memory can subdue the terrors of its monstrous 'backward and abysm' by rescuing its fragments of the past from oblivion, as Miranda does in *The Tempest*.

Jacques's aria on the seven stages of man in *As You Like It* is a species of wisdom writing requiring the use of allegorical Everymen or types. Though the succession of the play's seven acts is inexorable, there is no need to be depressed by the two-dimensional quality of the acting. For at each stage every actor has a large repertoire of dramatic parts to play. Jacques celebrates the zest as well as the folly of the performance. He is melancholy without being melancholic: satiric without being cynical or disillusioned.

Progress through the stages of life is also the subject of Feste's lyrical soliloquy, 'Hey, ho, the wind and the rain,' which he sings alone on the stage at the end of *Twelfth Night*. The male member was only 'a foolish thing' when Feste was 'a little tiny boy.' But the clown has to do more than swagger about his male prowess when he comes 'alas! to wive.' Indeed, if the aging lover falls drunk on the beds of too many mistresses, his foolish 'toy' may fail him altogether.

As Feste says of the duped Malvolio, 'the whirligig of time brings in his revenges.' The most humiliating of these revenges is the lost innocence of the 'little boy,' the failed potency of the young man, the lost wisdom of age, which sedates its fall with drink. Only a clown's playful wit blunts the loss and balances with wise folly what one critic calls the clown's 'beautiful sadness of acceptance' (Bloom, 1998, 246). Most panoramic is the final stanza, which runs all times together.

> A great while ago the world begun,
>> With hey, ho, the wind and the rain,
> But that's all one, our play is done,
>> And we'll strive to please you everyday. (*Twelfth Night*, V.i.414–17)

The playwright's wisdom is not immortal: it is not immune to time's revenges. But like God's creation of the world 'a great while ago,' it is a light to order chaos and a power by which to live.

In his much darker quest for wisdom Macbeth is defeated by progressions that appear to repeat endlessly. Banquo's heirs retreat down history in unending succession. And instead of any quick succession of 'surcease' by 'success,' report of Duncan's murder is likely to reverberate like the echo of 'Might be' in 'be-all,' of 'be-all' in 'end-all,' of the first 'here' in the second 'here,' and so on forever.

> If the assassination
> Could trammel up the consequence; and catch
> With his surcease success; that but this blow
> Might be the be-all and the end-all here,
> But here, upon this bank and shoal of time,
> We'd jump the life to come.   (*Macbeth*, I.vii.1–7)

Equally alarming is the grating of hard 'c' sounds in 'could,' 'conse-quence,' 'catch,' 'success,' which like gossip or rumor seems to spread its harsh dissonances everywhere. Once pity strides the blast and heaven's cherubim are unleashed upon the couriers of the air, their onslaughts are interminable (I.vii.21–5). Nothing can deter the mes-sengers till Macbeth's horrid deed is blown in every eye.

Only in his final soliloquy, 'To-morrow, and to-morrow, and to-morrow,' does Macbeth confront without illusion the emptiness of a world in which time is just one tick-tock after another. This is the disin-toxicated time the drug addict fears, and its emptiness seems to be one precondition of wisdom both here and in Koheleth's hard sayings in Ecclesiastes. His wife 'should have died hereafter; / There would have been a time for such a word' (*Macbeth*, V.v.17). In a wisdom born of dis-enchantment and despair, Macbeth cannot accept a 'hereafter.' His expe-rience does not validate or justify it. Nor can he grieve for his dead wife. Like Sisyphus forever rolling his stone uphill, there is nothing he can feel. His soliloquy is too stunned and drained of energy for grief.

As in Ecclesiastes, it is the experience of nothingness itself that has to be understood, not just the prospect that Banquo's progeny will live on and prosper long after Macbeth has ceased to exist. We should not mistake his soliloquy for a meditation on mutability or a simple recog-nition that life goes on for only a limited span of time. Macbeth's expe-rience of nothingness is as startling as Koheleth's and just as terrifying. To gain some understanding of it we may compare Macbeth's solilo-quy to Hamlet's discourse in the graveyard. While contemplating Yorick's skull, Hamlet traces the dissolution of Alexander from world conqueror into dust, earth, and loam to stop a beer barrel. In reflecting on the nothingness of human matters, Hamlet anticipates the nihilism Lear confronts on the heath. In filial ingratitude, the pride of great ones, and the nothingness that comes of nothing, the king experiences a very strong form of emptiness.

There are qualities in Lear's daughter that defy acting out, and that disguise her virtues as animal-like stubbornness and cruelty. When her scheming sisters outbid her in the auction for their father's love,

Cordelia, like Actaeon confronted by the hounds about to tear him to pieces, struggles to say something to satisfy her father. But the only word that comes out is 'nothing.' To Lear Cordelia, like Ovid's Io, assumes the semblance of an animal. Though in contrast to her sisters, she never has the property of being an animal, Cordelia's 'nothing' appears as monstrous to her father as the non-human animalhood that prevents the enraged Othello and the murderous Macbeths from being persons.

In several reflective soliloquies earlier in the play, Macbeth has used conceited diction as a drug. The daggers that cause a breach or rent in nature are said to be breeched in the grooms' blood. Even Duncan's gilded gore and silver skin turn him from butchered guest into embalmed saint. As Macbeth continues to sedate himself with metaphor, the enormity of his conceits also swallows up the enormity of his crimes.

> Will all great Neptune's ocean wash this blood
> Clean from my hand? No, this my hand will rather
> The multitudinous seas incarnadine
> Making the green one red.   (*Macbeth*, II.ii.60–3)

Taking refuge in Latinate diction, Macbeth makes language as extravagant as his deeds. He crowds a hypermetric line with two polysyllabic words that push everything else to one side, including the lines' nominal subject, the enormous guilt and weight of his crimes.

I find it as difficult to extract wisdom from the disenchantment of Macbeth's last soliloquy as to extract wisdom from Koheleth. Each is full of emptiness. But in neither case can I find any trace of illusion or any retreat into dishonest metaphor or drugged diction. Instead of saying something fine which perpetuates illusion, both Koheleth and Macbeth say something exact which dispels illusion, as sun dispels mist or vapour. Even if the only light is now a flickering taper that casts a guttering flame on nothing more substantial than a shadow in Plato's cave, it is enough to bring strenuous illusion to an end.

> To-morrow, and to-morrow, and to-morrow
> Creep in this petty pace from day to day
> To the last syllable of recorded time;
> And all our yesterdays have lighted fools
> The way to dusty death.   (Macbeth, V.v.19–23)

Ironically, the words 'last syllable' and 'dusty death' appear in medial position: even the soliloquy's last phrase, 'Signifying nothing,' occupies a half-line of verse. It is as if Macbeth's strength gives out before he can reach the end of his blank verse lines. In appalling contrast, time creeps on forever. Its last syllable is never reached, not even in the line in which 'syllable' halts before a medial caesura. Macbeth wants to blow out the candle. But a last tiny increment or syllable of recorded time is something he continues to approach without ever reaching. It is like a limit in calculus or a target that Zeno's arrow moves toward but never hits.

1

One of the most accomplished masters of wise oracles is George Eliot, the sibyl of Victorian myth criticism. Her Delphi is Tübingen and her Apollo David Friedrich Strauss, the author of *Das Leben Jesu*, a work she translates into English. Eliot's best maxims are located somewhere between the two extremes of platitude and paradox. If her aphorisms veer too far in the direction of puzzle or paradox, they turn into unintelligible riddles. And if they go too far in the other direction, they dwindle into truisms. To retain her poise as a wise and judicious owl, Eliot also has to arrest her sibylline wit and check her impulse to demolish such targets of her satire as Casaubon and Bulstrode.

In chapter 29 of *Middlemarch*, the voice that interrupts George Eliot's narrator in mid-sentence asks questions that sound at first more riddling than wise. 'But why always Dorothea? Was her point of view the only possible one with regard to this marriage?' (1956, 205). Just when this quizzical sibyl seems to humanize Casaubon by saying he is spiritually hungry like the rest of us, she gently pokes fun at him. The sibyl implies that Casaubon marries a young bride, not because she is fresh and blooming, but because her husband feels 'she is more educable and submissive.' The unheard words behind her maxims come from Shakespeare's eleventh sonnet: 'She carv'd thee for her seal, and meant thereby / Thou shouldst print more, nor let that copy die' (ll. 13–14). But in Eliot's hands the similar sentiments that inform the couplets of sonnets 10 and 12 begin to erode. 'Times had changed,' she warns us. There is no Victorian equivalent of Shakespeare, no sonneteer like Christina Rossetti or her brother to urge Casaubon to leave behind a copy. The wise saying from Shakespeare provides Eliot, not with a confirming example, but with a damaging counter-example and pun.

Leaving behind no copies of his masterpiece, the key to all mythologies, Casaubon has no issue. The repeated pun on 'copy' and the double meaning of 'issue' drive home a point that makes the oracle more wittily destructive than wise.

Yet time, the enemy that conspires against Casaubon, enlists our compassion for him, too. When the sibyl announces that 'times had altered since then,' we are reminded that the alteration is true in a double sense. We are moderns, not Elizabethans. And if we live long enough, like Casaubon, we shall sooner or later experience the panic of the same closing door. The man who 'was fast leaving the years behind him' is at least evoked in the active voice. But the second time she expresses the thought, the sibyl turns the words just a little by changing Casaubon into a passive agent. His domestic delights, instead of leaving the years behind, are now 'left behind by the years.'

Eliot uses a trite but consoling aphorism to encapsulate male stereotypes of women. 'Providence, in its kindness, had supplied him with the wife he needed.' This value frame is destructive in its understated irony and wit. And the oracle it frames is a deadly commonplace, flattering to the male ego but a libel to women. 'With the purely appreciative, unambitious abilities of her sex,' Dorothea, we are told, 'is sure to think her husband's mind powerful.' There is a play here on the adverb 'purely.' Casaubon thinks his wife is uncontaminated by critical animus, too innocent to be unappreciative. But for Eliot 'purely' is also a synonym for 'merely.' The idea that Dorothea is merely unambitious and in that sense unappreciative is slanderous and self-deceiving. The dangerous prophecy about women who are timidly admiring begins to effervesce when the narrator uses the value frame a second time: 'Whether Providence had taken equal care of Miss Brooke ... was an idea which could hardly occur to him.' Deft inversion generates a final subversive thought. 'Society never made the preposterous demand that a man should think as much about his own qualifications for making a charming girl happy as he thinks of hers for making himself happy.' Allowing the etymology of 'preposterous' to come disconcertingly to life, Eliot uses a strident chiasmus ('man,' 'charming girl,' 'hers, 'himself') to mark the grave of a deficient male empathy.

To repair the oracles, Eliot must demolish axioms of bigotry and male prejudice. It seems irrational to Casaubon that 'a man could choose not only his wife but his wife's husband! Or as if he were bound to provide charms for his posterity in his own person.' And yet what could be more reasonable? Shouldn't a husband's greatest recommendation be a grace of self-command? And shouldn't we expect a father to endow his offspring with appealing attributes? We may laugh at Casaubon for expecting marriage to produce happiness automatically, like soda that pours out of a vending machine. But at the very moment Eliot seems to flatten Casaubon into a two-dimensional caricature, her sentences become more balanced and judicious.

> It is an uneasy lot at best, to be what we call highly taught and yet not to enjoy: to be present at this great spectacle of life and never to be liberated from a small hungry shivering self – never to be fully possessed by the glory we behold, never to have our consciousness rapturously transformed into the vividness of a thought, the ardour of a passion, the energy of an action, but always to be scholarly and uninspired, ambitious and timid, scrupulous and dimsighted. (Eliot, 1956, 206–7)

Keats says that Pope rode upon a rocking horse and called it Pegasus. Half satirist and half sibyl, Eliot rides upon the same horse and calls it prophecy. Her anatomy of Casaubon's psyche is neither wholly judgmental nor wholly approving. The march of negative phrases, 'uneasy lot,' 'small hungry shivering self,' 'uninspired,' 'timid,' 'dimsighted,' might serve as an epitaph for many a pedant's tomb. But even as she skewers Casaubon on a spit, she allows her vision of rapturous transformation and glory to stir her imagination of what a scholar might achieve.

Though Eliot alludes to Shakespeare's aphorism about the need to make copies of ourselves, she never quotes it. And when she cannot find an appropriate Greek epigram, she invents one: 'Doubtless some ancient Greek has observed' (1956, 207), she muses. Often she precedes a devastating critique with a warning sign, like a barrier at a railway crossing or a flashing red light. Casaubon's 'religious faith wavered,' we learn, 'with his wavering trust in his own authorship, and the consolations of the Christian hope in immortality seemed to lean on the immortality of the still unwritten Key to all Mythologies' (1956, 206). The repetition of 'immortality' imparts the shimmering illusion of a mirage. And the chiasmus is just as tremulous. The unstable turn on 'faith wavered,' 'wavering trust,' may imply that Casaubon's unfinished key is to be a religious apology. Or it may imply that Casaubon's religious faith is just as fragile as his scholarship. His real belief in immortality is based not on his Christian faith but on his hope of vicarious immortality as a scholar.

Often the wisest oracles in *Middlemarch* appear in epigraphs. They fall like shadows cast by more substantial oracles in the narrative to come. The marriage prayer from the Book of Tobit (the epigraph for chapter 74) prepares for the great aphorisms on marriage in the Finale. But the wise sayings about truth and candour that are ironically foretold by the marriage prayer, 'mercifully grant that we may grow old together,' are not true prayers but clever exercises in redefining words. The love of truth – 'a wide phrase' – is narrowed to mean 'a lively objection to seeing a wife look happier than her husband's character warranted' (1956, 543). Instead of reaping a harvest of memories in common with her husband, Mrs Bulstrode is the focus of vicious community gossip. Instead of bringing enlightened satisfaction, candour brings only unhappiness and gloom. There is more Schadenfreude than 'ardent charity' in the zeal with which 'the virtuous mind' sets about 'to make a neighbor unhappy for her good.'

Eliot's wisest oracles acknowledge the propriety of embracing silence and humiliation. They affirm the wisdom of renouncing wise sayings. Mrs Bulstrode is a wise wife precisely because she can survive 'the ardent charity' of her neighbours. She will be made 'unhappy for' her own 'good' – and for the good of her marriage – in a way her friends cannot begin to understand. At the moment Harriet joins Nicholas 'in mournful but unreproaching fellowship,' no wise saying or spoken word can accurately express the 'movement of new compassion and old tenderness' that passes 'through her like a great wave.' None of the words in quotation marks are actually spoken. Harriet shrinks 'from the words which would have expressed their mutual consciousness, as she would have shrunk from flakes of fire.'

Most harrowing is the wise saying about wives who merely feign intimacy with disgraced husbands, while silently admonishing their fall from grace. 'There is a forsaking,' we are told, 'which still sits at the same board and lies on the same couch with the forsaken soul, withering it the more by unloving proximity.' This wise saying concentrates its sting in the oxymoron of an 'unloving proximity.' A profanation of such intimacies as sleeping and eating together dramatizes what Yeats calls 'the perpetual virginity of the soul.' Its cruel pretences are a grotesque parody of Harriet's ritual act of sobbing out 'her farewell to all the gladness and pride of her life' and of remaining by her husband's side, united with him in 'shame and isolation.'

The aspirations of the Prelude are too protean to be fixed in any wise or witty oracle. But the Finale, which is more prophetic, opens with an oracle that limits the very idea of a last or conclusive word: 'Every limit is a beginning as well as an ending,' Eliot tells us. This wise saying invites us to peer over the edge or boundary of Eliot's novel. It teaches us what to 'overlook,' both in the sense of what to look over and what to remove from view.

Though marriage is the boundary of many novels, including *Middlemarch*, it 'is still a great beginning.' This observation launches Eliot into one of her most memorable prophecies. There are no guarantees: years may bring an 'irremediable loss,' since time is never the sample of an even web. Promises may be broken and 'an ardent outset may be followed by' loss and decline. But when 'latent powers ... find their long-awaited opportunity,' marriage, she foresees, may make the advancing years a climax and age the harvest of memories in common. This great oracle seems wise, because it rests upon two poles of truth, disillusionment and hope, honesty and expectation, each duly acknowledged, but each made to support and qualify the other.

Like the 'home epic' itself, the prophecy is ample and expansive. It seems to repose securely, like Fielding's novels, upon an axis of lived experience and truth. *Middlemarch* invites us to relax into the spacious similes, prophetic asides, and slow narrative pace favoured by a less frenzied age. In the past, we are reminded, 'the days were longer (for time, like money, is measured by our needs) ... summer afternoons were spacious, and the clock ticked slowly in the winter evenings' (1956, 105). In such a world even 'past error may urge a grand retrieval,' since in the ease of Eliot's great epic fiction people seem freer to acquire and exercise the leisure to be wise.

A wry aphorism gently deflates the pride of authors by equating the writing of books with the plagiarist's art: 'There was no need to praise anybody for writing a book,' the oracle assures us, 'since it was always done by somebody else.' Out of context, the aphorism sounds more cynical than wise. But restored to its context, it resonates in sympathy with the gentle humour of Eliot's portrayal of Fred Vincy and Mary Garth. Whereas the merit of Fred's book on agriculture is attributed to Mary, Mary's book on Plutarch's stories is ascribed to Fred, who had benefited from a university education. There is a left-handed justice in the indirect praise accorded ghost writers, even when justice is withheld from authors who write their own books.

As suits a Finale, many of the novel's concluding aphorisms are as bleakly concise in their strict autonomy as gravestone inscriptions. This is especially true of the epitaph the narrator plants on Lydgate, who fails to keep his most important promises, the ones he makes to himself. The light-hearted aphorism that Lydgate wrote a treatise on gout, 'a disease which has a good deal of wealth on its side' (1956, 610), cannot disguise the bitterness of his gibe that his wife is his basil plant, a herb which 'had flourished wonderfully on a murdered man's brains.' Ironically, it is Lydgate who is implicated in the homicide of Raffles. But the true murderer is Rosamond, who destroys her husband's most noble ambition, his dream of becoming a Victorian Vesalius. She is responsible for the sad conclusion of a life that describes a trajectory the exact opposite of her own: a sad 'declension' after the ardour of a signally promising 'outset' (1956, 607).

Outwardly, Lydgate is a success, even to his wife, who values income above achievement, and who is provided, not with the 'threatened cage in Bride Street,' but with all the 'flowers and gilding, fit for the bird of paradise that she resembled.' The oracle focuses on similarities between marriage and a prison, made tolerable only by the gold and tropical flora that cater to the whims of a rare exotic bird. And yet coming in a coordinate clause after a tribute to his well-remunerated medical skills, the judgment is crushing. Its disapproval of Lydgate is no less devastating for being all but buried in the inventory of achievement and apparent success that surrounds him: 'but he always regarded himself as a failure; he had not done what he once meant to do' (1956, 610).

Many of the oracles in *Middlemarch* are set in passages of free indirect discourse that allow Eliot to enter into the minds of Dorothea's complacent male critics while still exposing the smugness of their views. These wise but self-damaging oracles cluster round a nucleus of male prejudices, most flagrantly apparent in the paragraph beginning: 'And how should Dorothea not marry?' The question distantly echoes the opening words of *Pride and Prejudice*, whose epigrammatic wit harks back to an exemplum tradition Eliot shares with Austen: 'It is a truth universally acknowledged, that a single man in possession of a large fortune, must be in want of a wife.' A wife who reads theological books and fasts like a Papist may well devise utopian schemes to 'interfere with political economy and the keeping of saddle horses.' The undiscriminating male mind is gently mocked in the adage that places saddle horses on a par with politics. Only the insecurity of a reactionary like Mr Brooke, who is most 'watchful, suspicious, and greedy' about such personal items as his snuff-box, or of an egoist like Casaubon, would make a man 'naturally think twice before he risked himself in such fellowship.'

More alarming is the sentiment that 'women were expected to have weak opinions,' a male prejudice which Eliot immediately turns into the more radical and dangerous view that 'the great safeguard of society, and of domestic life was, that opinions were not acted on.' Lethargy is promoted as a civic virtue. Energy of mind is to be tolerated only in academic debates where it can be diffused at a safe distance from politics. The most preposterous oracle is the last one, which presumes to redefine the word 'sanity.' Samuel Johnson insists that all predominance of imagination over reason is a degree of insanity. Dorothea's male critics go one step further by associating all nonconformity with lunacy. Having narrowed the definition of 'sanity' to 'doing what one's neighbors do,' the oracle then calls any woman who refuses to conform a threat to civilized society. The free spirit praised by Mill in his essay on *Liberty* is now discredited as a madwoman. 'Sane people did what their neighbors did, so that if any lunatics were at large, one might know and avoid them.'

What complacent epicures like Brooke truly fear is that 'hereditary strain of Puritan energy,' so notably lacking in the aristocracy, but glowing intensely in his precocious niece. 'Riding,' we are told, 'was an indulgence which [Dorothea] allowed herself in spite of conscientious qualms; she felt that she enjoyed it in a pagan sensuous way, and always looked forward to renouncing it' (1956, 7). The ascetic pleasure of renouncing pleasure is as keen as the pleasure itself. Puritanism resurfaces in the 'glorious piety' Dorothea would willingly 'endure' as the wife of John Milton after his 'blindness had come on' (1956, 7). Her oddly ascetic view of marriage is expressed most memorably in her maxim that 'the really delightful marriage must be that where your husband was a sort of father, and could teach you even Hebrew, if you wished it' (1956, 8). This delusion comes to a focus in Celia's protest to her sister, which is as solemnly prophetic as it is wittily good-natured: 'O Dodo, you must keep the cross yourself.' That is, if you insist on such delightful delusions about the desirable qualities in a husband, then you are a more stupid misfit than the dodo bird and must suffer the consequence, which may include extinction of your species.

In an extraordinary passage, Eliot's narrator pretends to be unmoved by grief and indifferent to Dorothea's despair on her honeymoon. To our surprise, she focuses on what is ordinary or commonplace in most disillusion. We are told that 'many souls in their young nudity are tumbled out among incongruities and left to "find their feet" among them' (1956, 144). Eliot's wise sibyl treats Dorothea as a raw, uncultivated child who is no more capable of interpreting Rome, the city of 'visible history,' than of tracing the contours of her husband's mind. The oracle looks two ways at once. Does Dorothea stagger under 'the weight of unintelligible Rome' only because Rome, like Casaubon, is a labyrinth of 'deep degeneracy' and superstition? Or is the true labyrinth a maze of Dorothea's own making? Is it due to her ignorance as a child of meagre histories and starved Protestant sensibilities? When suffering has refined and matured her nude, untutored soul, perhaps her creator will show her more sympathy. Until then, Dorothea's dream of being married to a great scholar is rejected as indulgent and delusive. Even her 'faintness of heart' and 'discouragement' may be necessary as a precondition of learning to grow up.

Eliot inoculates her readers against any deep emotional response to her heroine by using an enthymeme to equate all moving experience with what is marvellous or extraordinary. It should be obvious that the disappointment of a bride on her honeymoon is not an uncommon event. It should therefore follow with the rigour of a syllogism that no reader should be deeply distressed by Dorothea's 'fit of weeping six weeks after her wedding.' But at the moment Eliot seems to clinch the argument, logic and feeling start pulling apart. We do not react as Eliot predicts. On the contrary, our hearts are as sharply wrenched as Dorothea's is. Eliot's two concluding oracles in this astonishing paragraph, which are as memorable as any she ever speaks, try to educate our emotional intelligence. They set readers in search of discovering why they are moved and why it is important that they should be moved if they hope to be deepened in their humanity while remaining critically aloof from life's predictable embarrassments and despairs.

The first oracle alerts us to the disturbing truth that if we are unmoved by Dorothea's grief, it is because our scale for measuring refined emotion is too 'coarse' and crude. Only creatures more finely tuned to suffering would be capable of responding sensitively to Dorothea's grief, which is now dignified with the grave attribute of 'tragic.' As a variation of the noun 'course,' the adjective 'coarse' means common or ordinary. But it also acquires a pejorative shadow meaning as a synonym for what is raw or unrefined. This secondary meaning comes to life in Eliot's disturbing oracle that the 'element of tragedy which lies in the very fact of frequency, has not yet wrought itself into the coarse emotion of mankind.' But as if to correct the discourtesy of making what is 'coarse' or ordinary a term of reproach, Eliot immediately adds the consoling afterthought that 'perhaps our frames could hardly bear much of it.' Far from opposing what is common to what is moving or extraordinary, Eliot confers a new value on what is commonplace, even when it is raw and unrefined (or 'coarse' in the less appealing sense of that word). Both the disappointment of the wedding trip to Rome and Dorothea's exalted imagination of what marriage ought to be are plainly present. As the young bride looks out on two worlds at once, the ordinary and the marvellous exist together in reciprocal dignity.

The providential quality of 'coarseness,' which exquisitely adjusts each perception to the viewer, is the subject of a final prophecy. 'If we had a keen vision and feeling of all ordinary human life, it would be like hearing the grass grow and the squirrel's heart beat, and we should die of the roar which lies on the other side of silence. As it is, the quickest of us walk about well wadded with stupidity.' The oracle turns on an axis of repose, poised between a fine appreciation of the ordinary and an exalted sense of wonder. The prophet who sees splendour in the grass and glory in the flower sees with the eye of an awakened imagination. But the sibyl also possesses the double vision that allows her to see two sides of the same event. To die of a rose in aromatic pain is hardly the height of felicity. Nor is it a consummation devoutly to be wished to die of the roar that lies on the far side of silence. Indeed, to be finely attuned to the marvellous or exquisite side of every commonplace event is to suffer a refined sense of torture. Though most progress is most failure, our defects of vision are protective covering, like knee or shoulder pads, which prevent our exposure to more pain than we can bear. This is why even 'the quickest witted of us' have to 'walk about well wadded with stupidity' (1956, 144). A fool like Celia or a clown like Mr Brooke can see why Dorothea's marriage to Casaubon is a subject for comedy. But it takes a wise sibyl like the narrator to see why our nerves or senses have to filter out experiences that might unbalance us or make us unstable. Perhaps, like Lear's madness, Dorothea's weeping during her honeymoon in Rome is 'what our sanity would be if it weren't under such heavy sedation all the time' (Frye, 1986, 119–20).

The discussion between Will Ladislaw and Dorothea on the subject of poetry culminates in Will's astonishing pronouncement that Dorothea herself is a poem (1956, 166). In his earlier praise of poets, he commends the emotional intelligence that allows 'knowledge' to pass 'instantaneously into feeling and feeling' to flash 'back as a new organ of knowledge.' Will's understanding of the poet has affinities with Coleridge's theory of primary and secondary imagination. Without actually writing any poems, a scholar or scientist may possess the synthesizing power of a poetic imagination. Whereas Ladislaw enlarges our understanding of poetry, Dorothea wants to narrow it: 'I think you leave out the poems,' she good-naturedly protests. Even in accepting the prize word 'poet' that Ladislaw generously bestows on her, she is amused that someone who shares 'the poet's consciousness in his best moods' should never feel inclined to write a sonnet or an ode.

Though Eliot's oracles are usually wise, they are also often wittily destructive. A philanthropist, she muses, is 'a man whose charity increases directly as the square of the distance' (1956, 281). It is easier to be charitable as the chairman of a trust, at a safe distance from the object of one's charity, than face to face with an importunate beggar asking for alms. Even the deceptive power of metaphor provides Eliot with a fund of critical aphorisms. Love and affection are not items that earn interest like a bank account. To think that a postponement of their use will be honoured like a bank draft is to be seriously misled by the metaphor.

> Poor Mr. Casaubon had imagined that his long studious bachelorhood had stored up for him a compound interest of enjoyment, and that large drafts on his affections would not fail to be honored; for we all of us, grave or light, get our thought entangled in metaphors, and act fatally on the strength of them. (1956, 63)

The treachery of language, which dupes us all, and the peculiar vulnerability of 'poor Mr. Casaubon' create a strong pole for sympathy. But compassion does not last long. For the more Eliot exposes metaphor's bewitchment of Casaubon, until only 'a certain blankness of sensibility' remains, the more crushing her judgments become.

2

By dramatizing the danger of too exclusive an optical selection, the epigraphs in *Middlemarch* often verify the wisdom of Eliot's parable of the pier-glass, which associates harmony with illusion and accurate perception with incoherence or disorder. For a flattering illusion of concentric arrangement, these epigraphs substitute two-way aphorisms and double meanings that put platitude or truism to the test. Some of these epigraphs challenge simpleminded criticisms of characters like Bulstrode and Lydgate. In chapter 53, for example, the opening aphorism attacks the critic who mistakes the logical inconsistency of the casuist, Bulstrode, for insincerity. Without condoning Bulstrode, the aphorism makes us aware of his intense inner life, of a 'living myriad' of concealed traps and self-deceptions, whose complexity no simple syllogism or enthymeme can hope to track or reconstruct.

> It is but a shallow haste which concludeth insincerity from what outsiders call inconsistency – putting a dead mechanism of 'ifs' and 'therefores' for the living myriad of hidden suckers whereby the belief and conduct are wrought into mutual sustainment. (1956, 380)

By opposing what is deep, devious, and organic to what is superficial and dead, Eliot confers a primordial energy on Bulstrode. To square his religious code with his criminal behaviour, Bulstrode has to writhe and squirm like an octopus or squid. Though the submarine monster may repel us, we have to concede that its sinister tentacles and 'hidden suckers' have more resilient life and suppler power than any logic machine operating with a calculus of hypothetical 'ifs' and syllogistic 'therefores.'

The masses of spider-web that Bulstrode uses to pad his moral sensibility give rise to another wise oracle, the epigraph from *Rasselas* that introduces chapter 61. '"Inconsistencies," answered Imlac, "cannot both be right, but imputed to man they may both be true"' (1956, 447). To make sense of what is said, we are sent in search of propositions that are logically inconsistent yet ostensibly true. Examples might include a cluster of contradictory propositions in modern physics, which asks us to believe that light is both a wave and a particle, for example. As a concession to human understanding, these inconsistent definitions are provisionally acknowledged to be true. But since a proposition cannot be both A and non-A, these antinomies are not unalterable facts but working fictions. Or to use Eliot's metaphor of the pier-glass, they are flattering illusions of concentric arrangement that may turn out be nothing more than the scratches on some larger pier-glass we cannot at present see. Though the epigraph may acquire an aura of wisdom in a Kantian world where truths are merely regulative, its defence of inconsistencies begins to unravel the moment the epigraph is applied to Bulstrode. What Bulstrode would like to see as the truth of opposites, we see only as inconsistencies between the principled believer and the immoral hypocrite, between the steadfast Christian and the slippery casuist.

In a wise aphorism, William James observes that 'wisdom is knowing what to overlook.' Like many of George Eliot's wise sayings, James's aphorism looks two ways at once. Is wisdom an inclusive power? Does it 'survey mankind from China to Peru'? Or like an aphorism, does it know what to 'overlook' in the sense of what to exclude? These two poles of aphorism are opposed most powerfully in the parable of the pier-glass. Exploring the mysteries of her art, Eliot speaks as a priestess of Delphi, an oracle of Apollo. She explains that even so ugly a piece of furniture as a scratched pier-glass of polished steel can yield a pregnant truth when lifted up 'into the serene light of science.' The illusion that the random scratches on the mirror are concentrically arranged is merely the result of candlelight falling on the surface of the metal 'with an exclusive optical arrangement.' Turning scientific fact into parable, Eliot reflects that 'the scratches are events, and the candle is the egoism of any person now absent – of Miss Vincy, for example' (1956, 195).

At this point a major quake rattles the temple at Delphi. Shock waves go out from its epicentre in several directions at once. Though the scratches' concentric arrangement is only a 'flattering illusion,' we are shocked to hear that the candlelight that creates the illusion is nothing more virtuous or worthy of being imitated than human egoism. And in case we should think there are noble egoists, Eliot immediately associates the quake's destructive energy with the most sinister and vicious of all egoists, the death-dealing Miss Vincy.

We can either see life steadily, as rings of planets orbiting the sun in predictable spheres, or else we can see it whole, as a random array in a much larger universe of suns. Wisdom is liberating when it links the centre of illumination provided by our own sun to the vastly different arrangements provided by countless other suns. Such wisdom is likely to produce either wonder or vertigo. A restrictive wisdom, by contrast, provides an illusion of order by narrowing our focus, like the self-centred Miss Vincy. What we call wisdom is too often the result of tunnel vision. But to be wise in this restrictive sense is also to be selfish or stupid, since it is to be blind to other ways of seeing. Eliot's parable of the glass creates a space for the reader's mind to grow in. If Miss Vincy and Bulstrode fail to see that the candle of their egoism creates only a 'flattering illusion of concentric arrangement,' then nothing can be done for them. Bulstrode is a self-censoring egoist, and though all censors are egoists, the self-censoring are the worst, since Bulstrode is trapped in the web of his own moral casuistry. A part of Rosamond wants to keep alive a sense of gratitude to Dorothea for helping her at the most critical moment in her life. But except for a resolve never to speak ill of Dorothea, Rosamond censors gratitude by erasing every generous impulse from her mind. T.S. Eliot says Rosamond Vincy frightens him far more than Goneril and Regan, because an 'admixture of weakness' and even a trace of gratitude make her vicious egoism plausible (1969, 101–2).

'When the commonplace "We must all die" transforms itself suddenly into the acute consciousness "I must die – and soon," then death grapples us, and his fingers are cruel; afterwards, he may come to fold us in his arms as our mother did' (1956, 311). The wrenching shift from death as a commonplace to death as an induced tremor is dramatized by the interval of silence after the second 'die' and by the switch in pronouns from 'we' to 'I.' The terror of the assassin, grappling us by the throat with his fingers, is aggressive and cruel. We experience it, not as a shock wave or a tremor, but as the impact of a blow that sends us reeling. A gentler more maternal death awaits us only later, folding the dead in her arms with a pitying caress.

Initially presented as a sinister, even ghoulish figure, walking by the yew-trees in 'mute companionship' with melancholy, Casaubon is also associated with Eliot's more maternal picture of death. As an imperfect Christian, Casaubon has certain dim hopes of a future life. But what drags him earthwards is not some 'distant hope' but an immediate, ignoble desire to cut Ladislaw out of his will. Eliot universalizes the tug of war between 'distant hope' and 'immediate desire' by introducing her powerful aphorism about the victories of imagination. 'The future estate for which men drudge up city alleys exists already in their imagination and love' (1956, 311). We are willing to perform the most squalid and commonplace tasks if they allow us to clear out the alley ways and slums and raise in their place the great mansions and estates where our mind longs to dwell. But the desire to live in these estates takes a less worthy turn in Casaubon. His 'immediate desire was not for divine communion and light divested of earthly conditions; his passionate longings, poor man, clung low and mist-like in very shady places.'

Aware of the plash of the oncoming oar, this companion of melancholy is consumed by desires unworthy of a Christian priest. No sooner is Eliot about to cast Casaubon off as a vampire, a ghoul unworthy of our pity, than she reaches out to this 'poor man.' Her gesture is a moving example of the blend of compassion and satire that W.J. Bate associates with Samuel Johnson (1975, 493–4). It is the kind of compassion that Dorothea herself will extend to her stricken husband in the scene that follows, when she feels 'something like the thankfulness that might well up in us if we had narrowly escaped hurting a lamed creature' (1956, 314).

Characteristic of the wise, judicious oracle is the axis of truth that balances a reader between poles of judgment and sympathy, satire and compassion. Some scholars are surprised that Eliot should model her unflattering portrait of Casaubon on her friend Mark Pattison, who had married a woman twenty-seven years his junior. The same can be said of Edward Casaubon, whose Renaissance namesake, Isaac, was the subject of a biography by Pattison. What these critics fail to see, however, is that, having skewered Casaubon on the spit of her exquisite and refined satiric intelligence, Eliot then does something more remarkable. She stands back to view him with compassion and understanding, just as Dorothea views Rosamond. Indeed we may say that Dorothea becomes the heroine of *Middlemarch* when she projects herself into Rosamond and assumes for a moment the affliction of her rival by asking the question: are suffering and abjection her own event only? As Simone Weil says, what people like Dorothea 'give to the afflicted whom they succour, when they project their own being into them, is not really their own being, because they no longer possess one; it is Christ himself' (1974, 95). Eliot has the power of grasping Casaubon entirely, a power which is incommunicable except for her astonishing intrusion into her fiction to claim she is 'very sorry for him' (1956, 206). This invasion of the reader's space is an act of total knowledge on Eliot's part, what Frye calls 'the divine comprehension which has sympathy but not affection, wrath but not resentment' (2004a, 172). In a form of 'satire *manqué*' or satire foiled, the wise moralist imitates Dorothea by reaching down to rescue her victim from her own sharpest blows. Arresting her wit and impulse to satirize, the sibyl lifts Casaubon up and folds him in her arms. Cradled like a child, Casaubon is rescued by his guardian in a scene each of us might hope to reenact when the hour is at hand when we shall act no more.

12 The Serpent of Irony: Wisdom or Guile?

This chapter explores the wisdom and guile of Pytho, the slain serpent who also serves Apollo as his priestess. When the Pythia replies to a question without answering it, her words looks two ways at once. She may speak with a serpent's forked tongue in order to deceive a suppliant. Or she may not know the answer to the question she is asked. In either case, out of Pythia's incoherent moans Apollo's priest polishes the oracles whose two-way meanings answer our desire. A classic example is the oracle's reply to Croesus, king of Lydia, who wants to know if he will defeat the Persians. The Pythia's response, 'If Croesus crosses the Halys, a great power will be destroyed,' is slyly ambiguous. When Croesus, interpreting the oracle in his favour, crosses the river Halys with a huge army and is defeated, the Pythia can disclaim responsibility by arguing that Croesus is a careless interpreter. As Heraclitus affirms, 'the Lord whose oracle is in Delphi neither declares nor conceals but gives a sign' (quoted in Kahn, 1979, 270–1). Since ancient Sumerian oracles were written in ideograms that, like characters in modern Chinese, had several meanings, they were Janus-faced, poised between pun and predictive riddle, word-game and prophecy. As Anthony Burgess explains, 'the oracle, telling a general both to stay at home and not to say at home, employed a pun: 'Domine, stes' sounds the same as 'Domi ne stes.' The enquirer took the latter meaning, went out to battle and was killed' (1973, 135). Apollo's epithet is Loxian, the Oblique One. A god who speaks through a priestess with the tongue of a serpent should not be taken to task simply because an unwary suppliant makes a wrong interpretation.

The oracles of the witches in *Macbeth* are as ambiguous in phrasing as they are unerring in prophecy. To relax his maddened mind

Macbeth reflects on the felicities of sleep. But these felicities are dearest to him when he has lost all chance of possessing them. The cry, 'Sleep no more! / Macbeth does murder sleep' is a voice from nowhere that has the authority of an oracle. It confirms the witches' strangely ambiguous prophecy that Banquo, though less happy than Macbeth, is also happier (I.iii.66). One of the witches' most unnerving oracles takes the form of a dumb show of phantom kings, followed by Banquo's ghost. The mirror in the last king's hand replicates endlessly the succession of Banquo's heirs. Reflecting the terrors of the mind's abyss, its cliffs of fall, the infinite regress prompts Macbeth to ask, 'What, will the line stretch out to the crack of doom?' (*Macbeth*, IV.i.117) In becoming what the witches prophesy, Macbeth loses peace of mind. Astonishingly, the most eloquent words on sleep come from a man who will never sleep peacefully again.

Macbeth is both the witch and sibyl of the play's darkest oracles. Without his overreaching ambition, the witches' prophecies would never have power to shake and move him as they do. Macbeth wants to practise sleight of hand upon himself. But subtler than the magician's art is the art of the self-deceiver who wants his eye to wink at what his hand will do.

> Stars, hide your fires;
> Let not light see my black and deep desires;
> The eye wink at the hand; yet let that be
> Which the eye fears, when it is done, to see.   (*Macbeth*, I.v.50–3)

The rhyming couplets impart to the moral witchcraft Macbeth practises on himself the force of a demonic rite.

The bastard Edmund in *King Lear* rejects oracles that foretell a bastard's fate for the same reason many readers reject the wisdom of a predestinating God in *Paradise Lost*. Milton's stern and unloving Father knows his children, Adam and Eve, will fall. But since he does not force them to fall, he disclaims moral responsibility. Edmund finds the base behaviour predicted of him by his father both illogical and unloving. In the litany of Edmund's grievances, 'base' keeps sounding as an insistent groundswell or basso ostinato: 'Why brand they us / With base? With baseness? bastardy? base, base?' (*King Lear*, I.ii.9–10). At best Gloucester's prophetic branding of his son deprives Edmund of his freedom. At its worst it turns an intelligent and resourceful son into a monster more heartless than his father in his worst nightmares can possibly imagine. No oracle in Shakespeare is more darkly fulfilled.

1

To turn from George Eliot to Thackeray or Swift is to turn from an oracle that uses arrested wit to hover judiciously between sympathy and satire to an oracle that is ironic, edged with guile, and capable of looking two ways at once. I argued in the last chapter that a wise oracle tempers the justice of strong moral judgments with the mercy of fellow feeling and compassion. One of its ablest English practitioners is Samuel Johnson, the great arbiter of value in morals and literature. As Walter Jackson Bate explains, 'ridicule, anger, satiric protest, are always in the process of turning into something else' in Johnson's hands (1975, 493). Often his most oracular judgments fall into the 'distinctive literary type' Bate calls 'satire manqué' or 'satire foiled.' As Bate says, satire manqué 'involves a kind of double action in which a strong satiric blow is about to strike home unerringly when another arm at once reaches out and deflects or rather lifts it' (1975, 494). In chapter 11 I showed how George Eliot uses arrested wit to humanize her satire. She mutes her mockery of Casaubon's pedantry by lifting it up and absorbing it in her fellow feeling and sympathy for all 'highly taught' scholars who are temperamentally unfit to enjoy what they know. After dissecting Casaubon on a mortuary slab, she reaches out to resuscitate him. In an astonishing gesture of sympathy, she protests 'for my part I am very sorry for him' (Eliot, 1956, 206). Softening her contempt for 'a small hungry shivering self,' she appeals to a wider understanding of all persons who are 'present at this great spectacle of life' without being 'fully possessed by the glory we behold' (1956, 206).

A strain of foiled satire pervades Johnson's poem 'The Vanity of Human Wishes.' Though its oracles are judgmental, they also melt with pity. Even when Johnson denounces the efforts of puny, short-lived people to destroy each other, he is moved by the sad trajectories they trace. Like evanescent fireworks, they mount and shine, evaporate and fall. As Bate says, these people 'start to stumble and weaken; disease, the envy of others, and old age club or push them into weariness, despair, and finally death. (One thinks of the remark Johnson was sometimes heard to mutter to himself: "And then he died, poor man")' (1975, 495). In 'The Vanity of Human Wishes,' the apparent satire of each portrait is softened by the judicious phrasing of the oracle, which turns the fate of each fallen hero or aspirant to fame into the fate of a wavering, allegorical Everyman. The satire inherent in 'glittering eminence' becomes unexpectedly literal in the fall of a great prelate like Wolsey or Archbishop Laud. But when swept up into a larger drama, one which is gravely announced as the universal 'massacre of gold,' the satire is made an occasion for compassion as well as judgment. As Johnson dramatizes the Fall, his satire is absorbed and swallowed up by a volley of anxious questions: 'Must no wishes rise?,' 'Must helpless man in ignorance sedate?,' which prepare for a final elevation of comedy into prayer.

In a poem like 'The Vanity of Human Wishes,' or in a novel like *Middlemarch* or *Barchester Towers*, it is possible to feel closer to such characters as the disgraced Wolsey, the ghoulish Casaubon, or the unsavoury Mr Slope than we wish to feel. Something similar happens in Thackeray's novel *Vanity Fair*, where we feel more sympathy for Becky than her behaviour warrants. Yet an important difference exists between the judicious narrator of *Barchester Towers* and the evasive, two-faced narrator of *Vanity Fair*. A connoisseur who speaks with a forked tongue about the dubious merits of Tudor architecture or the beauty of England's country houses may do so without offence in *Barchester Towers*. After all, aesthetic tastes may differ. Morality, however, is another matter. When Thackeray's narrator in *Vanity Fair* endorses opposite moral positions simultaneously, his two-way oracles begin to erode that centre of moral authority we expect a Victorian version of *Pilgrim's Progress* to possess and maintain.

At the end of the discovery scene, when Rawdon finds Becky and Steyne *in flagrante delicto*, Thackery repeats the question posed innocently by the French maid: '"Mon Dieu, madame, what has happened?" she asked. What had happened? Was she guilty or not?' (Thackeray, 1950, 556). We are never sure which team this oracle is on. Like the god at Delphi, he speaks with a forked tongue. Ostensibly, the narrator is addressing the wider moral audience. But he is also a go-between, defending Becky from conventional moral censorship. Instead of simply condemning Becky, as Steyne, Rawdon, and Lady Jane do, the narrator doubts Becky's technical innocence but concedes that the corrupt heart may in this instance have been pure. Surrounded by her 'tumbled vanities,' Becky is held responsible for her 'miserable ruin.' But in an oddly disturbing way she also seems to have commissioned Thackeray as her moral spy. She has hired him to unmask the hypocrisy of her censors and (strange as it may sound) to expose the double standards of most readers.

The harshest judgment passed on Becky seems to be that her past is 'profitless.' Lack of financial profit becomes a shockingly literal judgment that exposes the material basis of her censors' vaunted morality. Becky's boast that she could have been a good woman on five thousand pounds per annum plays upon the same confusion. If we attack Becky for moral casuistry, then we must also attack her critics for the same failing. Unlike Bunyan's narrator in *Pilgrim's Progress*, Thackeray's narrator is never a moral weather-vane. On the contrary, he is a two-way oracle and go-between, a double agent who plays one side against the other. His commission is never merely to act on Becky's behalf or on behalf of the society that condemns her. It is rather to expose the darkest secrets of both sides.

What is most subversive about *Vanity Fair* is the unexpected collapse of both Becky and her censors into a common front of cynicism and moral indifference. In the end no norms survive to differentiate them. The narrator uses moral words like 'bankruptcy' and 'vanity' without the expected moral meanings. When even the most ethical character in the discovery scene, the censorious Rawdon, complains that Becky failed to spare him a mere hundred pounds, he damages his cause by using an economic argument appropriate to Becky or the narrator rather than a moral argument appropriate to a censor. Brooding over the instability and strangeness of human affairs like the biblical Koheleth, Thackeray's narrator withdraws from the sequence of cause and effect. Instead of trying to possess time, he lets it pass. Watching with prescience, the narrator expresses views Thackeray himself may want to believe but half secretly doubts. Another unofficial voice, most often associated with Becky, expresses views Thackeray wants to deny but half secretly affirms.

2

Though the most salient features of Jonathan Swift's oracles are cunning and guile, the clarity of his own views in *Gulliver's Travels* is to the instability of Thackeray's views in *Vanity Fair* or to the confusion of tongues in Falstaff's soliloquies what the pole star is to Donne's trepidation of the spheres in 'A Valediction Forbidding Mourning' (l. 11). The King of Brobdingnag seems at first to approve Gulliver's panegyric on European civilization. But from the moment he strips off his mask of polite attention to launch a devastating attack on both European culture and its uncritical defender, we realize that Swift and the king are speaking in unison.

> My little friend Gildrig, you have made a most admirable panegyric upon your country; you have clearly proved that ignorance, idleness, and vice, may be sometimes the only ingredients for qualifying as a legislator; that laws are best explained, interpreted, and applied by those whose interest and abilities lie in perverting, confounding, and eluding them. (Swift, 1950, 148)

The torpedo touches come in triads: 'ignorance, idleness, and vice'; 'perverting, confounding, and eluding.' Though these triads have all the hallmarks of tantrum rhetoric, the prophet who detonates them with explosive force is acknowledged to be judicious and in possession of a balancing habit of mind. We accept the king's words as Swift's own, because up to this point his evaluations have been sane and moderate. If the king's language now seems intemperate, it is because the vices he lacerates are equally intemperate.

> I cannot but conclude the bulk of your natives to be the most pernicious race of little odious vermin that nature ever suffered to crawl upon the surface of the earth. (1950, 149)

Despite the savage indignation that ignites the words, the indictment itself has the ring of deserved censure and judgment.

Accepting preposterous court rituals at face value, Gulliver treats rope-dancing and minute differences in physical height with as much unthinking deference as the Lilliputians. 'Flimnap, the Treasurer,' we are told, 'is allowed to cut a caper on the straight rope, at least an inch higher than any other lord in the whole empire' (1950, 41). Swift the satirist reminds us of his presence by casually introducing a human scale, the inch, at the precise moment the tiny increments of size become the main measure of Lilliputian pride and rank. Even biblical oracles about the resurrection of the dead are placed in contexts that make them seem absurd to the learned and credible only to the literal-minded and gullible.

> They bury their dead with their heads directly downwards, because they hold an opinion, that in eleven thousand moons they are all to rise again,

in which period the earth (which they conceive to be flat) will turn upside down, and by this means they shall, at their resurrection, be found ready standing on their feet. (1950, 63)

A simple reversal of meaning also allows Swift to mock the four articles of impeachment drawn up against Gulliver, which redefine service as disservice, virtue as vice. The accused is denounced as a traitor for being a peacemaker. And for serving his Majesty he is to lose his eyesight. The final shock is that Gulliver is still too deferential to Lilliputian authority to insist on common sense. When the court decides to discharge 'very sharp-pointed arrows into the balls of [his] eyes, as [he lies] on the ground,' Gulliver confesses, without irony, that he is puzzled and confused. He is 'so ill a judge of things' that he cannot quite 'discover the lenity and favour of this sentence, but [conceives] it (perhaps erroneously) rather to be rigorous than gentle' (Swift, 1950, 79).

Like T.S. Eliot's Prufrock, who 'has measured out his life in coffee spoons,' Swift assails the luxury of serving exotic drinks in teacups made in China. Gulliver assures the Houyhnhnm master that 'this whole globe of earth must be at least three times gone round, before one of our better female Yahoos could get her breakfast or a cup to put it in' (1950, 286). Behind the oracle in which Gulliver declares that the benevolence of the Portuguese sea captain is only the civility of a despised and filthy Yahoo (1950, 326), we hear a second oracle: one in which Swift gently mocks Gulliver's own misanthropy. To treat the captain as a semi-rational Yahoo is to suffer from inverted pride. It is to hate all mankind for those very qualities Gulliver shares with other people. The final absurdity is Gulliver's affection for the conversation of his horses and his intolerance of both the companionship and smell of his family.

The two-way meanings of 'A Tale of a Tub' are more corrosive than the simple ironies in *Gulliver's Travels*. Unlike John Milton, who prays to be the oracle of heavenly wisdom, the modern poet wants to be secretary of the universe. He bears less resemblance to the poet who takes all knowledge for his province than to a coroner who dissects 'the carcass of human nature' (1950, 439). As his epic style disintegrates, Swift's critic betrays envy of his forbears. Though Homer had 'tolerable genius' for an ancient, modern scholars have detected 'many gross errors' in his epics. Despite Swift's pretended alignment with the moderns, the prophet behind the oracles is critical of

Homer's critics and continues to laugh up his sleeve at their nit-picking and envy.

Ostensibly, Swift is a critic of digressions: 'I have sometimes heard of an *Iliad* in a nutshell; but it has been my fortune to have much oftener seen a nutshell in an *Iliad*.' Except for the substitution of 'fortune' for 'misfortune,' which signals a simple verbal irony, the chiasmus neatly dramatizes the corruption of modern taste. Yet in poking fun at the moderns, Swift's censor also speaks with a forked tongue. He continues to say the opposite of what he means. 'I think the commonwealth of learning is chiefly obliged to the great modern improvement of digression.' By the time Swift concludes his praise of digressions, however, his tribute has started to effervesce. In improving the nation's diet, have digressions truly met the requirements of 'judicious taste'? Or is their refinement of taste not another name for the indiscriminate and decadent learning that dresses up culture 'in various compounds, consisting in soups and olios, fricassees, and ragouts' (1950, 453)?

At any randomly chosen moment it may be hard to tell whether Swift, the prophet behind the mask, is aligning himself with the oracle or making fun of it. And yet the values of the prophet's end games are seldom in doubt. When a heartless empiricist, a critic of the stripping away of masks, observes that he 'saw a woman flayed, and you will hardly believe how much it altered her person for the worse' (1950, 475), no sane reader would confuse the speaker with Swift. And yet when the same apologist proceeds to make a case for remaining only on the surface of life, without ever peering below, his casuistry begins to acquire a specious charm and seductive logic of its own. Where ignorance is bliss, is it not folly to be wise? 'He that can, with Epicurus, content his ideas with the films and images that fly off upon his senses from the superficies of things; such a man, truly wise, creams off nature, leaving the sour and the dregs for philosophy and reason to lap up' (1950, 475). Having caught us with the bait of a brain-numbing casuistry, Swift then springs the trap. He enters the mind of the sophist in order to blow it up from inside. 'This is the sublime and refined point of felicity,' he rhapsodizes, before giving the game away: it is 'called the possession of being well deceived, the serene and peaceful state of being a fool among knaves.' Stripping off the mask, the prophet behind the oracle lets us know what he thinks. The speaker is the dupe of con men who would bewitch him into taking truth on trust. He is the tool of demagogues who would enslave the ignorant by extolling their induced stupidity and stupor as the felicity of a 'serene' and 'peaceful state' (1950, 475). Anyone who denies it is blasphemous for a creature endowed with reason to offer God the sacrifice of a fool is not only stupid. He is also a 'fool' among deceivers and 'knaves.'

3

The torpedo touch of a two-way oracle is no less menacing for being silent and concealed. Indeed, in leaving a reader genuinely bewildered, its power to detonate two targets at once may put at risk so worthy a man-of-war as Matthew Arnold's collection of satiric prose monologues, *Friendship's Garland*. Who is the true target of Arnold's censure? Is it Arminius, the German critic of English culture, or its self-satisfied advocate? When the Anglophile used by Arnold as his letter-writer makes a commonplace book out of articles from *The Times*, which is the organ of atheism and *laissez-faire* liberalism in *Culture and Anarchy*, Arnold is clearly poking fun at his correspondent's ignorance and complacency. But no sooner has the letter-writer made a secular scripture out of such Satanic verses as essays from *The Times* than the focus of the satire starts to shift. Instead of mocking the letter-writer for defending an indefensible social system against Arminius's witty criticisms, Arnold allows his correspondent to piece together some fragmentary half-truths about the organic quality of a healthy culture: 'In England we like our improvements to *grow*, not to be manufactured' (1961, 398).

Most bewildering are the many passages in which Arnold speaks with so forked a tongue that it is hard to say which side of the cultural debate he is on. When pressed by Arminius about the education of aristocrats at Eden, it is unclear whether Arnold's letter-writer is defending or mocking the Englishman's eulogy of 'the grand, old, fortifying, classical curriculum.' If 'the most astonishing feats of mental gymnastics' at Oxford are feats of staying awake for four nights and consuming incredible quantities of 'wet towels, strong cigars, and brandy-and-water,' then Arminius, the arch-enemy and critic of English education, would seem to be vindicated. But Arnold, the Oxford Professor of Poetry, also seems to be endorsing his letter-writer's high-spirited praise of liberal learning for 'training and bracing the mind for future acquisition' (1961, 401). Since the abuse of a classical education is never a convincing argument against its right use, the only logical conclusion a reader can draw is that Arnold is arguing on both sides of the question at the same time.

As a prophet of culture who appropriates biblical language for his own satiric ends, one of Arnold's favourite tricks is to use religious allusions to discredit his religious adversaries. Alluding to the nuptial feast of the Lamb in Revelation, Arnold hilariously mingles the revels of a nudist colony with the solemn spectacle of the Philistines sitting down 'at the banquet of the future' with no wedding garments. In the nakedness and solitude of their unsocial natures, the Puritans will be bereft of clothing, and 'nothing excellent can come,' he warns, from their raw, uncultivated customs (1961, 423). Just as Paul tries to compass the mystery of love by saying what it is not ('Love is not jealous or boastful; it is not arrogant or rude. Love does not insist on its own way; it is not irritable or resentful' – 1 Corinthians 13:4–5), so Arnold tries to define culture by excluding from its charmed circle of attributes both hatred and machinery. 'He who works for machinery, he who works for hatred, works only for confusion. Culture looks beyond machinery, culture hates hatred' (1961, 426). When Arnold writes as a prophet of culture, he uses short, coordinate clauses that allow each idea to sink at once into the mind. If culture hates hatred, then it must loathe itself for hating anything. The paradox sends Arnold in search of better understanding, just as the mystery of love prompts Paul to conclude that his 'knowledge' and 'prophecy' are 'imperfect' (1 Corinthians 13:9). Introducing a hierarchy of virtues, Paul affirms that 'faith, hope, love abide, these three; but the greatest of these is love' (1 Corinthians 13:13). Having affirmed prophetically that 'culture has one great passion, the passion for sweetness and light,' Arnold then echoes Paul again by saying 'it has one even yet greater! – the passion for making them prevail' (1961, 426). Even as he kidnaps religion, allowing sweetness and light to swallow up the power of conduct, Arnold uses one of religion's great prophetic texts to authorize the takeover.

4

Though a satiric, two-way epitaph is likely to be deficient in sympathy, its wit may save an oracular Alexander Pope from platitude.

So unaffected, so composed a mind,
So firm yet soft, so strong yet so refined,

Heaven, as its purest Gold, by Tortures tried;
The Saint sustained it, but the Woman died.

('Epitaph. On Mrs. Corbet,' ll. 7–10)

The comparison seems strained until the last line, where the survival of the saint and the death of the woman gracefully combine to justify both the antithetical grammar and the culminating wit of the conceit. As an amalgam of antithetical virtues, 'firm yet soft,' 'strong yet ... refined,' Mrs Corbet is said to pass every test of genuineness posed by her breast cancer, which racks her body with pain even as it purges her soul with fire.

The same cannot be said, I fear, of Pope's epitaph for James Moore Smythe, which is too contrived to be moving. It may be clever of Pope in 'An Epistle to Dr. Arbuthnot' to subtract from the inventory of his father's achievements the lies of courtiers and the schoolman's wiles. But in the epitaph for young Smythe, the negatives are an unlikely blend of ingenuity and farce. Pope is amused by the absurdity of having to annihilate something so puny as a dwarf, a mere no-man or nothing.

Epitaph, On James Moore Smythe

Here lyes what had nor *Birth*, nor *Shape*, nor *Fame*;
No *Gentleman*! no *man*! *no-thing*! no *name*!
For *Jammie* n'er grew *James*; and what they call
More, shrunk to *Smith* – and Smith's no name at all.
Yet dye thou can'st not, Phantom, oddly fated;
For how can no-thing be annihilated?
        Ex nihilo nihil fit.

To prevent the oracle of Jamie's end from being an oracle that ends him, Pope contends that 'ex nihilo nihil fit.' If the major premise of Pope's syllogism is that 'a no-thing cannot be annihilated,' and if the minor premise is that little James is merely a 'no-thing' or a cipher, then it follows logically that Jamie's death cannot be an event that ends him. But Pope's syllogism betrays more conceited humour than conviction. It commands more admiration of Pope's mental agility than assent to what it says. To the degree it portends the contraction of the young man's life, the pun on the diminutive form of James is affecting. But there is no excuse for the frigid word play on 'Moore' and 'More' and for Pope's cruel strategies of belittling. Like the shrinkage of 'Smythe' to 'Smith,' the claim that (as a contraction of blacksmith) 'Smith' is an improper proper name is as contrived as learned parody as it is unpersuasive as argument. Even the decree 'ex nihilo nihil fit,' where the solemn tone seems to modulate at last into something more subtle and prophetic, contradicts a key biblical tenet, which maintains that God in Genesis did indeed create something out of nothing. And if Pope's only argument against annihilation is that the person who died was nothing in the first place, then, far from scoring a victory over death, he is merely moving the moment of annihilation from one side of the grave to the other. Such an epitaph is not only an oracle of our end. It is also an oracle to annihilate us before we die.

Reuben Brower calls the famous oracles of wit that open *Pride and Prejudice* 'Pope without couplets.' Every remark made by the sarcastic Mr Bennet and his mindless wife 'bounces off the magnificent opening sentence' (1962, 164–5). Another critic, Richard Jenkyns, traces Austen's aphorisms to a formula she would have encountered in the Book of Common Prayer, the use of a statement followed by a 'balancing contradiction.' Examples of this two-way construction can be found in the Anglican prayer for the conversion of the Jews. After commending the Jews as God's special 'inheritance,' the prayer balances its praise with mild criticism. It implicitly censures this 'ancient people' for closing their hearts to God and rejecting 'their true Messiah.' God is accordingly asked to open the Jews' hearts to his Son and to teach them to 'have life through his Name' (prayer 4, p. 41). As well as drawing upon the Prayer Book's predilection for balanced contradictions, Austen may have quarried from this specious 'prayer' the title of her novel: 'Take away all pride and prejudice in us that may hinder [the Jews'] understanding of the Gospel.'

Unsettling dualities also disturb Yeats's oracles. His poem 'Two Songs from a Play' wavers uneasily between cycles of classical and Christian civilization, of Doric discipline and a dangerous new barbarism.

> Odour of blood when Christ was slain
> Made all Platonic tolerance vain
> And vain all Doric discipline.   (ll. 22–4)

A similar duality animates the oracles of 'The Second Coming.' A revelation is imminent. But instead of evoking the Nativity in the stately cadences of Milton's famous hymn, Yeats intimates that anarchy and chaos are at hand. 'What rough beast, its hour come round at last, / Slouches towards Bethlehem to be born?' (ll. 21–2). The prophecy generates two-way meanings that are at worst frightening to contemplate and at best dark and ambiguous.

More moving because more deeply rooted in the holiness of the heart's affections and the truth of a humanized imagination is the two-way oracle that Yeats uses to end his poem 'The Folly of Being Comforted.' 'O heart, O heart! If you'd but turn your head, / You'd know the folly of being comforted' (ll. 13–14). The one who is comforted speaks with a forked tongue. It is hard to decide whether he is inconsolable or in no need of consolation. As the woman he loves grows older, her 'great nobleness' and grace of self-command make 'the fire that stirs about her when she stirs / Burn but more clearly' (ll. 9–11). The after-image of moving fire is Yeats's version of the halo or nimbus that floats in the air around sacred subjects. He tries to extract the loved one's essence, not by purging it of impurities in the refining fire of Byzantium's holy sages, but by steeping it in the destructive element of time. But how can the 'nobleness' of age compete with 'all the wild summer' of the woman's youth, which suddenly flares up in the poet's memory like flame from a collapsing funeral pyre? Though capable of being separately appreciated and appraised, the two kinds of fire are incompatible: nothing allows the poet to choose between them. The mystery comes, not from something unknowable in the subject, but from something unlimited in it.

5

A two-way oracle is often the prophet's equivalent of a mock-epic poem: it treats a low subject in a lofty style. Examples include Belinda's godlike act of naming in 'The Rape of the Lock': 'Let Spades be Trumps, she said, and Trumps they were,' and the Duke's marvel of prophetic conjuring in 'My Last Duchess': 'Fra Pandolf's hands worked busily a day, / And there she stands.' In each case the poet infuses a commonplace topic with the sublimity of God's creation by verbal fiat at the opening of Genesis. 'God said Let there be light, and there was light.' Shakespeare uses a similar trick to make the weaver Bottom's dream as oracular as possible. In a fumbling attempt to recall his vision, Bottom echoes St Paul's first epistle to the Corinthians (2:9). 'The eye of man hath not heard, the ear of man hath not seen, man's hand is not able to taste, his tongue to conceive, nor his heart to report what my dream was' (*A Midsummer Night's Dream*, IV.i.215–18).

As Keats recognizes, Shakespeare has more wise reserve or negative capability than most poets. Unlike Coriolanus, the inflexible, single-natured man of practical capacity, who is as austere in peace as he is in war, Aufidius is a poet like Shakespeare who rests in uncertainties and looks two ways at once. This is a gift Aufidius accuses Coriolanus of lacking. His friend, he says, is

> Not to be other than one thing, not moving
> From the casque to the cushion, but commanding peace
> Even with the same austerity and garb
> As he controlled the war.   (*Coriolanus*, IV.vii.42–5)

Coleridge claims he can make little sense of Aufidius's speech: Frank Kermode acknowledges a similar bewilderment (2000, 15–16). Though I defer to the judgment of both critics, I must confess that in my simplemindedness Aufidius's speech has always seemed clear enough to me. Its perceived difficulties may come from Aufidius's negative capability, his ability to see all sides of an issue and entertain like Shakespeare several ideas at once. If Coriolanus is as 'the osprey to the fish, who takes [its prey] / By sovereignty of nature' (ll. 34–5), is it because the hawk, a king among raptors, is predatory by disposition? Or is it because, as a sovereign, it takes the fish as its due? The jury is out: Coriolanus may be only an unscrupulous predator. Or a judge may decide that Coriolanus is entitled to his prey because of his superior gifts. Since Shakespeare is transcribing thought in rapid progress, he allows Aufidius to correct his first ideas even as he amends his second ones.

> but one of these –
> As he has spices of them all – not all,–
> For I dare so far free him, – made him feared;
> So hated; and so, banished; but he has a merit
> To choke it in the utterance.   (ll. 45–9)

In an effort to be precise and fair, Aufidius concedes that it is not exactly true that Coriolanus, despite his lack of negative capability, has a spice of all faults. 'Not all,' he concedes: 'I dare so far free him.' Aufidius here displays the scrupulous honesty and balanced judgment he immediately praises in Coriolanus, the 'merit' of 'choking' an unworthy thought 'in the utterance.' Though self-correction and two-way syntax continue to pull his mind in opposite directions, I am less baffled by the contrary pulls of Aufidius's negative capability than by the motives of Iago, Hamlet, and Brutus (in the orchard), which often seem inscrutable and deeply puzzling.

Also puzzling is the Bastard Faulconbridge, whose first soliloquy in *King John* is a sustained exercise in double talk, in which the speaker both attacks and defends expedience or commodity. And since he is both a censor and witty evader of censorship, he also outwits and censors himself. The soliloquy's first two lines compose a diverting prophecy of the Bastard's fate.

> A foot of honour better than I was,
> But many a many foot of land the worse.   (*King John*, I.i.182–3)

The primary meaning of 'foot' is the standard unit of measurement. But in the hypermetric second line, 'foot' acquires a secondary meaning in what seems to be the 'many a many a foot' of dragging verse that draw his speech out. To compensate for his loss of feet, the Bastard must take measures to secure 'the footsteps of his rising.' Hovering inventively between literal and figurative meanings of 'foot' and 'bastard,' Faulconbridge predicts his 'mounting spirit' will be only a hostage to fortune, a mere 'bastard to the time,' unless it can use the backs of flunkeys as a footstool or ladder in its scramble for power. As Voltaire jokes, history is the sound of heavy boots clambering up society and of velvet slippers coming down.

In his better-known second soliloquy, the Bastard prophetically denounces all triumph of expedience over virtue and principle. But the syntax is too unwieldy and fractured to acquire the authority of a wise saying we might ascribe to Shakespeare himself. The words bear marks of contiguity-disorder, stranded or forgotten grammatical subjects, and reductive jokes. In one of the complex word structures that William Empson analyses, the minor sense of a word is made clear only in retrospect. His example comes from the end of *Hamlet*: 'give order that these bodies / High on a stage be placed' (V.ii.388–9). 'Stage' means platform. But the planting of theatrical ideas twenty lines earlier allows Shakespeare to carry the theatrical stage as a subsidiary meaning. The Bastard's outcry in his second great soliloquy, 'Mad world! mad kings! mad composition!' denounces the dishonourable peace agreement that King John has just concluded with the King of France. Yet the Bastard's talent for inventing highly spirited but equivocal speeches allows him to harbour in the word 'composition' – the 'composing' of political differences – a submerged secondary meaning: the 'composition' of his mad outburst of invective. In keeping with the Bastard's genius for double irony, with his capacity (as Bloom says) to be 'both in and out of the game, watching and wondering at it' at the same time (1998, 55), is his ability to float two meanings of a word in a single line. Alas, the Bastard admits, I have no 'power to clutch' or withdraw 'my hand' when the 'fair angels' of the god Commodity 'salute my palm.' The radiant 'angels' or ministers ('the better angels of our nature') are his ostensible subject: his reductive minor meaning does not register until we reach the end of the line. The mercenary appeal of the coins or angels thrust as a bribe into the Bastard's hand is deliberately suppressed: when it surfaces in 'palm,' we are meant to take pride in our cleverness at deciphering a little word game or joke.

Lacking the weight and brevity of an oracle, the Bastard's prophecy soon loses its way in a maze of digressive, ill-tempered attacks. Once the desultory genius of expedience starts whispering in France's ear, the Bastard's grammar wanders with it. We search in vain for any principal verb to go with 'France,' the grammatical subject of the Bastard's loose harangue. As syntax loses direction, it manifests several symptoms of 'contiguity-disorder.' The soliloquist displays great facility in piling up word lists: 'Of kings, of beggars, old men, young men, maids' (King John, III.i.570). But he has more trouble identifying and placing in context the 'purpose-changer' and 'sly divel,' the 'smooth-faced,' 'tickling' gentleman, Commodity, despite the ease with which he loads abusive epithets upon him. The etymology of 'broker' comes disconcertingly to life in the decline of the broker Commodity, the middleman or agent, into a hired pimp, bawd, or pander: 'this commodity, / This bawd, this broker.' In the 'daily break-vow' Shakespeare also revives the origin of 'broker' in the tapster or broacher of casks. This commission-agent, Commodity, is literally a breaker of heads, including the maidenhead of virgins. 'Having no external thing to lose / But the word "maid,"' Commodity 'cheats the poor maid [even] of that' (King John, III.i.572).

Similar two-way oracles and prophecies abound in the monologues of Robert Browning, who is astonishingly adept at making out a case for an adversary or opponent. In 'Bishop Blougram's Apology,' for example, a speaker who combines wisdom with guile, and whom we initially distrust, trespasses on our sympathy by replacing a fiercely partisan defence with a voice more discerning and prophetic.

> Just when we are safest, there's a sunset-touch,
> A fancy from a flower-bell, some one's death,
> A chorus-ending from Euripides, –
> And that's enough for fifty hopes and fears
> As old and new at once as nature's self,
> To rap and knock and enter in our soul,
> Take hands and dance there, a fantastic ring,
> Round the ancient idol, on his base again, –
> The grand Perhaps!   ('Bishop Blougram's Apology,' ll. 182–90)

The fugitive impressions from nature are designed to disquiet an empiricist entrenched in his scepticism. Behind the disturbing fact of death and the solemn chorus ending, the prophet intuits an attitude of flickering hesitation, wavering in emphasis between the death of day and the glory of nightfall. Even in discrediting idolatry, such disturbing intimations leave Blougram suspended between the gallantry of Rabelais, setting off in quest of his 'grand Perhaps,' and one of the great choruses of Euripides, in which the playwright tries to comprehend and define Zeus even as he prays to him.

As a last oracle in an age of unbelief, the final stanza of Philip Larkin's poem 'Church Going' displays a comparable power to unsettle and disturb. Having viewed the church with 'awkward reverence,' Larkin suddenly affirms, without apparent irony, 'A serious house on serious earth it is' (l. 55). The poet is surprised by this heresy against his atheism. A prophetic impulse seems to trespass on his unbelief before he knows what is happening. But does his compulsion to be the mouthpiece of an open oracle overtake the poet? Or is Larkin overtaking the compulsion of a 'hunger in himself to be more serious' (l. 60)? Is he lightly mocking the gravity of the oracle by wrestling it the ground of the half-comic superstition that the dead who lie scattered round the church may also instruct the living? The prophet who deepens into seriousness means the former, but the unbeliever who distrusts the oracle's trespass on his sympathy seems to mean the latter. Though religion cannot always see life steadily, at least it tries to see it whole. Larkin acknowledges its power to hold 'unsplit' what is too often found 'Only in separation – marriage, and birth, / And death, and thoughts of these' (ll. 48–51). He also concedes that a religion that allows 'all our compulsions' to meet in 'its blent air' (l. 56) will never be obsolete. Even in turning a life of inconsequence into magnificent theatre, however, and even in robing our compulsions as 'destinies' (ll. 56–7), religion can seldom abate the tyranny of these compulsions or tame their terror. The question is whether Larkin abandons himself too readily to the unbeliever's self-pity and despair. Or does he submit that self-pity to scrutiny in an alert refusal to discredit belief uncritically? Behind Larkin the sceptic we hear the voice of a prophet like Karl Jaspers, who fears that when philosophy ends its debate with faith all that remains will be an 'empty seriousness.' Seldom are the conflicting impulses of a two-way oracle, wavering between unbelief and an impulse to be serious and prophetic, so precariously balanced.

6

Like many of the speakers studied in this chapter, Shakespeare's Falstaff is a two-way oracle, a comical version of Thersites, a double agent who plays Trojan off against Greek. In his first great soliloquy, Falstaff is ostensibly a censor of thieves. As a 'squire of the night's body' whose horse has just been stolen by two fellow thieves, his commission is never merely to act on the thieves' behalf. Nor is to act on behalf of the society that censors thieves, since he is a thief himself. Falstaff is as bewitched by words as he is by the love potion he thinks Hal has given him to drink. He has to extol the claims of comradeship and trust in the language of thieves who betray such trust. The confusion of tongues comes to a focus in the oxymoron of a 'true thief.' 'A plague upon it when thieves cannot be true one to another' (1 *Henry IV*, II.ii.28–30). A 'true' or quintessential thief would not be true to anyone, including fellow thieves. But Falstaff is in love with thieves who are untrue to the craft of thieving by being true to each other. He has to express his love and trust in language that betrays (while still strongly intimating) what he feels.

Falstaff is bewitched by one of the great paradoxes of love poetry: he is vexed by what enchants him. His friends' greatest offence is that they have plied him, not with sack, but with love potions. If Hal has 'not given me medicines to make me love him, I'll be hanged' (1 *Henry IV*, II.ii.19–20). It seems impossible for Falstaff to avoid betrayal. To 'turn true man' by deserting Hal is to betray a friend he loves. On the other hand, everything Falstaff says he has done in jest to Hal and threatens to do to him in the future, Hal (we know) will do to Falstaff. With a swift, decisive cruelty that never ceases to shock and surprise an audience, Hal will put his old friend's heart in the grave the moment he comes to power as king. Though festive comedy, as Cesar Barber says, 'is always asking for amnesty' (1972, 186), its quality of mercy is seriously strained by Hal's ritual sacrifice of his friend.

Mocking the rituals of war and honour in a catechism that displays a soldierly command of a time-honoured question-and-answer formula, Falstaff plays the same double game that Faulconbridge plays. A double ironist whose catechism is highly patterned, built up of balanced questions linked by repeated words and driven by exuberant negative replies, Falstaff loves to run with the hare and hunt with the hounds. Just as Faulconbridge's talk against expedience is itself expedient, so Falstaff's anitwar talk takes place during a battle. As a knight, Sir John's social status is defined by war. And though he finds discretion to be the better part of valour, everything he says is shaped by military values. His soliloquy on honour is his answer, first to the Prince's taunt that Falstaff owes God a death, and then to his own Socratic questioning of feudal codes. In his catechism of sycophants in *King John*, Faulconbridge anticipates each rehearsed response. The answers are as predictable and rehearsed as the ryhming of 'Po' and 'so' (*King John*, I.i.203–4). But Falstaff, like Socrates, does not know the answers to his questions, and may be as surprised by them as we are.

Honour has less skill in surgery than Falstaff, who operates as a verbal surgeon on such words as 'honour' and 'counterfeit.' If a soldier acts honourably, will his action set to or heal a broken leg? Will it heal an arm? Will honour 'take away the grief of a wound'? As a word, 'honour' is mere breath or air, 'a trim reckoning' (1 *Henry IV*, V.i.137). Falstaff is not only a sceptic like Montaigne. He is also a medieval William James who redefines words like 'counterfeit' and 'honour' by examining their consequence for action. Can the hero who died last Wednesday feel or hear the honour he has won? Can the honour of the dead even abide with the living? Gradually, these heuristic questions turn into rhetorical ones, and the anticipated 'no' follows with the force of a refrain. The only honour that Falstaff's catechism leaves intact is the honour of a Socratic rationalist who shows that vainglorious military 'honour' is as ragged and devoid of substance as Falstaff's soldiers, who as scarecrows and ghosts bear an uncanny resemblance to the corpses of men taken down from their gibbets.

If Falstaff is the Socrates of Eastcheap, he is also the Wittgenstein of the war soliloquies. For he does battle, not only against Hotspur and Sir Walter Blunt, but also against the mind's bewitchment by words like 'counterfeit.' To this end Falstaff constructs a pragmatic enthymeme. If I am a person who merely counterfeits dying, I am the opposite of a counterfeit, because unlike the heroic but dead Hotspur I possess 'the true and perfect image of life' itself (1 *Henry IV*, V.v.120). Though the syllogism is logically sound, it harbours a material fallacy in the equivocal use of 'counterfeit' as a synonym both for an actor's 'feigning' or 'pretending' and for the spurious or the fake. The less creditable form of 'counterfeiting' is immediately dramatized in Falstaff's laying claim to a 'counterfeit' honour by giving Hotspur a fresh wound in the thigh. In his great anti-war speeches Falstaff puts in doubt the heroic view of war held by Hotspur and Prince Hal. Both *Henry IV* and *Henry V* express stirring patriotic views that Shakespeare himself wants to hold publicly but may privately question or doubt. Another voice, subversive and less heroic, and often associated with Falstaff, expresses views Shakespeare wants to reject but may secretly endorse.

The soliloquy in which Hal resolves to renounce Falstaff and his tavern friends is the prince's barest, most calculating example of forsaking the pleasures of double irony for the simpler satisfaction of abetting censors by banishing the festive comedy. It is as if Hal resolves to be a censor hereafter, but an offender now. He will offend by making offence a skill: an art of satisfying the censors in the long run. In the meantime, he will be a closet censor, a double agent who appears to be on Falstaff's side while secretly working for the other team. The double ironies of Falstaff and the Bastard have now turned into an art of cold-blooded duplicity designed to deceive Falstaff and his friends. To the audience and Falstaff the confessed doubleness of Hal's role must always seem a betrayal.

One unattractive feature of Hal's soliloquy is that he is too conscious of hearing himself say something quotable and fine. If poetry is overheard and rhetoric heard, then Hal's soliloquy is still too close to rhetoric and too far removed from the poetry of thoughts half evaded in the mind. The subversive but honest truth is that that his allegiances are divided. But this is a complex truth he cannot find language to express. The metaphor of the sun breaking free of clouds befits the prince's royal dignity. But it betrays his friends by demoting them to 'base contagious clouds,' strangling vapours, and foul, ugly mists. He seems to be rehearsing his rejection speech. This is something majestic and noble he thinks he ought to say, rather than something exact and truthful that expresses what he feels.

The Hal of the soliloquy is a professional actor, designed to make his reformation as spectacular as possible. It belongs to the stage rather than real life. A calculated reformation would seem to be as incompatible with a genuine reformation as a rehearsed martyrdom is with sainthood. As an artist in offence, Hal loses the identity we have come to know and love. He is the Frank Churchill of the play, professing a love for Falstaff he plans to betray. There is too much theatre and too little humanity in his performance. The concluding rhymes of the soliloquy – 'I'll so offend, to make offence a skill, / Redeeming time when men least think I will' (I.ii.239–40) – mock his facility. They show Hal is as easy with words as with people.

Hal's loss of self-identity through verbal trickery recurs in the choral line 'I do, I will' when he threatens to banish Falstaff during their role-playing at the tavern (II.iv.528). As the jovial banter deepens into momentary solemnity, the 'I do' of the play-actor modulates into the 'I will' of the future king. The illusion of play acting is shattered by the double force of the verb, which is not only the auxiliary of a simple future tense but also a threatening verb of volition — 'I will banish you.' As my considered decision and desire, this is my oracle as future king: it is the only promise I can make to you as a friend.

Hal is sensitive to the singularity of Falstaff as a comic genius who is not only witty in himself but also a cause of wit in Hal and his friends. Falstaff is someone Hal likes to be with. But he never loves Falstaff as Falstaff loves the prince and as we adore Falstaff. All such asymmetries are potentially grotesque and painful. Hal has many friends, but Falstaff's love for Hal constitutes his world. Falstaff *is* the prince: 'My king, my Jove, I speak to thee, my heart!' (2 *Henry IV*, V.v.50). Friendship is democratic, but love is totalitarian.

It is important in Shakespeare to distinguish between official and unofficial views, between what Falstaff and Hal think they ought to say and what they actually feel and sometimes say obliquely. The king's dismissal of Falstaff is a son's rejection of his father, a disciple's rejection of his mentor. In the soliloquy spoken over Sir John's supposed corpse, we want Hal to say 'Death has not struck so fat a deer to-day, / Though none so dear, in this bloody fray' (1 *Henry IV*, V.iv.107–8). Instead, the prince says, 'Though many dearer.' Hal is Falstaff's whole world, the object of his heart's love and desire, but for

Hal Falstaff is merely a fat deer. We would like to think that the pun on 'dear' is Hal's way of activating his mind and making a joke out of what is too painful to say: I loved that man dearly. He was a second father to me. But his word play on 'deer' is the opposite of 'endearing.' If reconciling love and friendship is one of the most important goals in Shakespeare, then is it not degrading for Hal to use puns to lower Falstaff in the scale of his affections? Yet Shakespeare in his greater wisdom may be holding other meanings in reserve. Who indeed is wiser? Falstaff, who believes that to lose love is to lose a world? Or Hal, who finds friendship must alter 'when it alteration finds'? Falstaff is more lovable than Hal. But in recognizing that Falstaff's love and his own genius for friendship are not in the end compatible, the king may be the sadder and the wiser of the two after all.

13 Groucho Marx to Bernard Shaw: The Irish Bull

When Groucho Marx quips that he would never join a club that would accept him as a member, his self-deprecating humour relaxes the strictures of an Irish bull. The *OED* defines a bull as 'a self-contradictory proposition; in modern use, an expression involving a ludicrous inconsistency unperceived by the speaker. The epithet *Irish* is a late addition.' If Groucho's desire to join a club depends on the club's refusal to admit him, then his wish is self-defeating. But the charming absurdity of his quip is instructive. For it deftly deflates the self-conceit of snobs who join a club to prove they are special. A witticism like Groucho's that begins in a tone of self-parodying exclusiveness may deepen by its end into an oracle that raises the ghost of bigotry and prejudice. Despite the joking, there is no loss of inner seriousness, for a bull is capable of lethal lunges and dangerous thrusts.

A deathly premonitory bull casts a shadow over Henry James's novella 'Daisy Miller,' when the heroine tries to extract from Winterbourne an invitation to meet his aunt. She begins by teasing him about his relative's patronizing assumption of superior worth.

> 'I want to know her ever so much. I know I should like her. She would be very exclusive. I like a lady to be exclusive; I'm dying to be exclusive myself. Well, we *are* exclusive, mother and I. We don't speak to everyone – or they don't speak to us. I suppose it's about the same thing.' (James, 1962, 109)

Daisy's first use of 'exclusive' verges on a parody of self-importance. A sense of social superiority prevents Mrs Costello from receiving Daisy. But despite being snubbed, Daisy professes to admire her enemy's discriminating taste: 'I like a lady to be exclusive; I'm dying to be exclusive myself.'

Later in the story Daisy will literally die to 'be exclusive.' She will contract fever after communing with the stars at midnight in the Roman Coliseum. Her 'dying' in the quoted passage is merely figurative. But it cannot disguise the growing seriousness of her tone, and is disturbingly prophetic. Desperate for connection, Daisy now claims that she and her mother are exclusive, not in the way Mrs Costello is exclusive – by snubbing others – but by being excluded by *them*. 'We don't speak to everyone – or they don't speak to us.'

The chiasmus here cannot quite disguise a miscarriage of logic (or the inconsistency of a bull). In claiming that she and her mother do not speak to everyone, Daisy is still trying to maintain a façade of polite respectability. But to make the chiasmus work, Daisy has to say that the people they decline to speak to do not speak to them. The pronoun 'they' has no grammatical antecedent. The closest pronoun it can attach to is 'everyone.' But to say that everyone declines to speak to them is to say that no one speaks to them. If so, their exclusion is complete: it is a disturbing omen of Daisy's final exclusion from life itself at the end of the story.

1

There is no solvent like laughter for extricating witty Irishmen like Oscar Wilde and George Bernard Shaw from the precious nonsense of their Irish bulls. When Wilde jokes that 'Meredith is a prose Browning, and so is Browning' (1968, 202), the shock depends on a miscarriage of logic. It is as if Wilde were to say that an oak is a member of the class, trees, and so is a tree. But what sounds at first like a category mistake or a clumsy tautology – 'and so is Browning' – is saved by Wilde's joke that Browning, though a poet, is a pedestrian poet. A witticism that ties itself into a knot may use humour to loosen the knot. Browning, Wilde would argue, is as prosaic as Meredith, who is as flat-footed and lame in his poems as he is poetic (by flashes) in his novels.

Some of Wilde's aphorisms teeter on the brink of nonsense. But when we ponder what he says, they usually disclose their own subversive sense. The joke about Browning immediately draws a laugh. But the violation of logic has its own critical point. It is like saying, 'Roman Britain was a small part of a great empire, and the empire was small, too.' How can X be a part of a great Y, if Y itself is then declared to be small? Only by altering the meaning of 'small' – to mean small-souled or paltry in spirit – or by some other twist of wordplay or grammar. To justify his bull Wilde asserts that Browning 'used poetry as a medium for writing in prose' (1968, 202). In other words, Browning uses verse, not to compose 'with the voice purely,' as Milton does, but with the hand and the eye also. Browning's oracles from the swamp 'stain' Shelley's 'white radiance of eternity,' not with a dome of many-coloured glass, but with impressions that are mudbound and viscous, 'Green-dense and dim-delicious, bred o' the sun' ('Caliban upon Setebos,' l. 40).

The paradox at the core of *Major Barbara* is the oracle: 'You shall save your soul by making money.' In *Saint Joan* Shaw dramatizes the paradox that the Church of Rome canonized in Joan the first Protestant saint. Many of Shaw's plays translate into dramatic prose oracles he first receives as aphorisms. Some of these kernels of wit and insight are strewn throughout the appendices and prefaces of Shaw's plays. In *Maxims for Revolutionists*, for example, Shaw says wittily, 'do not do unto others as you would that they should do unto you. Their tastes may not be the same' (*Maxims for Revolutionists*, *Man and Superman*, 1903). By retaining the archaic 'unto' he gives his subversion of the Golden Rule a prophetic ring. But behind the subversion lurks the nonsense of an Irish bull. Shaw is substituting for a charter of inalienable rights, duties, or freedoms, which are universal and unalterable, the mere 'taste' of some aesthetic or sexual preference, which may vary harmlessly from one person to another.

Shaw's witticism 'I don't believe in morality. I'm a disciple of Bernard Shaw' (*The Doctor's Dilemma*, III, 1906) extinguishes in laughter the emotion of placing trust in its author. To be a disciple, even of Shaw, is to profess belief in something. By raising the question of how faith in Shaw exceeds faith in morality, the witticism invites us to consider how Shaw operates as an ethical immoralist. By promoting ethical values like integrity Shaw has to battle against the seduction of his better impulses by the merely restrictive 'mores' or customs that society tries to impose on him in the name of 'morality.'

Shaw's witty oracles often combine precious nonsense in one direction with prophetic sense in another. Being Irish, Shaw allows his nonsense to take shape as an Irish bull. 'Being right when other people are wrong,' for example, is an oddly inclusive activity for Shaw to claim as his 'speciality' (*You Never Can Tell*, act IV, 1896). A wise or moral man would never presume to make a speciality of being right. Only a sophist would claim that a state of grace so liberal as wisdom or so unteachable as holiness is his special branch of learning, which he is clever enough to reduce to laws or presumptuous enough to formulate as rules. A species of Irish bull also animates Shaw's quip that 'no man is bad enough to tell the truth about himself during his lifetime' ('In the Days of My Youth,' 1900). In pretending to exonerate man from the charge that he is bad, Shaw actually does the reverse. It is because men are bad that they refuse to say how bad they are. In seeming to mark a limit to badness, Shaw cleverly does the opposite. But he also manages to extinguish in a joke the misanthropy that might make his claim more cynical than amusing.

In a letter to Frank Harris (20 June 1930), in which he professes a distaste for oracles and aphorism because they are only a 'way of being great by flashes,' Shaw boasts that the aphoristic 'English way' of Shakespeare, Ruskin, and Chesterton cannot disguise its incoherence from an Irishman like Shaw. But then Shaw is involved in the inconsistency of denouncing his own Irish talent for being paradoxical and witty. If what he says about his eye for incoherence in his letter to Harris is true, then Shaw is less Irish than English. And yet this concession offends 'his native [Irish] pride.' In truth, Shaw is never more Irish than when pretending not to perceive the charming inconsistency of his saying it is impossible to disguise incoherence from an Irishman, especially an Irishman who pretends to be as inconsistent as Shaw.

Shaw's most quotable sayings are often a blend of Irish blarney and English common sense. When asked about his reputation, Shaw replies: 'Which reputation? I have at least fifteen different reputations.' Like Arnold's claim that morality is three-fourths of life, Shaw's attempt to divide his reputations into fifteen parts sets up distinctions where they do not apply. As F.H. Bradley wittily remarks, 'a man's life, we take it, cannot thus be cut in pieces; ... in the saving one-tenth and the sweeping nine-tenths alike, we can see little more than the faltering assertion of one mistake, or the confident aggravation of another' (1876, 215). The more precise Shaw tries to be, the more fanciful he sounds. Since any number – fifteen or nine-tenths – imposes a limit on morality or genius as such, it also pokes fun at Shaw's claim to be a jack of all trades whose talents exceed any number he might assign to them. Intoxicated with the sound of his own voice, Shaw can often be exasperating. But who wants Shaw always to be talking sense?

Many of Shaw's political witticisms seem to nick their perpetrator as well as wound the bull he wants to gore. When he says that 'our political experiment of democracy' is 'the last refuge of cheap government' ('Epistle Dedicatory,' *Man and Superman*, 1903), he forgets that there is nothing cheap about educating a society of voters in order to give democracy a chance to work. In many of Shaw's other witticisms there lingers some 'doubt,' as one critic says, about 'which way' the Irish bull 'faces, whether it is two-faced as well as two-horned' (Ricks, 1993, 155). To maintain that 'Tom Paine has triumphed over Edmund Burke and the swine are now courted electors' is to deplore the decline in the quality, though not the size, of the electorate. But the folly is not all on democracy's side. The reduction of people to swine is Swiftian in its misanthropy; the curl of the cynic's tongue is tasteless and unpleasant. 'If Despotism failed only for want of a capable benevolent despot,' Shaw asks, 'what chance has democracy, which requires a whole population of capable voters?' ('Epistle Dedicatory,' *Man and Superman*, 1903). Like most advocates of despotism, Shaw fails to see that voters in a democracy do not have to be equal in ability to the rulers they elect. Instead of killing off democracy, Shaw's matador is seriously wounded by the bull he tries to gore.

At other times Shaw's foolery turns out to be wisdom in disguise. To reduce happiness to a commodity like wealth seems at first to degrade it. 'We have no more right to consume happiness without producing it than to consume wealth without producing it' (*Candida* I, 1895). An uncritical comparison of happiness with wealth falsely equates giving love with the manufacture of toys, or the receiving of life with the consumption of food. And yet the folly of quantifying happiness, as one quantifies wealth, may possess its own wisdom, too. It reminds us that if we hope to receive we must also give. It is better to bestow charity than to take it.

Though Shaw distrusts idealists, folly is seldom the monopoly of one side alone. Shaw's wit is a two-edged sword that acknowledges the idealist as a worthy enemy even as it seems to cut him down to size. 'The idealist is a more dangerous animal than a Philistine just as a man is a more dangerous animal than a sheep' (*The Quintessence of Ibsenism*, 1891). A merely figurative use of 'animal' in the first clause becomes shockingly literal in the second. Just as a sheep is a hapless victim of a werewolf, or of a wolf-man ready to feed on its prey, so a Philistine is an easy prey for an idealist. A wolf's craftiness and power to subvert may be more desirable qualities in a rational animal than the docility of a sheep. Shaw's true enemy, the sheepish Philistine, turns out to be as two-faced as it is two-horned.

Occasionally the deftly unsettling charm of Shaw's bulls seems simply wrong-headed: 'The worst cliques are those which consist of one man,' he says (Preface to *Back to Methuselah*, 1920, Part V). How can a clique, a group of conspirators, consist of a single person? Shaw's bull lends itself to the charge of being foolish or obtuse. And yet the bull reminds us that a tyranny of one can operate as a power block just as efficiently and perhaps as ruthlessly as a group of conspirators. Shaw's jest that 'Moscow is built of English history written in London by Karl Marx' is more amusing than persuasive (*The Apple Cart*, II, 1929). And it is outlandish for Shaw to claim that the Soviets owe more to Englishmen and Germans than to fellow Russians. But the wry and plaintive bull that 'revolutionary movements attract those who are not good enough for established institutions as well as those who are too good for them' (Preface to *Androcles and the Lion*, 1916) is both a witty indictment and a persuasive defence of revolutionaries. By disclosing an unexpected similarity between criminals and idealists and between insurrectionists and saints, Shaw repays the loan of our attention with ample interest.

In Sydney Smith's view, a bull is 'the very reverse of wit; for as wit discovers real relations, that are not apparent, bulls admit apparent relations that are not real' (Ricks, 1993, 191). More promising than Sydney Smith's indiscriminate attack on bulls is Christopher Ricks's clever defence of them for observing a three-stage evolution: 'apparent congruity, succeeded by a real incongruity, then issues in an unexpected congruity' (1993, 191). We can fault Smith for ignoring the last stage of this three-part process. Unlike Ricks, he fails to consider how expedient it may be for a wit like Shaw to keep his adversaries in doubt as to whether his bulls are simple blunders or shrewd political indictments. When Shaw says that 'excess of insularity makes a Briton an Imperialist' (*The Revolutionist's Handbook*, *Man and Superman*, 1903), he seems at first to be talking nonsense. Since an imperialist's agenda is global, it is surely the opposite of insular. But the more we ponder Shaw's Irish bull about English nationalism, the more unsettling truths it discloses. Only an imperialist, for example, would be insular enough to suppose that the idols of his cave are also gods of the universe.

Like a mule without pride of ancestry or hope of posterity, a sterile bull combines lust for progeny with a total incapacity to sire or breed anything. When Shaw announces that 'marriage, or any other form of promiscuous amoristic monogamy, is fatal to large States because it puts its ban on the deliberate breeding of man as a political animal'

(*The Revolutionist's Handbook*, 1903), opponents of eugenics are disposed to dismiss him as a simple anarchist. Shaw's reduction of people to political animals and of procreation to breeding seems initially as wrongheaded as his redefinition of marriage, which turns an institution usually thought necessary to the state's survival into something subversive and 'fatal' to it. But the bull that equates monogamy with its opposite, with the promiscuity that is best promoted by polygamy, is not as sterile or obtuse as it first seems. If 'marriage is popular because it combines the maximum of temptation with the maximum of opportunity,' then perhaps it satisfies the same selfish desires as polygamy without promoting polygamy's one desirable political objective: the breeding of a superior race. As Shaw says, 'the maternal instinct leads a woman to prefer a tenth share in a first rate man to the exclusive possession of a third rate one' (*The Revolutionist's Handbook*, 1903). With sly propriety, the advocate of selective breeding wittily turns his defence of eugenics into a vigorous and horny Irish bull.

2

If wits are sure to madness near allied, then so are many bulls that try to tell a difficult truth without lying. The apparent contradiction or lie may originate in the nothingness concealed in being. Many readers manage to discern some flicker of profound meaning at the end of Stevens's poem 'The Snow Man.' But more scrupulous interpreters might argue with some display of logic that the ending yields more confusion than sense. How can a 'listener' who is 'nothing himself' behold 'Nothing that is not there and the nothing that is.' (ll. 13–15)? To resist the temptation of reading human motives into winter sounds, the listener must have a soul of winter, Stevens tells us. The outer emptiness must mirror an inner emptiness, a 'nothing' in oneself. To experience this 'nothing' one must go into a closet and shut the door. As one observer says, 'this is the world of the individual experience that isn't just subjective and egocentric. It's also the nothing-world out of which nothingness grows into creation' (Frye, 2004a, 194). Since it is possible for 'a mind of winter' to behold 'the nothing that is,' it must also be capable of beholding the absence of something, the something that is not there. But this is precisely what Stevens has just said a mind of winter, if it is successfully to resist a seductive pathetic fallacy, cannot allow itself to discern. If Stevens's claim to see something that is absent is true, his claim to behold 'Nothing that is not there' must be false.

Stevens's profound (but counter-intuitive) insight is that only a 'mind of winter' can 'behold the junipers shagged with ice,' and *not* 'think / Of any misery in the sound of the wind.' His immunity to pathos parallels Frost's comparably strict and stoic claim that anyone with country sophistication will resist being deceived by the phoebes' song. In 'The Need of Being Versed in Country Things,' the light of the fire that burned the farmhouse has become a sunset glow. The house itself is a flower-like ruin. Even the song of the phoebes seems a sigh for the pity of human change. Yet instead of indulging this pathos, Frost explodes it from within by censoring the regret he fondly attributes to the birds' sigh-like murmur earlier in the poem. 'One had to be versed in country things,' he warns, 'Not to be believe the phoebes wept' (ll. 23–4).

Like Stevens, Frost is trying to retract with one hand what he offers with the other. Having endowed the phoebes with a human quality, the power to grieve, it is too late to deny them that attribute now. Like a judge who instructs jurors to ignore an argument that has moved them deeply, Frost is asking us to do what is not strictly possible. For we cannot separate the grievous reticence of Frost's poem from the extravagance of its surmise. Frost thinks he can reject the urban sophistication of pastoral poetry, which is the impulse behind the fallacy he finds both dangerous and enticing. But in this he is as surely self-deceived as that other Frost, the classical scholar and student of Virgil, who wants us to believe he is only a tough, down-to-earth New England farmer.

Though a bull's contradictions are subliminal, any oracular parody of a bull is on exuberant self-display for all to laugh at. In such prophetic verse as 'Hertha' and 'Genesis,' Swinburne teeters on the brink of the same inanities he mocks in his parody of Tennyson, 'The Higher Pantheism in a Nutshell.' Truist reductions of Hegelian axioms, 'More is the whole than a part' (l. 5), combine with absurd misstatements of these axioms, 'but half is more than the whole' (l. 15). The result is an inane violation of the law of contradiction: 'Doubt is faith,' 'faith ... is doubt' (l. 5), and trite truism: 'One and two are not one' (l. 17). One could say of these outrageous bulls what Samuel Johnson says of *Cymbeline*. 'To remark the folly of the fiction ... were to waste criticism upon unresisting imbecility.'

In 'A Nocturnal upon St Lucy's Day,' Donne's grieving lover is not content to be an ordinary nothing. In trying to magnify his loss, he says he is 'Of the first nothing the elixir grown' (l. 29). By his beloved's death Donne is made the 'elixir' or quintessence, not of ordinary nothing, which would be intelligible if not profound, but of 'the first nothing,' the nothing which preceded the world's creation in Genesis. This is certainly sublime or profound enough, but is it intelligible?

Though Donne makes his meditation on death a concentrated epitome of all that is dark and empty in the world, his lines themselves are the opposite of empty.

> But I am by her death – which word wrongs her –
> Of the first nothing, the elixir grown; ...
> If I an ordinary nothing were,
> As shadow, a light, and body must be here.
> But I am none; nor will my sun renew.
>
> ('A Nocturnal upon St. Lucy's Day,' ll. 28–37)

Abnormally compressed, Donne's verse never wastes a syllable. But packed as they are with supernormal meaning, do these lines make any sense? No human being, surely, can inhabit 'the first nothing' that precedes God's creation *ex nihilo*. It is even difficult for a human mind to imagine how God could inhabit it. The same problem bothers Augustine, who (as one critic notes) raises it 'in a famous passage in the *Confessions*, where in effect he answers the question, "What was God doing before creation?," by saying, "Preparing a hell for those who ask such a question"' (Frye, 1991, 42).

To revise Donne's paradoxes might deprive them of profundity and wit. But it might make more intelligible the mystery of 'creation out of nothing,' which (applied to God) is difficult to understand. However emotionally powerful and devastating Donne's conceits may be in a poem that gravitates naturally toward death, they abound in unperceived contradictions. If Donne's speaker were the 'none' he claims to be, instead of being melancholy or destroyed by the woman's loss, he would be a creature without qualities. To say that he is shadowless (since a shadow must be cast by light and a body, and he is now a dark ghost) confuses a mere property or accidental quality of the bereaved lover with the pure existence of a 'first nothing,' and hence with something devoid of qualities altogether.

When Milton's Satan claims that 'in the lowest deep, a lower deep / Still threatening to devour me opens wide' (*Paradise Lost*, IV.76–7), he is caught in a trap. For if there is still a 'lower deep,' 'the lowest' cannot be what he says it is, a use of the adjective in the superlative degree. As Edgar recognizes in *King Lear*, 'To be worst, / The lowest and most dejected thing of fortune, / Stands still in esperance, lives not in fear' (IV.i.2–4). Once we descend to what is worst, we can go in only one direction: up. Unlike Milton, however, Edgar forbids the use of such superlatives as 'lowest' and 'worst.' 'O gods! Who is't can say "I am at the worst"? / I am worse than e'er I was ... / And worse I may be yet' (IV.i.25–7). To avoid the exquisite and refined nonsense of worsening to an unimaginable degree or depth a torture that is 'worst,' Edgar immediately corrects the contradiction. 'The worst,' he concedes, 'is not / So long as we can say "This is the worst"' (IV.i.27–8). In saying, 'No worst, there is none,' Hopkins, like Shakespeare, is removing any foundation or basement to his despair. Disallowing the use of the superlative degree, he can envisage only a freefall through space.

3

Viola's soliloquy on wise fools and clowns in act III, scene i of *Twelfth Night* is as wittily definitive as Hamlet's address to the players on the art of acting. A true clown must be 'wise enough to play the fool, / And to do that well craves a kind of wit' (*Twelfth Night*, III.i.67–8). As much practice and art are required to be a fool like Feste as a wise man like Ulysses. A clever clown has to observe the mood of those he jests with. Feste has to amuse Viola without crossing or insulting her. And like the wise counsellor he must remain as alert and discerning as the hawk who checks every feather of his intended prey before swooping down to attack it.

A delight in bulls and wise wit is on exuberant display for all to relish in the clown Feste's exuberant exchange with Viola preceding her soliloquy. 'Dost thou live by thy tabor?,' Viola asks Feste, and the clown replies, 'No, sir, I live by the church.' The double force of 'by' generates double meaning that verges on a bull. It seems preposterous that a clown should earn his living as a clergyman. But if clowns are preachers, perhaps preachers are sometimes clowns. Feste is construing the preposition 'by' in its most literal sense, as a synonym for 'beside' or 'in spatial proximity to.' Amused by the equivocation, Viola refuses to let go of it. 'So thou mayst say, the king lies by a beggar, if a beggar dwells near him.' Though it may shock us to think of a king and beggar as neighbours, the proposition is logically convertible. If A lives near B, then B lives near A. But tenacious to the point of perversity, Viola turns the conversion into a perfect chiasmus, formulating the contradiction as a witty antithesis: 'Or, the church stands by thy tabor, if thy tabor stands by the church.' The metonymy that substitutes tabor for clown brings the two uses of 'by' into uneasy alliance.

The clown who lives beside or by the church earns his living by means of the tabor. But the two meanings that the metonymy wittily reconciles are likely to fly apart again into a bull at any moment.

Both dazzled and bewildered by Viola's wit, Feste exclaims: 'To see this age! A sentence is but chev'riled glove to a good wit.' The clown seems to be paying Viola a carefully considered tribute. Her witty thoughts, he says, fit into her precisely turned words as easily as a hand slides into a kid glove that fits it without a wrinkle. But then Feste qualifies his compliment by observing 'how quickly the wrong side may be turned outward!' Perversely turning the literal meaning of 'by' into a figurative one, Viola has forsaken a rational use of words for equivocations, bulls, and quibbles. Feste is anticipating the charge that Samuel Johnson will make against Shakespeare himself a century and a half later. A quibble for Shakespeare was the fatal Cleopatra for which he lost the world and was content to lose it.

Yet in a charming defence of wordplay, Feste suggests that any unequivocal use of language is a prison. Ever since the time 'bonds disgraced' words by binding them to a single meaning, words have proved resourceful in escaping their jailors. Indeed poetic words are so promiscuous and wanton that Feste declares he is 'loath to prove reason with them.' To call his bluff Viola charges Feste with being 'a merry fellow' who cares 'for nothing.' To defend his title as a 'corrupter of words' the clown plays exuberantly with the word she has given him. He refutes Viola's charge by protesting that if he cared for nothing he would care for *her*. We expect him to say that if he cared for nothing he would *not* care for her. But the use of a bull to reverse wittily what we expect to hear revives the equivocal force of 'nothing.' Does 'care for nothing' mean 'not care for anything?' Or does it mean care for that pure being or spirit which, since it is not some thing, is indistinguishable from nothing? Just when the clown's word play and bull seem to border on insolence by implying that in not caring for Viola he is caring for 'nothing,' a mere nonentity or cipher, he retrieves his balance. It is just as well, he seems wisely to observe, that in caring for you I am not caring for nothing, for that would turn you into a pure being or essence, and so 'make you invisible.'

Combining Viola's wit with Portia's intelligence, Beatrice's banter with the deep and spontaneous love of a mature Juliet, Rosalind is the most resourceful and multifaceted of Shakespeare's heroines. In her male disguise, Rosalind is as wittily critical of Orlando for arriving late as Beatrice is critical of Benedick (*As You Like It*, IV.i.44–9). An infinitesimal fraction of a minute is an enormity of time for any lover to keep his mistress waiting. Such a lover may protest that Cupid has arrested him and thrown him in prison. But he can never convince Rosalind that his heart has been touched or bruised, much less broken in two. Rosalind's claim that she prefers to be wooed by a snail than by a lover who is late for his rendezvous may seem too laboured to compete with the lighter wit of Viola. Armed with horns, the snail anticipates 'the slander of his wife,' whereas the lazy wooer is never prepared for the cuckoldry that wrecks his peace as a husband. Rosalind's wit has more bite than Viola's, but her conceit that the snail carries his house on his head and makes a better marriage settlement than Orlando is as wittily critical as charmingly clever. Rosalind also rivals the wise Portia in the advice she offers her lover. Instead of kissing his beloved before he speaks, Orlando should speak first and save his kiss for the awkward moment when words begin to fail him. Her observation that a kiss is the lover's equivalent of the orator's spit is as funny as it is shrewd. And when Orlando objects that no lover could ever be at a loss for words when face to face with a beautiful mistress, Rosalind's warning is as caustic as it is obliquely self-revealing. If Orlando were ever to be face to face with Rosalind, once her disguise is removed, his discovery that his mistress's candour is no less acute than her wit might leave him more speechless than he thinks.

As addicted to wordplay and bulls as Viola in her wordplay with the clown, Rosalind responds with a pun to Orlando's disbelief that his mistress would ever reject his proposal. 'What, out of my suit?' No, you won't be out of your apparel, she tells him; you won't cast your clothes aside and tumble into bed with your mistress. Instead, you will be out of your suit because your mistress will reject you. Appalled by the horny bull she brings to life only to fend back and repel, Orlando tells Rosalind he would die if he lost her. Though she is naturally enthralled to hear him say so, she has to conceal her joy in order to keep her disguise in place. To this end she assumes a tone more in keeping with Beatrice berating Benedick than with Juliet's candid outpouring of her love for Romeo. No man ever died for love, she bluntly tells him. The tone is rudely anti-heroic and burlesque. Far from dying for love of Cressida, Troilus 'had his brains dashed out with a Grecian club.' And though Leander is reported to have died for Hero, the unromantic truth is that he washed himself on a hot midsummer night in the Hellespont and was drowned when seized with a cramp. Rosalind uses this burlesque treatment of romantic subjects both to defend and discover. The low style conceals her identity and defends her against any premature trespass of intimacy. But by touching on heroic love it also helps her discover, refine, and celebrate what she feels for Orlando.

Rosalind has the genius to jest about what moves her. This is why there is pathos as well as wit, regret as well as irony, in her reflection that 'men are April when they woo, December when they wed; maids are May when they are maids, but the sky changes when they are wives' (*As You Like It*, IV.i.47–9). Countering without allaying the sadness inherent in any cycle of human change is Rosalind's determined claim that she will be as jealous of her lover as a Barbary cock-pigeon is of his hen. Furthering the reversal of sexual roles, she promises to be giddier in her desire for Orlando than a monkey for its mate. Rosalind's disguise allows her to assert the importunate needs and desires of a Cressida or Beatrice while preserving intact the modest restraint of an Imogen. Being both inside and outside the love games, Rosalind can disclose to her friend Celia after Orlando leaves that her love for him is as deep as Juliet's for Romeo. Like the boundless sea of Juliet's love, Rosalind's love cannot be sounded. 'My affection hath an unknown bottom, like the bay of Portugal.' By a strange arithmetic the infinite substance of love minus a partial reflection or shadow of it is still infinity. As a boundless sea can always be replenished, however much we draw from it, so the more love Rosalind gives to Orlando the more she has, for as Juliet says, 'both are infinite' (*Romeo and Juliet*, II.ii.135). Rosalind makes her discovery partly as a result of the bulls, quibbles, and jokes which are in keeping with her mask. The disguise she assumes allows her to be both a wise critic and apologist, a witty censor and an eloquent defender of love at the same time.

4

Witty bulls of a more philosophical breed than Shakespeare's have been known to charge and gore so mighty a matador as the redoubtable Hegel and even the great St. Anselm. According to Hegel's *Logic*, pure being is a predicate of everything that is. But it is not some *thing*. And what is not some thing is nothing. The conversion of Pure Being into its opposite, Non-Being, is a bull, since it boldly violates the law of contradiction. Equally suspect is the lofty nonsense of Anselm's proof that God exists. We are asked to believe that a God who exists is more perfect and sublime than a God who, possessing all the other attributes of perfection, lacks one quality: the perfection of being. But how does this philosophical bull differ from the proposition that a community of triangles, if it existed, would necessarily worship a triangular God? Except in the mind of a crazed mathematician, there is nothing to support the view that a community of triangles or a triangular God has ever existed. As George Santayana says, 'the foolishness of the simple is delightful; only the foolishness of the wise is exasperating' (1967, 139).

Finding the contradictions of the bull 'intimate with the great contradictions of life and death' (1993, 162), Christopher Ricks is amused that Samuel Johnson, a perpetrator of bulls himself, should attack the bull in John Gay's proposed gravestone inscription in Westminster Abbey. 'My own EPITAPH / Life is a jest, and all things show it, / I thought so once; but now I know it.' If only death reveals the justice of the sentiment that life is a joke, how can a dead Gay communicate it? And if the idea that life is a joke is Gay's present sentiment, how can death be said to confirm it while Gay is still alive? Johnson's verdict is harsher: 'these lines ... are impious in the mouth of a Christian, and nonsense in that of an atheist' (Ricks, 1993, 163). But Johnson lets slip his own bull when he says, according to Bombaugh, that 'every monumental inscription should be in Latin, for that being a dead language, it will always live' (Ricks, 1993, 176).

At its point of greatest instability, even a successful epigram may yield only the apparent incongruity of a bull.

Of treason

Treason doth never prosper; what's the reason?
For if it prosper, none dare call it treason.

It is surely contradictory to claim 'treason never prospers,' then immediately hypothesize: 'if it prospers.' Moreover, the epigram's first clause terminates in an apparent absurdity, since some traitors clearly do succeed and prosper. Yet the epigram's surprising conclusion converts its apparent bull into a witty redefinition. For if a subversive act does succeed, then a new emotive meaning must be found to match the sudden change in its descriptive meaning. A successful revolution is no longer treason but a blow against tyranny or a victory for democracy and freedom.

Equally effective and witty in converting a bull into a wise-sounding oracle is the epigram

All hastens to its end. If life and love
Seem slow it is their ends we're ignorant of.

If everything hastens to its end, then how can life and love be slow?
The solution to the bull lies in the pun on 'end' and 'ends,' which
contrasts a termination point with a final cause or goal. As one critic
says, it is the oracle's 'combination of surprise and fulfilment that
gives the last phrase its wit and the epigram its point' (Smith, 1968,
200–1).

Christopher Ricks believes that bulls 'are naturally childlike and
preternaturally poetic' (1993, 189). Though the ambitious word 'perpetuate' is an odd companion for the sad brevity of the phrase 'a little
while,' Coleridge is touched by the tender bull inscribed by Mrs
Cowley on her daughter's tomb: 'A little while to perpetuate my
memory' (Ricks, 1993, 175). Again, in Wordsworth's poem 'We Are
Seven,' the child's insistence that her family has seven members,
though two are now in heaven, is 'an inspired act of contradiction,' as
Ricks says, 'and is alive with naïve acumen' (1993, 189).

'How many are you, then,' said I,
'If there are two in heaven?'
Quick was the little Maid's reply,
'O Master! we are seven.'   (ll. 61–4)

It is discourteous, perhaps, for the maid and her brother John to play
round the grave of their dead sister. But it is even more discourteous
for death to force John to join his sibling and lie 'by her side' (l. 60).
Inspired by the contradictions inherent in all deaths, the young maid
rises to a contradiction of her own. Seven minus two, she insists, is still
seven.

'But they are dead; those two are dead!
Their spirits are in heaven!'
'T was throwing words away; for still
The little Maid would have her will,
And said, 'Nay, we are seven!'   (ll. 65–9)

Her absent siblings are still strangely present. We are touched by the
justified naïvety, the wise simplicity, with which the little maid
accepts and lives with contradiction. As in any tender bull, however,

we are also poignantly uncertain how far she registers the incongruity. Just how conscious is the child of keeping her two views of death in focus?

Samuel Goldwyn's bull, 'include me out,' hovers between paradox and solecism. Instead of saying 'count me out,' Goldwyn's imperfect command of English idiom commits him to the paradox that inclusion entails its logical opposite, exclusion. Other bulls entangle their speaker in a web of confused time sequences. 'Mr X said he was disappointed to find there was no suggestion box in the clubhouse because he would like to put a suggestion in it about having one.' If X's suggestion were acted on, there would be no need for him to put a suggestion in the box. But since no box exists, the idea of putting a suggestion inside it confuses something he wants to exist with what happens to be at the moment. At a more oracular level, Heraclitus's observation that 'there is nothing permanent except change' combines the shock effect of a paradox with the logical contradiction of a bull. For if change, which is impermanent, is the only exception to permanence, then nothing is permanent, and there can be no exception to the rule.

Other bulls are hard to distinguish from Zenlike paradoxes that turn bodies into ghosts by stripping gestures of their physical components. 'What happens to your fist when you open your hand?,' or the query: 'What is the sound of one hand clapping?' By peeling away attributes that normally define a subject, Lichtenberg performs a comparable operation on 'the handleless ax without a blade' (Hughes, 1975, 23). Less metaphysical but equally outrageous is the postscript that reads: 'If you don't receive this letter, it must have miscarried; therefore I beg you to write and let me know' (Hughes, 1975, 37). What begins as a tautology ends as a bull whose consequent, 'write and let me know,' negates what its antecedent affirms: namely, the non-arrival of the letter.

Sometimes a paradox that looks like a bull may be a wise owl in disguise. When Aleister Crowley observes 'it is no good trying to teach people who need to be taught' (Hughes, 1975, 42), we immediately object: 'what else is teaching for?' But if the most valuable skill a teacher imparts is the desire and aptitude to teach oneself, then someone who always needs to be taught is by definition 'unteachable.' There is also as much wisdom as bull in the Yiddish proverb: 'If the rich could hire other people to die for them, the poor could make a wonderful living' (Hughes, 1975, 62). What claims to be a wonderful livelihood or living is also its opposite: a wonderful form of dying. But even though acquiring wealth by dying for others achieves the opposite of what the proverb claims, the joke is not wholly gratuitous. For in inviting us to reconsider what wealth and poverty mean, the proverb also intimates that wherever wealth is found it must, in Ruskin's phrase, 'avail toward life.'

Ricks maintains that 'the best of the large Irish bulls is the thought of vacancy to which [Samuel] Beckett often and diversely returned: "Nothing is more real than nothing"' (1993, 202). What's on your mind, if you have a mind? Better a vacancy, perhaps, than the bull of a filled vacancy, which breeds only self-conceit and contempt. 'As to snobbishness,' says Shaw, inviting us to supply the missing terms of his enthymeme, 'ignorant men are always snobbish, because Nature abhors a vacuum' (*The Clerk*, February 1908). Like many observations about last or final things, the surmise that 'death is the last of our new beginnings' also conceals a bull. Death may be the last of the new beginnings we experience during our lifetime. But if death is not an end but a beginning, how can we say it is the last of such beginnings? If an end term can yield at least one new beginning, who is to say it may not yield more? Similarly, when the Quaker Isaac Penington says that every truth is substantial in its own place, but all truths are shadows except the last, he is hardly claiming that the last truth is his own aphorism. But if this is so, then his aphorism is just one more shadow in an infinite regress of shadows, and there need be no last or substantial truth after all.

Even the Anglican burial service for the dead refines the contradictions of a bull in ways that are both deeply affecting and (to me, at least) unnerving. 'Forasmuch as it has pleased Almighty God of his great mercy to receive unto himself the soul of our dear brother here departed, we therefore commit his body to the ground, earth to earth, dust to dust; in the sure and certain hope of the Resurrection to eternal life.' How could it please God to take from any of us our children, our parents, or the friends we love best? Samuel Johnson uses the same disturbing phrase when, after suffering a stroke, he writes to tell a friend that 'it has pleased God' to deprive him of speech. Just when God's will seems indistinguishable from the exquisite and refined pleasure a sadist takes in torturing a victim, the good offices of the liturgy come to our aid by assuring us that God in his mercy has taken the soul of our brother to himself. In case we dismiss this prayer as a tender bull, the burial service hastens to assure us that the act of committing earth to earth, heart-rending though it is, is offset by hope of a world to come. But we may wonder how 'hope' can be 'sure and certain' and still remain 'hope.' By setting doubt in motion, the prayer's apparent contradictions about the quality of hope, about the source of God's pleasure, and about the desirability of living in a world without end catch us off guard.

The burial service of the first Protestant prayer books directly addresses the person who has died. 'I commend thy soul to God the father almighty, and thy body to the ground, earth to earth, ashes to ashes, dust to dust.' As in Ben Jonson's great elegy, where the poet tells his dead son how to respond to a question: 'and, ask'd, say here doth lye / *Ben. Jonson* his best piece of *poetrie*' ('On My First Sonne,' ll. 9–10), an intimate conversation is still taking place. The living are addressing and being answered by the dead. But as Stephen Greenblatt reminds us, 'vigilant reformers felt that these words' of the original burial service 'had too much of the old Catholic faith hidden within them.' And 'so, a simple change was made: "We therefore commit his body to the ground" ... The dead person is no longer directly addressed, as if he retained some contact with the living. The small revision makes a large point: the dead are completely dead. No prayers can help them; no messages can be sent to them or received from them' (2004, 312–13). A sad recognition that the person we mourn is beyond reach may partly explain why the prayer for the dead leaves me poised on a knife-edge between consolation and despair. Instead of making an impact, its words induce a tremor. Every time I hear the burial service prayer it touches a nerve. It has the same effect as the closing lines of Johnson's incomparable poem, 'The Vanity of Human Wishes,' where everything the poet prays for reverses something he once stood for. If he were not so terrified of death and madness, so eager to melt away 'with unperceived decay' (l. 293), his confession would be much less wrenching and his prayer much less heartfelt than it is.

14 Oracles of Wit:
Oscar Wilde and Northrop Frye

Stephen Greenblatt's analysis of the decay of rituals during Shakespeare's lifetime applies with equal force to the damage sustained by oracles, myths, and what Tennyson calls 'the great vine of Fable' ('Timbuctoo,' l. 218) in nineteenth-century Britain. When the traditional consolations of theology are no longer intact, Victorian culture must experiment with new Sermons on the Mount and new forms of prophecy. Unprecedented new energies are released when oracles decay and poets must find new ways of focusing their powers. The genius of seers like Carlyle, Nietzsche, Wilde, and F.H. Bradley is inseparable from the wit that allows them to discard damaged oracles and salvage from their ruin a fragment of wisdom worth transmitting to posterity.

1

For the love of the Christian gospels, Oscar Wilde's Beatitudes substitute the good taste of an aesthete. Wilde's elect are not the meek in spirit, the peace-makers, or the mourners, but those 'to whom beautiful things mean only Beauty' (1968, 229). In the Gospel of Beauty set forth in his Preface to *The Picture of Dorian Gray*, hope, the second of the three Christian virtues, exists only for 'those who find beautiful meanings in beautiful things' (1968, 229). The closest equivalent of sin in Wilde's Gospel is the detection of 'ugly meanings' in beautiful objects. Such detection is 'corrupt without being charming,' and its trespass against good taste is said to be 'a fault.'

Beauty, not salvation, is Wilde's gospel. And since a disinterested (even useless) aesthetic must always be impersonal, the artist's aim 'is to reveal art and conceal' himself. But this axiom immediately begets a paradox. 'The highest, as the lowest, form of criticism,' Wilde tells us, 'is a mode of autobiography.' If art's aim is to reveal art and conceal the artist, why should the art critic not be equally self-effacing? We can see why art criticism might easily be marred by the confessional egoism of a critic who wants to talk about himself rather than Turner or Mozart. But why should the highest art criticism feature the critic rather than the artist? This precept seems contradictory, even the height of folly, until we realize that art criticism for Wilde is another form of art, one that translates 'into another manner or a new material his impression of beautiful things' (1968, 229). If a good critic were as self-effacing as a good poet, he could never turn criticism into a form of art, which must reveal itself as art while concealing the artist. As a creator, Wilde's critic has the difficult task of half-revealing and half-concealing the artist behind the mask.

As if to subvert the law received at Sinai, Wilde announces that 'there is no such thing as a moral or an immoral book. Books are well written, or badly written. That is all' (1968, 229). When art is deformed into propaganda, inciting hate or love in the spectator, it betrays its mission. Like Browning's Fra Lippo, who attacks a brother monk for scratching and prodding three slaves who 'turn the Deacon off his toasted side' in the painting of St Laurence ('Fra Lippo Lippi,' l. 328), Wilde decries any art that incites rage or loathing in a spectator. A stimulus-reaction theory of art breeds two perversions of taste: in the nineteenth century these distempers go by the names of 'Realism' and 'Romanticism,' respectively. 'The nineteenth century dislike of Realism,' Wilde quips, 'is the rage of Caliban seeing his own face in a glass.' And, by a corollary though opposite miscarriage of logic, 'the nineteenth century dislike of Romanticism is the rage of Caliban not seeing his own face in a glass.' Both oracles are appropriately distorted by Caliban's viewing the world from his swamp. They commit the identical error of assuming that art is a reflecting surface, a mirror rather than a self-illuminating candle or lamp.

Wilde's oracles are strongly judgmental. Though he is not a prophet of ethics or religion, he is as sternly prescriptive as Moses. If Wilde seems at first to be a witty but puzzling prophet, it is because he is moral in his proscription of moral sympathies, which he banishes from art as 'an unpardonable mannerism of style.' Wilde is, if you will, an amoral moralist. He is quite prepared to defend 'the morality of art.' But he parts company with such high Victorian defenders of art as

Arnold and Ruskin by insisting that 'the morality of art consists in the perfect use of an imperfect medium.'

By suppressing the minor premise of an enthymeme, Wilde can make an oracle sound as shocking or enigmatic as possible. Having asserted that 'no artist desires to prove anything,' he reaches the riddling conclusion that 'even things that are true can be proved.' In order to tease prophetic sense out of this apparent nonsequitur, Wilde must show that art does not aspire to the truth of logical demonstration, which is sequential and discursive. Instead, art possesses the truth of an oracle, which must be proved upon our pulses and intuited all at once, instantaneously and as a whole, or not at all. Far from denouncing art's inability to prove anything discursively, Wilde is celebrating it. The reversal comes with the use of the hinge word, 'even,' which replaces the word we expect to hear, the more logical 'only.' If we wish to restrict the word 'proof' to logical demonstrations, then only true things can be proved. But the mild shock produced by substituting 'even' for 'only' diminishes the status of a logical proof. Instead, like the words pronounced at Sinai or the Sermon Mount, the presentational truth of a great work of art is raised to a new plateau of discourse, which alone seem worthy of it.

Wilde expects each critic or reader to be Narcissus, for it is 'the spectator, and not life, that art really mirrors' (1968, 230). And since each Narcissus admires a different image in the mirror, art is also achieving its end most effectively 'when critics disagree' about what they are admiring. Since we tend to admire what we first romanticize, Wilde quotes appreciatively from Ouida's aphorisms on idealized love. The loftier the profession of faith the more prematurely it will perish. 'Half the passions of men die early, because they are expected to be eternal' (1968, 55). In professing more than it means to say, an oracle accomplishes not more, but less, than it is able to achieve. Though Wilde endorses Pater's axiom that all art aspires to the condition of music, he also accepts Henry James's teaching that art is good to the extent it is dramatic. Wilde tries to justify the paradox of being different things simultaneously by asserting that art is like music in its purely formal qualities, yet it resembles playacting by concealing behind a mask the personal feelings of the playwright. 'From the point of view of form, the type of all the arts is the art of the musician. From the point of view of feeling, the actors' craft is the type' (1968, 230).

Because of their rhetorical wit and elegance, Wilde's aphorisms often look simpler than they are. A critic's thankless task is often to show that these aphorisms are more complex than they seem. The only way we can draw the closing aphorisms of Wilde's *Preface* into a single web of sense is by turning them into the two premises and conclusion of a syllogism. What seems at first to be the conclusion, the oracular pronouncement that 'all art is quite useless,' is actually the major premise of a suppressed syllogism. All art is useless; useless things ought to be admirable; therefore art's only excuse for being is to be intensely admirable. Or as Keats would say, 'a thing of beauty is a joy forever.'

To attempt more than a superficial reading is to expose oneself to danger. For going below the surface is synonymous with reading symbols. And both activities are fraught with risk.

> All art is at once surface and symbol.
> Those who go beneath the surface do so at their peril.
> Those who read the symbol do so at their peril.   (1968, 230)

The repetition of the same principal clause in two successive aphorisms dramatizes the unspoken truth that reading symbols and probing beneath the surface of art are identical activities. And they pose a common danger of misjudging the formal qualities of art.

'To Parnassus,' Wilde says, 'there is no primer and nothing that one can learn is ever worth learning.' This new oracle from Parnassus seems to detonate in mid-flight. If nothing we learn is ever worth learning, why should Wilde think we have anything to learn from *him*? The contradiction begins to disappear the moment we realize Wilde is speaking as an oracle of the temple of art, and not as a prophet who aspires to teach a theory or explain a creed. We can learn the rules of discursive logic and argument. But Wilde believes that only the insights of a prophet or a seer are worth acquiring. And such insights, alas, can never be imparted in lectures, even those Wilde may give from halfway up Parnassus.

Suspicious of literary tastes that pretend to be universal, Wilde concludes that a reader who likes everything probably likes nothing. 'It is only an auctioneer who should admire all schools of art' (1968, 4). In a diverting aphorism from the drawing room, Wilde remarks that 'it is pleasanter to have the entrée to Balzac's society than to receive cards from all the duchesses in Mayfair' (1968, 10). But this pleasantry deepens into paradox when Wilde goes on to prophesy that 'a steady course of Balzac reduces our living friends to shadows, and our acquaintances to the shadows of shades.' Wilde's claim that fiction is more real than life is only partly explained by his shrewd saying that degrees of reality exist, even in fiction. We can all assent to Wilde's observation that Trollope increases 'the number of our acquaintances without adding to our visiting list; but after the *Comedie Humaine* one begins to believe that the only real people are the people who have never existed' (1968, 10). There is an oddly unsettling edge to this oracle, which turns fiction into substance and the world we inhabit into shadow or dream.

Wilde is seldom more scathing and judgmental than when condemning literary critics. Indulging a taste for oracular pronouncements, Wilde declares that 'the glib and shallow judgments' of a hapless detractor of Poe show 'that even dogmatism is no excuse for ignorance' (1968, 42). When the same critic claims that Longfellow had 'hundreds of imitators,' Wilde reserves his heaviest artillery for Longfellow, who 'has no imitators, for of echoes themselves there are no echoes and it is only style that makes a school' (1968, 41). Equally crushing is Wilde's judgment of a biography of Coleridge, which is 'so mediocre ... that not even accuracy could make it better' (1968, 44). The biographer 'has written the life of a great peripatetic philosopher and chronicled only the peripatetic' (1968, 43).

Since Wilde himself is an oracle of 'grave and chastened beauty' (1968, 60), it is surprising that his pronouncements on his fellow aesthete, Walter Pater, should be so full of contradiction. On the one hand, Pater is praised as an austere practitioner. Possessing 'the true spirit of selection, the tact of omission,' he is, if not 'among the greatest prose writers of our literature, ... at least, our greatest artist in prose.' On the other hand, Pater is praised without qualification as the supreme master of English style. His essays are unparalleled in our literature, and constitute for Wilde 'the golden book of spirit and sense, the holy writ of beauty' (1968, 61).

Perhaps Wilde would explain the contradiction as a consequence of Pater's being an artist: for a truth in art criticism, as in art, 'is that whose contradictory is also true' (1968, 157). Alternatively, we may ascribe the paradox to a change in Wilde himself. When criticizing Pater for being too discriminating, Wilde is simply imitating his master. He is trying to distinguish between Pater, the fastidious 'artist in prose,' and prose writers who are greater than Pater, because they are less strict in what they are prepared to include. In the later essay, however, Wilde is no longer willing to temper his enthusiasm. Even if he seems to exaggerate Pater's merits, Wilde now insists that 'where there is no exaggeration there is no love, and where there is no love there is no understanding' (1968, 61). Any memorable oracle or aphorism has a bias. And 'this is no doubt the reason why an unbiased opinion,' the idol of statisticians, robots, and simple-minded technicians, has never any value (1968, 62).

Wilde's aphorisms about Swinburne bristle with truth and cut deeply, partly because they address features of Wilde's own aesthetic. Swinburne's great limitation as a poet is his 'entire lack of any sense of limit' (1968, 83). The paradox of being limited by a refusal to recognize limits is converted into some semblance of logic by another figure of speech, the more reflective mirror trope chiasmus. 'It has been said of him, and with truth, that he is a master of language, but with still greater truth it may be said that Language is his master' (1968, 83). Like Wilde himself, who complains that 'everything about [his] tragedy has been hideous, mean, repellent, lacking in style' (1964, 125), Swinburne prefers art to life. He shows that Nature's oracle is rude, shrill, and breathless, and 'deafens us with her clangours' (1968, 85). Though Wilde's business is with Ariel, life sets him the ignoble task of wrestling with Caliban. Such, too, is Swinburne's fate. 'We have often had man's interpretation of Nature; now [in Swinburne] we have Nature's interpretation of man, and she has curiously little to say' (1968, 85).

Wilde's most devastating aphorisms are often deftly insinuating. A criticism that seems at first more witty than just acquires prophetic force when Wilde uses a triad of paratactic clauses to rise to a fine crescendo of indictment. 'As a novelist [Meredith] can do everything except tell a story; as an artist he is everything except articulate.' To create an impression of being a temperate critic, as discriminating as he is crushing, Wilde qualifies his flat assertion that 'whatever [Meredith] is, he is not a realist.' For that bald conclusion Wilde substitutes the more charming and inventive absurdity of 'a child of realism who is not on speaking terms with his father.' Having showered Meredith with ambiguous praise, conceding that his style, though 'chaos,' is 'illumined by flashes of lightning,' Wilde gently gives the scale a negative tilt by observing that 'as a writer' Meredith 'has mastered everything except language' (1968, 173).

Sometimes a single fertile aphorism by Wilde will breed a whole chain of witty sayings. When Wilde quips that 'one touch of nature may make the whole world kin, but two touches of Nature will destroy any work of Art' (1968, 176), he feels impelled to invent a third aphorism to tell us why. A sunset painted by Turner is at first so unique that Nature, forgetting 'imitation can be made the sincerest form of insult,' keeps on repeating the effect till no critic of taste can endure another sunset (1968, 188). Descartes says he exists because he thinks. If Descartes is intellectually a prisoner of his profession as a thinker, Wilde is imprisoned by his reputation as a wit. For Wilde, to know anything is to find a witty expression for it. Unfortunately, when a predictably witty aphorist like Wilde ceases to divert us, he also ceases to be interesting.

2

Like Wilde and Shaw, F.H. Bradley clusters many of his aphorisms around related topics. And like Shaw, he allows his best aphorisms to feed incestuously off other aphorisms. Instead of redeeming a platitude, Bradley will sometimes detonate its wisdom from inside. '"Everything comes to him who waits" – among other things death' (1930, aphorism 1). Patience is a virtue, provided we do not misuse it as a pretext for inaction. But if Shaw is a satirist with little sense of irony, often unconscious of his own contradictions and bulls, Bradley is an ironist with little sense of satire, often unconscious of what is absurd or grotesque in the aphorisms he proposes. According to La Rochefoucauld, for example, 'le soleil ny la mort ne se peuvent regarder fixement.' Bradley turns this aphorism into a solemn joke. If death, like the sun, is the one object we cannot view directly, then perhaps it is a stroke of providence that 'our life should set in clouds' (1930, aphorism 2). Browning's Pope believes that a cloud may soothe an eye made blind by blaze and better the very clarity of heaven. By taking Browning's metaphor as literally as La Rochefoucauld takes the sun, Bradley can playfully extol the decline in physical and mental powers that the clouds of encroaching senility may trail in their wake. The oracle is both a witty sally and a valiant effort to accept limits and live with setbacks as we age. But Bradley lacks the satirist's eye. He has none of Shaw's or Swift's sense of how monstrous it must be to decline into a *struldbrug*, or to expire like Swift, 'a driveller and a show.'

In a sequence of subversive oracles, Bradley offers persuasive definitions of 'optimism,' 'pessimism,' 'eclecticism,' and 'the unity of science.' Even in embracing the facile optimism of Leibniz, who announces that 'the world is the best of all possible worlds,' Bradley adds a gloss that sounds more like pessimism than unfettered optimism. For if 'every-thing' in the world is 'a necessary evil,' then the optimism that Bradley wants to define must be inclusive enough to embrace its logical oppo-site, pessimism. Bradley comes perilously close to saying, with Wilde, that a truth in metaphysics, like a truth in art, is one whose opposite is also true.

Bradley's two definitions of 'pessimism' are equally disturbing. 'Where everything is bad, it must be good to know the worst,' and 'where all is rotten it is a man's work to cry stinking fish' (1930, apho-rism 5). Bradley tries to wrest a bleak optimism from an imagined nadir of despair. His rock-bottom knowledge that 'everything is bad' affords the comfort of at least knowing 'the worst.' But if we never descend so low as to say with confidence, 'no worse, there is none,' then Bradley seems less wise in his confidence than Shakespeare. In Bradley's second oracle on pessimism, the protester who cries 'stink-ing fish' at least deserves credit for raising an alarm. But like a siren calling attention to a fog it does nothing to dispel, the alarmist's authority is sadly attenuated. To hold one's nose while calling 'stink-ing fish' is to substitute gesture for deed. It confuses an act of aesthetic revulsion with moral reform.

Bradley's oracle on eclecticism seems at first to produce more per-verse nonsense than prophetic sense. 'Every truth is so true that any truth must be false' (1930, aphorism 6). If everything is partly true, then nothing is wholly so. This is the kind of truth-claim that discred-its truth. The relativist defines truth in such a way as to dissolve it. But the self-destruction or suicide of truth is precisely Bradley's point. For an eclectic archivist, who is a collector of only partial truths, things fall apart: the centre will not hold. As an intellectual opponent of these rel-ativists, Bradley takes pleasure in his enemy's defeatist folly.

According to Isaiah Berlin, thinkers are either hedgehogs or foxes. They have either one big idea or many small ones. Like most utilitari-ans, J.S. Mill is a fox who breaks down complex problems into simple ones: in tackling each issue separately, he intentionally forgets the larger picture. Bradley, by contrast, is a hedgehog in a nation of foxes. His habit of first asking and answering the large questions may seem worthier and more ambitious. But by attempting more than the fox, the English hedgehog goes against the empirical grain of his culture and may accomplish less in the end. It is important to remember that Bradley's philosophy was highly heterodox in its time. As Richard Wollheim says, 'it is the unorthodox nature of Bradley's point of view that accounts for the blazing invective of his style, for those excesses of irony and rhetoric which sweep his thought along, only too often into obscurity' (1970, xiv).

Bradley's oracle on the unity of science is opaque in its very lucidness. Nothing could be more transparent than his bold assertion that 'whatever you know it is all one' (1930, aphorism 7). But how can Shelley's dome of many-coloured glass be blended back into the white radiance it has stained without trampling the glass to fragments? Bradley's unorthodox point of view as a monist accounts for the force and oddity of his style. However agile and foxy he appears to be in the first part of *Appearance and Reality*, Bradley turns out to be a stolid hedgehog in the sequel.

By indulging a witty play on words, Bradley converts propriety into its opposite. 'The propriety' of those people who appoint themselves custodians of public morality consists in 'having improper thoughts about their neighbours.' Equally perceptive is Bradley's aperçu about auricular confessions. If we are truly penitent, we won't confess to any priest or confidant. For 'true penitence condemns to silence. What a man is ready to recall he would be willing to repeat' (1930, aphorisms 9 and 10).

In describing 'states, moral as well as physical, where a jet of cold water may cause an explosion,' Bradley is describing the destructive potential of his own best aphorisms. A simple play on words, as on 'propriety' and 'proper,' has the force of gunpowder. Like Bradley's witty glosses on maxims by LaRochefoucauld or Leibniz, in which aftershocks prove more potent than the initial shock, explosive words have power to blow up a platitude from inside. Tennyson's maxim that it is 'better to have loved and lost / Than never to have loved at all' is memorable but trite. More alarming because of its shocking slide down a scale of scepticism and doubt is Bradley's aphorism that 'it is bad to doubt if one is loved, but it may be worse past all comparison to doubt if one loves' (1930, aphorism 11).

Some of Bradley's aphorisms adopt a brusque, dismissive style. 'It is not true that Mr. X never thinks,' Bradley quips. 'On the contrary, he always is thinking – about something else' (1930, aphorism 79). But the harder Bradley tries to be offhand and witty, the more personal barriers he also sets up. Instead of talking intimately with a friend, Bradley gives the impression of being on Delphi or Mount Olympus. What we hear is, not a confiding Fra Lippo Lippi, setting 'things straight now, hip to haunch' ('Fra Lippo Lippi,' l. 44), but a disembodied oracle speaking at a distance, often in riddles and dark sayings. 'He should be morally rich who can allow himself the luxury of repentance' (1930, aphorism 58); ''Unhappy those who seek to revive the intoxication and who cannot renew the mystery' (1930, aphorism 45).

An attractive feature of Bradley's oracles is their talent for self-deprecation. 'The hunter for aphorisms on human nature has to fish in muddy waters, and he is even condemned to find much of his own mind' (1930, aphorism 14). A writer of maxims is subdued to what he works in, like the dyer's hand. The gritty charm of this maxim casts a new light on one of Bradley's other aphorisms: 'Love is so much the habit of, and the need for, a certain tone of sentiment, that with some persons unfaithfulness in absence may be a species of fidelity' (1930, aphorism 13). As a mirror of its author's mind, the aphorism seems to be saying that Bradley, too, as an unfaithful lover and casuist, can best honour the woman he loves by loving someone else in her absence.

Bradley quotes Kant's celebrated oracle about the grandeur of the moral law, then detonates it with a single word. 'The moral law and the starry Heaven; each, according to Kant, overpowers us with reverence. We almost forget how to wonder that the latter should even know how to smile on disregard for the former' (1930, aphorism 15). If Kant is right, then the reverence we accord to an amoral cosmos is misplaced. The sublime folly of personifying and then venerating the starry Heaven is exposed in the verb 'smile,' which like the sun in Matthew's gospel seems to rise on the evil and the good alike (5:45), and to look on each with equal favour.

G.B. Shaw recognizes the danger of doing unto others as you would have them do unto you: their tastes may differ. Bradley is equally conscious that human nature, however poor in its essential unity, is rich in its accidental varieties. 'With one man resignation lays up treasure in Heaven; with another man it does but store explosives in the heart' (1930, aphorism 16). What is balm to the stoic is corrosive poison to the Faustian over-reacher, to Browning's Paracelsus, for example, who would love infinitely and be loved.

Some oracles tell us only half the story. It may be true that 'our pleasure in any one who in some way resembles those we love should warn us that no love is in its essence individual' (1930, aphorism 18). But it is equally true that, after opening our arms to the universe in a religious gesture, we close them again around an individual person. Our love of the unique and partial may be inseparable from our affection for wholes. But if love is a universal, it is also inescapably individual and specific. Bradley is trying to explore the difficult and finely faceted truth of what idealists call a concrete universal, or an individual that is also a whole.

Other oracles take the form of caveats. If one's obsessions cannot be mastered, they should be indulged moderately rather than totally repressed. For repression may merely double their strength. 'If in yourself you cannot break a spring, beware how much you compress it' (1930, aphorism 19). Bradley even issues a warning against the mere shock effect of oracles that are notable for being more witty than wise. 'There are persons who, when they cease to shock us, cease to interest us' (1930, aphorism 20). This aphorism is too often applicable to witty prophets like Nietzsche, Shaw, and Oscar Wilde, but seldom to Bradley himself.

Bradley's best oracles show a passionate absorption in his thinking as a philosopher. Combatting the errors of Cartesian dualism, Bradley wittily denounces the 'supposed independence' of body and mind as 'imaginary.' To 'overcome' their dependence by 'invoking a faculty such as Will is the effort to heal a delusion by means of a fiction' (1893, 296). Bradley's contempt for clichés and slogans comes from his conviction that, for any philosopher who is genuinely exploring an issue, thinking will be as risky and passionate as making love for the first time. He launches a bitter invective against Arnold's confusion of oracles with maxims because he thinks Arnold is offering what one critic, Alan Donagan, calls 'a faked report.' Instead of giving the public a God they can worship, Arnold offers it only 'an hypostasized copy-book heading.' Arnold's God 'is not much more adorable than "Honesty is the best policy," or "Handsome is that handsome does," or various other edifying maxims, which have not yet come to an apotheosis' (Bradley, 1970, 319). Arnold's rearguard religious skirmishes strike Bradley as fraudulent, because they seem 'designed to present himself as thinking and feeling in some approved way.' And as Donagan says, the 'betraying symptom' of such dishonesty 'is *cliché*' (1968, 55).

Bradley himself is a disarmingly honest aphorist whose best oracles cut deep and have the sting of truth. The most necessary empathy, he observes, is often the least glamorous. 'So it may happen that those who need empathy most attract it least.' And yet he is quick to assert the counter-truth that 'it is by a wise economy of nature' that this should be so. 'Those who suffer without change, and whom no one can help, become uninteresting' (1930, aphorism 22). For, cruel as it may sound, it is a waste of time to care for them. But what may be economical in the larger scheme is also inhuman and heartless to the individual who suffers and is in greatest need of our care. In a single aphorism, Bradley shows us his heart and pierces us.

Many of Bradley's most acute aphorisms explore the paradoxes of friendship and love. 'If any one is to remain pleased with you,' he observes, 'he should be pleased with himself when he thinks of you' (1930, aphorism 26). There is an irreducible minimum of self-love in even the most selfless love for others. Making love may also involve the make-believe of an actor. 'To feel too intensely is to play one's part badly. It is possible that, to make love perfectly, one always should more or less make it' (1930, aphorism 27). The word play on 'make' is Bradley's reminder that to play any part, including Romeo's, requires artifice and detachment. Even maternal love may be a mirror image of a girl's love for her doll. 'We say that a girl with her doll anticipates the mother.' But in a disturbing reversal, Bradley suggests 'it is more true, perhaps, that most mothers are still but children with playthings' (1930, aphorism 23).

Scepticism is the homage philosophy pays wisdom. Cleansing the temple of its idols, Bradley prefers a well-formed, chaste mind to a promiscuous, well-filled one. His oracles are most penetrating when they call for a searching internal evaluation. It is not enough to pass external judgment on a person. We must also try to see how that person sees himself. 'It is good to know what a man is, and also what the world takes him for. But you do not understand him until you have learnt how he understands himself' (1930, aphorism 31). Unlike a god or his oracle, a wise man may feel he has no authority to exact belief or pronounce judgment. He may not know enough himself to condemn ignorance in others. Bradley's invitation to take a sympathetic internal view recalls Coleridge's generous axiom: 'until I understand the cause of a man's ignorance, I presume myself ignorant of his understanding.'

A few of Bradley's oracles have the tail and sting of scorpions. Just when he seems to be extolling disinterested self-sacrifice or love, he exposes the whole delusive argument as a mirage. And he often does so with a bitterness and irony that rival the intensity of Swift's invective. 'In an intellectual aspirant the safest love is for an imaginary object, and that, perhaps, includes all love without possession.' This sounds safe and specious enough. But 'if we are to beget unrealities,' Bradley scornfully adds, 'we must know how to be happy with clouds' (1930, aphorism 35). However exalted such idealism may sound, Bradley casually deflates it. He exposes it as mere pretence and illusion.

The first part of an oracle often seems to announce a new Beatitude: 'The secret of happiness is to admire without desiring.' But then, as if to acknowledge that his Sermon from the Mount is too utopian, Bradley quietly inserts a counter-truth: 'And that is not happiness' (1930, aphorism 33). The irony is more devastating for being understated. Sometimes Bradley compresses an edifying truth and its qualifying counter-truth into a single sentence. 'There are things it is well to abstain from only upon the condition that we cease to desire them' (1930, aphorism 32). If ambition is the last infirmity of noble minds, then it may be edifying to lead a pastoral life. But if we are still secretly ambitious, even after we renounce ambition, our self-deception will be only a torment to us. The martyr must beware of cheap sacrifices. To give up what one does not really want is no more virtuous than 'the great sacrifice of trade,' which is 'the giving cheap what is worth nothing.' Though ambition may be worth renouncing, there may be more sacrifice involved in single-minded pursuit of a goal we genuinely desire. 'To know what one wants, and to scruple at no means that will get it, may be a harder self-surrender' (1930, aphorism 34) than an unworldly surrender of ambition.

By the end of *In Memoriam* the dead Hallam has faded into a 'diffusive power,' whose 'voice is on the rolling air.' Though Tennyson says he does not love his friend any less because he is now a presence in the running waters and the flowing wind, a genius of the rising and the setting sun, Bradley is less sanguine. 'When to love one must remember,' Bradley says, 'love will soon be a memory' (1930, aphorism 37). Tennyson wants to believe that Hallam is 'loved deeplier, as he is darklier understood.' But he asserts this belief in a poem called *In Memoriam*. We never forget that the friend whose hand he wants to grasp once more in Wimpole Street is a mere memory, the fading subject of a commemorative poem that only fleetingly revives his image.

Many of Bradley's oracles prove the truth of his oracle that '"one never tells more than half," and in the end perhaps one cannot. In the end one is alone' (1930, aphorism 44). It is never entirely clear, for example, why Bradley should say that 'it is natural, perhaps, to begin by despising those who are unable wholly to understand us, and it is natural, perhaps, to end by looking up to them.' Do we admire people who fail wholly to understand us because we cannot wholly understand ourselves? Or do we like to think of ourselves as complex and mysterious, and so not immediately intelligible to people who happen to take an interest in us? Perhaps the pleasure we take in people who fail to understand us is a symptom of our own humility, since 'the craving to be understood may in the end be merest egoism' (1930, aphorism 50).

Some oracles are true in a double sense. 'The deadliest foe to virtue would be complete self-knowledge' (1930, aphorism 68). In the mind of the Absolute, good, truth, and beauty cannot as such survive. As Emerson's Brahma says, 'Shadow and sunlight are the same; / The vanished gods to me appear; / And one to me are shame and fame' (ll. 6–8). Bradley seems to speak with a forked tongue when he says that 'up to a certain point every man is what he thinks he is' (1930, aphorism 72). The megalomania of the beggar who thinks he is Caesar is clearly delusive. But for an idealist like Bradley the world is also our idea of the world. And in a precise and literal sense, every person is what he perceives himself to be.

When the final clause of an oracle implies the futility of what it seeks, the interpreter is often left to make this damaging inference for himself. In aphorism 80, for example, Bradley first uses a chiasmus to contrast objects of approbation and love. 'We may approve of what we love, but we cannot love because we approve.' Bradley's next move is to demote approbation by reducing its concern for the type to the status of 'what is common and therefore uninteresting.' Love, by contrast, 'is the passionate attempt to find oneself in another. And oneself is unique.' Just when we think Bradley has made the case for love fool-proof and invulnerable, he demolishes that illusion by leaving a thoughtful reader to draw a subversive conclusion. If the self is 'unique,' then our 'passionate attempt to find' it in another is an act of sublime folly, for by definition the search of the unique for the same unique is doomed to fail.

Bradley's oracles often force us to consider two sides of an issue. It may be true that hypocrisy is the profession of 'moral sentiments which fail to pass into action.' But acting on every impulse would be equally disastrous. Or as Bradley wryly observes, 'there are few who would not be worse for complete sincerity.' Like 'hypocrisy,' even so despicable a practice as 'flattery' can suffer a sea-change that confers rare value on it. Flattery is deplorable, because it leads someone 'to feel or think falsely that he is what he desires, or is not what he fears, to be.' But when we remove the adverb 'falsely,' flattery becomes the desirable 'art of pleasing,' and when we 'add "truly"' it is nothing less than 'friendship' itself (1930, aphorism 84).

Like Matthew Arnold, Bradley directs some of his sharpest barbs against Puritanism. He mocks the prude who so dislikes 'the nude that [he finds] something indecent in the naked truth' (1930, aphorism 88). But the author of *Ethical Studies* is equally distrustful of 'pleasure for pleasure's sake.' He believes that husbands and wives should be partners in mind and soul as well as in body. And so to the biblical adage that 'Adam knew Eve his wife and she conceived,' Bradley adds a witty gloss: 'it is a pity that this is still the only knowledge of their wives at which some men seem to arrive' (1930, aphorism 94).

Though Bradley has a talent for dissolving every platitude about Romantic love that comes his way, he does so without diminishing the value of love itself. Taking the commonplace that 'absence makes the heart grow fonder,' Bradley reflects that 'distance can lend no charm to the woman who is really amiable.' Without in any way dimming the fair and shining memory of people we have loved, Bradley soberly reminds us that 'love that absence does not lessen, or modify, can hardly be genuine' (1930, aphorism 97). He is equally critical of soul-love. 'The soul's immutable core – if there is one – can hardly be amiable. And to love any one for himself perhaps in the end becomes unmeaning' (1930, aphorism 95).

Most heretical of all is Bradley's claim that 'love in its essence tends to be immoral.' If morality is the great solvent of egoism, romantic love is surely its nutrient, 'the instinctive reference of all to the pleasure of one being' (1930, aphorism 96). Having cut love down to size, however, Bradley surprises us by raising it to new heights in his last oracle: 'To love unsatisfied, the world is a mystery,' he says, 'a mystery which love satisfied seems to comprehend.' But Bradley does not want an uplifting a sentiment to be his last word on the subject. In case a gratified love should become self-satisfied and complacent, he is quick to remind us that a satisfied love 'is wrong only because it cannot be content without thinking it is right' (1930, aphorism 100).

3

Bradley is most often moved to aphorism when a topic stirs his caustic intelligence or sense of the absurd. It is important that Bradley should maintain critical distance from the subject of these aphorisms. Oracles, by contrast, are reserved for occasions when a subject absorbs and transforms a speaker. As Frye observes of Longinian ecstasis, oracles posit 'a state of identification in which the reader, the poem, and sometimes, at least ideally, the poet' or the prophet 'also, are involved' (1957, 67).

Such states abound in *Sartor Resartus* where, even as metonymies are materializing people into 'Clothes-screens,' metalepses are melting them into shadows by substituting remote causes for present effects.

> Their solid Pavement is a Picture of the Sense; they walk on the bosom of Nothing, blank Time is behind them and before them. Or fanciest thou, the red and yellow Clothes-screen yonder, with spurs on its heels and feather in its crown, is but of Today without a Yesterday or a Tomorrow; and had not rather its Ancestor alive when Hengist and Horsa overran thy Island? (Carlyle, 1970, 49)

The owlish solemnity of Carlyle's reflection that people with spurs on their heels and feathers in their crowns are mere 'Pictures of the Sense' alternates with unmistakable accents of hysteria and panic. For the oracle predicts that, even as these fantastically attired phantoms tread the 'solid Pavement,' they also walk 'on. the bosom of Nothing.' By contracting space and time, these oracles allow Carlyle to conflate the nineteenth-century English gentleman with such ancient Saxon ancestors as Hengist and Horsa, leaders of Germanic invaders of the fifth century. 'Friend, thou seest here a living link in the Tissue of History, which inweaves all Being: watch well, or it will be past thee, and seen no more.'

In the chapter 'Natural Supernaturalism,' the prophet is both absorbed and transformed by his contemplation of miracles. Since every commonplace is a miracle when viewed from a lower link in the scale of marvels, it is idle to denounce miracles as events that mock nature. An icicle is a miracle to the King of Siam. And by substituting a part of a floating ship, the iron hulk, for the whole vessel, synecdoche can turn even a feat of nautical engineering into the miraculous trick of teaching iron to swim (1970, 235). Here we reach that 'mysterious area' in Carlyle where, as one critic says, 'the oracular and the witty seem different aspects of the same thing' (Frye, 2004a, 186–7). Metaphor provides a fresh picture of the world by coining such phrases as the statute book of Nature or the 'star-domed City of God.' Similarly, metalepsis dismantles the two great illusions of space and time by assimilating the minnow, man, and his creek, the planet earth, to the ocean of the immeasurable All. Even the minnow's 'Monsoons and periodic currents' become 'the mysterious Course of Providence through Aeons and Aeons.'

Left to hover between what can be named and computed, on the one hand, and what is nameless and beyond computing, on the other, Carlyle's prophet finds that the 'signless Inane' has as much power to dizzy and appal a spectator as to ennoble or exalt him. When the Time and Space Shadows are dispelled, will they reveal a star-domed city or a chaotic nether deep? Geological time, which levels mountains and creates seas, discloses that earth is but a film that cracks in two. Yet geological time also proves the durability of the human species, which leaves its footprint in the fossil record. 'The last rear of the host,' as it gropes its way to a void as bottomless as Blake's nether sky, will still 'read traces,' he predicts, 'of the earliest Van' (1970, 243). In their dialogue with the void, these oracles are as aloof and enveloped by silence as the reverberation of the verb 'despair' in Hopkins's lyric 'The Leaden Echo.'

Whereas Ernest Renan sleeps with a revolver under his pillow for fear of a revelation, Carlyle finds an oracle in every creek and clothes-screen that he sees. If the Holy Ghost appeared to Renan, he would commit the unpardonable sin of denying that any ghosts exist. But since obliquity is the core of revelation, its light is also withheld from Carlyle, who sees oracles in everything. The trick is to relax the will, cultivating a readiness to experience whatever comes along. As one commentator says, 'you can't expect something, or you'll find an oracle in every spiritual breeze that passes over you: you can't expect nothing, or you'll have in yourself no principle of escape' (Frye, 2004a, 199).

Some of Nietzsche's wittiest and most subversive oracles are delivered from the Sermon Mount of a self-professed Antichrist, beyond the pale of good and evil. 'Jesus said to his Jews: "The law was for servants – love God as I love him, as his son! What are morals to us sons of God,"' who love the author of the laws as our Father (1989, 91, aphorism 164)? Whereas Jesus in the Beatitudes comes, not to abolish, but to fulfil the law, Nietzsche's Jesus is an antinomian, an ethical amoralist. 'Whatever is done from love always occurs beyond good and evil' (1989, 90, aphorism 153).

Nietzsche accuses Christianity of damaging the Greek oracles. Though its attempt to murder the Greek god Eros was a botched job, the harm Christianity inflicted proved irreversible. 'Christianity gave

Eros poison to drink; he did not die of it but degenerated – into a vice'
(1989, 92, aphorism 168). Nietzsche finds Christianity's scandalous
assault on Eros sublimely ironic in light of the fact that underneath 'the
holy fable and disguise of Jesus' life there lies concealed' a demand to
love and 'be loved and nothing else.' The Gospels according to Nietzsche tell 'the story of a poor fellow, unsated and insatiable in love,'
who invented 'hell in order to send to it those who did not *want* to love
him' (1989, 220).

   If we are to love our neighbour as ourselves, then surely Nietzsche's
sixty-seventh aphorism in the fourth section of *Beyond Good and Evil* is
a corollary. Love of only one person 'is a barbarism; for it is exercised
at the expense of all others,' including God. Even the Decalogue tells
us that our love of God should not be an exclusive love. It must be
comprehensive enough to take in our neighbour. And yet collective
love may entail compassion for no one. As Nietzsche says in his
eighty-second aphorism, '"pity for all" – would be hardness and
tyranny to you, my dear neighbour! – .'

   'In the mountains the shortest route is from peak to peak, but for
that you must have long legs. Aphorisms should be peaks, and those
to whom they are spoken should be big and tall of stature'(Nietzsche,
1961, 67). When Nietzsche boasts that every aphorism is a peak and
that it takes a giant mountaineer to leap from one peak to another, he
is flirting like all prophets with danger. Yet as Stephen Booth points
out, daredevils like Nietzsche 'let you know that they are married
forever to particular, reliable order and purpose' (1983, 35). The bold-
ness of the rebel is inseparable from the depth and range of his
systematic thinking, as Arthur C. Danto has shown in *Nietzsche as
Philosopher*.

   One of Nietzsche's subtlest oracles accuses God himself of subtlety.
'It was subtle of God to learn Greek when he wished to become an
author – and not to learn it better' (1989, 86, aphorism 121). In the civilized word of Christ's time the Septuagint could presumably circulate
more widely than a text written in Hebrew or Aramaic. But what are
we to make of Nietzsche's claim that God was an imperfect Hellenist?
It is sly of Nietzsche to suggest that Hebraic and Christian monothe-
ism could not be imported readily into a polytheistic Greek culture.
And ideas that resist translation may be more seductive because they
sound darkly oracular, more secretive and sibylline than an immediately intelligible idea. Nietzsche seems to imply that the Bible would
have been less influential if it had been perfectly comprehensible to

Greek and Roman pagans. Part of the Bible's power and charm may have been its imperfect translation of Hebrew and Aramaic prophecies into an alien Greek idiom.

I find Nietzsche's oddest but most haunting aphorism the ninety-ninth: 'the voice of disappointment: "I listened for an echo and heard nothing but praise"' (1989, 83). If we were to omit the first sentence, we might interpret the oracle as a gloss on Frost's poem 'The Most of It' or Wordsworth's 'There Was a Boy.' To replace the copy-speech of an echo with the counter-love of praise (either praise of God or praise of the poet's godlike mind) would seem to be a cause for joy or celebration. To make sense of Nietzsche's oracle, which associates the echo with 'the voice of disappointment,' we may have to consult his later aphorism that 'praise is more obtrusive than a reproach' (1989, 92, aphorism 170). If we want to be lulled asleep by the predictable consonance or flattering rhyme of an echo, we may find a sudden assault of praise both disturbing and unwelcome.

In rewriting the Sermon on the Mount, Nietzsche affirms that those who suffer and mourn are blessed, not because they will be comforted, but because difficult pleasures that once caused pain etch them more deeply. As experiences we remember, the trials of adversity do more to enhance and glorify our lives than the pleasures of lotos land. Prosperity may be the blessing of the Old Testament, but adversity is the blessing of the New. And yet it is painful to be in love with a world we must leave before long. If we train for death, as 'we train our conscience' to be moral, our taking leave of this earth should 'kiss us while it hurts us' (aphorism 98). As Nietzsche advises in one of his most beautiful aphorisms, 'one should part from life as Odysseus parted from Nausicaä – blessing it rather than in love with it' (1989, 83, aphorism 96). Nietzsche's best aphorisms penetrate and bite. It matters less whether Nietzsche is right or wrong than whether his mind is alive or dead. As one critic quips, 'Christ speaks in aphorisms, not because they are alive, but because he is' (Frye, 2004a, 13).

4

Few modern prophets move as deftly from aphorism to wit and from wit to oracle as Northrop Frye. In one of his stirring defences of Blake in *Fearful Symmetry*, Frye struggles to maintain a balance between the obvious disadvantage of Blake's public neglect and the less apparent advantage of his independence. 'The public's contemptuous neglect of

Blake was as wrong and foolish as it could be,' Frye concedes, but he nevertheless claims that 'Blake owes much of his integrity to his isolation' (1947, 413). So painful, however, is the public's contempt and neglect of Blake that, even in extolling Blake's 'precious quality of mental independence' (1947, 413), Frye launches into a wittily satiric account of how Blake took delight in spreading 'banana peelings in the paths of heroes.' Frye tries to be as judicious as the 'incorruptible mental court' before which Blake himself arraigns and judges all defences of tradition and convention. But even as Frye applauds Blake's 'Cockney cheek' and 'Nonconformist conscience,' and praises his hero as a courageous 'saboteur' of 'the dark Satanic mills in English life,' the trauma of his hero's lifelong neglect wrecks in the end the balance of his prose.

> We have said that Blake's theory of poetry would have been more easily accepted had he lived in the Renaissance, but as he lived when he did, we have a unique example of an artist saying what he pleased without the least tendency, which social recognition often encourages, toward the parasitic in literature, the sycophantic in politics or the malignant in religion. (1947, 413–14)

The final adjectives – 'parasitic,' 'sycophantic,' 'malignant' – fall like hammer blows. As anger and frustration overpower Blake's champion, there is more fear than symmetry in his rhetoric. Indeed the energy with which the satirist lashes forth in the last three phrases betrays an intemperance that is more typical of Swift's invective than of Frye's.

It is impossible, Frye says, to explore the nature of Blake's so-called madness without being haunted by one of Blake's own epigrams. 'The man who pretends to be a modest inquirer into the truth of a self evident thing is a Knave.' But what exactly is 'self-evident'? If we assume it is Blake's sanity, we are in for a surprise, for 'that Blake was often called mad in his lifetime is of course true' (1947, 12). A further shock awaits us when Frye announces that 'the point is, not that the word "mad" applied to Blake is false, but that it is untranslatable.' After showing how the meaning Samuel Johnson assigns to madness has 'dropped out of our language,' Frye demonstrates how Blake combines Johnson's understanding with the later Romantic view. The energy and enthusiasm that inspire great art are the opposite of the socially useless sterility and chaos Johnson castigates in madness. If society mocks Blake, who is the antithesis of mad in Johnson's sense, then 'it is society that it is mad, not the artist' (1947, 13). And if we judge Blake by Romantic definitions of madness, which view art as 'a disease that cures the world homeopathically,' then Blake is insane only in the sense Ezekiel is mad. The prophet eats dung and lies on his side, we are told, in order to raise 'other men into a perception of the infinite.' Frye's conclusion, which carries the logical force of a syllogism, is best expressed as a paradox that reverses normal expectations. 'What Blake demonstrates,' Frye says, 'is the sanity of genius and the madness of the commonplace mind' (1947, 13).

In his essay 'The Keys to Dreamland,' Frye seems at first to be quoting Wilde, who tells us that 'there's no such thing as a morally bad novel' (Frye, 1963a, 39). But if Frye sounds like an aesthete, he surprises us by withholding the aesthete's conclusion. After announcing 'there is no such thing as a moral or an immoral book,' Wilde says 'books are well written, or badly written. That is all' (Preface to *The Picture of Dorian Gray*). For Wilde's aesthetic explanation Frye substitutes the paradox that a novel's 'moral effect depends entirely on the moral quality of its reader, and nobody,' including the judges at the trial of *Lady Chatterley's Lover*, 'can predict what that will be' (1963a, 39). Even more paradoxical is Frye's claim that, far from being immoral, Lawrence's novel suffers from the opposite vice of being too 'preachy and self-conscious.' The book accused of being pornographic and obscene is like 'the Sunday-school novels of my childhood.' Though thought to be immoral, Lawrence bores Frye because he tries so hard to do him good (1963a, 39).

It is sometimes hard to tell whether Frye is uttering an oracle with a dead-pan countenance or making a joke at the sibyl's expense. According to Macaulay, the Puritans suppressed the sport of tying a bear to a stake and allowing dogs to kill it, 'not because it gave pain to the bear but because it gave pleasure to the spectators' (Frye, 1963a, 41). Are Frye and Macaulay making fun of the Puritans or of the cruel sport they suppressed? At first Frye, like Macaulay, seems to be poking fun at the killjoy Puritans. They are less opposed to the cruelty of blood sports than to the pleasure offered by any public entertainment, including the pleasures of Shakespeare's playhouse. But Frye's joke has two edges. He surprises us by saying that 'whatever their motives, the Puritans and Shakespeare were operating in the same direction' (1963a, 41–2). Lest we be taken in or deceived by the anti-Puritan joke, Frye now turns the tables on Macaulay. He 'may have intended his remark to be a sneer at the Puritans,' Frye remarks, 'but surely if the Puritans did feel this way they were one hundred per cent right. What other reason is there for abolishing public hangings?' Shakespeare shares with the Puritans 'the exhilaration of standing apart' from cruel and inhuman things like bear-baiting and the blinding of Gloucester 'and being able to see them for what they are' (1963a, 42). And just as Frye is about to lose his balance by sounding too homiletic in his praise of the poet's power to 'refine our sensibilities,' he pokes fun at the 'fine mouth-filling' phrases (1963a, 42) of Puritan sermons while delivering one himself.

Frye sees the relation of critic to poet through a prism of paradox. Though the critic has been called a judge of literature, it may not be the poet but the critic who is judged. Having mocked pretension through the demeaning wit that likens criticism to the award of ribbons at a 'cat-show,' Frye now lifts up the critic in one of his boldest prophecies. 'Literature is a human apocalypse, man's revelation to man, and criticism is not a body of adjudications, but the awareness of that revelation, the last judgment of mankind' (1963a, 44). The critic, in other words, is not so much a judge as a witness of judgment, the judgment of literature itself. Turning an objective genitive into a subjective one, Frye audaciously substitutes literature's last judgment for God's.

Often Frye startles us into attention with a paradox. 'All the arts are dumb,' he announces. 'There is an important sense in which poems are as silent as statues' (1957, 4). It is not just 'strained wit' that leads Archibald MacLeish to call the language of poetry 'mute,' 'dumb,' and 'wordless' (1957, 5). Though the poet probably knows something, Frye insists he cannot talk about it, at least not in a direct or forthright way. The curiously indirect, often oracular, quality of literary writing leads Frye to be equally oracular himself. 'Part of the critic's reason for feeling that poets can be properly assessed only after their death is that they are then unable to presume on their merits as poets to tease him with hints of inside knowledge' (1957, 5). What exactly is the oracle saying? Keats claims that the Grecian urn teases him out of thought as does eternity. Why is it undesirable to be teased? We have to read the rest of the paragraph to find out. Poets not only tease the critic by covering their tracks with false clues. They also claim an authority that, as poets rather than critics, they do not possess.

It is sometimes hard to tell whether Frye is formulating a paradox or an antinomy. He tells us that 'the framework' of literary criticism 'is not that of literature itself, for this is the parasite theory again.' On the other hand, the framework is not 'something outside literature, for in that case the autonomy of criticism would disappear ..., and the whole subject would be assimilated to something else' (1957, 6). But if criticism cannot be located either inside or outside literature, no third alternative appears to exist. X must be either Y or Z, but both Y and Z are untenable. Just when we think Frye is formulating a logical contradiction or antinomy, he reminds us that there is in fact a middle term he has excluded. Criticism can be based on literature itself, not in the sense that the critic is a parasite or jackal feeding off the carcasses that poets leave behind, but in the sense that the framework a critic uses is derived from an inductive survey of literature. The presence of induction, Frye argues, changes the character of criticism 'from the casual to the causal, from the random and intuitive to the systematic, as well as safeguarding the integrity of that subject from external invasion' (1957, 7). What Frye is seeking is not just an inductive process that is as predictable in its results and as mechanical in its operation as a computer program. He needs a method both intuitive and systematic, a procedure resembling Whewell's 'consilience of inductions,' which combines the poet's flash of insight with the scientist's experimental rigour. A straight induction can never develop a theory, either in science or the humanities. What induction needs is a 'jump start,' a leap of logic to fire the mind, as a 'jumper' restarts a dead battery with a sudden surge of electric energy.

The Romantic error of confusing poetic creation with barbarism prompts some of Frye's sharpest aphorisms. 'It is hardly possible,' he observes, 'to accept a critical view which confuses the original with the aboriginal.' The cognate forms ('original,' 'aboriginal') may trick an unwary critic into a fatal error of judgment. Nor does the poet, like God, produce his poem 'in a special act of creation ex nihilo' (1957, 97). More solemn, less witty, is Frye's aphoristic corollary that 'originality returns to the origins of literature, as radicalism returns to its roots' (1957, 97–8). To be original is to recover one's origins, and hence to be traditional – or the opposite of original in the popular Romantic sense. To justify this near-paradox, Frye shows how the Romantics' invention of the copyright laws have made 'it difficult for a modern novelist to steal anything except his title from the rest of literature' (1957, 98). But just when we think Frye is deviating once more into solemnity, he utters an aphorism that sounds more like a joke than an oracle. 'As with other products of divine activity,' he announces, 'the father of a poem is much more difficult to identify than the mother' (1957, 98).

This astonishing aphorism requires a little parable to justify and explain it. 'The mother is always nature,' we are told, but the 'poet who writes creatively rather than deliberately, is not the father of his poem; he is at best a midwife, or, more accurately still, the womb of Mother Nature herself; her privates he, so to speak' (1957, 98). For a moment the metaphor of Mother Nature carries Frye away. Struggling to find more accurate analogies for the poet's relation to the mother, he first calls the poet a midwife, then the womb of nature, and, finally, in a triumph of Donne-like wit and indiscretion, the private parts or pudenda of the procreative power itself. Frye seldom carries a metaphor to the breaking point. But in this rare instance, caught in the umbilical cord of his own obstetrical analogy, he cannot let go of it. Frye insists that the poet is 'responsible for delivering [his creation] in as uninjured a state as possible, and if the poem is alive, it is equally anxious to be rid of him, and screams to be cut loose from all the navel-strings and feeding-tubes of his ego' (1957, 98).

Frye's habit of ironically denying the opposite of what he means often makes even the most commonplace fact interesting. The task of illustrating his aphorism that 'humor, like attack, is founded on convention' might easily become dreary. But Frye entertains instead of bores the reader by wittily itemizing, not what 'rigidly stylized worlds' include, but what they invariably leave out: 'generous Scotchmen, obedient wives, beloved mother-in-laws, and professors with presence of mind' (1957, 225). When Frye is not speaking as a prophet of apocalypse, he is able to make even dull behaviour interesting by considering its opposite. It is hard to satirize people who make 'convention' their 'deepest conviction.' But Frye animates stylized behaviour by considering its counterpart. 'Anyone with a new theory of behaviour,' he reflects, 'even if saint or prophet, is the easiest of all people to ridicule as a crank' (1957, 226).

As an oracle of wit, Frye exhibits the same 'perilous balance' that he finds in punsters like Joyce: a balance 'between verbal wit and hypnotic incantation' (1957, 276). When Frye is both oracular and witty, prophetic and funny at the same time, a reader will be absorbed enough to be moved by his thought but still detached enough to be amused and critically diverted. Just because Frye has made use of terms like 'archetype' and the 'unconscious,' he has been mistakenly confused with Jung and Maud Bodkin. Using the accident of alliteration to mock the folly of such fanciful associations, Frye wittily protests that he resembles Miss Maud Bodkin about as closely as he resembles the late Sarah Bernhardt. In a witty aphorism that sums up his impatience with literary critics who fail to find a centre in literature itself, Frye compares criticism to Los Angeles, 'an aggregate of suburbs' (1971, 18) with no urban core.

Only when Frye indulges wit or exuberance for its own sake does he sometimes appear irritable or unfair. Twice in the first chapter of *The Critical Path* he accuses Marshall McLuhan of exaggerating the distinction between medieval manuscript culture and the printed page of a later era (1971, 21, 26). Far from being the portentous historical distortion Frye claims it is, McLuhan's discerning contrast has stood the test of time. Frye the fox is being cunning rather than judicious, clever rather than convincing, in pointing out that all types of media permit both 'linear' and 'simultaneous' responses. Of course, Frye is right: there are qualifications to everything. But his sly point that there is a 'simultaneous' response to print as well as the obvious 'linear' one, and vice versa for painting, is too clever by half. Bizarrely enough, it prompts Frye to observe that 'there is a preliminary dance of the eye before we take in the whole picture,' and that even 'music, at the opposite end of experience, has its score' (1971, 26). Surely Frye's ingenious swordplay does nothing to wound McLuhan, whose thrusts in this duel seem more on target than Frye's. Though McLuhan's thinking, like Frye's, is oracular rather than logical, aphoristic rather than causal and sequential, it is surely a triumph of paradox over fact for Frye to reflect that 'something about greatness *ended* around 1940. We're doing different things now. Marshall McLuhan is a typical example: a reputation as a great thinker based on the fact that he doesn't think at all' (Frye, 2002, 146).

Changing just one key adjective in a familiar truism often allows Frye to say something witty. 'Civilization,' he observes in passing, is 'the sane (rather than the white) man's burden' (1971, 157). Imperialism may be the legacy of racists like Kipling. But civilization, which only sanity can preserve, is the fragile alternative to anarchy. Frye discerns a paradox at the heart of J.S. Mill's energetic defence of free thought and discussion in the essay on liberty. If we think of society 'as a kind of intellectual counterpart of Parliament,' we can see that one difference between society at large and the parliament at Westminster is that 'the liberals' in society 'can never have a majority.' This explains 'why democracy has to function as an illogical but deeply humane combination of majority rule and minority right' (1971, 163). Frye's aside that liberals 'can never have a majority' sounds at first cynical.

But it grounds his idealism, and justifies his paradox of an arrangement that is both 'illogical' and deeply civilized which can remain
intact 'only so long as the university keeps operating' (1971, 164).
Plato's idea that the wise man's mind provides an analogy of the ideal
state enriches Frye's thought in several ways. It stands behind his
claim that Mill thinks of free thought as an 'intellectual counterpart of
Parliament' (1971, 163). It also informs More's idea that Utopia is 'the
social vision of the wise counsellor's mind, founded on a humanistic
education' (1971, 164). One corollary of this analogy is that society and
the individual are no longer feuding with each other, since 'the real
Utopia is an individual goal, of which the disciplined society is an allegory' (1971, 165).

One of Frye's most luminous aphorisms – 'Death is a leveler, not
because everybody dies, but because nobody knows what death
means' (1982, 230) – touches on a paradox. Only knowledge about a
subject deserves Frye's involvement; but an intense involvement with
death also precludes any dispassionate understanding of it. As one
philosopher says, how can knowledge 'accommodate at its full subjective value the fact that everyone, including oneself, dies' (Nagel, 1986,
230)? What is a wisdom writer to do with 'the thought of this perpetual cataract of catastrophe in which the world comes to an end hundreds of thousands of times a day' (Nagel, 1986, 230)? Any claim to
understand death varies inversely with our personal involvement *in* it.

Eager to escape from the language of argument and dialectic, a 'two-
edged sword that cuts and divides' (1982, 231), Frye is alarmed to discover that 'after all the centuries of sacramental processing, [the]
whole subject [of death] seems to be as much up for grabs as it ever
was' (1982, 230–1). Frye wants the mind to expand 'from the closed
fortresses of believer and skeptic' into what he calls a 'community of
vision' (1982, 230) where death's 'prospect of nothingness' will no
longer be what Thomas Nagel calls it, 'the ultimate form of abandon-
ment' (1986, 226). But the only way Frye can achieve such an expanded
view of death is to replace the language of understanding with 'the
language of love, which, as Paul reminds us ... is likely to outlast most
forms of communication' (1982, 231). Frye would be less prepared to
admit that 'nobody knows what death means' if he were not also
aware that the emotional overload of even the most dispassionate,
objective view of death is too great for us to handle.

Frye notices that in Newman's lectures on education the normally
calm and reasonable tone becomes 'edgy and nervous' whenever

liberal theology comes up for discussion. Frye's own style becomes nervous and edgy when he asserts that 'criticism does not aim at evaluation' (1971, 127). He cites as a reason the absence of any literary hell to which censors have a right to send works of literature. The implication is that because no vision is negative, there is no place for evaluative criticism. But the premise is invalid. The Marquis de Sade is hardly a 'positive contributor to man's body of vision' (1971, 127). And even if he were, Frye's conclusion is surely a non sequitur. We may accept Frye's premise that every writer makes a potential contribution to the total body of imaginative vision and yet still insist that some writers contribute more than others. It does not follow that critics should never evaluate the different qualities that distinguish the contributions of different writers. But at this point Frye loses his own balance by charging any 'critic who wants to get into the concern game' with the crime of making 'literature a single gigantic allegory of his own anxieties' (1971, 127). Pejorative terms like 'concern game' combine with the hyperbole of a 'gigantic allegory' to betray Frye's own anxiety.

Frye insists with some exasperation that only a writer who has 'drifted' into criticism 'without any vocation for it' would claim he is writing literature. Such a misunderstanding might be intelligible 'in outsiders, or in poets, but how a critic himself can be so confused about his function as to take the same view I could not (and cannot yet) understand' (1971, 14). It is hard not to detect anxiety in this disclaimer, as if Frye were protesting too much. As a disinterested study of myths of concern, Frye's criticism should, I suppose, suppress anxiety and concern. But Frye is a very human and committed critic, whose prose occasionally 'betrays' his own ideal in both senses of that verb. Moreover, the more we study what Frye has to say about the prophet's oracles, aphorisms, and proverbs, and about the parables and pericopes of the Gospels, the more we realize that such forms are important elements of Frye's own prose style. He would be less disturbed by misguided efforts to make criticism a branch of literary art if he did not nourish secret ambitions to climb Parnassus himself.

PART FOUR

Wisdom at Gettysburg: Rewriting the Oracles

The fourth section of the book explores the difficult idea of an open oracle, a covenant or contract that unites the authority of a decree with the risk and freedom of a genuine experiment in living. Such an oracle is usually found in a culture that is the opposite of authoritarian. An ideology or creed is crustacean, not built to stand the strain of innovation or experiment. By contrast, an open culture is organic; like liberal education or science, it carries its skeleton inside a body that is flexible and growing.

Oracles are created out of a tension between what Northrop Frye has called 'concern' and 'freedom.' The concern of a sect or party is seldom free from intolerance and prejudice. And freedom without concern has nothing to attach to. To communicate with a finite mind, an infinite mind may have to resort to an oracle which speaks 'of a world that may not exist' but which nevertheless 'completes existence' (Frye, 1971, 170). To the degree that an oracle is partisan and a voice of concern, it exhorts us to create and belong to a 'society of neighbors' (Frye, 1967a, 27). It is better to be Blake's 'clod,' 'something attached to the rest of the earth,' than an isolated 'pebble.' Or as Frye's aphorism puts it, 'we belong to something before we are anything, nor does growing in being diminish the link of belonging' (1967a, 28). An oracle of concern asks us to expand our horizon without losing the 'primitive function of religio' (Frye, 1967a, 25), a binding together by means of shared beliefs and values. To the degree, however, that an oracle is disinterested and a voice of freedom, it invites us to replace an explanatory system with a poetry that provokes explanation but accepts none.

To balance the claims of concern and freedom an oracle may combine the seriousness of an end game with the irony of a joke. When Isaac asks his father, 'where is the lamb for a burnt offering?,' Abraham's reply that 'God will provide himself the lamb' has the solemnity of a divine contract or covenant. But the oracle is also unsettling, for it includes the dark possibility that Isaac is the lamb. An oracle that commands us to submit to God is coercive. But since any expression of an infinite mind in finite language implies more than it says, it may also provide a fire exit or escape clause. As Kierkegaard shows, Abraham combines his faith in a God of love with self-critical irony, for he knows he has answered Isaac without saying anything.

To assert that Rome is the new Troy or that 'our America is here or nowhere' is to consecrate the ground we stand on. It is to affirm we dwell in a sacred region, a holy land, and proudly possess a code of true commands or laws. Quite different from this oracle of concern, which binds us by obligation and affection to the 'life of significant soil,' are the oracles of freedom that move a culture beyond boundaries of class and race toward a horizon that is always retreating from view as we approach it. When Martin Luther King says he has 'a dream,' his vision of freedom promotes more vision. His oracle is also a view from nowhere, since the freedom it celebrates never fully exists at any given time. Though we are moved by the rhetoric of the Decalogue, which is an oracle of God's concern for his people, we are touched by the poetry of the Sermon on the Mount, which (like King's dream) is an oracle of personal emancipation.

Oracles of freedom remind us that, though people may believe a kingdom of ends exists, such a kingdom is 'not to see but to see by' (Frye, 1971, 165). In other words, it is 'an informing power rather than an objective goal to be attained' (Frye, 1971, 165). By a bold leap of induction, Frye finds a host of Buddhist, Platonic, and biblical examples of a 'world which may not exist but is pointed to by the articulate orders of experience' (1971, 168). In a wise aphorism that revives the latent pun in Utopia (the good place is also the no-place), he goes so far as to suggest that 'the lively feeling' of Utopia's absence 'is what accounts for the quality of pleasure in the arts' (1971, 168). Only literature, Frye believes, can 'reflect the world escaped from, in its conventions of tragedy and irony and satire, along with the world escaped to, in its conventions of pastoral and romance and comedy' (1971, 169). He leaves us at the end with a troubling paradox, with a glimpse of a world that may not exist and yet informs existence, 'the world of the definitive experience that poetry urges us to have but which we can never quite get' (1971, 170–1).

We should distinguish between oracles of science, which make confident predictions about the future, and the oracles of prophets and poets, whose concern is the potential, what is imaginatively conceivable or possible. To judge the poet's oracles by the oracles of science is to forget that art and religion are neither logical nor anti-logical, but counter-logical. As the breath and finer spirit of knowledge, poetry is what Wordsworth calls the 'countenance of all science.' Since science is the ascendant force in our culture, a tendency exists to make all oracles as predictive and knowledgeable as possible, with all the hope and wisdom smoothed out. Unfortunately, the oracles of prophets and poets are all hope and wisdom. They cannot be assimilated to phenomena that are somewhat rashly said to be predictable, like stock markets or the weather.

At a time when all knowledge that is not reducible to rules is in danger of being relegated to the dustbin of obsolete belief and superstition, a culture may wish to redress the imbalance by removing weight from the heavier scale. Though wary of bardic solemnity, its prophets may try to lighten gravity with grace. They may try to turn the shadow of lost knowledge into the substance of vision. A culture that respects tradition but distrusts authority faces a double challenge. To respect tradition, it must repair or keep intact its wisdom writing and oracles, without allowing them to turn into petrified ideas or confiscated myths of concern. But in challenging authority, a culture faces an opposite problem. An oracle is a centre of moral and spiritual authority. Even when it offers ambiguous advice, an oracle's authority is not itself ambiguous. If a culture consistently subverts authority, it may have few end games to modify and no wisdom to live by or replenish.

The hope that grows with wisdom is the master of the possible or the potential, and its adversary is despair. The faith that grows with knowledge is the master of prophecy or prediction, and its adversary is doubt. The popular 'foretelling' aspect of oracles is now the province of science, which has learned to control and predict a few events in the natural world. Outside science, the future is no longer a metaphor for events we have enough knowledge to foresee or enough faith in reason to predict. The most resonant oracles today use the future as a metaphor for the potential, not the predictable. The great resource of wisdom is an ability to tap into this potential by relaxing the will and being ready to hear an oracle when it speaks.

For a prophet of freedom like Irenaeus the glory of God is man alive. In Hegel's view the most insidious slavery is a tacit willingness to live at any cost, even at the cost of losing one's freedom. In his great essay on 'Fate,' Emerson even 'hazard[s] the contradiction' that 'freedom is necessary. If you please to plant yourself on the side of Fate, and say, Fate is all; then we say, a part of Fate is the freedom of man' (1965, 610). Sooner or later, however, a prophet of freedom faces the disturbing possibility that his search for value in an open world is both necessary and impossible. If an inquiry is genuinely open and subversive, with the result that nothing concludes or ends, then nothing can be concluded or decided either. Conversely, when a prophet of genius like St. Paul or Moses delivers to the world hermetic instructions or a new code of laws, the covenant he reveals will be sealed off and closed. It will retain authority but lose its power to subvert. As one critic comments, 'the test of every revolutionary movement ... comes when it must establish continuity with what has preceded it' (Frye, 1976a, 144–5). A prophet is unlikely to embrace a new decalogue or supersede his first revelation with a second announcement of novelty or surprise. Though St Paul believes the truth will make us free, he is suspicious of any freedom that makes a parody of grace or that appeals to the heart in protest against the notion of original sin. Even a prophet of freedom like Thomas Jefferson, the author of the Declaration of Independence, cannot be expected to endorse a second revolution when delivering his first inaugural address as president of the republic he recently helped found. In a thoughtfully disturbing book, *The Religious Case against Belief*, James Carse argues that 'belief marks the line at which our thinking stops' (2008, 44). Only poets who promote wonder and prophets who reinvent their world can push against the doors that every belief system tries to lock and keep shut. In a truly open culture, Socrates and Jesus, Marx and the revolutionary Jefferson, are still alive, and their ideas continue to be dangerous.

15 From Delphi to Gettysburg: Changing the Covenant

Thomas Jefferson is the rationalist of the Enlightenment, who seals his Republican covenant with the smile of reason. Abraham Lincoln comes from a darker time. He believes like Jefferson in meaningful history. But unlike earlier champions of America's manifest destiny, who insist that only fools or traitors forget what it is, Lincoln maintains that, though there is a providence at work in history that makes it purposeful, only blind patriots or fools will presume to say what that purpose is. Lincoln never allows us to forget that 'the Almighty has his own purposes.'

The ambiguity and sublimity of most oracles are attempts to remove a declaration of our destiny from partisan bias. They are antidotes to fanaticism. Reinhold Niebuhr compares Lincoln to the Hebrew prophets, since both see time under the aspect of eternity and both believe in purposeful history. 'It was Lincoln's achievement to embrace a paradox which lies at the center of the spirituality of western culture; namely, the affirmation of a meaningful history and the religious reservations about the partiality and bias which the human actors and agents betray in their definition of meaning' (1964, 77). The absence of partiality and party zeal makes it easier for Lincoln to display a spirit of magnanimity toward the end of his second Inaugural, when he looks toward the future 'with malice toward none' and 'with charity for all.'

1

Jefferson's first Inaugural address is a republican covenant. It has the defining features of a secular oracle, a renewal of old law and newly discovered liberty. Instead of sanctioning a second revolution, like the

Declaration of Independence, the Inaugural address initiates an experiment in government under Jefferson's own presidency. With great dexterity Jefferson navigates between descriptive and performative uses of language. From 'will of the law' and 'will of the majority' he unobtrusively moves to the use of 'will' as a future auxiliary verb (Jefferson, 1801). He resolves or wills to serve well a republican democracy whose will it is that he should govern.

Jefferson approaches the 'first executive office' of his country in the same mood of contrition and unworthiness as a penitent might approach the communion table or as a suppliant might approach Delphi. What could convince Jefferson, a man of strong intellect and vision, that his powers are too 'weak?' Why is he humbled and overwhelmed by the magnitude of his summons? Even before we realize that the destiny of the new republic is worthy of another oracle at Delphi, the new president dramatizes the monumental scale and difficulty of his task. He confesses that he assumes the burdens of office with 'anxious and awful presentiments.'

Jefferson makes it easier for Federalist opponents to support his presidency by calling the bitter disputes of the past decade a 'contest of opinion.' Far from teetering on the brink of anarchy, as John Adams and other members of the Federalist opposition may fear, the debates of the recent past were only a free play of ideas, a spirited display of how a democracy should work. But now as he calls for a new unity of purpose, Jefferson concedes to his Federalist opponents that the minority who declined to vote for him must possess its 'equal rights, which equal law must protect, and to violate would be oppression.' To prevail, the will of the majority must be 'rightful.' Jefferson is not so utopian as to suppose that what is 'rightful' will always be strictly rational, capable of withstanding the scrutiny of political scientists and philosophers. It is enough that the views of the majority should appear prudent and reasonable. But if prudence or complacency is all we can reasonably expect from a powerful majority, then a minority that may have reason on its side, that may be rational as well reasonable, must 'possess [its] equal rights,' too, 'which equal law must protect.' The chiasmus of sound and meaning, locked into place by the pivotal comma after 'rights,' secures the point: 'possess, equal, equal, protect.' Jefferson's political oracle looks two ways at once. Majorities and minorities are in one sense unequal, since the will of only one can prevail. And yet they are also equal in the sense that matters most, for they both have equal rights.

Sometimes attacked as a master of duplicity, as an apostle of liberty who owned slaves, a partisan who pretended to be above partisanship, Jefferson does (it is true) allow double, even opposite meanings to grow from the centre of his address. 'The conflicting elements of a troubled world' are very much a part of Jefferson's two-way grammar and prophecies. Even the innocuous concessive phrase 'of course' acquires in its context a double force. 'All will, of course, arrange themselves under the will of the law.' Coming from Jefferson, the author of the Declaration of Independence, the prophecy contains a paradox. Though every revolution hopes to transcend the law, hope recedes in proportion as the revolution succeeds. Jefferson's casual idiom does not quite conceal this paradox. If revolution was once the will of nature and nature's God, the course of history now runs elsewhere, 'under the will of the law.' Civic virtue complements and fulfils republican liberty and revolution. As a prophet of the new nation, Jefferson sustains a two-way vision. Undeniably, revolution was the condition of America's birth. But the republic also has to learn federalist virtues as it grows older: the will of law is the natural, conservative sequel of an unnatural, revolutionary beginning.

Nowhere is Jefferson's two-way vision more strikingly expressed than in his reminder that 'liberty and even life itself,' the great goals of the Revolution, 'are but dreary things' without 'harmony and affection.' We may be surprised to hear the champion of liberty and revolution sounding more like Edmund Burke than Thomas Paine or John Stuart Mill. For the liberty Jefferson seeks is not the freedom of an eccentric or recluse. It is the liberty to cultivate qualities of intellect and sympathetic imagination, faculties that nourish moral sentiments and that are essential to 'the pursuit of happiness' as Jefferson conceives it.

In keeping with his talent for two-way meaning, Jefferson's odd use of 'wonderful' fleetingly discloses a palimpsest of suppressed or reinvented narratives. Having evoked a nightmare vision of regicide and slaughter, as nations like France sought through blood their 'long-lost liberty,' Jefferson reflects that 'it was not wonderful that the agitation of the billows should reach even this distant and peaceful shore.' What does seem 'wonderful' is the isolation of the new republic, founded by revolution, from the agony of France's bold but terrifying experiment. As observers like Edmund Burke point out, the relative stability of the successful American experiment, when set against the anarchy in France, is worth admiring. We half expect Jefferson to say that 'it was wonderful that the agitation' in France should not reach us. Though honesty compels him to revise this statement, the substitution of 'wonderful' for the more logical 'surprising' ('it was not surprising that the revolutionary fervor should reach even America') allows the censored contrast between two revolutions – American and French – to enjoy a subliminal half-life of its own.

Jefferson's ringing affirmation that 'we are all Republicans, we are all Federalists' might seem a mere trick of rhetoric. It may be less a mastery of two-way vision than of double talk, a triumph of self-deceiving hope over expectation. Like a Colossus of Rhodes, however, Jefferson is resolved to straddle both political partisanship and prophecy. In the 'contest of opinion' that divided the two political parties during the 1790s there seemed little to unite them. Yet in his handwritten copy of the speech, Jefferson refrains from capitalizing the two party labels. Only false divisions can permanently separate small-letter federalists from small-letter republicans. Jefferson is not denying that it is possible to 'dissolve the Union or to change its republican form.' Nor would he suppress such changes, if most Americans willed them. For essential to Jefferson's republican faith is a conviction that both monarchists and anarchists can easily be defeated in public debate when 'reason is left free to combat' the errors of both sides. Jefferson shares Mill's faith in free discussion. Errors of political opinion, including Jefferson's own mistakes, can be left undisturbed as quaint monuments of Enlightenment thought or as antiquated ideas about slavery. Provided they are subject to vigorous refutation or disproof in a free exchange of ideas, obsolete beliefs are no more dangerous to a democratic state than other discarded idols of the marketplace or tribe.

The buoyant resilience of Jefferson's vision is most apparent in the blend of high promise and peril he discerns in America's maritime commerce, crossing 'all the seas with the rich productions of [her] industry.' Since America's destinies, like her ships' trajectories, lie far 'beyond the reach of mortal eyes,' Jefferson can boldly transform the literal ships of commerce into a metaphoric vessel of state. Navigating 'the conflicting elements of a troubled world,' this republican ship is buffeted by billows of agitation and unrest reaching it from Europe. Though 'launched on the full tide of successful experiment,' the ship is exposed to risks that are commensurate with the great rewards that await the nation should the venture succeed. After all, what are the alternatives? If a citizen cannot be trusted with self-government, can he be trusted to govern others? 'Or have we found angels in the form of kings to govern him? Let history answer this question.'

Once we accept Jefferson's democratic axiom that political liberty promotes civic virtue, all the oracles of his republican creed fall naturally into place. Unlike the theorems in Euclidian geometry, these axioms are not the conclusions we reach at the end of a logical proof. Instead, since each conclusion is implicit in each premise, and all the axioms imply and sustain each other, any argument that Jefferson conducts is necessarily circular, a form of *petitio principii* (or begging the question). As both a transmitter and receiver of truth, Jefferson can easily, in his own apt phrase, 'close the circle of our felicities.' Their right constellation or circle includes 'freedom of religion, freedom of the press, and freedom of person under the protection of the habeas corpus, and trial by juries impartially selected.' But the only proof Jefferson can finally offer of the truth and value of these 'felicities' is the probation or proving ground of American democracy and the republican experiment itself.

In an Inaugural address, as in any ascent to a mount of prophecy and vision, a suppliant who is about to speak as an oracle of state approaches the temple of power with commingled humility and awe. Though few presidents have been better qualified for their office than Thomas Jefferson, he feels impelled to confess his unworthiness. His podium is not Mount Sinai, nor is he Moses about to receive commandments from God. His prophecy of state will succeed only if it fosters reconciliation and hope by allaying distrust. Just as an elegy helps its speaker perform what Freud calls 'the work of mourning,' so Jefferson's oracle of state performs the work of prophecy, vision, and renewed commitment to republican democracy.

But is Jefferson's anti-partisan claim that 'we are all Republican, we all Federalists' not itself a partisan disclaimer? Is the Inaugural address a Republican manifesto? Or does it 'manage somehow to transcend the very political realities that elevated [Jefferson] to executive office' (Browne, 2003, 8)? Ostensibly, Jefferson's address purges the young republic of the contagion of partisanship. But Stephen Howard Browne believes that, even in transcending the conditions of their own making, Jefferson's most oracular pronouncements still constitute a 'profoundly political act, in motive, function, and form' (2003, 15). Since oracles often disguise their practical functions, they may also disclose what Fredric Jameson calls a 'political unconscious.' Though Jefferson seems to do everything in his power to make the Republicans a 'party to end parties,' he never forgets that he is the head of the political coalition that elected him to office.

2

A partisan is an uncritical believer whose faith is unquestioning. A prophet, by contrast, is a sceptical believer: he has faith in tradition but is critical of authority. A contest between two partisans ends when one of the players wins. But in an open culture the purpose of an end game is to keep all the pieces in play. To see how far political rivals may contribute to the character of a democracy, I want to digress for a moment to two earlier defining episodes in American political mythology. What begins as a battle between loyalists and revolutionaries in Hawthorne's short story 'My Kinsman, Major Molineux,' or between Puritans and aesthetes in 'The Maypole of Merry Mount,' ends with the prophecy of a more inclusive whole. As a team of rivals, both contestants will be united in a more harmonious culture, where each fulfils and sustains the ambitions of the other. Robin, the Anglophile, is invited to join the revolutionaries, and Edgar and Edith, while not exactly converted to the Puritan cause, learn to look their last on all things lovely, without wasting 'one regretful thought on the vanities of Merry Mount.'

When Hawthorne's Robin takes refuge in a Boston church in 'My Kinsman, Major Molineux,' he asks in some confusion, 'Am I here, or there?' Suspended between dream and waking reality, he wanders between two worlds, one dying and the other struggling to be born. In theory, Robin still belongs to the rural loyalist world of his clergyman father. 'Dear remembrances' still allow him to 'keep his heart pure by refreshing memories of home.' But Robin's disturbing night in Boston is beginning to shatter that spell. How long can he be charmed by venerable traditions? How long can he play the ritual end games – those 'old thanksgivings' and 'old supplication for continuance' – that are repeated to the point of 'weariness' in his family circle?

The Boston revolutionaries prepare for a different end game, for a ritual of tar and feathering, in which Major Molineux, the loyalist and Anglophile, will be publicly humiliated. But rising above partisan politics, Hawthorne's prophecy is disinterestedly inclusive. Like 'the double-faced fellow' whose face is painted half black and half red, the anticipated game of ritual hazing prepares *for* and not *against* surprise. Everything about the end game throws us off guard by looking two ways at once. The initial shock is that Robin is no longer a passive spectator. He is compelled instead to entertain the 'indefinite but ... uncomfortable idea that he was himself to bear a part in the pageantry' (1959, 31). Having shunned Robin earlier in the evening, the revolutionaries are about to conscript him into a grotesque farce. Everything converges on him like a recognition scene in a play.

The original puzzle is why Robin's mention of Major Molineux's name should shock and agitate the citizens he questions. Though called, ironically, a 'shrewd youth,' every time Robin tries to explain something he misconstrues it. The old man with the sepulchral cough takes offence, not because he is unfamiliar with the Major (as Robin supposes), but because he knows the Major too well. The innkeeper is polite, not because he sees a resemblance between Major Molineux and Robin, but because he values Robin as a rural youth with no Old World connections. Robin is being obtuse, not 'shrewd,' when he concludes that people at the inn despise him for lacking money. He is ostracized, not for being poor, but for airing genteel pretensions.

We half expect the ritual hazing to be a simple exposure of Robin's fantasy creation, of his patronizing assumption of superior worth, and of the social pride of his kinsman. But Hawthorne keeps the end game open by striking a fine balance between sympathy and moral judgment and by maintaining two-way cultural associations in the phrasing.

> [The Major's] whole frame was agitated by a quick and continual tremor, which his pride strove to quell, even in those circumstances of overwhelming humiliation. But perhaps the bitterest pang of all was when his eyes met those of Robin; for he evidently knew him on the instant, as the youth stood witnessing the foul disgrace of a head grown gray in honor. They stared at each other in silence, and Robin's knees shook, and his hair bristled, with a mixture of pity and terror. (1959, 31)

Though nothing can mitigate 'the foul disgrace,' it is the infamy of a 'head grown gray in honor.' The 'mixture of pity and terror' that overcomes Robin elevates the spectacle above mere misrule and farce. By replacing coarse humour with the two emotions Aristotle associates with tragic drama, Hawthorne turns a hazing ceremony into a prophecy about the cultural heritage of New England.

The oxymoron of a 'tar-and-feather dignity' erodes any claim to grandeur. But however shaken by his enemies, vestiges of 'a steady soul' survive in the Major's 'strong, square features' and his large, 'majestic person.' The more fiendish and mocking the mob becomes, the more sympathy Hawthorne elicits for the Major. Our affection for a potentially pompous Colonel Blimp is most intense when a single metonymy brings his humanity unexpectedly to life by contrasting it with the inhumanity of the frenzied crowd, 'trampling' without feeling 'on an old man's heart.'

Though 'mighty no more,' the Major is 'majestic still in his agony,' like a 'dead potentate' or a waning but once great imperial power. Robin feels a strong urge to leave Boston, the city of revolution, for the more conservative culture of the countryside. But the Boston gentleman's parting words to Robin are prophetic. Refusing to direct him to the ferryman, Robin's new mentor invites him to stay a while before deciding whether to leave Boston or join the cause of a republican America. 'If you prefer to remain with us, perhaps, as you are a shrewd youth, you may rise in the world without the help of your kinsman, Major Molineux' (1959, 33). Forward-looking and inclusive, the oracle's last use of 'shrewd' is the only use that does not resonate with irony and that opens on a cultural horizon instead of closing on a boundary.

In another parable of cultural destiny, 'The Maypole of Merry Mount,' Hawthorne keeps open the contest between jollity and gloom that will determine, according to his oracle, the 'future complexion of New England' (1959, 145). Even after the apparent victory of the Puritans seems to tilt the balance in the direction of gravity and gloom, Hawthorne manages to add weight to the lighter scale. Though the Lord and Lady of the May belong to the band of vanquished revellers, Hawthorne protects them from the Puritans' savagery and celebrates them as the true heroes of his story. In the nocturnal adventures of Young Goodman Brown, Hawthorne examines a paradox within Puritanism itself. He shows how a strict doctrine of election may breed its apparent opposite: an antinomian contempt for law that threatens to abolish moral rule altogether. In 'The Maypole of Merry Mount,' his parable of New England's seventeenth-century religious and political culture, Hawthorne dramatizes a related contest for empire: he explores the same conflict between Puritanism and pagan culture that Arnold examines in the contest between Hebraism and Hellenism in *Culture and Anarchy*.

In a balanced portrait of the revellers, Hawthorne combines a charming evocation of the aesthetes' talent for pleasure with a gentle mockery of their decadence. We applaud the citizens of Merry Mount for gallantly pouring sunshine over New England's rugged hills. Yet we are mildly shocked to learn that they 'scatter flower seeds' instead of grain 'throughout the soil.' After a harsh winter and belated spring, no one grudges 'the gay colony' its right to celebrate May's long-deferred bounties. But our assessment of the colony may be less generous when we learn that, in violation of nature's seasonal cycle, 'May, or her mirthful spirit, dwelt all the year round at Merry Mount' (1959, 138).

Hawthorne's attitude to the Puritans is ambiguously sly. 'Let us thank God,' he says with caustic wit, 'for having given us such ancestors; and let each successive generation thank him not less fervently for being one step further from them in the march of ages' (quoted in Kazin, 1997, 24). Instead of ending his tale with a confident declaration of a Puritan victory, Hawthorne raises two of the revellers, Edgar and Edith, above the status of partisans. As Lord and Lady of the May, the newly married couple enjoy the prophet's privilege of playing with cultural boundaries and enlarging them.

The most oracular words in the story echo Milton, the sublime Puritan who in *Paradise Lost* and *Samson Agonistes* writes, like his senior contemporary, Shakespeare, not for an age but for all time. The high priest of Merry Mount, the clerk of Oxford who marries Edgar and Edith, is an Arminian, an advocate of free will who speaks for the Cavalier or Royalist cause in the Civil War. The Puritans, by contrast, are stern Calvinists, the New England counterparts of the Roundheads and Milton. But the Milton we hear is not the Latin Secretary of Oliver Cromwell. He is the poet of the masque *Comus*, whose crew appears in Hawthorne's tale as lewd revellers, 'midway between man and beast' (1959, 140). Like Milton's companion poems 'L'Allegro' and 'Il Penseroso,' Hawthorne's story of Edgar and Edith is a prose poem of contrasting moods and tones.

> 'Edith, sweet Lady of the May,' whispered he reproachfully, 'is yon wreath of roses a garland to hang above our graves that you look so sad? O, Edith, this is our golden time! Tarnish it not by any pensive shadow of the mind; for it may be that nothing of futurity will be brighter than the mere remembrance of what is now passing.' (1959, 141)

As both Keats and Milton understand, 'in the very temple of Delight / Veiled Melancholy has her sovereign shrine' ('Ode on Melancholy,' ll. 25–6).

Like a voice from Sinai, a prophetic Hawthorne lets us know that, even before the Puritans destroy Merry Mount, the married lovers have already decided to leave their paradise. 'From the moment that they truly loved, they had subjected themselves to earth's doom of care and sorrow, and troubled joy, and had no more a home at Merry Mount' (1959, 142). As George Eliot says, Adam and Eve 'kept their honeymoon in Eden, but had their first little ones among the thorns and thistles of the wilderness.' Like Walter Scott, Edith and Edgar realize that one crowded hour of glorious life is worth an age without a name. They would rather ease gracefully into a fulfilled old age than suffer the ennui of perfection, at a standstill through eternity.

Substituting horizons for boundaries as they pursue their way 'heavenward,' the newlyweds support each other 'along the difficult path ... it was their lot to tread' (1959, 149). The oracular coda of Hawthorne's tale resonates with an echo of the closing lines of *Paradise Lost*:

> The World was all before them, where to choose
> Their place of rest, and Providence their guide:
> They hand in hand with wandering steps and slow,
> Through Eden took their solitary way.   (XII. 646–9)

The skewered pathos of Merry Mount's attempt to live in a paradise remote from history is Hawthorne's reminder that the only Eden is the one we have lost. Though a Puritan sermon on the vanities of Merry Mount might move or persuade us, we are touched by the spirit of Edgar and Edith. For like Milton's Adam and Eve, these exiles from Eden are prophets rather than partisans, poets rather than preachers and zealots. After experiencing the transience and therefore the seriousness of pleasure, their decision to leave Merry Mount is not a course of action forced on them by the Puritans but a decision they themselves have already made. Once again, as in 'My Kinsman, Major Molineux,' Hawthorne bursts into impulsive prophecy about the promise and future character of both New England and America.

3

Jefferson says in his Inaugural address that Americans 'possess a chosen country,' ample enough in its geography and wealth to include and support diverse groups for generations to come. We must beware, however, of assuming that oracles of state are purer than political history, that they are somehow more privileged and disinterested than the agendas of evangelicals and atheists, of Federalists and Republicans, who want their concerns addressed. Herodotus reminds us that during their invasion of Greece the Persians bribed the Greek oracle to predict a victory for their side. Since any oracle can be bribed, it is tempting for an ascendant political ideology to kidnap the oracles of state by pretending that an address like Jefferson's is what one commentator calls 'a secular analogue to the Mosaic tradition,' an 'image of a people guided by the laws to its destined fulfillment' (Browne, 2003, 128). Jefferson, it seems to me, is too self-confident and rational a prophet to experience the fear and trembling of Abraham or the sublime moral imagination of a Hebrew prophet. Perhaps the most telling criticism of Jefferson comes from Charles Francis Adams, who complains of his 'placidity.' 'One would like more evidence that the iron had some time or other entered his soul, more evidence of having profoundly reflected on the enigma of existence, of having more deeply felt its tragic import' (Browne, 2003, 130). For such iron and grit we must turn from Jefferson, a prophet of sweetness and light, to a more tortured republican prophet, Abraham Lincoln.

Though Jefferson approaches his high office with appropriate humility and even awe, he is also Olympian and serene. As an oracle of those same republican principles to which he gives eloquent expression in the Declaration of Independence, Jefferson is a model of controlled energy and optimism. Nothing could afford a greater contrast to the fearful fatalism of Lincoln's Last Inaugural address: the reelected Civil War president seems stunned by all the blood and trauma of a conflict that rolls on like a Juggernaut, refusing to end. In seeking guidance from an oracle he only imperfectly understands and that he can in no sense manipulate as his mouthpiece, Lincoln is subject to much deeper misgivings than Jefferson. He seems as shocked by the blood and carnage of the great Civil War as any solider on the fields of Gettysburg.

Indeed there is something grotesque as well as miraculous about what Lincoln modestly, half humorously, calls his 'second appearing.' Though his reelection was unexpected, there he stands like Hamlet's ghost, gaunt and grave, half apparition and half saviour. Like Christ's Second Coming, Lincoln's 'second appearing' may be a providential return. But for Lincoln's enemies, spooked by fantasies of a resurrected messiah of the slaves, the phrase is electrifying. His 'second appearing' is their worst nightmare come true.

Lincoln allows a civil war to take place when the threatened secession of the southern states endangers boundaries. But in his Second Inaugural address, Lincoln opposes factions that engender boundaries. By confronting his southern opponents, not with power and violence, but with malice to none and charity to all, he uses the oracles of law and religion to oppose rancour with vision. Like any great prophet, Lincoln has the power to show the secessionists that what seems necessary – the break-up of the union – is only possible. Instead of meeting argument with counter-argument, Lincoln's non-partisan use of biblical prophecy engages a people in transition with emotions of shock, wonder, and bold surmise that help put the boundaries of a whole and undivided nation back into play.

Lincoln first apologizes for what he will be leaving out of his Second Inaugural. He is already warning his audience that the unheard words, the subtext, will be more important than anything they hear. Unlike Jefferson, who mounts to his plateau of civic instruction with an assured blend of optimism and humility, Lincoln approaches the oracle with fear and trembling. Brought low by a battery of impersonal passive verbs ('to be pursued,' 'could be presented,' 'is well known,' 'is ventured'), he is too stunned, it seems, to take responsibility for any firm course of action. Even when Lincoln tries to be more assertive by tentatively expressing 'high hope for the future,' he seems to censor or withdraw that hope in the second half of his sentence. Too prudent to make a wager, he cautions that 'no prediction in regard to it is ventured' (Lincoln, 1865).

In the second paragraph of his address, Lincoln performs a delicate balancing act. While justifying the Union, Lincoln does everything in his power to unite North and South in the great venture that divides them. Though one side tried to save the Union and the other to destroy it, they both shared a deep aversion to war. Muting the harsh clash of opposites, of '*saving* and *destroying*,' which Lincoln places in italics, his repetition without change of a phrase used by both parties – 'without war' 'without war' – vindicates his claim that North and South agreed on at least one matter. But a common deprecation of war can do nothing to delay or soften the drum roll of antitheses – 'make war' and 'accept war'; 'let the nation survive' and 'let it perish' – which set the two sides apart, like opposing armies on a great field of battle. Given the rift, the doom announced by the final four-word sentence ('And the war came'), alarming in its brevity, seems both scandalous and inevitable.

Instead of giving a sermon on the evils of slavery, as Jefferson gives a lecture on the virtues of republican democracy, Lincoln shares with the audience his perplexity and doubts. Trying to find common ground with the enemy, he uses anaphora to bind North and South together: 'All knew,' 'Neither Party expected,' 'Neither anticipated,' 'Each looked for,' 'Both read,' 'each invokes.' The warring factions are joined by the very actions that divide them. Even when Lincoln ventures onto the dangerous ground of their deep disagreements, he euphemistically invokes the institution of slavery, not as the evil that it is, but as 'a peculiar and powerful interest.' He even allows an anti-pun to flicker briefly before the conscious mind before consigning it to darkness. The offence precipitating civil war is not just the offence of slavery. It is also, the anti-pun suggests, the offence of 'fences,' of allowing a House divided to use the fence of schism and secession to shut out far more brotherhood and civic goodwill than it can ever enclose or fence in. In a civil war of words, the 'offence' of slavery builds a fence between neighbours. Nothing can quite fence out the violence of the flickering anti-puns and the offences they commit against the proprieties of civilized discourse and good breeding.

In seeking light from an oracle that is as dark as it is wise, Lincoln concedes his own learned ignorance about the cause of the conflict. Slavery was, somehow, the root of the problem, he thinks. But the two pregnant pauses, coming both before and after 'somehow,' are as sharp and incisive as knife wounds inflicted on the corpse of the Union. The weighted adverb dramatizes not only Lincoln's inability to understand the justice or wisdom of the god to whom both sides pray. It also magnifies the mystery of the great iniquity that comes in war's wake: the incremental force of a Juggernaut nothing seems able to slow down or stop. Lincoln feels nothing can temper the cruelty of slavery, an institution that incorporates the harshness, though not the justice, of God's punishment of Adam and Eve, who after their expulsion from Eden have to earn 'their bread from the sweat of [their] faces.' But unlike the God of Genesis, Lincoln seems more baffled than angry.

Even the South's appeal to God in its defence of slavery strikes Lincoln not as an evil practice or even a hypocritical one, but merely as 'strange.' It is paradoxical, perhaps, or at most inconsistent. No sooner has Lincoln expressed his surprise, however, than he checks any impulse to condemn the South. Instead he tempers justice with mercy by appealing to a second passage of Scripture, this time from the gospel of Matthew: 'but let us judge not that we be not judged' (7:1).

In a conciliatory coda, Lincoln assures his opponents that the 'government will not assail you. You can have no conflict without being yourselves the aggressors. You have no oath registered in Heaven to destroy the Government, while I have the solemn one to "preserve, protect and defend it."' Even when Lincoln has exhausted the subject and has nothing more to say, he seems loath to close. We are not enemies, but friends, he insists. Though passion may have *strained*, it must not *break* the bonds of what we share and have in common. David Bromwich justly notes that William Seward's original draft of the Inaugural's last paragraph is 'a touch orotund and front-heavy.' Lincoln's 'greatest change is a small one that transforms the sense.' By substituting 'the better angels of our nature' for Seward's 'cliché of patriotic feeling' (the phrase 'guardian angel of the nation'), Lincoln can appeal 'to a power of admonition and charity that is broadly human' (Bromwich, 2006, October, 48–9). He can prophesy, more inclusively now, that when touched again by 'the better angels of our nature,' the mystic chords of a memory stretching from every battlefield and patriot grave to every living heart and hearthstone will once again swell the chorus of the Union.

Arnold says that religion is morality tempered with emotion. We can say the same of oracles, which place powerful exclamation points after their prophecies and injunctions. But as one commentator warns, 'because of its appeal to the absolute,' an oracle 'is capable of the most awful pretension.' It may clothe 'immediate causes with ultimate sanction' (White, 2002, 115). To reduce this danger Lincoln offers 'not only the edge of affirmation, but interrogation' (White, 2002, 113). In his letter to the Hebrews Paul says 'the word of God is quick, and powerful, and sharper than any two-edged sword.' White adds that 'Lincoln liked to wield the Bible as a sword, using one edge to affirm and the other to question' (2002, 113). When Lincoln, the oracle of Gettysburg, is not speaking with a forked tongue, he is replacing a tribal god with a universal one, a deity that resists alignment with either party.

Though Lincoln quotes twice from Matthew, once from the Psalms, and once from Genesis, the biblical text that resonates most powerfully, the book of Job, is never quoted. For 'stranger' than the invocation of God in a cruel cause or than the prayers of enemies to the same God is the silence and apparent withdrawal of God himself. The oracle conceals more than it reveals. It can offer only the cryptic, Delphic comment that 'the Almighty has his own purposes.' But a suppliant who tries to fathom these 'purposes' does so at his peril. It would be consoling if Lincoln, like Moses, could transcribe God's words or receive them on a tablet. But the oracle must be oblique: its 'silent-speaking words' must be riddling and enigmatic. The indirection is the result of a logical dilemma. Since a free state is not a slave state, and a divided nation cannot be a united one, the prayers of North and South are in logical contradiction. God *cannot* answer both of them, and he *may* answer neither. Satisfaction of both parties is *impossible*; even the victory of only one side is merely *probable*.

Two Lincolns can be heard in this majestic address: Lincoln the partisan, who believes he has a divine mandate for going to war, and Lincoln the agnostic, the prophet of a higher ignorance. As re-elected leader of the winning side, Lincoln is at first confidently in control of what he says. One party 'would rather *make* war than let the nation survive; and the other would *accept* war rather than let it perish.' The artful contrast between 'make' and 'accept' is the rhetoric of a partisan claiming authority for what he has done. But a few sentences later Lincoln hits bedrock. He strikes a core of mystery and paradox that forces him to abandon his role as knowledgeable protector of the state and acknowledge his profound ignorance of God's will. The best comments on this second Lincoln come from James Carse. 'All claims that anyone including [Lincoln] himself, is acting on a divine mandate are at best an illusion.' With the words 'both sides read the same Bible, and pray to the same God,' Lincoln 'has placed all ideology, indeed all belief, under the final unintelligibility of a God who answers prayers, if at all, as he wishes, not as we wish. No longer can any one of us claim God as an authority. Inasmuch as God was generally thought of as Supreme Authority, Lincoln is declaring by implication that there is no authority at all to whom we can turn for a final claim to truth. This Lincoln is no ideologue, not even a true believer; he is the very portrait of higher ignorance' (2008, 89).

Lincoln's dilemma, which is familiar to students of agnostic theology, is explored at length by H.L. Mansel in *The Limits of Religious Thought*, published in 1858, seven years before Lincoln delivered his Second Inaugural address. According to Mansel, the divine nature can never be logically grasped by the mind's logically exclusive conceptions of a supreme being that is at once Absolute, Infinite, and a First Cause. No more can the will of Lincoln's oracle be compassed by the prayers of Americans who want to be at once divided and united as a nation, both in possession of slaves and free of 'offence.' It is possible, of course, that those who 'read the same Bible, and pray to the same

God,' yet seek each other's destruction, are guilty not just of a moral or theological error, but also of a fallacy in logic: they may each be excluding a middle term. It may, after all, please an inscrutable God to ignore the prayers of both parties. As Lincoln says, 'the prayers of both could not be answered; that of neither has been fully answered.' Lingering as a disturbing afterthought is the fear that neither side will be fully answered either now or in the dark days ahead. This excluded possibility haunts Lincoln like a nightmare. The darkest of his Job-like premonitions is the scourge of protracted war. In a gruesome vision that dizzies and astounds all suppliants of the oracle, Lincoln foresees a time when 'every drop of [slave] blood drawn with the lash shall be paid with another drawn with the sword.'

The false comforters in Job defend the heartless premise that a just God would never afflict a just man. There must be a causal connection between what people do and what happens to them. Lincoln is tempted to use this same argument himself. But he proceeds to do so hesitantly, with a cautious indirection, first by framing the argument as a hypothesis and then by turning it into a question. 'If we shall suppose that American Slavery is one of those offences which ... [God] now wills to remove, shall we discern therein any departure from those divine attributes which the believers in a Living God always ascribe to him?' A Living God is not the President Emeritus god of Thomas Jefferson and the deists. Presumably justice and retribution are attributes of the very potent and judgmental God we meet in Revelation and Genesis. But the sheer length of Lincoln's complicated sentence, from which I have deleted several subordinate clauses and phrases, may require even an attentive reader to circle back in search of a missing prodosis for the long-delayed question.

> If we shall suppose that American Slavery is one of those offences which, in the providence of God, must needs come, but which, having continued through His appointed time, He now wills to remove, and that He gives to both North and South this terrible war, as the woe due to those by whom the offence came, shall we discern therein any departure from those divine attributes which the believers in a Living God ascribe to Him?

As one commentator says, 'a curious reservation gives a conditional cast' to this 'all-important sentence ... What is strange is the third-person reference to "the believers in a Living God." Would someone sure of his own belief have chosen this long way round the saying of it?' (Bromwich, 2006, November, 28). Though this is true and well said, I think Lincoln's reserve has a deeper cause than Bromwich suggests. It is as if the oracle itself were reluctant to pose the question. Lincoln half expects the reader to forget something that he wants to forget himself. This is the alarming fact that Lincoln's own speculation originates in an uncharitable and unworthy impulse – in a desire to blame the South for its great affliction, as the comforters blame Job.

But before Lincoln can fully formulate his disconcerting question, he begins to censor and amend its implicit censure of the South by conceding that God has given to both parties, North as well as South, 'this terrible war.' The higher power whom Lincoln supplicates is not the benign God of Thomas Jefferson or James Monroe, the God of a manifest providence or destiny. It is rather the God of a strangely mysterious providence, the good but inscrutable deity of Ecclesiastes and Job. If the unthinkable should happen, if the oracle should decree that war will continue until the nation is broken and destroyed, then Lincoln can only conclude, with Job, that 'the Lord has given and the Lord has taken away, blessed be the name of the Lord.' Ronald C. White discerns the influence on Lincoln of Phineas Densmore Gurley's sermons at the New York Avenue Presbyterian Church in Washington. A Calvinist of the Old School, Gurley never preached politics, but he did emphasize the importance of an inscrutable providence, while acknowledging 'the elements of ambiguity and mystery in discerning' God's will (White, 2002, 140). As David Bromwich says, 'Lincoln seems to have wished for a faith his reason could not grant to any religious institution; and some way into his speeches and writings, one is struck by his habit of using other words for God: "providence," "my maker" – as if he were groping for a truer term' (2006, 28).

Having been humbled and even humiliated by what the oracle both discloses and withholds, Lincoln concedes that everyone had 'looked for an easier triumph, and a result less fundamental and astounding.' As Lincoln descends, like Moses, from his mount of vision, he seems chastened by a power whose judgments are as dark as they are fearful, as terrible as they are irreversible and true.

> Let us strive on to finish the work we are in, to bind up the nation's wounds, to care for him who shall have borne the battle, and for his widow and his orphans; to do all which may achieve and cherish a just and lasting peace among ourselves and with all nations.

After his contact with the 'one who walked the waves' in 'Lycidas,' Milton is prepared to return to the world with fears set aside and hope renewed. In a similar mood, Lincoln in his coda uses a series of slowly expanding infinitives – 'to strive,' 'to finish,' to bind up' – to open a window on the tenseless (and hence timeless) future of 'a lasting peace, among ourselves, and with all nations.'

4

Robert Lowell thinks that only Lincoln and Jefferson among American presidents combine a poet's command of words with a prophet's power to shape history. In joining 'Jefferson's ideals of freedom and equality ... to the Christian sacrificial act of death and rebirth,' Lincoln's address at Gettysburg has given to posterity a universal oracle, a prophecy that outlives its historical occasion. 'It still rings today,' Lowell says, 'when our country struggles with four almost insoluble spiritual problems: how to join equality to excellence, how to join liberty to justice, how to avoid destroying or being destroyed by nuclear power, and how to complete the emancipation of the slaves' (1964, 89). At Gettysburg Lincoln asks if the nation's dedication to the Declaration's key proposition (human equality) can survive the test of struggle in the day-to-day world of injustice and prejudice, relieved only by occasional acts of sacrifice and moral daring. His words possess what Lowell calls 'the gravity and brevity of an act of state' (1964, 88).

A great wisdom writer does not merely chronicle history: he also makes history. The best comments on the performative power of Lincoln's words at Gettysburg come from Gary Wills. Lincoln's address 'was the perfect medium for changing the way most Americans thought about the nation's founding acts,' Wills claims. 'Lincoln does not argue law or history, as Daniel Webster did. He makes history. He does not come to present a theory, but to impose a symbol, one tested in experience and appealing to national values, with an emotional urgency entirely expressed in calm abstractions (fire in ice). He came to change the world, to effect an intellectual revolution.' If Wills is right, then Lincoln's address at Gettysburg is a model for all future oracles. 'No other words could have done it. The miracle is that these words did. In the brief time before the crowd at Gettysburg he wove a spell that has not, yet, been broken – he called up a new nation out of the blood and trauma' (Wills, 1992, 174–5).

Ever since the *Iliad* was written, epic poets have been saying that the deeds of heroes like Hector or Achilles are more important than anything the poets can say about them. Lincoln's prediction that the world will not remember what he says at Gettysburg, though happily reversed by the judgment of history, draws upon a highly derivative trope, the so-called topos of modesty. Whatever thrilling magic adheres to his words cannot be separated from conventions as old as Greek epic. 'Nobody can remember the names and dates of battles unless they make some appeal to the imagination: that is, unless there is some literary reason for doing so. Everything that happens in time vanishes in time: it's only the imagination that, like Proust ... can see men as "giants in time"' (Frye, 1963a, 53). Like many prophets, Lincoln is derivative at a deep but original level. Gettysburg like Marathon carries an 'evocative ring *to us*' because Lincoln has made it 'a battle of literary' as well as historical 'importance.' Indeed nothing could be more unexpected, more oracular and radically prophetic, than Lincoln's address. 'If the name "Gettysburg" evokes strong feelings when it is as far away from us as we are from Marathon, it will do so only because of whatever literary tradition may have been begun with Lincoln's speech' (Frye, 1963c, 47).

As an elegy for those who fell at Gettysburg, Lincoln's address purifies the blood and trauma of the battle, and sends away the mourners 'in calm of mind, all passion spent.' To achieve catharsis Lincoln balances each impression of catastrophe and carnage with a countervailing impression of renewal and rebirth. The power that Lincoln supplicates is not the inscrutable oracle of his last Inaugural address, but a text of civic instruction already inscribed for all to read in Jefferson's great Declaration. Surprisingly, however, Lincoln gives to the Declaration itself, as he gives to the nation, a 'new birth of freedom.'

> It is rather for us to be here dedicated to the great task remaining before us; that from these honored dead we take increased devotion to that cause for which they *here* give the last full measure of devotion; that we here highly resolve that these dead shall not have died in vain; that the nation shall, under God, have a new birth of freedom, and that government of the people, by the people, for the people, shall not perish from the earth (Lincoln, 1863).

According to one commentator, James Carse, the American Revolution, 'a creation of highly educated upper-class gentlemen, had a different outcome [from the French Revolution] because of a simple but profound intellectual insight: they developed a belief system that did not completely believe in itself' (2008, 35). Jefferson's declaration that all men are created equal was not intended to include the equality of slaves to their masters. But in filling one of the holes that Jefferson left open, Lincoln is giving the dedication to equality a 'new birth of freedom' and reinventing the meaning of the nation's founding fathers. As Carse concludes, 'we easily speak of the "idea of America," an often unaware acknowledgment that it is not a fixed political entity but an accidental community of persons whose collective identity is under the constant recreation of its *thinkers*' (2008, 35).

Like Heine, Lincoln knows that freedom is a prison song: those who want it most, the American slaves, have lost it. Oracles of freedom are words of power. In 'words that remade America,' as Garry Wills has said, Lincoln is not merely citing the Declaration of Independence: he is also transforming it. The 'new birth of freedom' that confers equality on all Americans, and not just on white supremacists, is a form of 'doing-by-saying.' It carries moral as well as political authority, since it expands instead of limits the dignity of everyone who accepts it. Lincoln's address brings into being a new republic that did not authentically exist until his words are spoken.

When an oracle that proclaims 'a new birth of freedom' becomes one of the defining charters or creeds of a culture, its members no longer understand the oracle in terms of their experience. They understand their experience in terms of the oracle. Prophecies of enduring power, such as the oracles of the Bible or the aphorisms of Shakespeare, are luminous touchstones that 'verify our singularity,' as Seamus Heaney says, and 'stake out the ore of self which lies at the base of every individuated life' (2002, 189). Reaching down through time, these oracles touch each one of us and define who we are. As one commentator says, 'experience is the result of this generative touch, not its cause' (Carse, 1986, 167). Without the oracles and founding myths, few shared values would continue to affect or move us. Our culture as we know it would cease to exist.

As in Othello's dying plea, 'Nothing extenuate, / Nor set down aught in malice' (V.ii.342–3), there exists in Lincoln's 'malice to none and charity to all' a gentleness of attitude that is closer to Virgil than Homer. Lincoln harks back to the Sermon on the Mount rather than the speeches of Pericles or Caesar. He says during the Civil War that 'the things I have to deal with are too great for malice.' As one critic remarks of Shakespeare in *King Lear*, Lincoln knows 'there is another way than the heroic of meeting "the worst," the way of submission and suffering, of selflessness and compassion' (Brower, 1971, 411). With a Shakespearean poise that inhibits both simple partisanship and simple enmity, Lincoln invites us to see that 'the rarer action is / In virtue than in vengeance' (*The Tempest*, V.i.27–8). It takes a certain charity in the hearer not to fall into the reductions that fuel a great conflict like the Civil War.

An oracle like the Gettysburg address or the Sermon on the Mount does not only repair the Declaration of Independence or the Decalogue: it also reinvents it. Each is an example of an unusual literary form: unconsciously great art not originally conceived as art. A wholly invented oracle may lack the authority of precedence. But a merely bandaged or refurbished oracle may look anachronistic. To reinvent the Declaration of Independence is to keep one eye on history and the other on the altered circumstances of present and future generations. A prophet like Lincoln or Jesus who tries to transmit to posterity an original but just interpretation of the Declaration of Independence or the Decalogue has to walk a tightrope. The oracle he reinvents must be neither too rigid nor too fluid. If the oracle is too yielding, if it merely abolishes the law instead of fulfilling it, it will be displaced by unworthy rivals and retain no discernible identity. But if it is too rigid, if it makes spiritual life infinitely more strenuous, or if it banishes from its field of vision a new birth of freedom, no worthy opponent of Pharisees or racists may have the will to challenge or the energy to change it. An oracle that hopes to survive must have adversaries worthy of attacking or even trying to destroy it, and so of enlarging or contracting what it has to transmit.

16 Coleridge and Huxley: Experiment or Decree?

As Bacon foresees when he distinguishes between magisterial and probative aphorisms, the new gods of Delphi are experiment and decree. Whatever its syntax, the deep grammar of a magisterial oracle is descriptive. It is either a decree that has the force of law ('Let there be light, and there was light') or an authoritative summary of what is declared to be the case, as with an axiom in logic or a law in physics. By contrast, the grammar of a probative oracle, which catches an explorer in the act of discovery, is what J.L. Austin calls 'performative.' Like Jesus' prophecy, 'Blessed are the pure in heart, for they shall see God,' or Lincoln's prediction about a 'new birth of freedom,' a probative oracle conducts an experiment. What is the result of entertaining its words of power or believing they are true? In this chapter and the next I examine oracles of experiment and decree in such masters of prophetic speech as Coleridge and Huxley, Hopkins and Donne, G.B. Shaw and J.H. Newman. As we might expect, most oracular turns of phrase in poems and sermons by G.M. Hopkins and John Donne are both experimental and witty. But we may be surprised to find that T.H. Huxley, the scientist, is more dogmatic and magisterial than Samuel Taylor Coleridge, whose *Aids to Reflection* conducts a series of innovative experiments in the philosophy of religion. It may also come as a surprise to discover that Newman's exploration of a theory of theological development in his Oxford sermons is more probative and playfully experimental than Shaw's comically solemn exposition of evolutionary theology in *Back to Methuselah*, *Man and Superman*, and the Preface to *Saint Joan*.

1

In his sermons and poems, Hopkins, the Victorian Jesuit, is just as daring and probative as his seventeenth-century precursor. But at the centre of his faith Hopkins is also more tortured than Donne. In his sonnet 'Show me, dear Christ, thy spouse, so bright and clear,' Donne's address to the church is a progress in insolence. From a 'richly painted' bride, the church declines into a robed and torn waif, then, in a last blow to her dignity, into a whore, who is most 'pleasing' to her bridegroom when most unfaithful to him. Even when verging on blasphemy, however, Donne is always in control of these contending voices. In allowing his 'amorous soul' to 'court' God's 'mild dove,' he never loses his knightly decorum. By contrast, in his sonnet 'Thou art indeed just, Lord,' Hopkins teeters on the brink of despair and defeat. So risky is his experiment in invoking a friend who seems also to be his enemy that he finds a way to control the confusion of tongues only in a final prayer: 'Mine, O thou lord of life, send my roots rain.' His 'victory is hardly won,' as one critic says, 'and perhaps only temporary' (Brower, 1962, 27).

As in 'Show me, dear Christ,' Donne's great meditation on 'no man is an island' develops with shocking literalness the metaphor of the church as Christ's body. 'When she baptizes a child, that action concerns me; for that child is thereby connected to that body which is my head too and ingrafted into that body whereof I am a member' (mediation 17, Donne, 1946, 68). Donne experiments with his oracle by identifying the whole body with a mere portion of itself, its head. But the body that is Donne's head or master is no mere paradox. For the baptised child and the believer who has just been buried are so ingrafted into the body of the church that, like Donne himself, they are as literally its members as an arm or a leg are parts of a single person.

By reviving the etymology of 'translation' as a transferring or carrying over, Donne can explore different ways in which crossing the divide between life and death can be a turning from one language to another, as when we read a Hebrew text in Greek.

God employs several translators; some pieces are translated by age, some by sickness, some by war, some by justice; but God's hand is in every translation, and his hand shall bind up all our scattered leaves again for that library where every book shall lie open to one another. (Donne, 1946, 68)

The repeated use of two-way meanings allows the oracle to hover between the library and the Judgment seat. In a final translation God will bind the leaves or relics of the dead into the leaves of the great book of life, where the story of each translated soul can be read and judged.

Since the desire of the heart for recovered wholeness is endless, readers are still drawn in funeral services to that part of Donne's meditation in which the metaphor of wholeness shifts from the library of open books to the geography of an undivided continent or sea.

> No man is an island entire of itself; every man is a piece of the continent, a part of the main. If a clod be washed away by the sea, Europe is the less, as well as if a promontory were, as well as if a manor of thy friend's or of thine own were. Any man's death diminishes me, because I am involved in all mankind, and therefore never send to know for whom the bells tolls; it tolls for thee. (Donne, 1946, 68)

No man is an island because the terror of our perishing each alone, sundered by an 'unplumbed, salt, estranging sea' from other islands, is too harrowing to contemplate. The progression in intimacy from 'Europe,' to 'promontory,' to the 'manor' house of one's 'friend,' inches us toward the final shock of previewing in anyone's passing from the world the time at hand when we, too, shall do no more.

We can say of Donne what T.S. Eliot says of Lancelot Andrewes: 'in an age of adventure and experiment in language,' he 'is one of the most resourceful of authors in his devices for seizing the attention and impressing the memory' (1932, 349). Admonitions like 'no man is an island' or 'never send to know for whom the bell tolls; it tolls for thee' combine the impersonal authority of an oracle with advice so personal and intimate that it seems spoken in confidence to each of us alone.

Even in his powerful sermon on death the last enemy (sermon 15, folio of 1640), Donne is as confident of victory as he is in 'Death be not proud,' a sonnet which culminates in the boast that death itself will die. Donne's claim that death is invisible, like God, and that no one can look upon it and live, is in one sense a tautology. To see death face to face is, of course, to die. But why do we feel a sublime twinge in Donne's claim? Perhaps because his assimilation of death to God speaks to us across our own death of something we never see or experience while alive. As Eliot says of Andrewes, Donne has a talent for 'purifying a disturbed or cryptic lecture-note into lucid profundity' (1932, 347). 'Militio and malitia,' the learned homilist reminds us, 'are words so near in sound ... that the Vulgate edition takes them as one' (Donne, 1946, 72). By clamping two words into an alliterative vise, the phonetic similarity reinforces a necessary connection between war and misery, but not between our enemies in war and death, an enemy 'no man ever saw ... and lived' (1946, 70). Donne reminds us that even the metaphor of death as a terrifying adversary in war tells us more about its devastating impact than about the so-called power that wreaks the havoc.

Pope's *Essay on Man* is a majestic long-playing record of counterpointed judgment and wit. But Donne's sermons, though equally gorgeous and brocaded, are also impromptu personal experiments in the understanding of complex words. What does it mean to see through a glass darkly or to say that death is the last enemy to be destroyed? The insidious horror of death the enemy consists in its beginning even before our birth (at the moment of conception) and in its extending far beyond the moment when body and soul are separated at death. Donne's redefinition of death, however, also has an opposite effect. In dramatizing the long detaining action that keeps body and soul apart until the Last Judgment, it also attenuates death's power.

Donne is a kind of Hamlet among the homilists. In his meditation on the decay of the world and on the decay of man as a microcosm of that world, he traces dissolution beyond the indignity of death to the ruin wrought on the human corpse by corruption and worms. Unlike J.H. Newman or Lancelot Andrewes, Donne is obsessed by self-consciousness, consumed by introspection, and easily disturbed by the presence of ghosts. No one can belittle the intensity or depth of his vision of universal decay. But it is graphic and grotesque to the limits of endurance. As T.S. Eliot says, Donne is 'the religious spellbinder,' 'the flesh-creeper, the sorcerer of emotional orgy.' And about Donne, as Eliot says, 'there hangs the shadow of the impure motive.' Eliot thinks Donne's 'experience was not perfectly controlled, and that he lacked spiritual discipline' (1932, 345).

Donne's best oracles abound in paradox. When he meditates on Christ, he transforms the infamy of an 'ingloriously apprehended' thief and traitor into a God to whom we 'look for glory and all glory and everlasting glory' (Donne, 1946, 118). To secure a maximum shock effect, Donne also combines the most familiar experiences of a human family with the knowledge of Jesus' brothers and sisters that he had 'a father in another place' and that he was also 'as old as his father.' His siblings also had to believe that their brother, the carpenter's son, had 'set up a frame that reached to heaven out of which no man could and in which any man might be saved' (Donne, 1946, 118). More importunate, less gracious, than George Herbert's suppliant in 'Love (3),' Donne imagines his resurrected body pleading its case to the angel of the council, the Son of God himself. 'I am of the same stuff as you, body and body, flesh and flesh, and therefore let me sit down with you at the right hand of the Father in an everlasting security from this last enemy, who is now destroyed, death.'

Donne's oracles and paradoxes are least successful when they make eccentric fancy or conceit the fulcrum of his universe. We are asked to believe, for example, that the act of lifting a corpse before burying it is a token of raising the body at the Last Judgment (Donne, 1946, 73). But unless an undertaker rolled a corpse to the side of a grave then unceremoniously dumped it over the edge, it is hard to see how he could bury a body without first lifting it. It is also difficult to see what comfort one should take from the fact that life traces out a circle. Since our passage is from ashes to ashes, and ends where it began, Donne believes we should be consoled by the fact that our life describes the most perfect geometric shape. But surely a spiral that ends on a higher plane than it begins would constitute a truer image of perfection. As Santayana says, Donne's thoughts 'are often like the Sibylline leaves, profound but lost' (1967, 43).

We are never sure how far a metaphor or trope will take Donne. His prophetic use of the reversing trope, chiasmus, may perfectly convey the levelling power of death. 'It comes equally to us all and makes us all equal when it comes' (1946, 74). But less equable and measured are the many passages in which Donne makes the paradoxes of death and resurrection as jarring and grotesque as possible. Joining an 'arm that was lost in Europe' to a 'leg that was lost in Africa or Asia scores of years between,' God, we are told, is a collector of dust and an archivist of tears who 'does not forget the dead' (1946, 112). We may marvel at the ingenuity that invents such conceits as the joining of arms lost in Europe to legs lost in Asia. But Donne is prompt to assure us that the only way to present death as a high adventure of the soul is to make the body's prior dismemberment as jarring as possible. His imagination is so perversely fertile, and so in danger of breeding the opposite of what he wants to say, that few would dispute Coleridge's claim that Donne 'was an orthodox Christian, only because he could have been an Infidel *more* easily' (1984, title 12, 2:220).

2

In his sermons and meditations, Gerard Manley Hopkins often sounds more like Matthew Arnold than George Herbert. He is a soul-mate of Oscar Wilde, not of John Donne. Unlike the latter's sermons, which are at least shaped by stable doctrine, the swift jumps and turns of Hopkins' meditations are idiosyncratic and wayward. Drawn to Christ by the beauty of stories that 'stand off' from other sayings like 'stars' or 'lilies in the sun,' Hopkins is just as entranced by aesthetics as theology.

> No stories or parables are like Christ's, so bright, so pithy, so touching; no proverbs or sayings are such jewellery; they stand off from other men's thoughts like stars, like lilies in the sun; nowhere in literature is there anything to match the Sermon on the Mount. (Hopkins, 1953, 140)

> When these sayings are gathered together, though one cannot feel sure of every one, yet reading all in one view they make me say, 'These must be Christ's, never man etc.' One is: Never rejoice but when you look upon your brother in love. Another is: My mystery is for me and for the children of my house. (Hopkins, 1953, 140)

Taking selected sayings as touchstones of value, Hopkins uses art to prove the power of prophecy and style to validate the articles of faith. Like Newman, Hopkins is also a creative rhetorician. An artist of occasions, he has a gift for personalizing prayer and making poetry out of a sermon.

Hopkins's portrait of Christ is a lover's portrait, a picture of a young man, 'majestic and strong,' yet 'lovely and lissome in his limbs,' physically attractive to the homilist. The precious calamity of the Passion is that 'this lissomness' should be 'crippled, this beauty wrecked, this majesty beaten down.' Like Donne, Hopkins uses the Ignatian meditation as a chance to experiment. Though the protocol is prescribed, the composition of place is unique to each interpreter, and there is a distinctly homoerotic turn to Hopkins's homily. His meditation runs a course of lucky accidents and ends with the shock of a minor discovery. To our surprise, the pulse on which he proves his text is a sublimated erotic pulse, never quite foreseeable in advance.

Even when meditating on Loyola's *Spiritual Exercises* during a retreat at Liverpool in 1880, Hopkins playfully substitutes for the strong sense of closure that Loyola's own meditations traditionally impose a thought experiment that is dangerously solipsistic. Preoccupied with the mystery of selfhood, Hopkins is at a loss to see how his own unique self can be made to rhyme or chime with Christ, or indeed with the distinctive pitch of anything. The self's items of ecstasy are 'more distinctive,' he finds, 'than the taste of clove or alum, the smell of walnutleaf or hartshorn, more distinctive, more selved, than all things else and needing in proportion a more exquisite determining, selfmaking power' (Hopkins, 1953, 148). Hopkins is unwilling to have the pitch of this distinctive self absorbed into the 'pitch of a great universal mind,' whether it be the *intellectus agens* of the Latin Averroists or the universal mind of Hegel's Absolute. But he is equally eager to find some escape from the prison house of self. Otherwise, how can he boast that he is 'all at once what Christ is, since he was what I am' ('That Nature Is a Heraclitean Fire,' l. 22)?

3

We might expect that, as a great adversary of dogmatic finality in all branches of learning, T.H. Huxley would be a more probative, less magisterial thinker than S.T. Coleridge, who in *Aids to Reflection* and *The Statesman's Manual* writes as a free-thinking philosopher of religion. But Darwin's bulldog is a more pugnacious oracle than the sage of Highgate. Whereas Huxley embraces a gladiatorial theory of existence in order to overthrow the high priests or 'Levites in charge of the ark of culture' (1904–25, 3:136), Coleridge is both a stout polemicist and a gracious apostle of sweetness and light. The aphorisms of Archbishop Leighton that Coleridge quotes with approval in *Aids to Reflection* are as tentative and self-critical as the axioms of any investigator in the experimental sciences. 'Dubious questioning is a much better evidence' of faith, Leighton claims, 'than that senseless deadness which most take for believing' (aphorism 87). This aphorism's corollary is that the more sectarian or partisan an oracle sounds the less it can be trusted. 'He, who begins by loving Christianity better than Truth, will proceed by loving his own Sect or Church better than Christianity, and end in loving himself better than all' (aphorism 88).

Aids to Reflection consists of aphorisms designed to renovate received truths by making them as fresh and shiny as newly minted coins. As Coleridge explains in a footnote, aphorism derives from 'the Greek *ap*, from; and *horizein*, to bound or limit; whence our horizon.' To understand the meaning of aphorism, he invites us to 'draw lines of different colours round the different counties of England.' We are then to 'cut out each separately, as in the common play-maps that children take to pieces and put together – so that each district can be contemplated apart from the rest, as a whole in itself' (1905, 17). According to Coleridge, 'this twofold act of circumscribing, and detaching, when it is exerted by the mind on subjects of reflection and reason, is to *aphorize*, and the result an *aphorism.*'

In aphorism 27 Coleridge cryptically observes that 'exclusive of the abstract sciences, the largest and worthiest portion of our knowledge consists of aphorisms.' Presumably Coleridge is making a metaphor out of the word's etymology. If the cutting out of jigsaw pieces and the contemplation of each piece as a whole is what Coleridge means by aphorizing, then any concrete fragment of the truth that we contemplate as a whole functions as an aphorism. As a kernel of verbal perception, an aphorism is a folded map which a prophet or poet may slowly spread out before him until it discloses 'a World in a Grain of Sand' or 'Heaven in a Wild Flower' (Blake, 'Auguries of Innocence,' ll. 1–2). Aphorisms, like oracles, are designed to awaken and energize the 'power of truth' whenever it lies 'bed-ridden in the dormitory of the soul' (aphorism 1, 1). To this end aphorism 30 introduces an ingenious analogy between language and ethics. 'In general, Morality may be compared to the Consonant, Prudence to the vowel. The former cannot be *uttered* (reduced to practice) but by means of the latter' (1905, 23). Prudence is morality at work in the world. As its faithful steward, prudence is to morality what 'the lungs are to the heart and brain' (1905, 22). To turn commonplace maxims into living aphorisms and oracles, Coleridge believes all we have to do is reflect on them in reference to personal experience. 'To restore a commonplace to its "first *uncommon* lustre," you need only *translate* it into action. But to do this, you must [first] have *reflected* on its truth' (aphorism 3). The images you see behind you when you face a mirror are to the images at the same apparent distance in front of you what reflection is to forethought. And both are essential parts of thinking.

In aphorism 104, section 5, Coleridge introduces an important distinction between analogy and metaphor, which he explains at greater length in *The Statesman's Manual*. According to Coleridge, 'analogies are used in aid of Conviction; Metaphors, as means of Illustration' (1905, 181). Divine justice is not just a metaphor: it is part of the divine nature, an analogy between God's moral nature and our own. 'Language is analogous, wherever a thing, power, or principle in a higher dignity is expressed by the same thing, power, or principle in a lower but more known form' (1905, 181). Coleridge's example is John 3:6, Jesus' prophetic words to Nicodemus: 'That which is born of the Flesh, is Flesh; that which is born of the Spirit, is Spirit.' The latter half of the verse contains the fact asserted; the former half the analogous fact, by which the oracle is made intelligible. The fleshly origin of flesh is an analogy of the spiritual origin of spirit. It is not a mere metaphor, because it expresses the same subject with a difference and not a different subject with a resemblance.

Coleridge is a more restless, less predictable apologist than Huxley. There are few scientific dogmas that Huxley is not willing to defend. But Coleridge is as quick to attack an orthodox idol as he is ready to defend a heretical truth. To treat analogy as mere metaphor is to erode belief. But to treat a metaphor as a genuine analogy is to assume more knowledge than we have. To avoid a superstitious or idolatrous profanation of the doctrine of Atonement, Coleridge argues that a genuine similarity exists between the gratitude we feel to a friend who pays our debts and the gratitude we feel to a just and loving God. But the similarity between these two effects does not mean that their causes are the same. We are grateful to God, not because he has literally ransomed us or satisfied our creditors by paying off our debts, but because his benevolence is the effect of a much greater cause.

The gratitude and sense of obligation we feel for someone who pays our debts is a metaphorical way of expressing the gratitude and worship we owe God for his mercy and forgiveness. The intercessor on our behalf is A and our consequent sense of obligation to him is k. But A + k is not an analogy. It is a mere 'metaphorical exponent' of the gratitude and love we ought to feel for a transcendent cause X, which operates outside the banker's world of debts and credits altogether. To mistake the economic metaphor for an analogy is to take a mere counter or token for coin of the realm.

The cancellation of a financial debt is different in kind, Coleridge argues, from the satisfaction of a moral obligation. And because the analogy breaks down, any comparison of God to a redeemer is not, in fact, a true analogy at all. A third party C can readily discharge a bond by paying to B, on A's behalf, the thousand pounds that A owes. But when the debt a son owes his mother is not financial but filial, he must repay a 'worthy and affectionate' parent with honour and love. We cannot suppose that a third party can discharge the debt as a 'vicarious Son' (1905, 293). Indeed the merits of such a surrogate son serve only to embitter the mother by magnifying her own son's unworthiness. The mother will be satisfied only if the virtuous example of the substitute son inspires comparable behaviour in her offspring.

The metaphor of a redeemer, then, is not a genuine analogy of God's relation to man, because there is an important difference, Coleridge argues, between a debtor and an undutiful son. In both cases, the person who owes a debt is liberated from a burden, and in both cases he owes his liberation to the 'free grace of another' (1905, 296). In the first case, the person whose debt is discharged is not required to do anything: the third party, acting singly and alone to pay off the debt, is the liberating agent. But if spiritual redemption is a contract, it is, as F.H. Bradley says of marriage, 'a contract to pass out of the sphere of contract' (1876, 174). To be sure, its precondition is God's grace. But that grace must be 'co-efficient' with an active acceptance and reformation on the part of the person who is freed.

Unlike Newman, who is deeply suspicious of fallen reason, Coleridge insists that 'whatever is against right reason ... no faith can oblige us to believe' (aphorism 119). Perhaps his impatience with arrogant decrees and his preference for patient experiment and inquiry explain the offence he takes at Pope's epitaph for Newton's tomb in Westminster Abbey. 'Nature and nature's laws lay hid in night; / God said, "Let Newton be!" and all was light.' Coleridge denounces the epigram 'as nothing better than a gross and wrongful falsehood conveyed in an enormous and irreverent hyperbole' (1905, 306). Given the intemperance of Coleridge's attack, one might think that Pope had ascribed the oracle to Newton himself rather than to God. Yet we know what Coleridge means. Any suggestion that Newton knows God as well as God knows himself is an insult to Newton's own professed humility.

Coleridge is as independent and tough-minded in his attack on Jeremy Taylor's misconception of original sin as he is vigorous in his assault on the Pauline doctrine of redemption and atonement. After quoting Taylor's text on original sin and reflecting on it critically, Coleridge takes issue with Taylor's obscure definition. A sin, according to Coleridge, 'is an Evil which has its ground or origin in the Agent, and not in the compulsion of Circumstances' (1905, 231). Sin is never a mere link in a chain of effects, where B is a cause of C and an effect of A. When we call B a cause of C, we mean merely that it is the conductor of a causative influence. But Coleridge protests that this so-called chain of nature is merely natural, and 'no natural thing or act can ... be truly said to have an origin in any other' (1905, 232). A true origin in nature is above nature and assumes a supernatural agent. If sin, by definition, originates in the will of an agent, then all sin must be original and the phrase 'original sin' is a tautology. An act that does not originate in the will is circumstantial. It 'may be calamity, deformity, disease, or mischief; but a Sin it cannot be' (1905, 235).

Why, then, does Taylor call Adam's sin 'original'? Since the only origin of a chain of natural causes and effects is outside or above nature, in a supernatural power, we must assume that sin is a form of spiritual evil. But we cannot say that this spiritual evil is God. 'Inasmuch as it is evil, in God it cannot originate' (Coleridge, 1905, 237). The only place evil can come from is man himself. Once we reject the postulate of a responsible human will, Taylor's doctrine of original sin would seem to fall into place, with irrefutable logic and rigour. But if we grant the postulate Taylor refuses to allow, that 'the will is ultimately self-determined' (Coleridge, 1905, 250), then the spectre of man's original sin dissolves in thin air.

As the aphorisms on original sin unfold, they exhibit fewer features of an experimental inquiry and more signs of a withering polemical attack on Jeremy Taylor. Coleridge rejects Taylor's traditional doctrine of original sin because, by turning Adam's demerit into a penalty imposed on all posterity, it inhibits free will. In repeating his tribute to the great churchman's acknowledged erudition and eloquence, Coleridge allows a tone of mockery to enter his voice. 'Sufficient to have stood, but free to fall,' says Milton's God of Adam. By denying such sufficiency, a doctrine of original sin forces Adam to fall. In Coleridge's view, Taylor degrades the individual will beneath its innate dignity by substituting a constraining external circumstance for a condition internal to the will itself. If sin is not spiritual evil, it is not sin at all but mere misfortune or calamity. To impose sin as a penalty on all mankind, or as a legacy of the ruined millionaire, Adam, is to misconstrue the nature of sin. An original or originating sin must have a transcendent or spiritual cause. And since evil cannot originate in God, it must originate in what is most godlike in each of us: the human will.

Coleridge treats all religious language as an experiment. If the first Person of the Trinity is to the Second as a Father to his Son, then the language is analogical, for Coleridge can think of no equally powerful or accurate way in which the identity of God and Christ could be expressed. The same cannot be said of metaphors, however, where other better or equally appropriate comparisons might be used. Indeed metaphors of a benefactor redeeming our debts or of a sin originating outside our will tell us less about our relation to God than about the limits of the tropes we are using. Coleridge recognizes that all religious language is a wall. His task is not 'to destroy' the wall, but, as one commentator says, to 'show the openings' in the wall (Carse, 2008, 83) through which the poetic horizons of a belief system like Christianity can come into focus for us, especially through a deft use of aphorism, which Coleridge calls the horizon trope. As Carse explains, 'the operative principle here is that if vision is restricted to a belief system, or if it is divorced from all belief systems, it ceases to be vision. What is necessary is that it not restrict itself to a belief system but that belief systems always fall within the scope of poetic horizons' (2008, 83).

4

In principle, T.H. Huxley is as relentlessly sceptical as Coleridge. By exposing the verbal fictions that masquerade as scientific and theological truth, Huxley is as hostile to scientific materialists as he is to religious dogmatists. In practice, however, Huxley passes the mantle of authority from the theologian to the scientist. The transfer of authoritarian religious rhetoric to a new subject – to scientific testing and faith in empirical verification – may be felicitous stylistically, but it is logically invalid. For in appropriating the oracles of religion, science is also threatening to become the new religion, the new Vatican of unquestioned authority. And it is precisely such use of oracular decrees that science is pledged to root out and banish wherever found.

In Huxley's view, the true oracles of science are not to be confused with the utopian dreams of pragmatists resolved to exploit scientific technology. Science is not an Aladdin's lamp, nor does it exist in order to provide us with 'telegraphs to Saturn' (1904–25, 1:30). Huxley is at once the most consistent of pragmatists and one of pragmatism's sharpest critics. No empiricist is more outspoken than Huxley in his attack on authority. On the other hand, the mere utility of science is its least important function. Science is useful because its experimental methods disclose new truths: it is not true because its discoveries merely happen to be useful. Science's original purpose may have been to make useful discoveries. But it flourished because it enchanted and beguiled the mind and led to surprising discoveries that were not immediately useful. Aristotle says that men came together for the sake of mere life and remained together for the sake of the good life. Huxley says, in effect, that men became scientists to be useful to society, and they remained scientists because the discoveries they made disclosed new and deeper puzzles than the mysteries they first set out to solve.

In one of his striking oracles, the prophet of science declares that experimentalists 'ask for bread and receive ideas' (1904–25, 1:36). Scientists begin by pursuing what is useful and end by discovering what is true. Providential explanations of the plague of 1665 or the Great Fire of 1666 produce less understanding than scientific ones. Indeed, both the fire and the plague wane in importance when compared with the founding of the Royal Society and the increasing importance of scientific explanations. But the more intelligible such phenomena as physical matter and the heavenly bodies become, the more mysteries they disclose. Just as matter turns out, to our surprise, to be infinitely subtle, full of seething particles in a surging sea of atoms, so astronomy reveals a universe infinitely more spacious than the solar system we inhabit.

Huxley's new god of Delphi is experiment, not decree. Why, then, should Huxley use oracles of decree to banish magisterial arguments of authority and set up scientific experiments in their place? Everything Huxley values in the honest inquirer, his authoritarian opponents denounce as impious or immoral. Whereas religion brands doubt a moral defect and scepticism a sin, science reverses the process by calling faith blind and scepticism sharp-sighted. In an oracle of decree that substitutes proof by experiment for all future decrees, Huxley announces that 'the man of science has learned to believe in justification, not by faith, but by verification' (1904–25, 1:41). This oracle of decree is couched in the very language of authority it sets out to reject. Even in renouncing 'faith' Huxley uses the theological concept of 'justification' and retains a religious infinitive, 'to believe.'

Huxley's use of religious rhetoric to demolish the oracles of decree might seem at first a clever rhetorical ploy. But the risks, I think, outweigh the gains. If science is authoritative in the way its oracle proclaims, then it loses such authority as 'its absolute refusal to acknowledge authority' entitles it to claim. Paradoxically, science retains authority only to the degree it subverts authority. In becoming the new Delphi, science is betraying its claim to legislate. Since science is experimental, it cannot include in its oracles any of the authoritative decrees it has to abolish in order to survive and prosper.

Huxley compares nature to a hidden player in a chess game. The chessboard is the world, the pieces are physical phenomena, and the game's rules the laws of nature. Everything would seem to be as intelligible and complex as chess, a pursuit of deep fascination. But the game is made more baffling because 'the player on the other side is hidden' from view (1904–25, 1:82). Since Huxley wants to substitute experiment for decree, he has to establish as his first postulate of faith a universe that is intelligible and law-like. To this end he ascribes specific attributes to the hidden player in the game. He affirms without proof that the chess player is 'always fair, just, and patient.' If the player is hidden, however, how can Huxley know this? Should Huxley not be just as agnostic in withholding attributes from an unseen player as he is in withholding attributes from the unseen God of Kant, Mansel, and Sir William Hamilton, the so-called agnostic theologians? Of if Huxley persists in using figurative language to describe nature, how can he consistently attack the figurative language of religion? Perhaps it is impossible to discard figurative language in either area, and 'Jehovah, who would suffer no statues, [is] himself a metaphor' (Santayana, 1967, 128). One problem with Huxley's chosen metaphor is that playing chess is a less accurate symbol of the game science plays with nature than is card-playing, where 'the logical pattern is part of a haphazard chance chaos with fitful glimpses of patterns – runs of luck and so on' (Frye, 2004b, 30). Though science, like card-playing, requires a degree of skill, its deep ignorance in many areas has more affinity with fate-worship than chess.

When Huxley transfers his allegiance to the new god of science, which is experiment, not decree, he still relies on magisterial oracles of decree, the language of the old god, to make the transfer credible. Why should Huxley take on faith the attributes he ascribes to nature but is unwilling to ascribe to God himself? To the degree the player in the chess game is truly hidden from us, his attributes are unknown. To the degree the attributes are known, the player is not truly hidden. Surely it is just as true to describe the hidden player in the chess game as indifferent and impersonal as 'always fair, just, and patient.' According to Einstein, God is subtle but not malicious. What entitles Huxley to say anything more? Perhaps the hidden player is Satan playing chess for Job's soul. Half sensing the fallacy, Huxley seems to realize that what is at stake are postulates of faith – metaphoric proposals about the kind of ethical world, the kingdom of ends, we want to live in – and not true-or-false propositions about the physical world we actually inhabit.

Indeed, the Nature who brutally exterminates her slow learners, and who treats incapacity as sternly as crime, never truly conforms to ideas of 'fair, just, and patient.' Nature may be less elitist than English universities. She has no Test Acts, and we all attend her school. But her discipline is so severe and her punishments so swift that she often strikes us as arbitrary and cruel. Nature's 'discipline is not even a word and blow, and the blow first; but the blow without the word' (1904–25, 1:85). The more unpredictable the outcome of Huxley's experimental method of inquiry, the more misgivings he begins to entertain about the chess player's character. If sphinx-like Nature hides a secret, perhaps Huxley is betraying (both in the sense of disclosing and distorting) it when he presumes to speak of Nature as a person. So far is Huxley from accepting nature as his nurse or guardian that he even amends his original postulate of faith to include the possibility that nature's methods are blundering and 'defective.'

As in Darwin's phrase 'natural selection,' the use of diffused personification in his picture of nature as a chess player deeply troubles Huxley. In conducting a new experiment in metaphor, Huxley wonders if it might be preferable to think of nature as a beneficent stepmother. As her adopted son, the scientist is meant to function only as her obedient minister or servant. But how free is such a stepson if he acts as a mere mouthpiece, and if the superior power continues to pull the strings like a ventriloquist controlling a puppet? This is hardly the equal partnership of a marriage, but a despotic arrangement in which the mind of the truly liberated scientist might wish to sue for a divorce.

In truth, the more closely Huxley studies nature, the less benign she appears. If Clerk Maxwell is right to predict that the earth like the sun is gradually cooling down, then 'the time must come when evolution will mean adaptation to an universal winter.' Then 'all forms of life will die out, except such low and simple organisms as the Diatom of the arctic and antarctic ice and the Protococcus of the red snow' (Huxley, 1904–25, 9:197). The whimsical, unpredictable sibyl that pronounces such an oracle is sometimes liable to tantrums and at other times she is smiling and serene. In either mood she possesses 'a different sort of benevolence from that of John Howard.'

Since nothing can reverse the downward turn of the sun, even as it reaches its zenith, there is an old melancholy mixed up with the highest pleasure. 'The most daring imagination will hardly venture upon the suggestion that the power and the intelligence of man can ever arrest the procession of the great year' (Huxley, 1904–25, 9:86). Like the end of the *Dunciad* and Pope's fourth *Moral Essay*, *The Prolegomena to Evolution and Ethics* brings the shattering, door-smashing intrusion of huge new thoughts: death everywhere, the dying of everything, the running-down of universal nature and the end of humanity as we know it now. Huxley dramatizes the depressing implications for culture and civilization of the Second Law of Thermodynamics. It is a vision in which matter, energy, and the saurian mind itself usurp roles that once belonged to the oracles of Apollo, the god of wisdom and light.

In an oracle of decree to end all future oracles of the kind, Huxley announces that 'the Nemesis of all reformers is finality' (1904–25, 3:149). In his epistle to the Philistines, the chief Levite of culture, Matthew Arnold, keeps proclaiming that culture is a criticism of life. Instead of sounding his trumpets against the walls of science 'as against an educational Jerhico' (1904–25, 3:146), Arnold should have been civil enough to concede that 'we cannot know all the best thoughts and sayings of the Greeks unless we know what they thought about natural phenomena' (1904–25, 3:151). Huxley seems to have won the argument, convincing us that scholars have no monopoly on curiosity or criticism. But then he seriously damages the case for science by announcing with as much dogmatic finality as any apostle to the Philistines that 'the free employment of reason, in accordance with scientific method, is the sole method of reaching truth' (1904–25, 3:151). Here in all its dangerous arrogance we find festering even in Huxley that cancer of modern learning, the 'research fallacy,' which assumes that all knowledge must aspire to the condition of a physical science.

More faithful to the new gods of Delphi, testing and experiment, is Huxley's claim that science has to be self-critical to remain true to its mission. Rejecting all arguments from authority, science must candidly admit that all its 'interpretations of natural fact are more or less imperfect and symbolic' (1904–25, 3:150). Huxley warns against the delusion of scientists like Lord Kelvin, who maintained that nothing in science is genuinely intelligible or worth paying serious attention to until stated in exact mathematical terms. In fact, quantification can be just as dogmatic and egregiously wrong-headed as any other method. Misunderstanding the sources of energy and underestimating its loss, Kelvin concluded that the earth and sun were much younger than they are. 'Physics envy,' the desire to convert all evidence into numbers and equations, may mystify the layman. And it can also mislead a mathematical expert like Kelvin.

Though Huxley realizes that the progress of science is discontinuous, moving ahead in lurches at unprecedented speed, he himself does not live to see the full dissolution of the old physics. For Whitehead and scientists of the next generation, hard facts seem to melt away overnight, vanishing under the pressure of astonishing new discoveries. As Lewis Thomas sums up, the universe is 'alive with ambiguities, but it can be read' and interpreted intelligibly (1983a, 75). Since facts can be changed by our ways of seeing and interpreting them, Thomas compares the scientist's world to Wallace Stevens's blue guitar. 'They said, "You have a blue guitar, / you do not play things as they are." / The man replied, "Things as they are / are changed upon the blue guitar."' The things for which Huxley's scientist shows greatest respect are not man-made computers or mathematical equations, but things he does not understand, like his own mind and a scientist's gift for conducting experiments and making discoveries. It is in this sense that nothing remains stable but the arts and nothing truly improves but the sciences. What Huxley worships is the scientific gift for progress and invention, 'fallible, error-prone, forgetful, unpredictable,' and always 'ungovernable,' as Lewis Thomas finely says (1983b, 90). But like every other gift of the Muses, it seems way over Huxley's head.

17 Evolving Oracles:
Newman, Browning, and Shakespeare

In a colloquial, discursive passage of 'The Dry Salvages,' T.S. Eliot tries to replace mere sequences from the past with patterns of a different order. Without diminishing the past, he wants to evolve some meaning from experiences that seemed devoid of meaning at the time they occurred. But Eliot fears his quest for meaning will be mistaken for a quest for mere development or progress. Such development, he cautions, is 'a partial fallacy, / Encouraged by superficial notions of evolution, / Which becomes, in the popular mind, a means of disowning the past' (II.39-41). The oracles he seeks never supersede or suspend the past. On the contrary, like the figural antitype of a historical type in Scripture, they grow out of history and fulfil it.

Though a progressive science is committed to the thesis that knowledge evolves, an oracle that substitutes a belief in progress for a theory of process is in danger of diminishing the value of past achievements. This is why a culture devoted to historical as well as scientific discovery may have to invent new ways of stepping off the moving platform of the present if a potential asset is not also to become its greatest liability. Scientists are encouraged to refine and supersede the models of Newton and even Einstein in ways that no literary scholar can ever forget the achievements of Dante and Milton. Every scholarly community has to honour the god Janus, who looks backward and forward simultaneously. But a scientific culture has tunnel vision, which it directs exclusively toward the future. A culture is more likely to honour history and tradition when the meaning of its experiments evolves gradually over time. Instead of supplanting the past, an oracle that comes into focus for its prophets slowly, over a protracted time span, is better positioned to build memorials to past greatness.

1

Indeed the past experience that Eliot's oracle hopes to keep alive and fulfil in 'The Dry Salvages' 'is not the experience of one life only / But of many generations' (II.50–1). Eliot tries to prevent his prophet from being so securely in possession of a figural meaning that he minimizes the value of its literal or historical meaning. To this end Eliot shows how much harder it is to say the exact truth about his 'sudden illuminations' than some fine extravagance that is not the exact truth.

> The moments of happiness – not the sense of well-being.
> Fruition, fulfilment, security or affection,
> Or even a very good dinner, but the sudden illumination –
>
> ('The Dry Salvages,' II.42–4)

Eliot's prophet may seem slightly incoherent. The abrupt turns, the negative examples, and, above all, the absence of grammatical completions all suggest a momentary wandering of the mind as it circles round a dark, elusive subject. Far from endorsing a comfortable doctrine of progress, Eliot registers a sudden tremor of fear and misgiving. He cannot quite suppress a dread of recidivism or reversion as, looking back over his shoulder, he glances furtively behind 'the assurance / Of recorded history' 'towards the primitive terror' (II.53–5).

The most haunting prophecies in *Murder in the Cathedral* are shrouded in comparable misgivings and mystery.

> But now a great fear is upon us, a fear not of one but of many,
> A fear like birth and death, when we see birth and death alone
> In a void apart.   (Eliot, 1935, 20)

The quintessence of fear is to apprehend ends and beginnings in a void, with no chain of intermediate links, as a victim of amnesia apprehends them. The chorus is most afraid of indefinable terrors, whose precise origin will not quite come into focus for it. Even the grammar of the chorus looks two ways at once. Is its 'fear not of one but of many' a subjective or objective genitive? Is its foreboding communal? Or is it an unfocused fear, directed not at a single enemy of the archbishop but at many indeterminate ones? As Becket explains to the second priest, the Canterbury women are oracles of a mystery they only partly apprehend. They know and do not know what it is to act or suffer.

They know and do not know, that action is suffering
And suffering is action.   (1935, 22)

Actively to aspire to martyrdom is incompatible with being a martyr.
For agent and patient must be neither active nor passive, but 'fixed in
an eternal patience / To which all must consent that it may be willed
/ And which all must suffer that they may will it' (Eliot, 1935, 22).

When the Fourth Tempter repeats this oracle verbatim to Becket
later in the play, he becomes to Becket what Thomas is to the chorus in
the earlier scene: the prophet of a higher truth. Or it might be more
accurate to say that, since the subtlest temptations are always internal
temptations, the Tempter and Becket are one. In both cases, the chorus
and later the Tempter have to remind Becket that in order to suffer
martyrdom he may have to act decisively. He may have to incite the
knights to murder him. 'The last temptation,' he realizes, 'is the greatest treason; / To do the right deed for the wrong reason' (1935, 47).

The oracles of the chorus pass from the horrors of assassination and
death to the Last Judgment and then to a final 'Emptiness, absence,
separation from God' (1935, 77). Behind the visible agents of death,
beyond the cramped thin spondees of 'the white flat face of Death,'
and even behind the throne of Judgment itself, stands the great reflex-
ive image of the Void, collapsing everything inside it like a black hole
or burned-out star. The effect is extraordinarily like Dante's 'kingdom
of perpetual night,' which greatly impressed Eliot. If the caesuras were
not so weighted, the progression not so relentless, and the logic not so
inexorable, we might be tempted to repudiate the passage altogether.
For despite its prophetic reach, the chorus is also a 'miserable bureau-
cratic parody of religion' which tells us, in one critic's words, 'that all
those who are not good enough for heaven must be bad enough for
hell, when it's so obvious that nobody is fit for either' (Frye, 2004a,
166).

Though less tormented than the chorus in *Murder in the Cathedral*,
Eliot's wise man in 'The Journey of the Magi' is just as baffled in his
effort to discern some prophetic meaning in a Birth that strangely
resembles Death. The 'three trees on the low sky' ('Journey of the
Magi,' l. 24) are types of the crosses on which Christ and the two
thieves were crucified. But like the 'Six hands at an open door dicing
for pieces of silver' (l. 27), their figural meaning escapes his understanding. Unlike the oracles of Huxley's evolutionary new science,
which dispenses altogether with obsolete fictions, Eliot's oracles are

firmly anchored in history. They also enforce upon a reader the 'concrete presence' of Lancelot Andrewes's great seventeenth-century sermon on the Magi, whose 'flashing phrases ... seize the attention and impress the memory' (Eliot, 1932, 349–50) in the poem's opening lines.

> 'A cold coming we had of it,
> Just the worst time of the year
> For a journey, and such a long journey:
> The ways deep and the weather sharp,
> The very dead of winter.'   (ll. 1–5)

Since there 'was no information,' however, and their destination was 'merely satisfactory' (ll. 29, 31), the wise man seems ready to concur with Eliot's speaker in *Four Quartets*, who concludes with some exasperation that 'We had the experience but missed the meaning' ('The Dry Salvages,' II.45).

2

Even if the wise man were able to attain the knowledge of Eliot himself or the insight of an informed reader, his understanding of events would not be evolutionary. For in biblical typology, a historical type never develops into its figural antitype. Just as Christianity is not a higher form of Judaism, nor the rabbi of Galilee a worthier Moses, so the Decalogue, even in adumbrating the Sermon on the Mount, retains its separate value and identity.

Evolutionary thought is more congenial to ancient Greek religion than it is to biblical theology. Just as the titan Hyperion evolves into the Olympian sun god, Apollo, so Zeus in the *Oresteia* abolishes the revenge code of blood for blood by establishing a higher moral law. Though we can trace outlines of a bleak evolutionary theology in Thomas Hardy's poems, its most memorable nineteenth-century developments are found in Browning, Tennyson, and Swinburne.

A secularized version of Hegel's theology of self-making appears in Tennyson's late poem 'The Making of Man,' which is the babble of a soul in ecstasy, a triumph of rapture over poetic form. According to Tennyson humanity has only a negative identity until it has earned the right to say, in a final oracle of praise, 'Hallelujah to the Maker. "It is finished. Man is made"' (l. 8). More sustained and complex are Swinburne's two oracles of self-making, 'Hymn of Man' and 'Hertha.'

Though Swinburne may have known nothing of Hegel's thought directly, he seems to have encountered, in William Blake, in Jacob Boehme, and perhaps even in Indian thought, a form of Hegel's spiral journey out of being into non-being, then back into becoming. Such is the trajectory of Hegel's Idea, which at the end of the *Logic* returns to a higher form of its original unity.

All Victorian readers of Benjamin Jowett's *Essays and Reviews* (1860) would be indirectly familiar with Hegel's idea that, in order to complete his original creation, a God of becoming requires his worshippers to actualize the freedom that is his greatest gift. They would also have encountered a version of this doctrine in Jowett's influential essay 'On the Interpretation of Scripture,' which applies Hegel's principle of development to Christianity just as resourcefully as Jowett's commentary on Plato's *Dialogues* applies Hegel's ideas to Greek philosophy. The method is carried furthest in the substitution of human self-making for God's creation in such radical Hegelians as David Friedrich Strauss and Ludwig Feuerbach, whose legacy leaves its dissolving trace on Browning's 'Development' and his 'Epilogue' to *Dramatis Personae*.

In Browning's theological monologues, Christ is the Hegelian spirit (love), God is the Hegelian idea (power), and the world is the Hegelian nature, which Browning associates with knowledge. If Christ is to unite these two Trinities, he cannot be described as a mere moral teacher. To venerate Christ as a Jewish Kant, who instructed man in the 'simple work' of moral 'nomenclature,' is like praising, 'not nature, / But Harvey, for the circulation' of the blood ('Christmas Eve,' ll. 971–3). But just as Christ overreaches the law he expounds, so Browning believes that both God (or the Hegelian idea) and love or spirit overreach the world. Instead of being a mere good man, Christ must be an infinite God-man. He must form the middle term of a double Trinity, directing Browning, as it directs Hegel, 'from the cistern to the river' and the source ('Christmas-Eve,' l. 1015).

In the most evolutionary of his theological monologues, 'Caliban upon Setebos,' Browning's precocious savage entertains the hypothesis of a god who evolves from brute power into persuasive agency and love, like an insect that grows from grub into butterfly. However inspired and daring Caliban's evolutionary theology may be, Browning keeps its defects in focus. Creating the world out of hate instead of love, and using the island and its inhabitants to amend his own deficiencies, Caliban's god is a grotesque parody of the God envisaged by

Joseph Butler in his *Analogy of Religion*. Just as Butler finds a corresponding anomaly in nature for every anomaly in revealed religion, so Caliban – a kind of Butler in reverse – finds a corresponding contradiction in religion for every contradiction in the order of nature. Browning operates on Karl Barth's principle that God is never identical with what we call God – not even with Caliban's 'the Quiet,' the god who rules over Setebos and who made him. Browning is also as critical of natural theology as Blake, for whom it is a sin against the Spirit, a 'Synagogue of Satan.' As Caliban turns into a vengeful David Hume, he teaches lesser forms of life that causality is one of natural philosophy's obsolete fictions – a mere psychological feeling rather than a logical necessity.

> 'So must he do henceforth and always.' – Ay?
> Would teach the reasoning couple what 'must' means!
> 'Doth as she likes, or wherefore Lord? So He.
>
> ('Caliban upon Setebos,' ll. 238–40)

In a bold redefinition of deity, Caliban asserts that to be a divine First Cause is to dispense altogether with the hypothesis of any casual connection between the way creatures behave and what happens to them. No sooner has Caliban ascended to his Sermon Mount of antinomian vision, however, than he reverts to the hysteria of a juvenile delinquent. Afraid that God has overheard his blasphemous prophecies, Caliban cowers in fear as he counts off in each successive thunder roll a further proof of God's displeasure and desire to be avenged. By exhausting the freakishness of arbitrary caprice, Caliban's anthropomorphic God falls as far below a reasonable understanding of deity as the sublime God of the psalmist rises loftily above it.

3

In theory, a creative evolutionist like George Bernard Shaw should be a more progressive, experimental prophet than J.H. Newman, who seems to write on the development of religious doctrines because, as a contemporary of Darwin, he realizes that evolution is a popular and influential subject. In practice, however, just as Coleridge, the sage of Highgate, proves a less dogmatic oracle than Darwin's bulldog, T.H. Huxley, so the brooding, introspective Newman makes suppler, more innovative use of evolutionary thought than Shaw.

No one has ever doubted the hardness and clarity of Shaw's mind or his genius as a preacher of evolutionary religion and socialist Christianity. But since Shaw turns his deepest convictions into the wildest witticisms, and often cracks his best jokes with a dead-pan countenance, it is hard to separate his beliefs from his bluster and his oracles from his jokes. As a disciple of Samuel Butler, Shaw is as deeply critical of Darwinian evolution as Tennyson or Bishop Wilberforce. Equally critical of any form of benignly progressive evolution is G.B. Shaw's devil in *Man and Superman*. In contrast to Huxley, who believes that each individual is a potential explorer in the heroic mould of Tennyson's Ulysses, Shaw's devil is a determinist for whom nothing original is possible. His oracles proclaim that in a mechanistic universe, rich in its accidental varieties but poor in its essential types, the profoundest truth is 'the saying' of his 'friend Koheleth, that there is nothing new under the sun' (1967, 31). Rejecting as 'an infinite comedy of illusion' the quaint belief that 'every swing from hell to heaven is an evolution,' the devil is equally contemptuous of the delusive counter-fiction that 'every swing from heaven to hell is an emancipation' (1967, 30).

The devil turns out to be a convenient prop or puppet that Shaw sticks up to spout forth his own attack upon the Darwinists. The determinist devil has more spirit and wit than any creative evolutionist. But as the determinists' bleak oracles continue to darken the Preface to *Back to Methuselah*, we are warned that 'a hideous fatalism' cripples their prophecies. What seems at first to be an innocuous 'chapter of accidents' is in fact 'a ghastly and damnable reduction' to mere randomness 'of beauty and intelligence, of strength and purpose, of honour and aspiration.' Indeed the determinists commit a blasphemy against Nature by reducing evolution to 'such casually picturesque changes as an avalanche may make in a mountain landscape, or a railway accident in a human figure' (1967, 101). For if Nature is in charge of such selections, her 'casual aggregation of inert and dead matter' cannot be that nurse, guide, or guardian of our moral being praised by Wordsworth in 'Tintern Abbey.' She has more in common with the monster of tyranny and violence that congeals our blood in Mill's essay 'On Nature.' In an oracle that is less memorable for apocalyptic fervour than for bathos, Shaw predicts that the result of natural selection will be 'to modify all things by blindly starving and murdering everything that is not lucky enough to survive in the universal struggle for hogwash' (1967, 102).

More successful as prophecy than the Preface to *Back to Methuselah* is Shaw's play *Man and Superman*. In this 'dramatic parable of Creative Evolution,' Shaw hopes, he says, to have written the first book in his new Bible of Evolution. He exhorts future playwrights to follow his example of taking 'the Garden of Eden in hand' and of 'weeding it properly.' He predicts that if they do so, their new secular scriptures will leave testaments like *Man and Superman* and *Back to Methuselah* as 'far behind as the religious pictures of the fifteenth century left behind the first attempts of the early Christians in iconography' (1967, 123).

As prophet of the Life Force, Shaw is usually witty and amusing. But too often we can predict what he will say. Shaw may draw a smile when he calls Darwin 'an intelligent and industrious pigeon fancier' (1967, 103). And his paradoxical disclaimer that Darwin himself was not a Darwinist, since he refused to quarrel with the theists, is true enough to be diverting. But Shaw cannot restrain his 'blasphemous levity' for long. And in preaching creative evolution 'in the manner of a man who insists on continuing to prove his innocence after he has been acquitted' (1967, 105), Shaw is often as tediously predictable in his homilies as he claims Darwin is.

4

Though J.H. Newman is more orthodox than Shaw, his application of evolutionary thought to the development of religious doctrine is more original and genuinely experimental than anything we find in Shaw's theology (if we can call Shaw's 'Bible for Creative Evolution' a theology) (1967, 123). Shaw uses an extraordinarily witty and paradoxical style to make even ordinary ideas sound original. Newman, by contrast, uses a measured, academic prose to make innovative ideas sound traditional. When his prose is arcane, it is because his theology is complex and difficult. His style is never difficult because his ideas are obscurely expressed.

Unlike Shaw, Newman never affirms that religious truth evolves. And he disapproves of Tennyson's evolutionary notion that men rise on the stepping stones of their dead selves to higher things. Aquinas denies that any creature can attain a higher grade of nature without ceasing to exist. Though less in sympathy with Aquinas than with the Church Fathers, Newman would agree with St Thomas that there are some kinds of wisdom one has to die to attain. According to Newman, all that evolves is religious doctrine, which is our way of expressing and trying to understand the truth. Written at the height of his private crisis of faith in 1845, Newman's *Essay on the Development of Christian Doctrine* is an attempt to identify by historical example the marks of an authentic development of early Christian teachings. Far from dispensing with history, Newman's search for the signs of genuine development is a sympathetic study of the historically changing moods, attitudes, and axioms for judgment of the early church. In his portraits of the principles and attitudes of the first Christians, Newman is consistently fresh and striking. As Owen Chadwick says, 'startling judgments [are] thrown off in page after page; judgments always personal, usually original, sometimes brilliant, occasionally wild, very occasionally shocking' (1983, 46).

Though both works were written before *The Origin of Species* appeared, Newman's *Essay on Development* is as suffused as *In Memoriam* with the genius of evolution. Newman wants to know when a development like monasticism, for example, or the veneration of relics is a genuine growth, and when it is a corruption. A grub may evolve into a butterfly, as Browning's Caliban says, and by a more circuitous route even a hippo may develop into a whale. But in any pilgrimage back to the dawn of life, as Richard Dawkins has shown, our ancestors' tale discloses many developments doomed to fail as well as countless other experiments rewarded with success. To recognize the difference between true and false developments Newman devises seven tests. Chadwick justly observes that 'no one believed in them when the book first came out and no one has believed in them since' (1983, 47). Nevertheless, Newman's idea of development is important to anyone who is intellectually honest and wants to reconcile faith with current developments in philosophy or science.

On the deathbed of his faith in Anglicanism, Newman wants to prove for his own peace of mind that, whereas Catholicism stands in the same relation to the early church as a man stands to a higher primate, Protestantism is related to it as a lungfish to a bird. Unfortunately, as an intellectual historian Newman knows far less about the Reformation than about the early church. He is attempting to define Protestantism in terms that few Protestants or few historians of the Reformation would accept. And yet whenever Newman enlarges his own predicament and openly recognizes the troubling yet necessary impact of history on religion, he speaks as an authority who generally commands assent. For passages in the *Essay on Development* that trace the ways in which ideas are 'received, corrupted, and adapted, and made institutional' are usually more prophetic than partisan. As Chadwick concludes, 'no one can understand Newman without studying the *Essay*. This was that unusual combination, a book unconvincing and yet seminal' (1983, 47).

More persuasive but equally seminal, I think, in its anticipation of evolutionary ideas is Newman's last university sermon, 'The Theory of Developments in Religious Doctrine' (1843). One mark of heresy, Newman contends, is that 'its dogmas are unfruitful.' The higher criticism of Strauss or works of natural theology like Paley's *Evidences of Christianity* 'end in themselves, without development, because they are words; they are barren, because they are dead' (1887, 318). But if death is a sign of falsehood, does it follow that fertility and life are necessarily attributes of truth? Surely Bacon's spiders can propagate their webs of falsehood and deceit with as much cunning and tenacity as any Levite of culture can diffuse his gospel of light.

The harsh oddity of dogma seems to be a shock effect of meeting an idea in a medium that is not native to it. It is like confronting a Mercator projection of the Rockies and failing to recognize in a map of western Canada any facsimile of that region's spectacularly mountainous terrain. When the mind entertains impressions of supernatural facts, it has to move out of a multidimensional world onto a two-dimensional plane. Dogmatic statements transform 'what was at first an impression on the Imagination ... [into] a system or creed in the Reason' (1887, 329). Poets and prophets have ideas or visions of God 'as one, and individual, and independent of words, as an impression conveyed through the senses' (1887, 331). But the mind can reflect upon the full magnitude of such an impression only 'piecemeal.' 'A Divine fact,' as Newman says, 'far from being compassed by [the propositions of a dogma], would not be exhausted, nor fathomed, by a thousand' (1887, 332).

J.M. Cameron has observed that 'there are many striking parallelisms between the thought of Newman and that of Hume, and this far-reaching similarity represents a certain affinity in spirit and method, though not in conclusions' (1962, 222). On the three occasions when David Hume is mentioned in the Oxford sermons, he is represented as a sceptical enemy of religion. And yet Newman is never more daring and resourceful than when stealing weapons from the enemy's arsenal. Refining a technique of Locke and Hume, Newman tries to differentiate between impressions of God that are clear and distinct and less precise impressions of material objects. As the empiricists had argued, impressions are fleeting, fugitive, unrecallable, until the imagination has fashioned them into more stable and recurrent ideas of sense. Though the mind of Newman's believer may be prepared in a different way from Locke's mind or Hume's, the actual receiving of the divine impressions is as involuntary and mysterious as the receiving of a sensible impression. Religious creeds are 'a chief mode of perpetuating' the fugitive impressions that the empirical philosophers consistently associate with sense experience.

As Cameron says, it is 'tempting to suppose ... that there is an affinity between idealist metaphysics and the sacerdotal mind; and that empiricism in philosophy is logically implicated with hard-headedness, agnosticism, the movement for social reform and what have you. Many as well as Pattison have encountered this temptation and have succumbed to it. In general the supposition is absurd; and it is especially absurd in the case ... of Newman' (1962, 220). A visit to the Birmingham oratory reveals that one of Newman's most copiously annotated volumes is by Thomas Reid, the eighteenth-century Scottish philosopher, author of *Inquiry into the Human Mind on the Principles of Common Sense* (1764). Ever practical and empirical, Newman has as much affinity with Locke and Hume as with Plato. Newman is a sceptic, a sly fox like Hume, adept at making agile moves. He is too English to be a hedgehog, a thinker like Aristotle or Aquinas, who uses a few big ideas to build a system. Before the introduction of Platonic studies at mid-century, Aristotle was worshipped at Oxford as a fourth person of the Trinity. But in his essay 'Poetry, with Reference to Aristotle's *Poetics*' (1829), Newman is clearly drawing more on Plato's thought than on Aristotle's. He argues that poetry should become to representational genres like history and biography what mathematical laws in physics are to natural phenomena. It should operate as their Platonic model or type. Newman is attracted by the speculative genius of Augustine and Origen, Tertullian and Pelagius, whose volumes surround him in the working library still preserved at the oratory on Hagley Road. But Newman apparently found Aquinas too scholastic and abstract. Whereas he extensively annotated the library's volumes of Athanasius, a theologian whom he edited as a labour of love toward the end of his life, Newman's copy of Aquinas's *Summa Theologica*, presented to him by Jesuits in Dublin, is barely marked. Carlyle exhorts Teufelsdröckh to close his Byron and open his Goethe. It appears that some tutelary genius told Newman to close his Aquinas and open his Athanasius and Thomas Reid instead.

In the *Apologia* Newman says that the heavenly facts that fill eternity are locked forever within the embrace of the church and her sacraments. But in the sermon on development, a tidal wave of melancholy hits Newman. As a great surge of sadness and self-scrutiny passes over him, the voice of a sceptical anti-self can be heard as part of the sermon's subliminal message. To a critical opponent of religion there seems to be no truth outside the church, not so much because the church is infallible as because the idea of any independent truth is rejected as a fiction. Newman's Oxford sermons are remarkable for their self-criticism and honesty. They display the sympathetic imagination of a scholar who knows his adversary's position almost as well as he knows his own. When the homilist is trying to explain how the development of true doctrine is possible, his sceptical opponent seems to claim at once too little and too much for language. On the one hand, to speak of God at all is to take his name in vain. On the other hand, 'our ideas of Divine things are just co-extensive with the figures by which we express them, neither more nor less, and without them are not' (1887, 338–9). To apply an implicit empirical theory of language rigorously is to reach sceptical conclusions Newman wants to reject. But his Oxford sermons keep wresting truth from experience by demolishing the enemy from inside. Even when Newman tries to refute the sceptic by moving from nature to grace, traces of a sceptical Humean argument are still discernible. Any attempt to represent supernatural or eternal principles in intelligible oracles or signs must compromise, he concedes, the mystery of their subject. Like Johnson's poem 'The Vanity of Human Wishes,' Newman's sermons move Trojan horses into the enemy's citadel, where troops can be released for night battle. But victories are precarious and not easily won. Like Johnson, Newman arrives at truth only because he finds himself forced into ever-darker corners of a world where phantoms betray each wanderer in the mist. The solution each prophet finds is the last refuge of a sceptical and critical mind in retreat from alternative positions, successively found untenable.

The paragraph in the fifth and last chapter of Newman's *Apologia Pro Vita Sua*, beginning with the phrase 'To consider the world in its length and breadth,' has the majesty, weight, and authority of an oracle. Like 'The Vanity of Wishes,' it searches every state and canvasses every prayer. A reader keeps waiting for the inventory of items to end. Spilling over sixteen lines of print before providing a long-deferred grammatical object for the infinitive 'consider,' the suspended sentence and its abrupt conclusion are used by Newman like a weapon. Part of its prophetic power lies in an oddly literal use of the verb 'inflicts.'

> – all this is a vision to dizzy and appal; and inflicts upon the mind the sense of profound mystery, which is absolutely beyond human solution. (Newman, 1968, 186–7)

Though 'a sense of profound mystery' is not something usually 'inflicted' on the mind, like worry or disease, Newman's sensation is as sharp as pain and as acute as an attack of migraine or nausea.

As a prophet of mystery rather than a religious partisan, Newman finds his reason bewildered and affronted. 'Either there is no Creator, or this living society of men ... is discarded from His presence' (1968, 187). Either God is absent, or he never existed. As if to temper the audacity of these two heretical surmises, Newman immediately considers the analogy of the refined and handsome youth, without memory or birthplace, disinherited, it seems, by parents he has shamed. The analogy deftly corrects a material fallacy in the prophet's distressing logical dilemma, which too carelessly implies that in discarding his children God left behind no tokens of his presence. If the world is a fact, then so is God, and so is the terrible sundering that tears God apart from his creation. Like Spinoza's deft identification of substance with God in the *Ethic*, the dogmas of the Fall and original sin have been creeping up on Newman the prophet as theological explanations, almost before we know what Newman the partisan is up to.

Dramatizing the fluctuations of his fallen reason, Newman is laying the groundwork for an unexpected logical inference. In the pull back and forth between belief and unbelief in his own mind, Newman discerns a defect of thinking in all matters of religious inquiry. There is no power on earth that can withstand the all-dissolving, all-corroding scepticism of the intellect. And from its corrosive influence Newman proceeds to a full-blown defence of papal infallibility, a move that might seem at first more polemically partisan than prophetically disinterested. The oracle has trespassed on our sympathy almost before we realize what has happened.

> I say that a power, possessed of infallibility in religious teaching, is happily adapted to be a working instrument, in the course of human

affairs, for smiting hard and throwing back the immense energy of the aggressive, capricious, untrustworthy intellect. (1968, 189)

I am still appalled by these words from the *Apologia*. Though I possess them by memory, they never lose their power to move and unnerve me. It is as if Newman the prophet, after scaling Mount Everest, has used his skill as a climber to gain admission to the local hiking club. Northrop Frye says that 'every religion is a sort of golfer's handicap; the question is, how much intellectual honesty can one attain in spite of it?' (2004a, 129). It must be said, however, that, unlike many partisans who spend their strength in channels of controversy or intrigue that are soon forgotten, Newman's genius is prophetic. As Frank Turner says, Newman's 'gift was to transform his concerns and passions over the particular into a larger vision to which he virtually always appealed for his own limited polemical purposes.' But 'as the memories of the polemic faded, [they] left the universal categories of his message standing' (2002, 640). Like Lincoln at Gettysburg, Newman rises above the occasion of his speaking. He looks for a larger purpose that unites friend and enemy in the strife that divides them. Behind Newman the polemicist and partisan looms the much greater presence of Newman the prophet and visionary.

5

Just as evolution may produce a creature too complex or specialized to adapt to its environment, so wisdom may evolve arguments that prove more than its spokesmen want or need to prove. Newman is too disinterested to be partisan and too far-seeing to be narrowly polemical. Shakespeare's Ulysses is too wise to be blind to the folly of what he urges Achilles to do. And Hamlet has too exacting a sensibility and too fine a mind to swoop down on Claudius like a hawk on its prey.

It is instructive to see what wisdom Shakespeare, the wisest of English poets, ascribes to Ulysses, the wisest Greek hero. In his great exhortation to Achilles to rejoin the battle, Ulysses applies to reputation and fame the same vortex of impermanence and flux that Ovid discerns in nature and in the transformation of persons into animals then back into people. The terror of being erased from memory, of being sucked down a black hole or void, is most apparent in the way expansive grammatical subjects are swallowed up in a short terminal predicate.

> For beauty, wit,
> High birth, vigour of bone, desert in service,
> Love, friendship, charity, are subjects all
> To envious and calumniating Time.   (*Troilus and Cressida*, III.iii.171–4)

Ironically, Ulysses' oration fails as applied persuasion. If oblivion is as all-devouring as Ulysses claims, why pay it any alms? If one more heroic act delays oblivion by a mere hour, why should Achilles leave his tent? The identical irony blunts the appeal of Tennyson's Ulysses. Why should the mariners follow Ulysses on a suicide mission, a voyage into death? Why pay oblivion the alms of a final heroic deed if the monster ingratitude is insatiable?

The antique wonder of huge rusty mail in monumental mockery is a memorial to the vanity of both action and inaction. There is no way in fact of keeping honour bright except in the specious present. And that 'instant way' is a perishing fiction. As applied persuasion, Ulysses' argument proves more than it need or should prove. Like Newman's great prophecy about fallen nature in the fifth book of the *Apologia*, the speech is more disinterested than partisan, and so self-destructive in any polemical context, whether it be Newman's attempt to win approval for papal infallibility or Ulysses' attempt to rouse the great Greek hero to action.

The most famous line in Ulysses' speech, 'One touch of nature makes the whole world kin' (III.iii.75), breaks down in context. We are all undone by the same enemy, Time, who is an ungrateful, hypocritical host. Anyone who has been pushed into retirement knows what Ulysses means. Welcome smiles but Farewell sighs, and we are no sooner pushed out the door than our host is embracing a new guest. Ulysses uses an unforgettable chiasmus (we give to 'dust that is a little gilt / More laud than gilt o'er-dusted,' ll. 178–9) to dramatize the elusiveness and illusion of value, which is at best a glimmering mirage.

Everyone is fooled by illusion and undone by time. Our envious and calumniating enemy effaces everything: an annihilating prospect. So why should Achilles stir? Not even the final touch of flattery, the reminder that Achilles' 'glorious deeds' drove Mars himself 'to faction,' succeeds in moving the great warrior. We are all pushed to the side of our own lives, and (contrary to Philip Larkin) we do not have to wait to be old to be pushed. Who, then, is wiser? Achilles, who recognizes the vanity of fame and refuses to renew the battle in the plain; or Ulysses, who wants to refurbish armour that will rust tomorrow?

Comparable puzzles disturb Hamlet in his great soliloquies. If Claudius is as base as Hamlet claims he is, and if Hamlet is as noble in reason as Shakespeare shows he is, then the prince is not too weak but too strong to succeed as an avenger. The task he is set is unworthy of him. The hunger of Hamlet's mind is always simplifying its needs into specific goals – the anguish of a mother's remorse, the exquisite and refined torture of an uncle's death – then finding these goals unsatisfying. Even if Hamlet were to succeed in everything he plots, he would still be unhappy.

Kierkegaard says we understand our lives backward but lead them forward.

> Sure, He that made us with such large discourse,
> Looking before and after, gave us not
> That capability and godlike reason
> To fust in us unused.   (*Hamlet*, IV.iv.36–9)

The participial phrase, 'Looking before and after,' literally reaches back to the preceding line by attaching itself grammatically to 'discourse.' But it also looks forward to what follows, because it is still awaiting the completion of a grammatical subject. Hamlet knows that a mind noble in reason and infinite in faculty should in theory look back and forward at the same time. But Hamlet is so absorbed by the first task, the task of understanding his life backward, that he has no time for the second: the challenge of leading it forward. Even if Hamlet debases reason by quartering it into one part wisdom and three parts cowardice, the abuse of the faculty is no argument against its right and godlike use. 'Fust,' 'us,' 'unused': even tricks of language keep prompting Hamlet to pry the word 'us' loose from its prison in 'fust' and 'unused' and so give it a new life in 'use.'

The wisdom of Hamlet, the wisest of Shakespeare's spokesmen, is inseparable from the gnomic eloquence and restrained authority of his first great soliloquy. A Prometheus in prison, he seems to possess secret wisdom he is reluctant to share, even with himself. The war that threatens Denmark pales beside the drama of his inward insurrection. Curiously, Hamlet says at once too little and too much. His disillusion and sickness of soul are amplified at length. But the exact cause of his melancholy is never explained. There is something Hamlet keeps trying to say that he never says. In Newman's phrase, 'Secretum meum mihi.' Hamlet is torn between a death wish – a desire for his

'too too solid flesh' to 'melt' – and an impulse to abide on stage to lac-
erate his wound. Sometimes the two impulses run together. Though he
wants to erase all trace of his flesh, instead of wiping it out at a single
stroke, Hamlet uses three verbs to efface it: 'melt,' 'thaw,' 'resolve into
a dew' (*Hamlet*, I.ii.129–30). The flesh he abhors is associated with the
sexual appetite of Claudius and his mother. And the thawing of flesh
into dew anticipates the apparition of his father's ghost.

Torn between impulses to prolong his soliloquy and cut it short,
Hamlet launches into a denunciation of Gertrude – 'Frailty, thy name
is woman!' (I.ii.146), which rivals in intensity Posthumus's tirade
against Imogen and Lear's denunciation of his daughters. The simple
two-word clause, 'She married' (I.ii.156), is the deferred apodosis of an
extended grammatical subject launched ten lines earlier with the
words 'and yet, within a month, / Let me not think on't!' (I.ii.145–9).
This astonishing sentence seems to run on forever. It holds together
several grammatical fragments, including Hamlet's reflection that his
mother has committed incest by marrying his father's brother.
Depending on the punctuation, the twice-repeated phrase 'within a
month' (I.ii.145, 153) can modify either 'married with mine uncle' (l.
153) or 'She married' (l. 156). Like the two-faced Gertrude, who is also
the cause of self-division in her son, the syntax is Janus-faced, looking
two ways at once.

Hamlet's first long speech has to be a soliloquy, because its thoughts
are too seditious to be spoken aloud. Indeed Hamlet seems afraid even
to overhear himself, and precedes each deferred disclosure with some
expression of outrage and shock. The war in his mind even extends to
an imaginary war in heaven, in which the Everlasting has fixed his
cannon against self-slaughter. There is an intriguing oxymoronic
quality to Hamlet's God, who turns violent even in his war against
self-violence, and whose name is repeated three times, twice blasphe-
mously. Animating Hamlet's discourse and making it vividly physical
are the metonymies that substitute 'tongue' for words, 'galled eyes' for
grief, shoes for feet, and 'incestuous sheets' for sexual appetite and
lust. As a medial caesura breaks apart the blank-verse line, Hamlet
uses two powerful metonymies, 'heart' and 'tongue,' to show how
self-imposed silence throttles the affections. 'But break my heart, for I
must hold my tongue' (l. 159). Equally powerful are the buried
metaphors. Gertrude hastens with the wicked speed of a lusty mare to
her stallion's bed. The same phrases that Hamlet applies appreciatively to his mother's love for his father acquire a grotesquely insa-

tiable quality when applied with equal appropriateness to her lust for his uncle, which Hamlet refuses to dignify with the name of love.

> Why, she would hang on him
> As if increase of appetite had grown
> By what it feeds on.   (*Hamlet*, I.ii.143)

Like Gertrude herself and Hamlet, such phrases look two ways at once, and are either extolled or berated according to the nouns they attach to. Adding to Hamlet's stature as a possessor of wisdom and oracular authority is his response to the ghost's command: 'Hamlet, remember me.' The phrase keeps reverberating in an acoustic chamber of his mind, where the verb 'remember' is itself remembered as a word that continues to echo and re-echo: 'Heaven and earth! / Must I remember' (I.ii.142–3), 'Remember thee! ... Remember thee!' (I.v.95–7). Whether his apprehension of the ghost is angelic or demonic, Hamlet receives the ghost's commands as Moses receives the tables on Mount Sinai: 'My tables, my tables, – meet it is I set it down' (I.v.107).

Hamlet, like all of us, tends to think of himself as a set of ungrounded possibilities: in action he is like an angel and in apprehension like a god. It does not occur to him that his noble reason and angelic powers depend on his contingent status as an animal. It comes as a shock, then, for Hamlet to register the fact that his godlike potential will not only not be realized but will also vanish altogether. The alarming paradox that the paragon of animals is also the quintessence of dust destroys Hamlet's pride and shatters his illusions.

In his most famous soliloquy, 'To be, or not to be,' Hamlet's inability to imagine a time when he will experience neither pain nor pleasure, nor any sensation whatever, leads him to a strange conclusion: if death is only the termination of consciousness, Hamlet may be incapable of dying at all. As a suicide victim in danger of flying to ills he knows not of, Hamlet may be consumed by a cruel immortality, unable like Tithonus to shake off an infinity of torments.

His later reflection that 'the readiness is all' (*Hamlet*, V.ii.233) raises the more consoling possibility that death as the end of consciousness is not something we suffer, like a painful disease. Since it occurs at the boundary or limit of life, as something just outside it, 'when death comes,' as Epicurus says, 'we no longer are.' Death is a misfortune only if we make the mistake of bringing it forward in time and placing it, as Richard Wollheim says, 'within, rather than on the confines, of life' (1984, 268).

Like Edgar's assertion in *King Lear* that 'Ripeness is all' (V.ii.11), Hamlet's perception that 'the readiness is all' invites us to grow into death as the seasons grow into autumn. We should be no more appalled by our non-existence after death than by our non-existence before birth. Why should there be any asymmetry between the prospect of our not surviving in the future and our not existing in the past?

In his soliloquy 'O what a rogue and peasant slave am I,' Hamlet berates himself for *not* being a bad actor. If he were to saw the air with his hands and fall to the ground in a swoon, he would be breaking every rule in the actor's manual. But an actor who plays Hamlet can excel in the role precisely because Hamlet expresses significant emotion and seldom betrays the merely sincere emotion of a bad actor. Two Hamlets reveal themselves in this soliloquy. There is a strongly declamatory Hamlet speaking in histrionic, emphatically end-stopped lines and in chains of vituperative epithets that sometimes remind us of bad acting. And there is a more cautious Hamlet, whose deliberations carry him across line breaks in a carefully calculated plan to determine Claudius's guilt. The first style is found in Hamlet's explosive chiasmus: 'What's Hecuba to him, or he to Hecuba?' (II.ii.585). As the embrace of a repeated inner word by a repeated outer one (*a b b a*), chiasmus is usually a reflective figure, a trope of protective intimacy. But this chiasmus is a mere trick of stagecraft and rhetoric. Hamlet's play-acting reaches a climax in a hypermetric line consisting of four rhyming suffixes: 'Remorseless, treacherous, lecherous, kindless villain' (l. 609). Incapable of turning such Marlovian rant into a heroic enterprise, Hamlet opts for a suppler, more judicious blank verse that carries him across line breaks and allows him to pause thoughtfully at the middle of lines.

Like his predilection for hendiadys (the splitting of a locution in two), Hamlet's addiction to double nouns – 'in our circumstance and course of thought' (III.iii.83) – provides him with an important weapon in his well-stocked arsenal of delay. But weighty phrasing can also prove functional. 'Course of thought' revives the metaphor gone dead in 'circumstance' by evoking Hamlet's constant mental circling round forbidden topics. If it lies 'heavy' with his father, who was murdered grossly, 'full of bread,' the burden of his son is no less weighty. Hamlet's own 'circumstance' is to stand round and brood, weighed down by two alliterating nouns. As Frank Kermode explains, 'hendiadys is a way of making a single idea strange ... so that it calls for explanation as a minute and often sinister metaphor' (2000, 15). When Claudius dies Hamlet wants his heels to kick at heaven so that the inverted villain may land in hell upside down, like Ugolino in the *Inferno*.

In his great soliloquy, 'How all occasions do inform against me,' Hamlet wields hendiadys as a two-edged sword. In deploring that the physical needs of sleep and food have become 'the chief good and market' of a man (IV.v.34), Hamlet is contracting the first noun of the hendiadys into the second one. It is as if a man's chief end and virtue were to hawk wares at a farmer's market and spend his life buying or consuming food. He is more generous in commending Fortinbras's army, which is said to have both 'mass and charge' (IV.v.47). Lest we think a massive army is also unwieldy, Hamlet uses the second noun of the pair to animate the army's mass. He tempers it with the response of a high-spirited horse or charger, attuned to the command of 'a delicate and tender prince' (IV.v.48). Yet a discerning playgoer overhears Shakespeare in this soliloquy, sharing wisdom with the audience that he seems to withhold from Hamlet. If the small plot of ground Fortinbras fights for is 'not tomb enough and continent / To hide the slain' (IV.v.64–5), then the hendiadys that stretches a burial place into a land mass as wide as Asia raises doubts about the wisdom of so rashly heroic an enterprise.

> Rightly to be great
> Is not to stir without great argument,
> But greatly to find quarrel in a straw
> When honour's at the stake.   (*Hamlet*, IV.v.53–6)

The reflective turn on 'great' and its cognates ('Rightly to be great,' 'great argument,' 'greatly to find') has gnomic authority. But that authority erodes when honour trumps reason. Hamlet's wise-sounding chiasmus of sound and sense is an implicit censure of the rashness he presumes to applaud in the hotheaded Fortinbras, who foolishly equates 'great' or weighty argument with something so lightweight as quarrel over a straw.

When ideas evolve and clash in unforeseen ways, wisdom tries to savour the contradictions that knowledge prefers to explain away or dissolve. If Claudius is the eggshell and cipher Hamlet says he is, then Hamlet's dilemma is that there is only one deed more base than a cowardly refusal to kill Claudius: and that is the squalid act of killing him at all. Hamlet faces the same paradox as Ulysses in *Troilus and Cressida*. If his rhetoric succeeds, it also fails. If time is as all-devouring and calumniating as Ulysses says it is, then there is no reason for Achilles to leave his tent. If Achilles is not forgotten today, he will be tomorrow. A comparable fate awaits Newman. If the ruin of man's angelic destiny is as total as he says, how can Newman the theologian continue to honour the wisdom of Newman the scholar? In order to promote a doctrine of papal infallibility, Newman has launched an attack upon the scepticism of the intellect in matters of religious inquiry that degrades the mind below its natural dignity, a dignity that the great defender of liberal education is eager to protect and preserve. Hamlet faces a similar dilemma. What delight can a prince of men expect to find in the expense of his talent in a waste of shame? What fulfilment can there be in Hamlet's expending his godlike reason and infinite capacity in the extinction of so worthless a victim as Claudius? The English reader will always seek wisdom in Shakespeare. And the wisest, most intelligent of Shakespeare's spokesmen will always be Hamlet.

18 An Underground Oracle: 'Look in Your Heart and Write'

Though Christianity demonizes oracles from the underworld, they are kept alive by the prestige of Virgil, who associates prophecy with Aeneas's descent to hell in book 6 of the *Aeneid*, where he meets the archetypal prophet-poet, the Cumaean Sibyl. The moment in which Apollo possesses the Sibyl, making her his own, is Virgil's equivalent of Leda's possession by the swan. Like Tithonus, the Sibyl is granted immortality but not perpetual youth. As Lawrence Lipking says, 'she is filled by a genius both hysterical and fruitless' (1981, 90). Any seer who, as the mere mouthpiece of a god, is the puppet of a divine ventriloquist suffers the fate of the priestess at Delphi. Like Yeats's Leda, she is torn apart by the divine and animal forces contending for her soul. She is both more and less than human. According to Virgil, the Sibyl's name, Deiphobe, is derived from the god who possesses her. As Lipking says, 'to be a vates under such circumstances – a worn-out puppet in the hand of a divine ventriloquist – may be more than flesh can bear' (1981, 90). The Sibyl's predicament is the dilemma of every bride of darkness and of every oracle from the underground. She aspires not only to give voice to the god but also to interpret him. Both human and divine, she mediates between two worlds. Like the raped virgin in 'Leda and the Swan,' the Sibyl wages a losing struggle against the god who masters her. Lipking describes the process as 'a horrible parody of labor pains – labor in reverse, since the god compels an entrance. Her fate is to lose herself' in his power (1981, 90).

1

From Juliet to Desdemona, from Lady Macbeth to Goneril and Regan, Shakespeare fills his tragedies with spectral brides, murderous wives, and heartless daughters. Juliet's gruesomely prophetic imagination of dying strangled in the tomb before Romeo can rescue her is graphic to the limits of endurance. The only event that exceeds her morbid fantasy is the tragedy of the last act itself, which takes place in the tomb's foul mouth, a place where Juliet can breathe no wholesome air and where she foresees her doom as a bride of darkness trapped in a crypt.

> O, if I wake, shall I not be distraught,
> Environed with all these hideous fears,
> And madly play with my forefathers' joints,
> And pluck the mangled Tybalt from his shroud,
> And, in this rage, with some great kinsman's bone
> As with a club dash out my desp'rate brains? (IV.iii.50–5)

Portending the double suicide, and dramatizing Juliet's heroic resolve to be drugged and then entombed, these horrors prove all too prophetic. Before the bride can muster courage to drink the potion, she has to imagine that her bridegroom, Romeo, is calling for her to come, desperate that she should stave off the vengeful deeds of Tybalt in his crypt.

Equally harrowing is Desdemona's fate as a bride of darkness in *Othello*. To displace the ugliness of his sexual jealousy and lust, Othello weaves an enchanting love spell just before strangling his ravishingly beautiful bride: 'Yet I'll not shed her blood, / Nor scar that whiter skin of hers than snow, / And smooth as monumental alabaster' (V.ii.3–5). Denied a chance to make a final prayer, Desdemona is destroyed by a desperate black man who, 'like the base Indian, threw a pearl away / Richer than all his tribe' (V.ii.347–8). And yet Shakespeare invests this dark groom, 'not with witchcraft and devilry,' as we might expect, but 'with the true power of love,' as he had endowed Shylock 'with the voice of humanity' (Bayley, 1981, 216).

If we see Desdemona as the dupe of a dupe, as the victim of a man who is himself the victim of sexual intrigue, then she shrinks to a figure of jokes and farce. As a subject of gross gossip, casually pictured 'naked with her friend in bed, an hour,' she maddens her dark groom. But if Othello can substitute for sex the exalted language of love, if he can protect its sublime but fragile fabric from the coarse assaults of Iago, then Desdemona becomes, not just a bride of darkness or a wronged wife, but a martyr of love. Unfortunately, the only person who believes that Othello is 'one that loved not wisely but too well' is Othello himself (Bayley, 1981, 201). To see events from Othello's point of view is to be a spectator of a tragedy. To see the play from any one else's perspective is to be present at 'a bloody farce,' as Thomas Rymer says, 'without salt or savor' (1971, 164), because the proximity of love to sex inexorably squeezes out the tragedy.

Lady Macbeth is a far more fearful bride of darkness than the witches in Macbeth. And since she is more strong-willed and prophetic, Lady Macbeth is also more frightening than Medea. Although she resembles Seneca's heroine in her power to precipitate disaster, she contributes more than Medea to the play's tragedy of consciousness. She makes us feel less intimate with Macbeth, who is not the person she describes, than with the seething ferment of her own mind, which boils and bubbles like the witches' cauldron. Though Lady Macbeth loves her husband deeply, she loves him as a child, fed with milk that she alone provides. In her prophecies, strength of purpose confers on her the authority of the oracle at Delphi. 'Glamis thou art, and Cawdor, and shalt be / What thou art promised' (I.v.12–13). There is a terrifying discrepancy between the husband she pictures yearning to be great, but 'without the illness' that 'should attend it,' and the man she calls the 'dearest love' and 'partner' of her life. Ironically, the qualities Lady Macbeth pretends to despise in her husband, his innate kindness and his deep and intimate reliance on his wife, are also the qualities she loves best in him. And yet she is ready to unsex herself in order to turn her consort into a caricature of the man she knows him to be. She thinks she can love Macbeth only if she can feed him, not on the milk of human kindness, but on that milk which her steely ambition and her murderous schemes will slowly but relentlessly turn to gall.

Like her husband, Lady Macbeth has too much imagination to succeed as a killer. She says she could not slay the groom because he resembled her father. Her imagination draws her outside the murderous act. She views it from the groom's perspective, as if she were both the hangman in a play and the audience of the hanging. It is extraordinary that the words 'my father' and 'my husband' should appear at the beginning and end of the same line.

Had he not resembled
My father as he slept, I had done't – My husband! (*Macbeth*, II.ii.12–14)

Lady Macbeth makes demands of her husband that are both unloving and illogical. It is as if Ophelia were to ask Hamlet to kill someone who looked like her father – Laertes, for example.

In context, Lady Macbeth's obsession with progressions that refuse to end is just as devastating as her husband's. Against the integrity of 'the poor and single' she opposes expanding phrases that approach unity only as a limit.

> All our service
> In every point twice done and then done double
> Were poor and single business to contend
> Against the honors deep and broad wherewith
> Your majesty loads our house. (*Macbeth*, I.vi.14–18)

Combined with the abstract hyperboles of a Goneril or Regan, the interest in mathematical progressions and the studied use of chiasmus ('twice done and then done double') exaggerate the want of feeling. Collapsing under their weight are the honours Duncan loads upon Lady Macbeth and her own integrity and honour. After the arrival of Duncan at their castle, the courtesy of the Macbeths is less a piece of courtly behaviour than a mechanical exercise of vocal cords, bowing backs, and scraping knees. If Lady Macbeth and her husband can still do things that gracious hosts can do, they do them as robots rather than people.

In Lady Macbeth's final soliloquy, the last bonds to give way are bonds of reason and ligatures of syntax.

> To bed, to bed! there's knocking at the gate. Come, come, come, come, give me your hand. What's done cannot be undone. – To bed, to bed, to bed! (*Macbeth*, V.i.72–6)

Though Lady Macbeth is marvellously adept at multiplying impressions of the murky hell she lives in, the words that disappear in her speech are the connecting words, the prepositions and conjunctions. Since each phrase she repeats can be located at a precise moment in the past, however, her soliloquy retains a confused limpidity. The playgoer can easily provide the spatial and temporal connections that the sleepwalker's own diseased mind can no longer supply. We feel her repetitions of 'to bed, to bed, to bed!' will echo endlessly, since she is already in the world of infernal time Macbeth inhabits in his soliloquy, 'To-morrow, and to-morrow, and to-morrow.' In a world where things repeat, repeat, and repeat again down to the last syllable of recorded time, it is as impossible for her to arrive at a last receding increment of time as it is for Zeno's arrow to reach its target. It is no wonder she ends her agony by committing suicide.

When Gertrude marries Hamlet's uncle, the prince spurns his mother as a bride of incest and dark intrigue. But Gertrude is not a murderess like Lady Macbeth. She knows nothing about the murder of her first husband in the orchard. Nor does she have an affair with Claudius before his brother dies. Hamlet wants to portray his mother as a bride of darkness. 'Look here upon this picture and on this,' he tells her. But for Gertrude the difference is never black and white. She loves King Hamlet and her son with a lasting and tested affection. Though it is true that Gertrude has 'no life to breathe' or betray the confidences Hamlet shares with her, it is equally true that she has no intention of betraying Claudius either. Despite the enormity of his crime, Claudius inspires trust in his bride and has a dignity and strength of his own. Just as Hamlet casts his mother as a blacker bride of darkness that he needs to, so he makes Ophelia's situation worse than necessary. We sense that Hamlet has loved Ophelia honourably. But by humiliating her publicly, sending her to a nunnery, then being indirectly responsible for her suicide, he makes it harder to find peace in a world he finds sordid and rotten to the core.

As a darker bride of darkness than even Lady Macbeth or the witches, Goneril uses a veneer of words to hide the evil in her heart. She expresses her love for her father in a drum roll of abstractions: 'grace, health, bounty, honor' (I.i.58), and later she rejects him with cold deliberation. The Fool's ironies blunt themselves on Goneril's inhumanity. Banal and unimaginative in her total incapacity to imagine what her father feels, she possesses stupidity's stubborn strength. When Lear, as an oracle through whom the gods speak, calls down his worst curses upon his daughter with calm and dreadful strength, nothing seems to move her, even though her husband Albany is visibly shaken. In the end Goneril poisons her sister Regan and compasses her own ruin by lusting after Edmund. In contrast to the rhymed couplets of the honourable King of France and to the imaginative villainies of Edmund, which Shakespeare lifts into lively blank verse, Goneril and Regan speak in straight prose – the perfect medium for two heartless schemers.

Leda, the mother of Helen, becomes a bride of darkness when raped by Zeus in the guise of a swan. Compressed into a fearful oracle in Yeats's poem 'Leda and the Swan,' the doubleness of Leda's fate foretells a comparable ambiguity in the destructive beauty of Leda's daughter, Helen, which leads to the Trojan war and the murder of Agamemnon. The indicative verbs of the third stanza consist of prophecies as well as statements.

> A shudder in the loins engenders there
> The broken wall, the burning roof and tower
> And Agamemnon dead.
>
> (ll. 9–11)

After the moment of rape and rapture, when Leda dies for an instant to the rush of time, the poem consists entirely of questions and discrete fragments: 'a sudden blow,' 'the great wings beating still,' 'her thighs caressed' (ll. 1, 2). These absolute constructions leave Leda suspended, grammatically as well as spatially. Equally suspenseful are the questions, which range in kind from the merely rhetorical – 'How can those terrified vague fingers push / The feathered glory from her loosening thighs?' (ll. 5–6) – to the enigmatic and unanswerable: 'Did she put on his knowledge with his power?' (l. 13)

As a priestess of dark oracles that rise from the sea of the unconscious, like a lost Atlantis submerged under Blake's 'Sea of Time and Space' (Frye, 1990, 247), Emily Dickinson is just as resourceful as Blake or Yeats in thinking up ways of being posthumous. Married in her lyrics of consciousness to a dark double, the poet can no more divorce herself from her role as a self-conscious spectator than she can unhinge the world of her sense experience from a perceiving subject. She is the Bishop Berkeley or J.F. Ferrier of American sibyls.

In lyric 894 Emily's dark bridegroom, her 'awful Mate,' undergoes rapid transformations. At first he resembles the pursuing hound of lyric 822. The Soul 'cannot be rid' of this avenger. But then, in a surprising move, Dickinson compares her groom's penetrating gaze to the eyes of God. The Consciousness has more in common with Francis Thompson's Hound of Heaven than with the dark bridegroom to whom Emily's soul is shackled in the earlier lyric.

> Of Consciousness, her awful Mate
> The Soul cannot be rid –
> As easy the secreting her
> Behind the Eyes of God
>
> (ll. 1–4)

Her Mate is 'awful' in a double sense. He pursues her as relentlessly as a hound. But he also incites her awe, since he penetrates the inmost chambers of her mind. It as futile to seek refuge from her Mate as it is to escape God's gaze by trying to inhabit his skull or by hiding behind eyes that cut like X-rays through her own.

> The deepest hid is sighted first
> And scant to Him the Crowd –
> What triple Lenses burn upon
> The Escape from God   (ll. 5–8)

Despite her petty stratagems of disguise, the more Emily tries to mask her identity, the more visible and transparent she becomes. When her dark bridegroom turns upon his vagrant bride the 'triple Lenses' of his Eye, any planned escape becomes a mere evasive prank, a child's game of hide-and-seek.

2

What act committed by a bride of darkness would cause a mourner to grieve and still find her act wholly senseless and unintelligible? The answer, of course, is suicide. But it is easier to solve this riddle than explain it. And it is typical of such a subject that we should want to draw a circle of words around it. Most of us need to approach it indirectly, as we approach a riddle. We never want to confront an experience of violent death head on. I find, however, that only when my daughter's terrifying plunge into darkness is recalled and relived in a mood of reflective tranquillity can I begin to understand her deed and begin to find an answer to the question: after such knowledge, what forgiveness?

A well-known book, *Night Falls Fast*, is subtitled 'Understanding Suicide.' But anyone who is touched by suicide knows that 'understanding' is the last thing one achieves. For most of us the suicide of someone we love is beyond telling or knowing. In the familiar biblical phrase, it 'passeth understanding.' When my daughter died, she took my heart out of the world with her. Was it a senseless loss? Unfortunately, a lucid comprehension of suicide, if it comes at all, is a function of recollecting and not of mere remembering. I recall what Norman's father tells him in 'A River Runs through It,' my favourite short story. If you would understand your brother's death, you must write a story about it. As Kierkegaard keeps reminding us, repetition is never tedious to those who recollect instead of merely remember the past. To remember is to recollect, in Kierkegaard's sense of the word. Keeping a journal about Margaret might seem an exercise in self-indulgent morbidity. But for me it has been a daily life-or-death need.

As long as we are searching for meaning, life cannot be totally devoid of meaning. By remembering the past, giving it the shape of a descent to the underworld by a bride of darkness, I may also make it more intelligible. When I remember Margaret's suicide I restore the experience of that event in a different form, even though the experience itself is far removed from anything I could call a consolation or catharsis.

> We had the experience but missed the meaning,
> And approach to the meaning restores the experience
> In a different form, beyond any meaning
> We can assign to happiness.   (T.S. Eliot, 'The Dry Salvages,' II.45–8)

The grief I felt at Margaret's funeral was an intensified reliving of earlier griefs, and the grief of recollecting those griefs, though less acute, may restore the experience in a more manageable shape, one I may someday begin to understand.

The underworld journey of any bride of darkness confronts us with a double mystery. It is the mystery of how strong mourners grieve, and the more universal mystery of why devastating afflictions must be borne by people who do nothing to deserve them. The Eleusinian rites were a set of secret ceremonies, mysteries that initiates were forbidden to reveal. How then can we expect one mystery – the anabasis of Kore – to resolve another mystery? How can pagan mourning, even if it is (as I suspect) more human and accessible than Christian mourning, lighten the burden of the more universal mystery: why terrible things happen to innocent people. I could make only one comment to my oldest daughter, after leaving unit 2-5 at Queen Street when Margaret was first confined there: this is a circle in Dante's hell; what have they done to deserve their torment?

The safer Margaret seemed to be, protected in a hospital, the more at risk she was. The affliction of Wordworth's Margaret was the affliction of a woman deserted by her only son. The affliction of my Margaret was her abduction by a dark power. She was literally a bride of darkness, a Persephone kidnapped by her unrelenting inner voices. Persephone was abducted from without, by her soul-mate and future husband. But Margaret was abducted from inside, by voices that told her to take her own life.

When Margaret played Gluck on her flute, she was Orpheus guiding Eurydice back from the underworld. Her first flute was mangled during one of her bursts of mania in the hospital. But later I bought her another flute, at Long and McQuade. We had it adjusted, and she played it like Orpheus in efforts to rescue her own Eurydice from hell. My wife and I bought her sheet music for it. She played this music for her brother and sisters, but after her death the flute and music books were lost. When I went through her effects in the hospital room after the funeral, I threw aside her clothes and art books in a desperate search for the flute and music. 'Ours, the treasure!' I wanted to cry, like Browning's Guido Reni and 'all Bologna.' But 'suddenly, as rare things will, it vanished' ('One Word More,' ll. 30–1). I never saw either the flute or music books again.

After a suicide it is impossible to attain Milton's confidence in 'Lycidas': 'Tomorrow to fresh woods and pastures new.' All one can hope for is the lucid consciousness of Sisyphus. Though bravely aware that his task is absurd, Sisyphus is content to know and perform it conscientiously. 'One must imagine Sisphyus happy,' Camus oddly but wisely tells us. The bracing words are simple ones, words honoured by Camus: 'comprehension,' 'modesty,' a 'lucid consciousness' and mind.

> It is during that return, that pause, that Sisyphus interests me. A face that toils so close to the stones is already stone itself! I see that man going back down with a heavy yet measured step toward the torment of which he will never know the end. That hour like a breathing-space which returns as surely as his suffering, that is the hour of consciousness. At each of those moments when he leaves the heights and gradually sinks toward the lairs of the gods, he is superior to his fate. He is stronger than his rock. (Camus, 1955, 89)

Unlike raw grief, an educated or intelligible grief is lucid. At first the anguish is raw, heart-piercing, brutal, and untamable. Later it becomes subdued, more manageable. 'The heavy yet measured step' of Sisphyus remains. But it becomes steadier, and 'the breathing-space,' the moment of gentle obstinacy, more regulated and assured. I understand now what Camus means by the pause of Sisyphus, or by the 'time out' that Frost commends, 'the slant / As of a book held up before his eyes.'

'The thing was the slope it gave his head; / The same for reading as it was for thought, / So different from the hard and level stare' ('Time Out,' ll. 2–3, 8–10).

There are two kinds of underworld journey. One is 'the confrontation with nothingness' and the other 'the creative descent that finds a treasure.' Do we come back from the underworld, dazed and witless like Browning's Lazarus, with soot on our face? Or do we 'simply slough off the lower world as an encumbrance' (Frye, 2004a, 158)? Do we have a resurrection or ascension? The more I seek a bracing oracle or Word, the more it eludes me. I am afraid that any rope-bridge I throw over the gorge will be a rope to hang by. The strongest rope may be some oracle from the underworld, some victory over memory and time such as Demeter achieves over Zeus, or such as Persephone achieves in her accord with Pluto, her groom of darkness, lord of the underworld and death.

After his son Lionel's death in 1886, Tennyson uses the myth of Demeter and Persephone to master subversive thoughts he could not subdue in any other way. As the oracular coda of 'Demeter and Persephone' focuses, with full pathos, on 'the Stone,' 'the Wheel,' and 'the field of Asphodel,' the prophetic certitude of 'see no more' is quietly discarded.

                              and see no more
The Stone, the Wheel, the dimly-glimmering lawns
Of that Elysium, all the hateful fires
Of torment, and the shadowy warrior glide
Along the silent field of Asphodel.   ('Demeter and Persephone,' ll. 147–51)

The eye registers the undulations, phrase by phrase, waiting to locate Sisyphus and Achilles in their twilight world, until Demeter's prophecy of obliterating that world is all but forgotten. Achilles moves softly in the last great lines, and twilight descends in the way Persephone, a bride of darkness, might hope to meet her consort in a world of shades. As each phrase subsides, knowing its inevitable direction but pausing and hovering before descent, prophetic assurance is replaced by a natural dignity of movement that precludes lament. So authoritative is Tennyson's sense of what produces the quarrel of life with the conditions of life itself, and so powerful is the catharsis he achieves, that after finishing 'Demeter and Persephone,' a short dramatic monologue, we feel we might be at the end of a tragedy or epic poem.

3

Adept at serious play, any master of oracles should also be a wise fool who traffics in logical absurdities and takes delight in cosmic jokes. Why is death a leveller? Not because everybody dies, but because nobody knows what death means. To be enlightened is to get the joke, to appreciate the humour of an answered riddle. As Frye muses cryptically, 'the door of death has oracle on one side and wit on the other: when one goes through it one recovers the power of laughter' (2002, 162).

A philosopher with an aptitude for oracular wit and witty prophecy is Ted Cohen, who admits to feeling 'a sacred twinge' in someone's laughter (1999, 59). To be welcomed for its lightness of spirit, the paradox of wise or noble folly is the great solvent of self-importance and pretension. It is also a reminder that the soul of adventurous learning is the pursuit of knowledge in a spirit of serious play. Alcibiades registers the playful, foolish side of Socrates by comparing him in the *Symposium* to an ugly Silenus or pug-nosed satyr. And Erasmus uses the pagan female figure of Folly to celebrate Jesus as a wise fool who cures the 'folly of mankind' by choosing 'the foolishness of the Cross.'

Cohen believes there is a 'biblical, and even Talmudic' sanction for jokes. Many of them display the 'crazy logic' we find in paradoxes and bulls. Like the sayings of the Fool in *King Lear* or Yeats's Crazy Jane, 'they have an insane rationality, a logical rigor gone over the edge' (1999, 46). To demonstrate the humour of twisted logic, Cohen tells a joke in which a statement 'It's cold outside' functions as the antecedent of a conditional proposition. If it's cold outside and the husband closes the window in response to his wife's request, does the wife now want her husband to open the window because then the outside should be warm (1999, 46)? If a, then b; not b, therefore not a. Though the denial of a consequent is a valid operation in formal logic, it may also represent a rationalism that has lost direction. In a similar vein God has to tell the rabbi that if he wants to win a fortune in the lottery it is not enough to pray: he must first buy a ticket. As Cohen says, 'the rabbi is made to consider the Leibnizian question of whether even God can work a logical contradiction' (1999, 47).

Many bulls and jokes exhibit an absurd response to a normal occurrence 'or a kind of doubling of absurdity.' To show how logic may run wild, Cohen tells a joke about a taxi-driver who takes a customer from Manhattan to Chicago only to have a woman get into the taxi and tell the driver she wants to go to Flatbush. Then the cabbie tells her, 'I don't go to Brooklyn' (1999, 48). When God tells the elderly Sarah she is about to conceive, she laughs at the improbability. But sometimes God devises absurd outcomes that prompt laughter. He uses them as signs of his presence in a world that, in perfecting the science of statistics and the laws of probability, has lost its faith in miracles.

When Sarah conceives a son, as God predicts, she calls him Isaac, which means 'laughter.' And when God later directs Abraham to sacrifice a ram and free Isaac, Cohen wonders whether God is directing laughter to 'be freed and let loose in the world. Let us hope so' (1999, 55). As Kierkegaard understands in *Fear and Trembling*, humour is a religious category, and irony a way of speaking without saying anything. When a puzzled Isaac asks his father what animal he will sacrifice, Abraham replies – with superb indirection – that God himself will provide the offering. As soon as Abraham understands that he cannot understand why God should command him to sacrifice Isaac, he substitutes for the science of lying to his son the art of Socratic irony and paradox.

Cohen thinks an 'intense concentration on logic and language' (1999, 62) is an abiding feature of Jewish humour (and, one might add, of paradoxes and bulls). The absurdity of logic as an end in itself devours Cohen's rabbi, who would rather trap his student in a logical dilemma than teach him philosophy. Having caught the neophyte in a web of refutations, the rabbi tells him that before he can study the Talmud he must first master the rudiments of 'Jewish logic' (1999, 66). A student of the Talmud 'argues, debates, contests, criticises, and learns; he does not stop. Indeed it is possible to be so consumed by this study that one loses one's bearings' (1999, 66).

There is a touch of logical imbalance in Cohen's joke about the painting commissioned to commemorate Lenin's time in Zurich. The picture displays Mrs Lenin in bed with Trotsky. When asked, 'Where is Lenin?,' the painter says, 'He's in Zurich.' The absurdity of being present only in one's absence derives from the logic of language. We can discern it lurking behind Hegel's laboured paradoxes about being and non-being in the *Logic*. Traces of it can even be detected in the less solemn verbal jokes of Wallace Stevens, especially in 'The Snow Man,' which invites us to play with the difference between the 'Nothing that is not there and the nothing that is' (l. 15).

To refract an oracle through a prism of wit is to dissolve its solemnity in reflective laughter. For the genius of oracles is nothing more nor less than an ability to discern the difference between wisdom and folly, between the spirit of a great biblical prophecy and the absurdities of a Delphic or an Irish bull. An oracle often contrasts seriousness with play. It opposes what is clear in a command with what is indeterminate or baffling in a mystery or enigma. Like the songs of the wise fool in *King Lear*, the oracles of Auden's lover in the ballad 'As I Walked Out One Evening' take urgent possession of his listener. They combine the authority of a biblical prophecy with the absurdity of nonsense poetry and the charm of a nursery rhyme.

> I'll love you, dear, I love you,
> Till China and Africa meet,
> And the river jumps over the mountain
> And the salmon sing in the street.   (ll. 9–12)

Only a fool would think that a fish, taken out of its natural element, the water, would sing instead of perish in the street. And it would take a lunatic to suppose that a river, in defiance of the laws of gravity, could jump over a mountain. And yet the lover's hyperbole is a powerfully prophetic way of saying his love will last forever.

> I'll love you till the ocean
> Is folded and hung up to dry
> And the seven stars go squawking
> Like geese about the sky.   ('As I Walked Out One Evening,' ll. 13–16)

The unobtrusive shock of the ocean's being folded and hung up to dry, like linen, depends on our expectation of some grander outcome. 'I'll love you till the ocean' does what? Is the lover a fool or a connoisseur of bathos? An apocalypse of singing salmon in the previous quatrain may lead us to expect: 'I'll love you till the ocean surrenders its dead or meets the Alps.' Auden jolts the reader by domesticating the mystery. But instead of evoking the idea of apocalypse only to rescind it, he allows his repressed prophecy to resurface in the spectacle of an ocean that has been dried out at the end of time, like the sea in Revelation, when the deep will give up its dead.

A true prophet may make fun of prophecy. The subversion of oracles is typical of both Abraham's ambivalent response to Isaac, his assurance that God himself will provide a burnt offering, and God's superb taunt to Job, his rebuke that Job is trying to make a covenant with a sea beast: 'Canst thou draw out Leviathan? ... Will he make many supplications unto thee? Will he speak soft words unto thee?' (Job 41:1, 3). The prophet may also suffer the indignity of a modern Quixote, tilting at windmills whose vanes keep turning on him. He may seem to play God's fool after God has disappeared and the wisdom of Socrates has been replaced by the mentality of a microchip.

4

The modern world pays little respect to people with ecstatic powers. Their rhapsodies are usually a passport to the nearest madhouse. Yet in Plato's dialogue *Ion* the rhapsode is to Greek poetry what the inspired prophet is to biblical history. Jesus invests prophets with more authority than the 'chief priests and scribes' (Matthew 5:12). And so great is Moses' regard for oracles that he wishes all God's people would be prophets (Numbers 11:29). Both wisdom and prophecy individualize a revolutionary impulse. Jefferson's first Inaugural address is wise, a personal appropriation of republican principles and laws. By contrast, Lincoln's Gettysburg address is prophetic, geared to the future rather than the past and to a new beginning that is already present. By dissolving time and making the present real, a prophecy offers an enlarged vision of the world we now live in. As Frye says, 'space vanishes when we are told ... that the kingdom is entos hymon (Luke 17:21), which may mean among you or in you, but in either case means here, not there' (1982, 130). And yet every oracle is also a shadow of the disturbing truth that 'society will always sooner or later line up with Pilate against the prophet' (1982, 133). Shaw's *Saint Joan* shows that society cannot distinguish a false oracle from a true one: a Deborah from a Witch of Endor.

Dostoevsky's story of the Grand Inquisitor is often interpreted as a condemnation of the church for betraying its founder. If Christ were to come back to earth, the church would find means of crucifying him again. Presumably Christ is a revolutionary who substitutes for the church's closed repository of faith the risk and challenge of a religion that exhorts each believer to be free. In spurning Christ's potentially subversive appeal to cultivate the divinity *entos hymon*, the Inquisitor, like Satan, offers the believer material rewards, including the benefit of turning the stones of the desert to bread. He also gratifies the superstitious habits of the faithful by embracing miracles, and even satisfies a lust for power by forming an empire, the successor of imperial Rome.

But there is another side to Dostoevsky's story. His Inquisitor also wants us to ponder the counter-truth that no society can found its charter or constitution on the oracles of a prophet or a saint. From Spain to Salem, theocracies have proved the soundness of Alexander Pope's insight that the worst of madmen is the saint run mad. The Sermon on the Mount is a moving vision of a highly integrated individual life. But it would be a formula for tyranny if a society were to adopt it as a blueprint for reform. Neither Jesus nor Socrates could survive in such a world. On the contrary, both remind us that no society can absorb a complete human individual. Jesus is a radical and extremist. In Frye's terse phrase, he is 'the one figure in history whom no organised human society could possibly put up with' (1982, 133).

The riddling prophecies of the witches in *Macbeth* detach the mind, but the oracles chanted by Tennyson's lotos-eaters charm and absorb it. As Northrop Frye observes, a riddle is a charm in reverse. Whereas the witches' riddles activate the mind and make it critical, the chant of Tennyson's mariners lulls the mind and puts it to sleep. Jonathan Raban speaks of a 'vein of oracular sad gravity' running through Lowell's late letters (2005, 10). 'Even as one eavesdrops on Lowell's private despair, one can't help admiring the careful eloquence in which it's phrased. He'd always managed to give anguish a voice of memorable grandeur –

> Pity the planet, all joy gone
> from this sweet volcanic cone ...

– and there was a kind of tragic grandeur, tempered with irony, in the way he wrote and rewrote his last days, in both letters and poems' (2005, 10). A similar 'sad gravity' and fitful 'grandeur,' achieved in part by the perfect (if sometimes too predictable) repose of the tranquillizing tetrameter quatrains, remove the mourner in *In Memoriam* from the actual experience of loss by suspending his breath and laying him asleep in body till he becomes a living soul.

A seer who wants to beguile his readers should chant his oracles and punctuate his aphorisms with silence. Even as he charms and seduces the listener, he should suggest aloofness by intimating 'that there are riches in his mind which his actual writing gives no more than a hint of' (Frye, 1963b, 86). As Frye explains, 'the use of discontinuous aphorisms suggests to the reader that here is something he must stop and meditate on, aphorism by aphorism, that he must enter into the writer's mind instead of merely following his discourse. What one says is surrounded by silence, as though a hidden context of mental activity lay behind every formulated sentence' (1963b, 87).

5

All wisdom literature is oracular, but not all oracles are wise. From Ecclesiastes to *The Rambler*, from Johnson's moral essays to 'The Auroras of Autumn,' the achievement of great wisdom writing is its mastery of loss. The balanced phrasing and honest assessments of its oracles compose a kind of liturgy that releases emotion even as it controls the unmotivated depression and grief Freud associates with melancholia. Wisdom literature is often melancholy but seldom melancholic. As Harold Bloom says, 'Johnson is very close to Ecclesiastes and Proverbs, and in their wake he tends not to associate mourning with melancholia, from which he perpetually suffered' (2004, 174).

There is extraordinary pathos in the concluding prayer of 'The Vanity of Human Wishes.' I find it odd that Johnson should warn us of the dangers of a 'specious prayer' (l. 354) at the very moment he invites us to pray. To 'pour forth' one's 'fervors for a healthful mind' would be unremarkable in a Methodist. But this injunction comes from a poet who is just about to invoke the aid of heaven against the charms of false similitude and the baleful fantasies that make a man mad.

> Yet when the sense of sacred presence fires,
> And strong devotion to the skies aspires,
> Pour forth thy fervours for a healthful mind,
> Obedient passions and a will resigned;
> For love, which scarce collective man can fill;
> For patience sovereign o'er transmuted ill;
> For faith, that panting for a happier seat,
> Counts death kind Nature's signal of retreat:
> These goods for man the laws of heaven ordain,
> These goods he grants, who grants the power to gain;
> With these celestial wisdom calms the mind,
> And makes the happiness she does not find   (ll. 357–68)

The author of *Rasselas* is not noted for according a high place to happiness. But now he praises 'celestial Wisdom' for making 'the happiness she does not find' (ll. 367–8). Though a final chiasmus clinches the argument – 'These goods he grants, who grants the power to gain' (l. 366) – the reversing alliterative pattern is persuasive primarily because everything that Johnson the Christian now prays for reverses something that Johnson the stoic and moralist once stood for. Though wisdom can chasten the poet, only religion can teach him patience. Many oracles use incantation and repetition to drug the mind and lull an auditor into easy acceptance. Their use of hypnotic anaphora ('These goods for man,' 'These goods he grants'), of seductive truth claims ('Verily, verily, I say unto you'), and of enchanting exhortations ('Go and do likewise') charm and absorb the mind. 'The Vanity of Human Wishes' is not world-weary or despairing. Like Ecclesiastes, the poem is what one critic calls 'a shrewd, tough-minded attack on the bromides of popular proverbs' (Frye, 2004a, 286). 'With his touchstone of *hebel*, mist or vapors' ('They mount, they shine, evaporate, and fall,' l. 76), Johnson writes as an eighteenth-century Koheleth, collecting but testing the formulas for happiness of many two-dimensional Everymen. The incantatory power of 'The Vanity of Human Wishes' releases an energy that its majestic couplets can barely contain. When we hear the words intoned, their effect is bracing rather than defeatist. Despite the undertow of melancholy, they suspend disbelief and create in each listener a will to affirm.

Frye believes that a wisdom writer's oracles have their own distinctive rhythm, which is 'meditative, irregular, unpredictable, and essentially discontinuous.' We can identify it by unexpected 'coincidences of the sound pattern' (1957, 271) and by 'sound-links, ambiguous sense-links, and memory-links very like that of a dream' (1957, 272). Intuitive and for the most part unconscious, an oracular rhythm cutting across the four-stress metrical rhythm gives power to Claudio's great mediation on death in *Measure for Measure* (1957, 271). To bring out this oracular, associative rhythm Frye graphs the speech's opening line as a pair of internally rhymed phrases followed by an unrhymed unit.

Ay:
But to die ...
    and go
    we know
        not where ...

To loosen rhyme, as in Emily Dickinson, or to free the accents in a line of verse from a fixed number of syllables, as in Hopkins's use of sprung rhythm, is not to abandon an oracular rhythm but to make it more potent and supple.

A less technical way of understanding an oracle is to think of it as a seed-phrase ('I am that I am,' 'You have seen what you have seen') which requires a parable to save it from redundancy. The great command to love one's neighbour as oneself is an oracle, because it is a seed-phrase in search of embodiment. And Christ's parable of the Good Samaritan is precisely the kind of story for whose sake the oracle exists, since only such a story can give the words flesh in a community of people we see and feel concern for.

An oracle often functions as the specifically formal cause that holds a work together. Pumblechook's prophetic words in *Great Expectations*, '"Take warning boy, take warning!" as if it were a well-known fact that I contemplated murdering a near relation, provided I could only induce one to have the weakness to become my benefactor,' have a reverberating power. They catch echoes of words that intimidate Pip elsewhere in the novel and that express the guilt he will feel for causing Magwitch's death and the comparably violent fate of such other 'near relations' as Miss Havisham and Mrs Joe. Again, spoken over Tess just after his marriage, and rippling out into the rest of *Tess of the d'Urbervilles*, there sound and resound Angel Clare's powerfully prophetic words, 'Dead, dead, dead.' As a ghastly commingling of marriage and funeral rites, the words are the buried seed, the apocryphon waiting to be unsealed in Tess's deferred honeymoon with Clare and her subsequent arrest and execution at the end of the novel.

The closing paragraphs of Joyce's short story 'The Dead' and Norman Maclean's 'A River Runs through It' also haunt us like an oracle, because many phrases used earlier in the stories converge on their endings like a paradox on its mystery or a tragedy on its recognition scene. Something similar occurs at the end of *Four Quartets*, where Eliot returns us to 'the unknown remembered gate' in the rose garden at the beginning of 'Burnt Norton.' As a burning bush that is never consumed, the rose plant itself is now on fire. As 'the tongues of flame are in-folded / Into the crowned knot of fire, / And the fire and the rose are one' ('Little Gidding,' V. 44–6), the fire which is torment to the damned and purgation to the penitent turns into ecstasy for the blessed.

As Geoffrey Hartman explains, oracles in Greek tragedy share 'the characteristic of seeming to exist prior to the plays that embody them.' They appear to be 'riddles or gnomic words imposed by tradition and challenging an adequate setting. Take, for example, "So I too must die at the altar like my sister" (Orestes); or "I came to find my son, and I lose my own life" (Tydeus); Or, again, "Here we are doomed to die; for here we were cast forth" (Phineidae, *Poetics* 16.6). These phrases, over-heard, bring about a recognition. Like the voice of the shuttle they have little meaning without a story that sets them.' An oracle, then, is 'a part greater than the whole of which it is a part, a text that demands a context yet is not reducible to it' (Hartman, 1970, 337–8). Instead of leaving us detached or critical, like a witty epigram, an oracle absorbs us. It may daze our mind or even craze us, leaving us as witless for a time as Browning's Lazarus after his brush with infinity. In Northrop Frye's words, prophetic 'forces would not only absorb but annihilate us if they entered ordinary life, but luckily the protecting wall of the imagination is here too. As the German poet Rilke says, we adore them because they disdain to destroy us' (1963a, 42).

Like any great oracle, the lofty coda of 'Lycidas' towers in the sun, partly because Milton, the poet-shepherd, and the author of Revelation speak together for the first time in the poem.

> For *Lycidas* your sorrow is not dead,
> Sunk though he be beneath the watry floar,
> So sinks the day-star in the Ocean bed,
> And yet anon repairs his drooping head,
> And tricks his beams, and with new spangled Ore,
> Flames in the forehead of the morning sky:
> So *Lycidas* sunk low, but mounted high,
> Through the dear might of him that walk'd the waves
> Where other groves, and other streams along,
> With *Nectar* pure his oozy *Locks* he laves,
> And hears the unexpressive nuptiall Song ...   ('Lycidas,' ll. 166–76)

At first a series of strict couplets ('bed,' 'head'; 'sky,' 'high') confine the sound in a narrow channel. But like a voice compressed in a trumpet, the proclamation then springs out more briskly and strikes us with greater impact in the more widely distanced rhyming of 'watry floor' with 'spangled Ore' and of 'waves' with 'laves.' Milton also uses the mid-line caesura – 'So Lycidas sunk low, but mounted high' – as a great cantilever or hinge on which the drowned youth can pivot. If the mourner's own ascent had been less sheer and precipitous, it would have been harder to recognize the depth of the abyss out of which he has climbed. Without the majestic reversals of sound and sense ('Lycidas sunk low,' 'mounted ... might of him'), it would also have been harder for the poet to achieve his own reversal and turn.

As the mourner swivels on the hinge of the spacious phrase 'And yet anon,' the relentless sinking of both the drowned Lycidas and the daystar is spectacularly reversed. The pivot upon that phrase is made more expansive by the chiasmus of sound, which repeats the rhymes in reverse order: 'floar,' 'bed,' 'head,' 'Ore' (ll. 167–70). 'Floar' and 'bed' are literally 'repaired' in the second pair of end words. And with the repairing of the rhymes comes the great reparation of Lycidas, mounted high like the sun, made golden now and lucid. Though the reparation of the sun, flaming in the forehead of the morning sky, is logically the end of one unit of thought, the solemn break after 'sky,' made more emphatic by the colon, is partly bridged by the deft use of a couplet: 'sky' and 'high.'

> Flames in the forehead of the morning sky:
> So *Lycidas* sunk low, but mounted high ...   ('Lycidas,' 171–2)

The break is not as great as we might first think. The chiasmus of sound and sense in the daystar's reparation can also be appropriated by Lycidas, who is now assimilated by the bridging rhyme to the same pattern of reversal.

The power to touch common emotions demands from Milton both a confidence in the natural cycle of setting and rising suns and faith in the dear might of a much greater Sun. The dominion of truth that can be felt repairing the sun and exalting Lycidas is an obvious appeal to emotion, and believer and atheist alike are poorer in spirit if unable to respond to it. As conclusive couplets anchor the causeways on secure pillars of sound, dispersed rhymes can be used to throw an arch forward, building a bridge into an uncertain future. Prophecy and hope turn the most ordinary analogies between the drowned man and the sun into oracles of such renovating power that few lovers of poetry can 'peruse the climax ... without a thrill such as scarcely any other verses in the language excite' (More, 1961, 93).

To create the impression of depth beneath a surface of inarticulate speech, a wisdom writer may repeat the same words, charging them with new meaning each time they are used. When Frost's farmer says 'I have promises to keep, / And miles to go before I sleep, / And miles to go before I sleep,' the drowsy rhythm pulls us into the orbit of a mind that is half in love with easeful death. The repetition makes us intimate with his inmost fears and desires. Equally compelling but more disturbing is the fivefold repetition of 'never' in *King Lear*. As Stephen Greenblatt explains, 'repeated words of this kind are drained of whatever meaning they may have started with; they become instead placeholders for silent thinking' (2004, 281). Brought too close for comfort to the suffering Lear, a listener may find that each repetition shrinks the distance between himself and the oracle, making it impossible to achieve stable critical detachment. Like Macbeth's 'Tomorrow, and tomorrow, and tomorrow,' Lear's 'Never, never, never, never, never' has nothing to do with dictionary definitions. As R.P. Blackmur observes, the repetitions are 'an obsessive gesture of the poet himself, made out of the single iterated syllables intensified into a half-throttled cry' (1954, 17). Lear feels existence until he can no longer stand it, and is made wordless as a result.

Imaginative generosity on the part of poets may turn even the most familiar words into engulfing gestures. It may also create a measure of dramatic confusion, as when Yeats cries out in ecstasy or anguish (it is hard to tell which): 'O heart, O heart! if she'd but turn her head / You'd know the folly of being comforted.' Is he protesting that he has no need of consolation or that he is inconsolable? Like many oracles that look two ways at once, the impassioned words give voice to depths of feeling that overwhelm the poet by dragging after them their own opposites, not for contradiction but development. Even as they release a great cry or gesture, such words acquire the anonymous authority of an oracle. As Elizabeth Drew says, 'Yeats is *inside* [the poem], and so are we as we read it.' The prophetic repetition of 'O heart, O heart' expresses 'the whole heartache of the world at the inexorable coming of age, as well as the personal passion of revolt of the poet himself at the change in his beloved' (1933, 109).

When Lear swears by Apollo after banishing Kent from his sight, Kent cuts him short with an oracle of his own devising: 'Now by Apollo, King, / Thou swear'st thy gods in vain' (*King Lear*, I.i.160–1). In his hideous rashness, Lear offends the god of light, the oracle of Delphi, by failing to know himself. A man who is wise must avoid the error of both a comic prophet like Malvolio and a tragic prophet like Macbeth, who are each deceived by oracles of fate. As a comic prophet of his own greatness, Malvolio shows there is a way things are and only a fool forgets what it is. As a tragic prophet building on the prophecies of the three witches and the will to power of his ferociously determined wife, Macbeth demonstrates that there is a way things are and only a fool presumes to know what it is. Without assuming that character drags fortune in its train and moulds the gods to its own shape, a wise man has enough trust in reason to heed the injunction of the great oracle at Delphi: 'know thyself.'

Instead of commanding silence, like a magisterial Moses, Jesus uses silent-speaking parables to help us find and develop our own voice. The alternative is to turn thinkers into slaves who fear the freedom of a bold idea. As Nietzsche's Zarathustra predicts, a slave morality throws 'injustice and dirt at the solitary' and crucifies 'those who devise their own virtue' (1961, 90). A slave lacks the spark of invention, and rejects the challenge of contributing to knowledge. He commits the ultimate treason of renouncing the demanding but liberating high adventure of a life devoted to thinking for oneself. When a daughter I love commits suicide, I ask grotesque and dreadful questions. Did I murder my daughter? What could I have done to avert the horror of her end? To live with these questions and their answers is to turn oracles of our end into life-and-death issues. I am appalled that Dante, our greatest poet of the underworld, should dispatch all suicides to a low region of hell. If Virgil offered me the same safe conduct he offered Dante, I would willingly take a tour of hell in order to produce a better estimate of it. In my audit of punishments, the Christians who demonized the underworld would receive a harsher penalty than Virgil. And Dante would be surprised to find himself in hell for having invented it. His only extenuation would be his secret rebellion against the terrors he creates. His *Inferno* embodies views that Dante the Christian thinks he should hold. Half secretly he repudiates them. Another unofficial view, most often associated with Dante the pilgrim, extends a compassionate and understanding heart toward people in torment. Dante the poet of Christian eschatology thinks he should discourage compassion, but often he embraces it. The *Inferno* would be unreadable if Dante, like Shakespeare, were not also a poet of inward insurrection. His pilgrim is so at war with the hell invented by Dante the prophet-poet that, face to face with Piero delle Vigne in the circle of suicides, he utters a poignant cry to Virgil: 'Ask him again ..., for I cannot, such pity fills my heart!' ('Domanda tu ancora / ... ch'i' non potrei, tanta pietà m'accora!,' *Inferno*, canto 13, ll. 82, 84).

Though Oscar Wilde foretells that each man kills the thing he loves, I hazard a counter-prophecy: that lost souls 'form part of the resurrection because their lives have been part of the divine agony and endurance' (Frye, 2004a, 171). My daughter and I loved each other, and I know love is the only language we can be sure God understands and speaks. When an oracle from the underworld leaves us badly shaken or unnerved, it should prompt us to invent our own oracle: '"Fool," said my Muse to me, "look in thy heart and write"' (Philip Sidney, *Astrophel and Stella*, sonnet 1, l. 14). According to legend, in her last oracle, a funeral epigram to the cult of Apollo, Pythia counselled the suppliant to consult hereafter, not the shrine of the god, but the temple of his own heart and mind, the haunt and main region of her prophecies.

Since most believers do not reason, and hardly ever can, they may find like Wordsworth, in his movingly honest 'Ode to Duty,' that an 'unchartered freedom' to question the gods and interpret their oracles is a burden and oppression. Feeling 'the weight of chance desires,' Wordsworth exercises his freedom not to be free. Unlike Sartre, who believes we are all condemned to freedom, Wordsworth seeks in bondage to a stern lawgiver a control or 'quietness of thought' that always is the same (ll. 35–40). And yet to maintain that a Father of light would require or for that matter even accept from the only one of his creatures whom he endowed with reason the sacrifice of a fool seems to Wordsworth's friend Coleridge the height of blasphemy. As Dostoevesky's Grand Inquisitor perceives, an oracle that takes away from its interrogators the freedom to interpret the oracle perpetuates this blasphemy. Simone Weil believes it is an offence against Christ himself, who said 'I am the truth,' to 'limit the operations of intelligence or the illuminations of love in the domain of thought' (1974, 712).

To shield wisdom writing from debate is like confining religion to the divinity schools, or putting literary sublimities in quarantine for fear of infecting the dialect of the tribe. Instead of starving on a poverty of readings imposed by canons of correctness, votaries of wisdom should feel free to feast off the rich variety of meanings that has always been a distinguishing property of great secular and religious writing. If 'the sacrifice of the intellect is an abomination to God,' then the citadel of faith is always in need of a counter-oracle. It requires a new prophet like Coleridge, someone who can 'put heart in all those queasy intellectuals who can't resist cutting the throats of their critical reason on the altar of an introverted acceptance of tradition' (Frye, 2004b, 146, 9). Montaigne complains that our wisdom writers 'stuff' the wise sayings of Cicero 'into our memory, fully feathered, like oracles in which the letters and syllables are the substance of the matter' (1958, 57). To be as sad and wise as his Ancient Mariner, Coleridge must become his own Delphi, a living oracle. When Tennyson says more things are wrought by prayer than this world dreams of, he is not thinking of the closed prayer of a suppliant, which is too often a disease of both intellect and will. He is thinking rather of the open prayer of a prophet, which is attentiveness without an object. Though it is hard for Dante the pilgrim to say farewell to Virgil in the *Purgatorio*, every student must outgrow his mentor in order to become himself. In an age of freedom a good disciple becomes a bad prophet when he is unable to survive his master.

Works Cited

Abrams, M.H. 1989. *Doing Things with Texts: Essays in Criticism and Critical Theory*. New York and London: W.W. Norton.

Armstrong, Isobel. 1994. *Victorian Poetry: Poetry, Poetics, and Politics*. London: Routledge.

Arnold, Matthew. 1960. 'On Translating Homer: Last Words.' In *The Complete Prose Works of Matthew Arnold*, ed. R.H. Super. Vol. 1. Ann Arbor: University of Michigan Press.

– 1961. *Poetry and Criticism of Matthew Arnold*. Ed. A. Dwight Culler. Boston: Houghton Mifflin.

– 1965. *The Poems of Matthew Arnold*. Ed. Kenneth Allott. London: Longmans, Green.

Auden, W.H. 1976. *W.H. Auden: Collected Poems*. Ed. Edward Mendelson. New York: Random House.

Barber, C.L. 1972. *Shakespeare's Festive Comedy: A Study of Dramatic Form in Its Relation to Social Customs*. Princeton: Princeton University Press.

Bate, W. Jackson. 1975. *Samuel Johnson*. Washington, DC: Counterpoint.

Bayley, John. 1981. *Shakespeare and Tragedy*. London: Routledge and Kegan Paul.

Berkeley, George. 1989. *Philosophical Commentaries by George Berkeley: Transcribed from the Manuscript and Edited with an Introduction and Index by George H. Thomas, Explanatory Notes by A.A. Luce*. New York and London: Garland.

– 1993. *George Berkeley Alciphron in Focus*. Ed. David Berman. London: Routledge.

Berlinski, David. 1997. *A Tour of the Calculus*. New York: Vintage.

Bishop, Jonathan. 1972. *Something Else*. New York: George Braziller.

Blackmur, R.P. 1954. *Language as Gesture*. New York: Columbia University Press.

Blake, William. 1965. *The Poetry and Prose of William Blake*. Ed. David V. Erdman, commentary by Harold Bloom. New York: Doubleday.

Bloom, Harold. 1961. *The Visionary Company: A Reading of English Romantic Poetry*. Garden City, NY: Doubleday.

– 1998. *Shakespeare and the Invention of the Human*. New York: Riverhead Books.

– 2002. *Genius: A Mosaic of One Hundred Exemplary and Creative Minds*. New York: Warner.

– 2003. *Hamlet: Poem Unlimited*. New York: Riverhead

– 2004. *Where Shall Wisdom Be Found?* New York: Riverhead.

Bolan, Anne C. 1973. *What the Thunder Really Said: A Retrospective Essay on the Making of the Waste Land*. Montreal and London: McGill-Queen's University Press.

Booth, Stephen. 1983. *King Lear, Macbeth, Indefinition, and Tragedy*. New Haven and London: Yale University Press.

Bourgeault, Cynthia. 2003. *The Wisdom Way of Knowing: Reclaiming an Ancient Tradition to Awaken the Heart*. San Francisco: Jossey-Bass.

– 2004. *Centering Prayer and Inner Awakening*. Cambridge, MA: Cowley.

Bradley, F.H. 1876. *Ethical Studies*. Oxford: Clarendon Press. Reprinted London: Oxford University Press, 1970. Edited by Richard Wollheim.

– 1883. *The Principles of Logic*. London: Kegan Paul, Trench.

– 1893. *Appearance and Reality: A Metaphysical Essay*. Oxford: Clarendon Press.

– 1930. *Aphorisms*. Oxford: Clarendon Press.

Bromwich, David. 2006. 'Abraham Lincoln.' *New York Review of Books*. October, 47–9, and November, 26–8.

Brontë, Charlotte. 1957. *Villette*. London: J.M. Dent and Sons.

Brower, Reuben A. 1962. *The Fields of Light: An Experiment in Critical Reading*. New York: Oxford University Press.

– 1963. *The Poetry of Robert Frost: Constellations of Intention*. New York: Oxford University Press.

– 1971. *Hero and Saint: Shakespeare and the Graeco-Roman Heroic Tradition*. New York and Oxford: Oxford University Press.

Browne, Stephen Howard. 2003. *Jefferson's Call for Nationhood*. College Station: Texas A and M University Press.

Browning, Robert. 1981. *Robert Browning: The Poems*. Ed. John Pettigrew and Thomas J. Collins. 2 vols. New York: Penguin.

– 2001. *The Ring and the Book. Robert Browning*. Ed. Richard D. Altick and Thomas J. Collins. Peterborough, Ont.: Broadview Press.

Bruns, Gerald. 1974. *Modern Poetry and the Idea of Language: A Critical and Historical Study*. New Haven: Yale University Press.

Buckler, William E. 1980. 'Tennyson's "The Lotos-Eaters."' In *The Victorian Imagination: Essays in Aesthetic Exploration*. New York and London: New York University Press.

Burgess, Anthony. 1973. *Joysprick*. London: Deutsch.

Bush, Douglas. 1971. *Matthew Arnold: A Survey of His Poetry and Prose*. New York: Collier.

Cameron, J.M. 1962. *The Night Battle*. London: Longmans, Green.

Camus, Albert. 1955. *The Myth of Sisyphus and Other Essays*. New York: Vintage.

Carlyle, Thomas. 1970. *Thomas Carlyle: Sartor Resartus and Selected Prose*. Ed. Herbert Sussman. New York: Holt, Rinehart and Winston.

Carse, James P. 1986. *Finite and Infinite Games: A Vision of Life as Play and Possibility*. New York: Ballantine Books.

– 2008. *The Religious Case against Belief*. New York: Penguin Press.

Chadwick, Owen. 1983. *Newman*. Oxford: Oxford University Press.

Chambers, Robert. 1844. 'Hypothesis of the Development of the Vegetable and Animal Kingdoms.' In *Vestiges of the Natural History of Creation*. London: John Churchill, 1844. Reprinted in *Nineteenth Century Science: A Selection of Original Texts*. Ed. A.S. Weber. Peterborough, Ont.: Broadview Press, 1999.

Chesterton, G.K. 1903. *Robert Browning*. London: Macmillan.

– 1936. *Autobiography*. London: Sheed and Ward.

– 1939. *Orthodoxy*. London: Sheed and Ward.

– 1947. *The Victorian Age in Literature*. New York and London: Oxford University Press.

– 1996. *The Man Who Was Thursday: A Nightmare*. New York and London: Oxford University Press.

Clampitt, Amy. 1985. *What the Light Was Like*. New York: Knopf.

Cohen, Daniel J. 2007. *Equations from God: Pure Mathematics and Victorian Faith*. Baltimore: Johns Hopkins University Press.

Cohen, Ted. 1999. *Jokes: Philosophical Thoughts on Joking Matters*. Chicago: University of Chicago Press.

Coleridge, Samuel Taylor. 1905. *Aids to Reflection*. Edinburgh: John Grant.

– 1969. *Coleridge on Shakespeare*. Ed. Terence Hawkes. Harmondsworth: Penguin.

– 1984. *Marginalia*. Ed. George Whalley. *The Collected Works of Samuel Taylor Coleridge*. Vol. 12. Princeton: Princeton University Press.

Cook, Eleanor. 2006. *Enigmas and Riddles in Literature*. Cambridge: Cambridge University Press.

Copleston, Frederick. 1967. *A History of Philosophy: Modern Philosophy Bentham* to *Russell*. Vol. 8. Part I: *British Empiricism and the Idealist Movement in Great Britain*. Garden City, NY: Doubleday.

Cox, Harvey. 2004. *When Jesus Came to Harvard: Making Moral Choices Today*. New York: Houghton Mifflin.

Culler, A. Dwight. 1977. *The Poetry of Tennyson*. New Haven and London: Yale University Press.

Davenport, Guy. 1988. 'Journal.' In *Our Private Lives: Journals, Notebooks, and Diaries*, ed. Daniel Halpern, 76–83. Hopewell, NJ: Ecco Press.

Dawkins, Richard. 1987. *The Blind Watch-Maker: Why the Evidence of Evolution Reveals a Universe without Design*. New York: Norton.

Desmond, Adrian. 1997. *Huxley: From Devil's Disciple to Evolution's High Priest*. London: Penguin.

Dickens, Charles. 1952. *Great Expectations*. London: William Heinemann.

Dickinson, Emily. 1955. *The Poems of Emily Dickinson*. Ed. Thomas H. Johnson. 3 vols. Cambridge: Belknap Press of Harvard University.

Didion, Joan. 2006. *The Year of Magical Thinking*. New York: Vintage.

Donne, John. 1946. Meditations from *Devotions Upon Emergent Occasions* and selected *Sermons*. *Seventeenth-Century Prose and Poetry*. Ed. Robert P. Tristram Coffin and Alexander M. Witherspoon. New York: Harcourt, Brace.

– 1967. *The Complete Poetry of John Donne*. Ed. John T. Shawcross. New York: Doubleday.

Douglas-Fairhurst, Robert. 2002. *Victorian Afterlives: Shaping of Influence in Nineteenth-Century Literature*. Oxford: Oxford University Press.

Drew, Elizabeth. 1933. *Discovering Poetry: An Introduction to the Nature of Poetry and the Poetic Experience*. New York: W.W. Norton and Co.

Einhorn, Lois J. 1992. *Abraham Lincoln the Orator: Penetrating the Lincoln Legend*. Westport, CT: Greenwood Press.

Eliot, George. 1956. *Middlemarch*. Cambridge, MA: Riverside.

Eliot, T.S. 1932. *Selected Essays*. London: Faber and Faber.

– 1934. *Collected Poems, 1909–1935*. New York: Harcourt, Brace.

– 1935. *Murder in the Cathedral*. London: Faber and Faber.

– 1943. *Four Quartets*. New York: Harcourt, Brace.

– 1961. *On Poetry and Poets*. New York: Noonday.

– 1964. *Knowledge and Experience in the Philosophy of F.H. Bradley*. Ed. Anne Bolgan. London: Faber and Faber.

Emerson, Ralph Waldo. 1908. *Emerson's Essays*, second series. New York: Thomas Y. Crowell and Co.

– 1965. 'Fate.' In *American Literary Masters*, ed. Charles R. Anderson, 602–20. New York: Holt, Rinehart and Winston.

Fackenheim, Emil L. 1961. *Metaphysics and Historicity*. Milwaukee: Marquette University Press.

Ferrier, J.F. 1842. 'Berkeley and Idealism.' *Blackwoods Edinburgh Magazine*. Vol. 51.

– 1854. *The Institutes of Metaphysics: Theory of Knowing and Being*. Edinburgh and London: Blackwood.

Forster, E.M. 1924. *A Passage to India*. New York: Harcourt, Brace.

Frost, Robert. 1968. *Selected Prose of Robert Frost*. Ed. Hyde Cox and Edward Connery Lathem. New York: Collier.

– 1969. *The Poetry of Robert Frost*. Ed. Edward Connery Lathem. New York: Holt, Rinehart and Winston.

Frye, Northrop. 1947. *Fearful Symmetry*. Princeton: Princeton University Press.

– 1957. *Anatomy of Criticism: Four Essays*. Princeton: Princeton University Press.

– 1963a. *The Educated Imagination*. Toronto: CBC Publications.

– 1963b. *The Well-Tempered Critic*. Bloomington: Indiana University Press.

– 1963c. *Fables of Identity: Studies in Poetic Mythology*. New York: Harcourt, Brace.

– 1967a. 'The Knowledge of Good and Evil.' In *The Morality of Scholarship*, Ed. Max Black. Ithaca: Cornell University Press.

– 1967b. *Fools of Time: Studies in Shakespearean Tragedy*. Toronto: University of Toronto Press.

– 1971. *The Critical Path: An Essay on the Social Context of Literary Criticism*. Bloomington: Indiana University Press.

– 1976a. *The Secular Scripture: A Study of the Structure of Romance*. Cambridge, MA: Harvard University Press.

– 1976b. *Spiritus Mundi: Essays on Literature, Myth, and Society*. Bloomington: Indiana University Press.

– 1982. *The Great Code: The Bible and Literature*. Toronto: Academic Press Canada.

– 1986. *Northrop Frye on Shakespeare*. New Haven and London: Yale University.

– 1990. *Words with Power: Being a Second Study of the Bible and Literature*. New York: Harcourt Brace Jovanovich.

– 1991. *The Double Vision: Language and Meaning in Religion*. Toronto: University of Toronto Press.

– 2000. *Northrop Frye's Late Notebooks, 1982–1990: Architecture of the Spiritual World*. Ed. Robert Denham. Toronto: University of Toronto Press.

– 2002. *The 'Third Book' Notebooks of Northrop Frye, 1964–1972*. Ed. Michael Dolzani. Toronto: University of Toronto Press.

– 2004a. *Wit and Wisdom from the Notebooks and Diaries*. Selected by Robert Denham. Toronto: House of Anansi Press.

– 2004b. *Northrop Frye's Notebooks on Romance*. Ed. Michael Dolzani. Toronto: University of Toronto Press.

Funk, Robert W. 2002. 'The Once and Future Testaments.' In *The Canon Debate*, ed. Lee Martin McDonald and James A. Sanders, 541–57. Peabody, MA: Hendrickson.

Gardner, Martin. 1996. *The Universe in a Handkerchief: Lewis Carroll's Mathematical Recreations, Games, Puzzles, and Word Plays*. New York: Copernicus.

Gartner, Bertil. 1961. *The Theology of the Gospel of Thomas*. Trans. Eric J. Sharpe. St. James's Palace: Collins.

Gilson, Etienne. 1941. *God and Philosophy*. New Haven: Yale University Press.

The Gospel of Thomas. 2003. Trans. Jean-Yves Leloup. Boston and London: Shambhala.

Gray, Thomas. 1937. *Works*. Ed. A.L. Poole and Leonard Whibley. Oxford: Clarendon Press.

Greenblatt, Stephen. 2004. *Will in the World: How Shakespeare Became Shakespeare*. New York and London: W.W. Norton.

Hair, Donald S. 1991. *Tennyson's Language*. Toronto: University of Toronto Press.

Halpern, Daniel, ed. 1988. *Our Private Lives: Journals, Notebooks and Diaries*. Hopewell, NJ: Ecco Press.

Hardy, Thomas. 1937. *The Complete Poetical Works of Thomas Hardy*. Ed. Samuel Hynes. 2 vols. Oxford: Clarendon Press.

Hart, Jeffrey. 2001. *Smiling through the Cultural Catastrophe: Toward the Revival of Higher Education*. New Haven and London: Yale University Press.

Hartman, Geoffrey. 1964. *Wordsworth's Poetry, 1787–1814*. New Haven and London. Yale University Press.

– 1970. *Beyond Formalism: Literary Essays, 1958–1970*. New Haven and London: Yale University Press.

– 2007. *A Scholar's Tale: Intellectual Journey of a Displaced Child of Europe*. New York: Fordham University Press.

Hawthorne, Nathaniel. 1959. *Selected Tales and Sketches*. New York: Rinehart.

Heaney, Seamus. 2002. *Finders Keepers: Selected Prose, 1971–2001*. London: Faber and Faber.

Hecht, Anthony. 2003. *Melodies Unheard: Essays on the Mysteries of Poetry*. Baltimore and London: Johns Hopkins University Press.

Hegel, G.W.F. 1975. *Hegel's Aesthetics: Lectures on Fine Art by G.W.F. Hegel*. Trans. T.M. Knox, 2 vols. Oxford: Clarendon Press. Originally published 1835.

Herbert, Christopher. 2001. *Victorian Relativity: Radical Thought and Scientific Discovery*. Chicago and London: University of Chicago Press.

Herbert, George. 1941. *Works*. Ed. F.E. Hutchinson. Oxford: Clarendon Press.

Hill, Geoffrey. 1983. *The Mystery of the Charity of Charles Peguy.* London: André Deutsch.

Hollander, John. 1975. *Vision and Resonance: Two Senses of Poetic Form.* New York: Oxford University Press.

Hone, J.M., and M.M. Rossi. 1931. *Bishop Berkeley: His Life, Writings, and Philosophy.* New York: Macmillan.

Hopkins, G.M. 1938. *Letters of G.M. Hopkins.* Ed. Claude Colleer Abbott. London: Oxford University Press.

– 1953. *Poems and Prose.* Ed. W.H. Gardner. Harmondsworth: Penguin.

– 1959. *The Sermons and Devotional Writings of Gerard Manley Hopkins.* Ed. Humphrey House and Graham Storey. London: Oxford University Press.

– 1967. *Poems.* Ed. W.H. Gardner and Norman Mackenzie. 4th ed. London: Oxford University Press.

Houghton, Walter. 1957. *The Victorian Frame of Mind: 1830–1870.* New Haven and London: Yale University Press.

Hughes, Patrick, and George Brecht. 1975. *A Panoply of Paradoxes: Vicious Circles and Infinity.* Garden City, NY: Doubleday

Huxley, T.H. 1904–25. *Collected Essays.* 9 vols. London: Macmillan.

James, D.G. 1937. *Scepticism and Poetry.* London: Allen and Unwin.

James, Henry. 1962. *The Turn of the Screw and Other Short Novels.* New York: Signet.

James, William. 1892. *Psychology: Briefer Course.* New York: Henry Holt and Co.

– 1909. *The Will to Believe and Other Essays in Popular Philosophy.* London: Longmans, Green, and Co.

– 1911. *Pragmatism: A New Name for Some Old Ways of Thinking.* London: Longmans, Green, and Co.

Jamison, Kay Redfield. 2000. *Night Falls Fast: Understanding Suicide.* New York: Vintage.

Jefferson, Thomas. 1801, March 4. *Jefferson's First Inaugural Address.* Raleigh, NC: Alex Electronic Catalogue.

Jenkyns, Richard. 2005. *A Fine Brush of Irony: An Appreciation of Jane Austen.* Oxford: Oxford University Press.

Johnson, Samuel. 1941. *The Poems of Samuel Johnson.* Ed. David Nichol Smith and Edward L. McAdam. Oxford: Clarendon Press.

– 1959. *Samuel Johnson: Rasselas, Poems, and Selected Prose.* Ed. Bertrand H. Bronson. New York: Rinehart.

Jonson, Ben. 1963. *The Complete Poetry of Ben Jonson.* Ed. William B. Hunter, Jr. New York: Norton.

Joyce, James. 1962. *Dubliners.* New York: Viking.

Kahn, C. 1979. *The Art and Thought of Heraclitus*. Cambridge: Cambridge University Press.

Kaplan, Robert and Ellen. 2003. *The Art of the Infinite: The Pleasure of Mathematics*. New York: Oxford University Press.

Kazin, Alfred. 1997. *God and the American Writer*. New York: Alfred A. Knopf.

Keats, John. 1978. *The Poems of John Keats*. Ed. Jack Stillinger. Cambridge, MA: Belknap Press of Harvard University.

Kenner, Hugh. 1948. *Paradox in Chesterton*. London: Sheed and Ward.

– 1962. 'Bradley.' In *T.S. Eliot: A Collection of Critical Essays*, ed. Hugh Kenner. Englewood Cliffs: Prentice-Hall.

Kermode, Frank. 2000. *Shakespeare's Language*. London and New York: Penguin.

– 2005. 'Arguing with God.' *New York Review of Books*, 1 December, 40–2. Review of Harold Bloom, *Jesus and Yahweh: The Name Divine* and Robert Pinsky, *The Life of David*.

Kierkegaard, Søren. 1960. *The Diary of Søren Kierkegaard*. Trans. Gerda M. Andersen. New York: Philosophical Library.

Landa, Louis A., ed. 1960. *Gulliver's Travels and Other Writings by Jonathan Swift*. Boston: Houghton Mifflin Co.

Larkin, Philip, 1989. *Collected Poems*. New York: Farrar, Strauss and Giroux.

Lewis. C.S. 1956. *Till We Have Faces: A Myth Retold*. Grand Rapids, MI: William B. Eerdmans.

Lincoln, Abraham. 1863. *Long Remembered: Facsimiles of the Five Versions of the Gettysburg Address in the Handwriting of Abraham Lincoln*. Ed. Lloyd A. Dunlap. Library of Congress, 1963.

– 1865, March 4. *Lincoln's Second Inaugural Address*. Champaign, IL: Project Gutenberg.

Lipking, Lawrence. 1981. *The Life of the Poet: Beginning and Ending Poetic Careers*. Chicago: University of Chicago Press.

Lowell, Robert. 1946. *The Mills of the Kavanaughs*. New York: Harcourt Brace.

– 1964. 'On the Gettysburg Address.' In *Lincoln and the Gettysburg Address: Commemorative Papers*, ed. Allan Nevins, 72–87. Urbana: University of Illinois Press.

Luce, A.A. 1945. *Berkeley's Immaterialism: A Commentary on His 'A Treatise Concerning the Principles of Human Knowledge'*. London: Thomas Nelson and Sons.

Mack, Burton L. 1990. *Rhetoric and the New Testament*. Minneapolis: Fortress Press.

Maclean, Norman. 1992. *A River Runs through It and Other Stories*. New York: Pocket Books.

Mansel, H.L. 1867. *The Limits of Religious Thought Examined in Eight Lectures.* London: J. Murray.

Martin, Robert Bernard. 1980. *Tennyson: The Unquiet Heart.* Oxford: Clarendon Press.

Melvill, Henry. 1838. *Sermons of Henry Melvill, B.D.* Ed. C.P. McIlvaine. New York: Swords, Stanford, and Co.

Merton, Thomas. 1981. *The Literary Essays of Thomas Merton.* Ed. Patrick Hart. New York: New Directions.

– 1989. *A Merton Reader.* Ed. Thomas P. McDonnell. New York: Image Books

Mill, John Stuart. 1962. *Earlier Letters, 1812-1848.* In *Collected Works of John Stuart Mill,* ed. J.M. Robson and Francis E. Mineka, vols. 12 and 13. Toronto: University of Toronto Press.

– 1974. *System of Logic: Ratiocinative and Inductive.* In *Collected Works of John Stuart Mill,* ed. J.M. Robson and R.F. McRae, vols. 7 and 8. Toronto: University of Toronto Press.

Milosz, Czeslaw. 1988. 'Fragments from a Journal.' *Our Private Lives: Journals, Notebooks, and Diaries,* ed. Daniel Halpern, 288–98. Hopewell, NJ: Ecco Press.

Montaigne, Michel de. 1958. *Montaigne Essays.* Trans. J.M. Cohen. Baltimore: Penguin.

More, Paul Elmore. 1961. 'How to Read Lycidas.' In *Milton's 'Lycidas': The Tradition and the Poem,* ed. A.C. Patrides. New York: Holt, Rinehart and Winston.

Murdoch, Iris. 1992. *Metaphysics as a Guide to Morals.* New York: Allen Lane.

Nagel, Thomas. 1986. *The View from Nowhere.* New York: Oxford University Press.

Newman, John Henry. 1887. *Sermons Preached before the University of Oxford between 1826 and 1843.* London: Rivingtons.

– 1906. *An Essay on the Development of Christian Doctrine.* New York: Longmans, Green.

– 1968. *Apologia Pro Vita Sua.* Ed. David J. DeLaura. New York: Norton.

Niebuhr, Reinhold. 1964. 'The Religion of Abraham Lincoln.' In *Lincoln and the Gettsyburg Address: Commemorative Papers,* ed. Allan Nevins, 72–87. Urbana: University of Illinois Press.

Nietzsche, Friedrich. 1961. *Thus Spoke Zarathustra.* Trans. R.J. Hollingdale. London: Penguin.

– 1989. *Beyond Good and Evil: Prelude to a Philosophy of the Future.* Trans. Walter Kaufmann. New York: Vintage.

Owen, G.E.L. 2001. 'Zeno and the Mathematicians.' *Zeno's Paradoxes.* Cambridge: Hackett.

Pagels, Elaine. 1979. *The Gnostic Gospels*. New York: Random House.
– 2003. *Beyond Belief: The Secret Gospel of Thomas*. New York: Random House.
Pearsall, Cornelia. 2008. *Tennyson's Rapture: Transformation in the Victorian Dramatic Monologue*. Oxford: Oxford University Press.
Petsas, Photios. 1981. *Delphi: Monuments and Museums*. Athens: Krene
Plath, Sylvia. 2008. *The Collected Poems*. Ed. Ted Hughes. New York: Harper Perennial Modern Classics.
Poirier, Richard. 1977. *Robert Frost: The Work of Knowing*. New York: Oxford University Press.
Pope, Alexander. 1963. *The Poems of Alexander Pope*. New Haven: Yale University Press.
Raban, Jonathan. 2005. 'A Tragic Grandeur.' *New York Review of Books*. 23 June, 9–12.
Ratzinger, Joseph. 2007. *Jesus of Nazareth*. Trans. Adrian J. Walker. New York: Doubleday.
Richardson, James. 1988. *Vanishing Lives: Style and Self in Tennyson, D.G. Rossetti, Swinburne, and Yeats*. Charlottesville: University Press of Virginia.
Ricks, Christopher. 1972. *Tennyson*. New York: Macmillan.
– 1987. *The Force of Poetry*. Oxford: Oxford University Press.
– 1993. *Beckett's Dying Words*. Oxford: Oxford University Press.
Rosenbaum, S.P., ed. 1971. *English Literature and British Philosophy: A Collection of Essays*. Chicago: University of Chicago Press.
Rossetti, Christina. 1979–90. *The Complete Poems of Christina Rossetti*. Ed. Rebecca Crump. 3 vols. Baton Rouge: Louisiana State University Press.
Rucker, Rudy. 1983. *Infinity and the Mind: The Science and Philosophy of the Infinite*. New York: Bantam.
Rumi. 1995. *Rumi, Selected Poems*. Trans. Coleman Barks. London: Penguin.
Ruskin, John. 1903–12. *The Works of John Ruskin*. Ed. E.T. Cook and Alexander Wedderburn. London: G. Allen, Longmans, Green.
Rymer, Thomas. 1971. *Critical Works of Thomas Rymer*. Ed. Curt H. Zimansky. Westport, CT: Greenwood Press.
Sagan, Carl. 1980. *Cosmos*. New York: Random House.
Salmon, Wesley. 2001. 'Introduction.' In *Zeno's Paradoxes*, ed. Wesley Salmon. Cambridge: Hackett.
Santayana, George. 1967. *Soliloquies in England and Later Soliloquies*. Ann Arbor: University of Michigan Press.
Schleiermacher, Friedrich Daniel Ernst. 1836. *Schleiermacher's Introductions to the Dialogues of Plato*. Translated by W. Dobson. Trinity Street, Cambridge: J.J. Deighton.
– 1928. *The Christian Faith*. Ed. H.R. Mackintosh and J.S. Stewart. Trans. of the 2nd German ed. Edinburgh: T. and T. Clark.

Shakespeare, William. 1942. *The Complete Plays and Poems of William Shake-speare*. Ed. W.A. Neilson and C.J. Hill. Cambridge, MA: Houghton Mifflin.

Shaw, G.B. 1946. *Man and Superman*. Edinburgh: Penguin.

– 1967. *Shaw on Religion: Irreverent Observations by a Man of Faith*. Ed. Warren Sylvester Smith. New York: Dodd, Mead and Co.

– 1993. *The Sayings of Bernard Shaw*. Ed. Joseph Spence. London: Duckworth.

Shaw, W.D. 1987. *The Lucid Veil: Poetic Truth in the Victorian Age*. London: Athlone Press.

Shelley, P.B. 1905. *The Complete Poetical Works of Percy Bysshe Shelley*. Ed. Thomas Hutchinson. London: Oxford University Press.

Smith, Barbara Herrnstein. 1968. *Poetic Closure: A Study of How Poems End*. Chicago: University of Chicago Press.

Sparshott, Francis. 1977. *Looking for Philosophy*. Montréal: McGill-Queen's University Press.

Spencer, Theodore. 1947. *Poems 1940–1947*. Cambridge, MA: Harvard University Press.

Stevens, Wallace. 1954. *The Collected Poems of Wallace Stevens*. New York: Knopf.

Strauss, David Friedrich. 1845–6. *The Life of Jesus, Critically Examined*. Trans. George Eliot. 3 vols. London: Chapman.

Suzuki, Daisetz T. 1964. *An Introduction to Zen Buddhism*. New York: Grove Weidenfeld.

– 1970a. *Zen and Japanese Culture*. Princeton: Princeton University Press.

– 1970b. *The Field of Zen*. New York: Harper and Row.

Swift, Jonathan. 1950. *Gulliver's Travels, A Tale of A Tub, The Battle of the Books*. New York: Modern Library.

– 1960. *Gulliver's Travels and Other Writings*. Ed. Louis A. Landa. Boston: Houghton Mifflin.

Swinburne, A.C. 1925–7. *The Complete Works of Algernon Charles Swinburne*. Bonchurch ed. Ed. Edmund Gosse and Thomas James Wise. 20 vols. London: Heinemann.

Tennyson, Alfred. 1908. *The Works of Tennyson*. Ed. Hallam Tennyson, vols. 8 and 9. London: Macmillan. [For quotations from the plays.]

– 1987. *The Poems of Tennyson*. Ed. Christopher Ricks. 2nd ed. 3 vols. London: Longmans, Green.

Thackeray, W.M. 1950. *Vanity Fair: A Novel without a Hero*. New York: Modern Library.

Thomas, Lewis. 1983a. *Late Night Thoughts on Listening to Mahler's Ninth Symphony*. Toronto, New York: Bantam

– 1983b. *The Youngest Science: Notes of a Medicine-Watcher*. Toronto: Bantam.

Tillotson, Geoffrey. 1968. 'Matthew Arnold's Prose: Theory and Practice.' In *The Art of Victorian Prose*, ed. George Levine and William Madden, 73–100. New York: Oxford University Press.

Trollope, Anthony. 1960. *Barchester Towers*. New York: Holt, Rinehart and Winston.

Tucker, Herbert F. 1988. *Tennyson and the Doom of Romanticism*. Cambridge, MA: Harvard University Press.

– 2007. 'When There's No There There: Mysteries of Matter.' Paper read at the conference of the North American Victorian Studies Association, University of Victoria, 12 October 2007.

Turner, Frank. 2002. *John Henry Newman: The Challenge to Evangelical Religion*. New Haven: Yale University Press.

Vendler, Helen. 1975. *The Poetry of George Herbert*. Cambridge, MA: Harvard University Press.

– 2003. *Coming of Age as a Poet: Milton, Keats, Eliot, Plath*. Cambridge, MA: Harvard University Press.

Weil, Simone. 1974. *Gateway to God*. Ed. David Raper. Glasgow: William Collins.

Welch, John W. 1981. 'Chiasmus in the New Testament.' In *Chiasmus in Antiquity*, ed. John W. Welch, 211–48. Hildesheim: Gerstenberg Verlag.

Wells, Stanley. 2002. 'God of Our Idolatry.' In *Shakespeare's Face*, ed. Stephanie Nolen, 15–31. Toronto: Alfred A. Knopf Canada.

Wheelwright, Philip. 1959. *Heraclitus*. Princeton: Princeton University Press.

White, Ronald C., Jr. 2002. *Lincoln's Greatest Speech: The Second Inaugural*. New York: Simon and Schuster.

Whitman, Walt. 1959. *Complete Poetry and Selected Prose*. Ed. J.E. Miller. Boston: Houghton Mifflin.

Wilde, Oscar. 1964. *De Profundis*. New York: Vintage.

– 1968. *Literary Criticism of Oscar Wilde*. Ed. Stanley Weintraub. Lincoln: University of Nebraska Press.

Williams, Charles. 1963. *The Descent of the Dove: A Short History of the Holy Spirit in the Church*. London and Glasgow: Fontana.

Wills, Gary. 1992. *Lincoln at Gettysburg: The Words That Remade a Nation*. New York: Simon and Schuster.

– 2006. *What Jesus Meant*. New York: Penguin.

Wittgenstein, Ludwig. 1961. *Tractatus Logico-Philosophicus*. Trans. D.F. Pears and B.F. McGuinness. London: Routledge and Kegan Paul.

Wollheim, Richard. 1970. Ed. *F.H. Bradley, Ethical Studies*. London: Oxford University Press.

– 1984. *The Thread of Life*. Cambridge, MA: Harvard University Press.

Wordsworth, William. 1940–9. *The Poetical Works of William Wordsworth*. Ed. Ernest de Selincourt and Helen Darbishire. 5 vols. Oxford: Clarendon Press.

– 1974. *Essays upon Epitaphs: The Prose Works of William Wordsworth*. Ed. W.J.B. Owen and Jane Worthington Smyser. Vol. 2. Oxford: Clarendon Press.

Yeats, W.B. 1960. *The Collected Poems of W.B. Yeats*. New York: Macmillan.

Index

Numbers in italics indicate the location of the main discussions.

By W. David Shaw

Babel and the Ivory Tower: The Scholar in the Age of Science
Origins of the Monologue: The Hidden God
Alfred Lord Tennyson: The Poet in an Age of Theory
Elegy and Paradox: Testing the Conventions
Elegy and Silence: The Romantic Legacy
Victorians and Mystery: Crises of Representation
The Lucid Veil: Poetic Truth in the Victorian Age
Tennyson's Style
The Dialectical Temper: The Rhetorical Art of Robert Browning